Crisis in Sociology

Crisis in Sociology

THE NEED FOR DARWIN

Joseph Lopreato
Timothy Crippen

TRANSACTION PUBLISHERS
NEW BRUNSWICK (U.S.A.) AND LONDON (U.K.)

First paperback printing 2002
Copyright © 1999 by Transaction Publishers, New Brunswick, New Jersey.

This book is printed on acid-free paper that meets the American National Standard for Permanence of Paper for Printed Library Materials.

Library of Congress Catalog Number: 98-50335
ISBN: 1-56000-398-7 (cloth); 0-7658-0874-9 (paper)
Printed in the United States of America

Library of Congress Cataloging-in-Publication Data

Lopreato, Joseph.
    Crisis in sociology : the need for Darwin / Joseph Lopreato and Timothy
    Crippen.
        p. cm.
    Includes bibliographical references.
    ISBN 0-7658-0874-9 (alk. paper)
    1. Sociology—Research. 2. Social Darwinism. I. Crippen, Timothy Alan.
    II. Title.

HM24.L82   1999
301'.07'2—dc21   98-50335
                                                                CIP

To Alan and Scott Schmidt,
Cherished Scions of a Beloved Child;
and
To Pam, Loving Wife and Loyal Friend

"Whatever long time has sanctioned,
that is a law forever;
the law tradition makes
is the law of nature."

—Euripides, *The Bacchae*.

"Humanity is exalted not because we are so far above
other living creatures, but because knowing them well
elevates the very concept of life."

—E.O. Wilson, *Biophilia*.

Contents

Tables and Figure   x

Preface   xi

Part 1: From Early Promise to Deepening Crisis

1. The Early Promise   3

2. The Deepening Crisis   21

3. Why the Crisis: A Sketch   49

Part 2: Elements of Evolutionary Theory

4. Darwin's Theory of Natural Selection   83

5. Elements of Evolutionary Behavioral Science   101

Part 3: Select Adaptations and Applications

6. Fundamentals of Sex Differences   135

7. An Uneasy Alliance   169

8. Fundamentals of Social Stratification   207

9. The Clannish Brain   247

   References   279

   Index of Names   311

   Index of Subjects   319

Tables and Figure

Table 5.1: Select Coefficients of Relatedness (r) in Species
Featuring Diploidy or Haplodiploidy   106

Table 6.1: Average Sex Differences in Select Aspects
of Sensation, Cognition, and Emotion   150

Table 6.2: Select Types of Sex Variations in Partner
Preferences   163

Figure 8.1: The Evolution of Dominance Orders   241

Preface

We are proud but concerned sociologists. We worry lest in the near future the current course of sociology will lead to academic self-destruction. We trust, therefore, that our readers will be influenced less by our criticisms of the current state of our discipline and more by our sincere, enthusiastic attempt to suggest a way out of what is by many accounts a very grave and deepening crisis.

Not all sociologists agree with this diagnosis. Many probably are so burdened by the heavy demands of their daily commitments to teaching and research that routine has become its own end. Others deny the crisis, or at least argue that it could be rather easily dispelled if only sociologists would make fairly minor adjustments in their practices. Some of the more common prescriptions would require fewer useless debates and mutually destructive critiques, a better integration of theory and methods, greater attempts at unification of existing theories, better public relations, and, among others, a greater objectivity so as to avoid ideology—of class, race, gender, and so on.

Still other members of the discipline share our own concerns in varying degrees. Some of these work outside universities, where demands on their craft tend to be practical and specific. There they often find that their skills are poorly valued because the "real world" and sociology have little or nothing in common. Others are academicians proud of their craft's potential but often exhausted by fruitless endeavors, their own included, to resolve the crisis and nurture the promise. Such scholars write books and articles on "the crisis in sociology," the "decomposition of sociology," the "trained incompetence" of sociologists, and related topics exemplified by journal symposia titles such as "What's Wrong with Sociology?"

The indictments, or mere analyses, indicate a disturbing state of affairs. For instance, sociologists repeatedly take one another to task for failing to define concepts clearly and to develop genuinely falsifiable theories. They engage in debates that, in modified language, recur every few years. They have produced "no sociological theory if you mean empirical relationships that are comfortably predictable and general enough to turn up across more than one topic"; that is, they may speak of sociological laws, but these are neither real nor recognized as such. There is widespread separation between theory and method; and even our statistics, a major portion of our "methodology," are almost entirely imported from such disciplines as economics and biology, and often employed to bewilder rather than to inform the reader. Further, most sociologists specialize in descriptive research that is motivated by "their personal interests and sometimes experience." And as if these were not problems enough, many sociologists are distressed that their once promising science is now awash in the flotsam of extreme cultural relativism and multiculturalism, postmodernism, political correctness, and, permeating these and other isms, an ideological agenda driven by provincial concerns of race, class, and the many grievances of a radical brand of feminism.

To a degree, our sister disciplines—for example, psychology, anthropology, political science—share our plight. But they—especially psychology and to a lesser extent anthropology—are being better steered by their long-entrenched linkage to evolutionary biology. From this perspective, they—along with various branches of zoology and several offshoots of sociology itself (e.g., urban studies, criminal justice, social work)—are actively cannibalizing sociology. The external threat feeds with little or no resistance on our internal shortcomings.

Our own fear is that the crisis in sociology is so grave and pervasive that the once proud science of society risks deletion from the academia in the next twenty-five to thirty years. Our problems are many. But fundamentally, the crisis is rooted in our failure to discover and utilize even a single law or principle general enough to suggest a large number of logically interrelated hypotheses. Inevitably such a tool would also provide the logic needed for coherent conceptualization and operationalization, appropriate methods of falsification, and hence the guidance toward a growing body of systematic, cumulative knowledge represented by a hierarchy of theoretical propositions cutting across the entire institutional framework.

We further hold that, given our failure to independently discover general principles, we, like modern psychology and anthropology, should borrow them, with whatever modifications may seem appropriate, from the natural science closest in subject matter to sociology. We should stress here that, for us, sociology must be a *science* if it is to be anything at all. Hence, those who do not share this vision will find our book irrelevant and even antithetical to their scholarly interests.

The natural science closest to sociology, as to other social sciences, is evolutionary biology. For 150 years, this branch of knowledge has constituted a marvelous scientific revolution. In recent decades, moreover, evolutionary biology has made giant strides toward the study of behavior, human conduct included, through refinements of Darwinian theory, several aspects of genetic science, and such evolutionary disciplines as human ethology, primatology, neurobiology, neuroendocrinology, and Darwinian psychology, among others. Here, more than anywhere else, is where the action is today in behavioral science. Sociology will participate in this revolution or it will be cancelled out of the intellectual landscape.

Accordingly, this volume is divided into three parts. The first, consisting of chapters 1–3, begins by offering a glimpse of the early promise of sociology—a promise that, however, may have contained the virus of the subsequent crisis. It proceeds, in chapter 2, to define the crisis, mostly in terms suggested by sociologists themselves, and then concludes with a brief discussion in chapter 3 of some of the basic causes of the crisis.

Given our view of the necessary tie between evolutionary biology and sociology, part 2 presents, first, the basic elements of Darwin's theory of evolution by natural selection (chapter 4) and then, in chapter 5, a brief discussion of basic elements of neo-Darwinian theory as it has evolved since around 1930.

The concluding part 3 consists of four application chapters. The sixth and the seventh are devoted to several aspects of sex-differentiated behavior, topics that of late have been monopolized by "feminist theorists." Here, especially in chapter 6, is where we find the detritus that may be most detrimental to sociological survival. As two women critics have put it, radical feminism constitutes a kind of "new creationism" that "defies common sense" and "ill suits an academic tradition rhetorically committed to human freedom." Our strategy in this part is to critically examine select feminist arguments and try to make better sense of them with a view to showing theoretical complementarity, where possible, between them and the material presented in part 2.

The remaining two chapters are devoted, respectively, to an attempt to (1) provide an evolutionary explanation of the rise, universality, and persistence of dominance orders (what sociologists term "social stratification") and (2) apply a corresponding approach to the universality and persistence of ethnicity and ethnic conflict in human society.

As is invariably the case in the writing of books, many good people have directly or indirectly influenced our work. In the indirect category belong several "neo-Darwinians" representing such fields as biology, primatology, anthropology, and psychology, among others. We are grateful for their powerful lessons, as the numerous references to their work indicates. More directly, several scholars have contributed to our thinking in various ways, including reading and commenting on all or part of an earlier draft of the volume. They include Dixon Benson, Amy Emery, Penny Anthon Green, Raina Hoover, Irving Louis Horowitz, Richard Machalek, Roy Smith, Jonathan Turner, and Pierre van den Berghe. We owe them a large debt, but we may also owe them our regrets for being less wise than their lessons could have made us. We are also pleased to acknowledge the assistance of our respective schools, the University of Texas at Austin and Mary Washington College. Both of us, for example, have profited from, among other things, a one-semester research leave granted during the initial stage of the project. Finally, Laurence Mintz, our editor, was helpful not only with the manuscript but also with various problems and questions that typically beset tired and eager authors. It was a real pleasure working with him.

Part 1

From Early Promise to Deepening Crisis

1

The Early Promise

Few cultural phenomena were more historically ordained than the rise of sociology in the eighteenth and nineteenth centuries. Its emergence exemplified the enduring élan of the Renaissance and the profoundly creative momentum of the Scientific Revolution and the Enlightenment. The human mind had probed long unimaginable laws of nature that placed our earthly plot in a cosmic context. It was now ready to turn to a more daring, reflexive inquiry of its more immediate environment. The question echoed broadly: Is a "science of society" possible? Equally resonant was the answer: It is an unavoidable necessity to find out. Those who unfolded the sociological frontier were polymaths proudly familiar with the scientific questions of their times, carefully bred in the cultivating currents of the humane disciplines, vigorously fascinated by the momentous encounter between ancient institutions and the emerging paradigms that inescapably challenged them.

None were sociologists in any of today's senses of the word. They may be best described as keen observers of the human condition who had been trained in philosophy, or literature, history, economics, jurisprudence, medicine, even engineering, among other specialties. They were all children of the Enlightenment and of the "evolutionary centuries," and were thus endowed with a sense of History writ large—with the burning conviction that little of enduring significance made sense if divorced from the roots that Time had wrought. The scientific revolution, the phenomenology of the mind, as Hegel termed it, the discovery of countless new peoples and cultures, and the expanding ethnography of the animal kingdom had constricted the Earth and thereby broadened intellectual horizons. Whatever else we may say of our progenitors, they were relatively free of parochialism and rigid habits. They replaced the old neophobia with an urgent need to discover and master the new. Above all perhaps, they were euphoric in the art of crashing disciplinary boundaries. Little wonder, then, that for a while matters went well with sociology. The beginning was glorious, good enough to fairly quickly establish it as a respectable academic discipline.

Unfortunately, sociology soon went astray, and, as is widely noted both within and without the profession, it has long been a discipline adrift. Scholars write of "the impossible science" (Turner and Turner 1990), "tranined incompetence" (van den Berghe 1990), and "the decomposition of sociology" (Horowitz 1993), among many other maladies. An essay solicited to celebrate the centennial of the *American Journal of Sociology* raised serious questions about the discipline's capacity to compete for scarce resources and respectability in the academic environment (Huber 1995). Symposia about "the crisis" produce few significant agreements on its causes but underscore its enormous scope (see, e.g., the June 1994 issue of *Sociological Forum* on "What's Wrong With Sociology?" and the debate on I.L. Horowitz's *The Decomposition of Sociology* in *Sociological Imagination*, nos. 3–4, 1996).

In this volume, we argue that the crisis in sociology became unavoidable when we strayed from the premise generally accepted by the Founders that there can be no scientific sociology without general laws. Moreover, sociology was born within the same intellectual milieu that produced Darwin's theory of evolution by natural selection and eventually population genetics and various evolutionary sciences that have developed toward the study of social, including human, behavior. For decades, this scientific revolution has unfolded at a rapid pace. Some human disciplines, for example, psychology and to a lesser extent anthropology, have entered the stream of this revolution. To survive as an academic discipline, sociology will have to do likewise—and very quickly, for cannibalization of our subject matter is proceeding at a most disturbing rate.

To state the point otherwise, sociological analysis is almost exclusively environmentalist, and thus produces discoveries and explanations that are at best ephemeral. To survive it must rediscover the brain, the circumstances of its evolution, and the evolution of its products. It needs to learn Darwinian lessons and contribute to their ever-expanding scope. Accordingly, part 2 of this book will provide some basic elements of modern Darwinian science. Part 3 will then endeavor to apply them to various crucial problems of sociological interest. But before that we must briefly visit the early promise of sociology and then proceed to define the crisis and its various causes.

Our Fathers Who Inherited the Enlightenment

Auguste Comte

Auguste Comte (especially 1830–1842, 1875–1877), our putative and very eccentric progenitor was, through his enormous debt to Henri de St. Simon (Comte 1854, I: 142), our direct link to the Age of Enlightenment. The Enlightenment had two passwords above all: Reason and Progress (Bury 1932). Together they implied many things. But first and foremost they urged thinkers to look forward, away from the old and decadent schemes. Copernicus, Kepler, Galileo, and Newton had cleared the mind of the prejudice of geocentrism. Was not the mind now ready to dispel the prejudice of temporecentrism, and with it the allied bias of anthropocentrism as well? Comte was one of the first to advocate the application of the scientific method to the study of society, and hence the quest for "invariable natural laws" analogous to "the doctrine of Gravitation" (Comte 1854, I: 5–6).

By the time of Comte, moreover, the evolutionary paradigm was insistently in the air. He avidly joined the pursuit and, in view of the search for general laws, he stated a "preponderant principle" of human evolution, underscoring the "progressive influence of reason over the general conduct of Man and society." Specifically: "The scientific principle of the theory appears to me to consist in the great philosophical law of the succession of the three states:—the primitive theological state, the transient metaphysical, and the final positive state—through which the human mind has to pass, in every kind of speculation" (Comte 1854, II: 522; see also Comte 1830–1842, I: 14). This is a vague and rationalistic conception of a prime mover. But Comte's Law is also tied to a Malthusian anchor, namely the natural increase of population; hence, it is to a degree reducible in the direction of the epoch-making Darwinian theory. Comte (1854, III: 305–8) specifically argued that increasing demographic density stimulates the "division of employments" and "better concerted energy against the expansion of individual divergences." At the same time, it creates new problems and promotes new technologies by reinforcing "innovating instincts" at the expense of "conservative" ones.

But it is perhaps when we focus on his "positivism," for which Comte is most widely known, that we make the most startling discovery. Contrary to the common equation of positivism with "raw empiricism" in sociology, Comte viewed empiricism as a "great hindrance" to scientific inquiry. " No real observation of...phenomena," he argued (1830–1842, IV: 418, 454–55), "is possible which is not initially guided and finally interpreted by some theory." Thus facts, even important historical ones, are useless if they consist of mere descriptions. They do not speak for themselves; the true value of facts appears only "in relation to social evolution," that is, to fundamental laws about social change.

Similarly, Comte drew a basic distinction between "static" and "dynamic" aspects of sociological analysis. In general, the former referred to today's sociologist's predilection for *social structure*. Little or nothing, he argued, could be said about the form of evolution, or the continutity of "consecutive social states," without a thorough knowledge of structure. But it was the dynamics that provided the *movers* of social evolution. "In this view, the object of science is to discover the laws which govern this continuity, and the aggregate of which determines the course of human development" (Comte 1854, II: 218–32). This was a promising start for a science of society. But only a century later, sad to say, sociologists were entangled in an acrimonious and sterile debate over whether the reigning "paradigm" of the time, "structural-functionalism" (e.g., Parsons 1951), was at all adequate to the study of social change. By then, the crisis in sociology was already a festering sore.

There are many other valuable aspects of Comte's work, and there are still others that we can easily do without (see Harris 1968: chap. 3, and Turner et al. 1998: chaps. 2–3 for informative discussions). A major example of Comtean error is the idealist philosophy that, his positivism notwithstanding, inhered in the law of the three stages. Social systems, according to Comte (1830–1842, I: 48–49) are "governed or overthrown by ideas: all social mechanisms rest on opinions." On this question, he was at least partly wrong, as K. Marx and modern evolutionary theory have firmly shown. But after all, Comte was a product of philosophy, and thus could hardly avoid this imperfection. It is the subsequent failure to correct it that constitutes the greater flaw.

Karl Marx

The preeminent social evolutionists who charted a course in some sense parallel to Darwin's extraordinarily fecund breakthrough were Karl Marx and, even more so, Herbert Spencer, one of the great giants often belittled with relish by subsequent generations of sociologists. Marx was both ideologue and scientist. As scientist, he was not hindered by narrow vision, whatever his language. Better than anyone else before and since his time, he rejected, in terms at once cogent and dramatic, Auguste Comte's, and G.W.F. Hegel's, excessively idealistic philosophies; at the same time he reinforced Comte's accent on the dynamics of social evolution.

Marx understood the Enlightenment's inability to escape the pincers of the rising capitalist order. Evasion required recognition that philosophical ideas are unavoidably the ideas of dominant groups, such as ruling classes. That amounts to saying that philosophical ideas are the secular means employed by the few in the subordination and exploitation of the many. Hence Marx rejected philosophy, what he otherwise termed ideology, in favor of what may be termed popular history, better known as "historical materialism." The substance of history, he argued, may be found in the productive actions of laborers, the true producers of wealth or "social power." Accordingly, the fundamental problem of history, especially urgent in his own time, concerned the means whereby the dominance inherent in social power could be transferred from the talkers-exploiters to the actors-producers. The deed would be performed by various forces allegedly inherent in the maturation of capitalism, for example, alienation, pauperization, urbanization, proletarianization, and so forth. In a seeming paradox, however, it would also be accomplished by the force of theoretically practical ideas: the ideas of the communists who, having a scientific understanding of the "true historical process," would clear away from the minds of the workers the "false consciousness" instilled by philosophical ideas. Freed from such deceit, the oppressed masses would mobilize as a "class *for* itself," thereby triggering revolutionary transformation of power relations toward a classless society. As ideologue as well as scientist, Marx fought ideology with ideology as well as with science.

It may also be argued that, given his general axiom that the dominant ideas of an epoch are the ideas of the dominant class, there is a marked Sysiphic dimension in Marx's thought. But Marx saw no inevitability in the axiom. It had been so. It need not be so forever. Accordingly, there is no irreperable fault in his attempt to descry the forces, even the "idealist" ones, that may rid the body social of exploitation and abuse, especially if in the process the effort also produces fundamental sociological lessons. In this he succeeded reasonably well. The following are some of these lessons: (1) the proper study of man is the study of change; (2) the proper means to the study of change is the study of competition and conflict; (3) if you would understand the forces of history, ask not what people think; ask rather what they do. In all these respects, most sociologists since Marx have lost their way; and yet, if paternity must be sought for our craft, Marx offers one of the more compelling candidacies.

"If in all ideology," Marx and Engels (1845–1846: 14) argued, "men and their circumstances appear upside down as in a *camera obscura*, this phenomenon arises just as much from their historical life-processes as the inversion of objects on the retina does from their physical life-process." If we are to understand human behavior, we must start by observing what people do, first and foremost in their productive activities, rather than by listening to what they say. The human being is a *homo faber*, producer and seeker of resources necessary to "the production of material life itself." Production is "the first historical act." Inextricably associated with it as "a double relationship" is the fact, manifestly Darwinian, that "men, who daily remake their own life, begin to make other men, to propogate their kind" (Marx and Engels 1845–1846: 14–22).

This position, stultified at every turn in today's theoretical babble as well as its very antithesis, the excessive reliance on survey research, has survived to our own time as one of the cornerstones of evolutionary behavioral science. Moreover, like his contemporary Charles Darwin, a more genial and fortunate giant of the nineteenth century, Marx proceeded to seek the fundamental mechanism underlying the historical process. He found it in the recurrence of the class struggle.

Now, he might better have served subsequent generations of sociologists if he had also paid more attention to what other sociologists have considered an even more basic type of struggle, that is, ethnic conflict (e.g., Pareto 1902–1903), which, as we shall see, links up very productively with a powerful tool termed kin selection by evolutionary scientists. It can hardly be gainsaid, however, that the human conflicts over appropriation of scarce material resources often take the form of clashes between coalitions of participants—whether social classes, political parties, ethnic groups, or even nations. *Conflict at the group level* is a constant fact of human evolution, and Marx made it the cornerstone of his theoretical edifice.

Marx's work is a huge mine of ideas, not all of which are relevant to our purpose. The crux of his general theory lies in the sub-mechanisms of the class struggle, and the heart of the matter may, with some obvious loss of ideological verbiage, be represented as follows: The greater the greediness of the more successful competitors for resources (the greater the stress between the "forces of production" and "the relations of production"), the greater the probability of widespread dissatisfaction (class consciousness) among the more assiduous producers, who, through a "revolutionary process," transfer the power of appropriation from one ruling coalition to another that at the time best utilizes the popular discontent. Dominant classes, in short, tend toward what may be termed crises of entropy, and fall prey to reenergizing classes rising from the very decay of the old order.

So viewed, Marx's (1867) historical materialism speaks a fundamental human truth. It also hints by analogy at a criticism of Darwin's allegedly "gradualist" conception of biological evolution. As we shall see in part 2, according to the "new evolutionary timetable" (e.g., Stanley 1981), the evolution of populations reveals extended time segments of relatively inactive selection pressures (little or no evolution) that are periodically "punctuated" by relatively rapid evolution or speciation. Marx's mechanism may thus be construed as the sociological analogue of "punctuation" in the new evolutionary timetable (Lopreato and Green 1990).

Of course, by present-day standards, Marx's evolutionism was only embryonic, and contained serious errors as well, such as his conception of a classless, and hence relatively conflict-free, future society. But it was a promising step in the right direction. Marx himself viewed his inquiry into human history as a quest for the general mechanisms responsible for the transformation of society. Moreover, his vision was so indebted to Darwin's *The Origin of Species*, which Marx read in 1860, that he reported as follows to Friedrich Engels: "Darwin's book is very important and serves me as a basis in natural science for the class struggle in history" (Marx and Engels 1935). Engels was even more sanguine about his friend's evolutionist accomplishments. "Just as Darwin," Engels (1883: 681) declared at Marx's burial, "discovered the law of development of organic nature, so Marx discovered the law of development of human history." With some little license, the alleged law may be interpreted in terms of Darwin's "struggle for existence" in view of the primacy attributed by Marx to the role played by the production and distribution of economic resources in human relations. In short, rightly or wrongly, Marx viewed the class struggle as the typical human struggle for existence, and hence the uniquely human mechanism of evolution. It is, therefore, mystifying to read some of the most hostile attacks on Darwinian theory precisely among self-proclaimed Marxist sociologists.

Herbert Spencer

Herbert Spencer was more thoroughly an evolutionist, and Darwin himself even claimed, wrongly, in a revised edition of *The Origin of Species*, that Spencer's concept of "the survival of the fittest" was "a more felicitous" expression for Darwin's concept of natural selection. The heart of Spencer's work is also harder to capture in a few paragraphs. The quick, and weak, way of representing his evolutionism begins with the theorized effect of population growth on evolution. As population ("mass") increases, there is also an increase in "the primary trait of evolution," that is, structural "integration." Population increase and integration are accompanied by "the secondary trait, differentiation" (Spencer 1876–1886, I: 471). This is the "law of evolution," which he defined as the "transformation of the homogenous into the heterogeneous," and is allegedly reducible to "a universal cause": "Every active force produces more than one change—every cause produces more than one effect."

The concern with change is very old in social thought. Few thinkers, however, have expressed more urgency about its centrality in human affairs than have Marx and Spencer. The lesson is of the essence, and constitutes a crucial promise of early sociology. Unfortunately, much of it has been lost. As J.D.Y. Peel (1972: vii–ix) notes in his excellent introduction to a Spencerian anthology, the theoretical constructions of sociologists "are dominated by the social forms of their own age." In fact, Peel may be a bit too generous, for the typical sociological focus is narrower than the term "age" would suggest. Certainly, as a group, sociologists suffer from a grievous scarcity of diachronic vision. Too often it seems that we are unaware of the very fact of time and of the roots that in time develop below the surface of human events.

A somewhat fuller glimpse of Spencer's evolutionism is possible by retrieving Spencer's Malthusian thesis that the increase of population entails a constant pressure on the means of subsistence. This excess of demand over supply stimulates the demand for "skill, intelligence, and self-control." These environmental pressures stimulate self-interested parties to design ever-more effective strategies for survival and success. It is this quest to satisfy selfish needs that, further, is alleged to be the fundamental source of human sociality: "Living together arose, because, on the average, it proved more advantageous to each than living apart" (Spencer 1892–1893, I: 134).

Up to a point, therefore, population increase is the mother of invention and "progress" (Spencer 1852). However, not all persons nor all peoples are equally endowed by nature to attain the higher levels of skill and inventiveness. Hence, "from the very beginning, the conquest of one people over another has been, in the main, the conquest of...the more adapted over the less adapted." The remark removes any doubt regarding Spencer's conception of the prime mover in human affairs. His ultimate mechanism of evolution is identical to Darwin's own: natural selection, or the differential contribution of offspring to future generations on the part of genetically diverse individuals and populations (see chapter 4).

Given the postulate of differential capabilities, the whole effort of nature, according to Spencer (1851: 414), is to rid itself of "feeble elements." The point is too starkly stated. It also gave birth to his erroneous and, Darwin's approbation notwithstanding, treacherous expression, the "survival of the fittest." More important, this conception unfortunately helped to inspire that intellectual pestilence, Social Darwinism, whose virus grew from the roots of classical capitalism and had little or nothing to do with Darwin's theory. Of course, it may reasonably be argued that Spencer intended to describe natural laws, not to prescribe social policy. But there was often gaucherie as well as error in his way of expressing evolutionary ideas. One error in particular was egregious, and its basis may be dismissed emphatically: *There was not then, and there is not now, any credible evidence that populations (e.g., societies) are "by nature" unequally endowed to attain high levels of civilization.* Still, Spencer's main point was the focus on competition and change—in itself hardly erroneous, trivial, or offensive. But affront it became, with the result that, while there was much that later sociologists could have learned from Spencer (e.g., Turner 1985; Turner et al. 1998: chaps. 4–5), he has been mostly reviled when not completely disregarded.

This dismissive attitude regarding Spencer's work reveals a more general characteristic of sociological discourse. Sociologists have been keener to the glare of blunders than to the promises of their overall contexts. That is easy scholarship. Successful scientists are more inclined to look for promising paths beyond the troublesome marshes. Consider the case of Charles Darwin. He committed his share of errors. For example, as noted, he allowed his key concept of natural selection to be coopted, at least in some circles, by Spencer's "survival of the fittest"; he accepted some of Lamarck's misconceptions regarding the inheritance of acquired traits; like the "progressivists" of his century, he frequently relied on over-adaptationist reasoning (e.g., Ridley 1993); and, as we shall see, he was confused about, among other things, the way in which "sexual selection," a crucial evolutionary mechanism, related to natural selection. But Darwinian scholars did not lose sleep over these blemishes; nor did they waste time making false capital of them. By 1930, they had mastered the good lessons of Darwin, discovered population genetics, and as a result produced a Synthetic Theory (e.g., Huxley 1942) that made the finer aspects of Darwin's theory look bigger rather than smaller.

Similarly, despite its flaws, there are many capital lessons in Spencer's evolutionary sociology. One of them is, ironically, considered by sociologists almost universally to be an error of major proportions. It refers to the so-called "organismic analogy." Spencer did draw an analogy between society and the organism (e.g., Spencer 1857, I). But there is nothing wrong with analogies *provided that* they are not used as means of demonstration. They are basic tools of science essential to the job of going, heuristically, from a better-known area to a lesser-known one. A careful reading of Spencer's work reveals that he used analogies in the proper fashion. He was careful, moreover, to enumerate the differences as well as the similarities that, as he saw them, existed between organisms and societies. Indeed, Spencer was one of the first to grasp the huge role played by "system" in scientific research (Spencer 1876–1886, I: 465–69, 613–16), so that the organismic analogy was drawn at the most abstract level in order to underscore the apparent mutual dependence existing among the parts of the social system. The following statement should leave no doubt on this point: "Here let it once more be pointed out that there exist no analogies between the body politic and a living body, save those necessitated by *the mutual dependence of parts which they display in common*" (Spencer 1876–1886, I: 613—emphasis added).

Whatever the misconceptions about Spencer's use of analogies, one thing should be clear. Analogies, by definition, stimulate comparative analysis. This is a major lesson from Spencer that has nearly vanished. His ultimate aim was a "theory of humanity," or "human nature," and this could only be accomplished through a comparative analysis of the various human institutions. Hence, for example, "the highest office which the historian can discharge is that of so narrating the lives of nations as to furnish materials for a Comparative Sociology, and for the subsequent determination of the ultimate laws to which social phenomena conform" (quoted in Harris 1968: 160).

One other virtue is especially noteworthy in concluding this necessarily brief note on Spencer's sociology. Unlike most other sociologists (but see, e.g., Pareto 1916; Homans 1967; Davis 1994), Spencer utilized the technique, virtually general in modern science, of "methodological individualism." Sociologists are torn between it and so-called structural analysis. For example, we probe into the "opinions" of individuals on the what and the why of various problems but then typically analyze the data from the viewpoint of various structural variables (e.g., family, religion, class, society). This sort of Hamletic stance constitutes the Scylla and Charybdis of sociological science. Whatever else this fascination with the "structural" dimensions of human life may have contributed to sociology's output thus far, we may be certain of at least one fact: It has produced no cumulative, nomothetically organized knowledge. Herbert Spencer was unequivocal about the method to follow in research. Stated in a nutshell, it was for him a "general principle that the properties of the units determine the properties of the aggregates" (Spencer 1873: 50–59); the laws of sociology should accordingly be stated with this principle clearly in mind. It may be that there is another way, as Émile Durkheim, next on our agenda, would have us believe, or at least is said almost without exception to have claimed. But it has not yet been discovered. In the meantime, the Spencerian strategy is increasingly reaping numerous and rich harvests—in disciplines other than sociology.

Émile Durkheim: Scientist and Metaphysician

If our task were to inventory even the most compelling highlights of the Founders' contributions, we would meet with a sizable group of distinguished minds, among whom the following, among others, would be inescapable: Max Weber, Vilfredo Pareto, Gaetano Mosca, Lester Ward, William Graham Sumner, George P. Murdock, Georg Simmel, Robert Michels, Robert Park, George H. Mead, Pitirim Sorokin. But our task demands a strict focus, and we shall close our remarks on the early promise of sociology with a brief comment on what some will consider an unlikely candidate: the cornerstone of Émile Durkheim's sociological analysis.

It has been said by many critics of mainstream social science (e.g., Lopreato 1984; Fox 1989; Tooby and Cosmides 1992) that Durkheim, like Boas in anthropology, did subsequent generations of social scientists a great disservice with his (1895) argument that social facts can be explained only by other social facts—that social and cultural facts are phenomena *sui generis* and thus endogenously explicable and autonomous from the realms of psychology and biology. Is the stricture valid? Yes and no. Equivocation is justifiable on several grounds. First, the Durkheim and Boas "schools" have certainly been influential among subsequent generations of scholars; but these have only been too eager to be influenced. The quasi-apotheosis of Culture (environmentalism) came about in part as a reaction to the erroneous and obscene use of biology made by some of the Social Darwinists. It also coincided with the making of modern America and the intellectual progress of humiliated newcomers for whom the very word "biology" became, and has long continued to be, a reminder of prejudice and arrogance.

We should also recognize that the logical structure of arguments is often concealed in precious lines of verbal hypertrophies. A close reading of Durkheim's work shows that he had something better to say, although he did often reveal a penchant for mixing an excellent song with an awful ruckus. For instance, Durkheim has apparently led many of his readers to conclude that he rejected evolutionism, allegedly replacing it with a type of theorizing that explains phenomena from the viewpoint of the functions they discharge; hence the common verdict that he was the father or at any rate the "main starter" of "functionalism" (e.g., Nisbet 1969: 229). But the verdict is erroneous as the following statement (Durkheim 1895: 89–97), among similar others, makes clear:

> Most sociologists think they have accounted for phenomena once they have shown how they are useful [functional], what role they play.... But this method confuses two very different questions. To show how a fact is useful is not to explain how it originated or why it is what it is...it is proper, in general, to treat the [cause] before the [function].... But if the usefulness of a fact is not the cause of its existence, it is generally necessary that it be useful in order that it may maintain itself.... [Else] the budget of the organism would have a deficit and social life would be impossible.

Obviously, something has gone wrong since this statement was written, for it manifestly states that causal analysis comes first. Moreover, function appears within an obviously evolutionary framework. In the aggregate, culture must be useful; else it ends by being acted upon unfavorably by natural selection (by having a "budget deficit"—by being maladaptive). Accordingly, it is questionable whether by "useful" Durkheim meant "functional" in any of the senses appearing later, say, in Mertonian or Parsonian sociology. In addition, the focus on the budget deficit of the organism reveals some commitment, however vaguely framed, to methodological individualism. Within this context, "useful" may be more appropriately translated into "adaptive," the same idea that, as we shall see, was central to the theory of Charles Darwin, one of the foremost nineteenth-century giants of behavioral science.

There is almost general agreement that *The Division of Labor in Society* (Durkheim 1893) represents an extraordinarily brilliant accomplishment in sociology. It is equally true, however, that sociologists do not know what exactly to make of it. It is still taught—or at least exegeses of it are taught. But with few exceptions such renditions suggest that Durkheim wrote not one but many books on the subject—nearly all of them poor and disconnected by objective criteria. Certainly, Durkheim is often vague and confusing. These defects have various causes, including indefiniteness of concepts, metaphysical expressions like "the soul of society," and above all the absence of an explicit *nomos* or law to anchor his reasoning. As noted elsewhere (Lopreato 1990: 190–93), however, the core of Durkheim's argument can be grasped fairly unequivocally. It also turns out to be quite relevant to one of the most productive theories in evolutionary behavioral science (Trivers 1971). We interpret it below in a series of brief statements.

1. In the primitive society (the clan), solidarity (the social order) is maintained by "a certain number of states of conscience which are common to all the members of the same society" (Durkheim 1893: 109).
2. Such states express themselves in the form of common interests, a common tradition, and a familistic organization. The solidarity is thereby said to be "instinctive" or "mechanical."
3. As society evolved through various technological revolutions, population size and density increased, thereby stimulating the frequency and intensity of social interaction ("moral density").
4. Such increase determined an ever more complex division of labor.
5. "All social links which result from likeness progressively slacken" (Durkheim 1893: 173), and in principle the old solidarity would break down and result in social and moral chaos. But the division of labor provides the basis of a new form of solidarity, which is termed "organic" in order to underscore by analogy the mutual dependence, moral as well as economic, of the various individuals and groups that constitute the complex society (Bellah 1973: xxiv–xxv).
6. If the basis of solidarity has shifted in the course of societal evolution, it must also be true that sanctions against breaches of the social order have also shifted in step with it. Indeed, a relative diminution of "repressive sanctions" has accompanied the relative waning of mechanical solidarity,

and concomitantly a relative strengthening of "restitutive sanctions" has accompanied the emergence of organic solidarity.

7. Moral and social institutions are anchored "not to reasoning or calculation, but...to subconscious elements"; hence, mechanical solidarity and repressive sanctions express strong states of "collective conscience." Conversely, restitutive sanctions "either do not totally derive from the collective conscience, or are only feeble states of it" (Durkheim 1893: 112). As a result, reaction to criminal behavior in the organic society is less severe than the reaction to offenses against the mechanical community (even though, it may be added, the former may have far more damaging incidental effects, as when bankers, for instance, rob the citizenry of billions of dollars that could otherwise be used for health care, medical research, public education, crime prevention, and so forth).

8. In short, "cheating," as today's sociobiologists would say, has become more subtle with the evolution of complex society (Trivers 1971; see also Machalek and Cohen 1991), and natural selection has had insufficient time "to act" against it ("the states of collective conscience" are still "feeble" in relation to recently emerged forms of social deviance).

9. Finally, the collective conscience is *ex initio* so structured as to accommodate "the free play of our initiative"—"to leave open a part of the individual conscience in order that special functions may be established there," and thus avoid hindering the evolution of organic solidarity (Durkheim 1893: 131). That is, the brain of primitive people was "preadapted" or preprogrammed to make possible the shift from mechanical to organic solidarity.

This is a causal, evolutionary theory, and the mechanism of evolution it proposes lies in the core of the current revolution in behavioral science. It bears stressing, first, that mechanisms come in various grades of causal relevance, and that the evolutionist is necessarily interested, at bottom, in the sort of mechanism that conveys the sense of causation that is most uniform and consistent. Accordingly, there are various kinds of mechanisms in Durkheim's theory: for example, population increase, division of labor, and sanctions against offenses to the collective conscience. But there is another of deeper significance, and, as in Spencer's work, it links up with Darwinian theory. "If work," for instance, Durkheim (1893: 266—emphasis added) adds, "becomes divided more as societies become more voluminous and denser, it is not because external circumstances are more varied, but because *the struggle for existence* is more acute." Again: "Darwin justly observed that the struggle between two organisms is as active as they are analogous. Having the same needs and pursuing the same objects, they are in rivalry.... It is quite otherwise if the co-existing individuals are of different species or varieties" (Durkheim 1893: 266). The result of the struggle for existence is natural selection (Darwin 1859: chap. IV), and this may rightly be considered as "the ultimate mechanism" in one of the most celebrated classics of social science.

We do not claim that Durkheim intended this construction of his work or even that he was fully aware of this possible interpretation. After all, one of Durkheim's rhetorical penchants consisted in first negating the validity of competitive theories relevant to his work (Durkheim 1897, 1912). He fancied himself thoroughly unique and crystal clear in what he wrote, despite the sobriquet of "metaphysician" earned early in his studies from his fellow students. Moreover, as noted, by the time Durkheim began to write, Darwin's theory of evolution by natural selection had been stained by Social Darwinism, and it simply was not safe for a sociologist to embrace it openly and without equivocation. But those who came after Durkheim could have freed themselves of this constraint and done better.

The End of the Promise

Our only claim is that the above interpretation of Durkheim's theory of evolution is justified by the text and made possible by the recognition that a fundamental goal of scientific theorizing is economy of expression—laying bare the logical structure of an explanation. Durkheim's argument contains details and radiations that the above representation does not comprise. Our aim was to capture the logical core of the argument. Much of what is at the margins consists of restatements, illustrations, and incursions into areas that, while informative in one sense or another, are superfluous to the main task of Durkheim's volume, and not infrequently misleading.

It is safe to maintain that scientific discourse is not possible without at least one general law. Laws perform many crucial functions in the production and accumulation of knowledge. They provide the logic wherewith to define terms and thus to grasp the kindredness existing between concepts in any given theoretical context. They provide the logic for the statement of hypotheses and for the grounds on which hypotheses are falsifiable. Again, laws supply the logic that ties hypotheses and their findings into a class of related statements, as contrasted to the congeries of loose statements that may be found in the typical argumentations. In short, laws help to explain and to place findings within a paradigmatic context and a body of "verified," cumulative knowledge (Pareto 1916; Kuhn 1962; Lenski 1988; Turner 1991).

The above rendition of Durkheim's argument represents an effort to extricate a nomothetic anchorage point from the camouflage of its metaphysics. The upshot is to link Durkheim's work to the theory of evolution by natural selection. As subsequent chapters will show, this theory contains a variety of tools, including a fundamental law that addresses explicitly the study of social behavior. The law in question, which will be central to this volume starting in chapter 4, states that *in the last analysis* organisms tend to behave so as to perpetuate the units of heredity they bear: their genes. But to obey this law, a number of activities are *in toto* or in part necessary, for example, eating, mating, and cooperating, *inter alia*.

Durkheim's (1893) study is a study in cooperation and is subsumable under modern evolutionary theory. The specific logic for this linkage may be found in the work of Robert Trivers (1971, 1985), among others (e.g., Axelrod 1984; Machalek and Cohen 1991). Trivers has systematically shown that cooperative behavior is favored by natural selection not only at the level of the kin group, wherein genetic relatedness is highest and cooperation (or "altruism") is most intense. He has broadened this context of natural selection, known as "kin selection," to comprise altruism between non-kin, indeed even between members of different species. What is important for cooperation to be practiced is that it be beneficial to the parties involved, though each is typically inclined to give less than he or she receives, and thus to "cheat" within a context of what Trivers calls "reciprocal altruism." Durkheim's study makes sense best as a study of the relative deintensification of nepotistic or kin altruism (mechanical solidarity) and a concomitant intensification or diffusion of "reciprocal altruism" (organic solidarity) within the context of a society evolving away from ties based primarily on genetic kinship.

In concluding this introductory chapter, we may ask, did sociology's Founders leave a legacy of scientific theory properly speaking? Hardly. For one thing, they tended to skirt the rising scientific paradigm of their time and subject matter instead of appropriating it and enriching it. But to a large extent, the answer depends also on what we can say about the perspicacity and creativity of subsequent generations of sociologists who have read the old texts in search of sociological theory. And here it is not easy to be proud. We have never effectively mined the intellectual strata laid out by the Founders. A beginning of sorts in the right direction was provided by scholars like Pitirim Sorokin (1928) and his Harvard colleague Talcott Parsons. By the 1930s both scholars had provided penetrating commentaries on many of the Founders, including Marx, Spencer, Durkheim, Pareto, and Weber. Parsons' (1937) *The Structure of Social Action* in particular could have acted as a powerful invitation to later generations of sociologists to carefully examine "the classics," retrieve those aspects that would help define the foundations of theoretical sociology, amend others, and of course discard the remainder. Unfortunately, such a development never took place. Sociology soon started moving away from such promising foundations in the direction of issues that were "relevant" to the immediate "problems" of an ever increasing number of academic parishes.

The failure was partly the effect of an at once strenuous and confining manner in which Parsons, who until the 1960s was the Pontifex Maximus of sociological discourse, produced his once-famous exegesis. The by-product of his analysis was alleged to be a "voluntaristic theory of action" on which such pioneers as A. Marshall, V. Pareto, É. Durkheim, and M. Weber presumably had converged. Now, such an output was not only to constitute the cornerstone of Parsons' subsequent theorizing. As a philosopher of science suggested in an evaluation of Parsonian theory (Black 1961b), the voluntaristic theory of action was also destined to become a major force in the theoretical trivialization of sociology. It follows that the work of the Founders was itself trivialized roughly in direct proportion to Parsons' influence on subsequent cohorts of sociologists.

Of course, some sociologists still read Marx, Durkheim, Weber, and so forth. Indeed, courses in sociological theory are still largely organized around the works of such scholars. But students typically read accounts of those who read those who read those who read.... When they read from the originals, they are treated to disconnected excerpts that tend to perpetuate superficial knowledge of a few concepts like class struggle, mechanical solidarity, ideal types, significant others, ethnocentrism, and little else. Matters are hardly encouraging when we recognize that, whether students are treated to primary excerpts or many-times-over digestions, in the classrooms they are subjected to disparate, sometimes diametrically opposed, typically ideological interpretations of the same materials, often in the various courses and seminars offered in the same department.

The resulting picture is not pretty. Nobody today knows what sociological theory is, or even if there is any such thing at all. At best, as

Robert K. Merton (1949) noted half a century ago, "sociologists tend to merge the history with the systematics of theory." It has hardly helped that Merton, intentionally or otherwise, invited sociologists to forget the Founders by quoting Alfred North Whitehead's equivocal apothegm: "A science which hesitates to forget its founders is lost." American sociologists were only too ready to forget. Most assuredly we did not hesitate. Nor, however, did we first explicate. That was also a time when the United States was exporting much more than goods to the rest of the world, especially to Europe. Consequently, European sociologists, too, soon learned to forget the Founders, despite, as Parsons (1954) himself noted, their deeper roots in the classical, historical, and philosophical tradition of social thought. Centuries earlier, a far greater scientist than Whitehead had claimed that if he had achieved much it was because he ha⌐ stood on the shoulders of giants. Perhaps we never had giants in sociology. But however tall or short our Founders, we have never really bothered to inconvenience their posture.

Nor have we, for nearly a century now, pursued a diet that might have independently improved our own stature. With little exception, what we call sociology today is, on the one hand, an awful extravagance of ideological debates—a forest of words—that go by the name of theory and, on the other, a miscellany of findings uninformed by theory and exhuding such quantity of trivia that even sociologists find the whole mortifying. We are in a deep crisis.

2

The Deepening Crisis

What is the crisis? For some sociologists, the very question is irrelevant, misguided, if not altogether offensive. For others it is both legitimate and compelling. Certainly the issue is controversial. In our own view the crisis is pervasive and profound. It may be grasped from various perspectives, though always with only partial success. We do not and cannot aim at an in-depth analysis. But difficult though it may be to grapple with, the crisis in sociology cannot be ignored if we intend to survive as a reputable academic discipline. For it is not only a problem recognized by many within the tribe. As we shall see, outsiders, too, are cognizant of our plight; and some of these—for example, administrators and legislators—control the resources on which our future depends. Thus a first step toward possible rectification is to identify the nature of our affliction.

In a nutshell, the crisis may be described as follows: *Sociology has failed to produce a recognizable body of nomothetically organized knowledge to guide further and cumulative developments. At the same time, research areas previously or presently claimed by sociology are increasingly appropriated by a proliferating number of Schools or Programs like social work, communication, business administration, criminal justice, and urban studies. More dangerously for our continuing existence, sociology is also being cannibalized by more academically prestigious social sciences—for example, anthropology and psychology—and by various behavioral branches of evolutionary biology that constitute the frontier of the current revolution in behavioral science. The predation is facilitated by the ever-greater self-isolation of sociology from the community of evolutionary disciplines whose business is the scientific study of human behavior. Sociology is still addicted to the increasingly implausible assumption that human behavior is solely the result of socialization. Accordingly, most sociologists are unaware of, or unable to cope with, the formidable challenge coming from without.*

Nor can we achieve awareness without broadening our training so as to grasp the new theoretical instruments that are making deep inroads into the once vast sociological landscape. Unfortunately, there is little evidence that the will is there to make the needed effort anytime soon. Most sociologists may be a little uneasy in the vague feeling that something is wrong, but they remain fairly comfortable in doing what they have for decades been accustomed to doing. Thus, more tersely it may be said that the crisis in sociology consists in the fact that sociologists have accomplished little or nothing of unequivocal and lasting scientific value and, while they may be a bit uneasy about the condition, they are also willful contributors to it. In the meantime the crisis deepens.

Before proceeding with a more detailed exposition we must add a hopeful note. It is just possible that the crisis of sociology lies less in the quantity and quality of our discoveries and attempts at explanation than in our inability to know with any precision what we have accomplished and what are some of the major problems awaiting rectification and/or further investigation. From our point of view, this is like saying that at the root of the sociological crisis is the absence of a general principle or pivotal law to guide research and provide the logic for the theoretical organization of our discoveries. We shall argue that such a law, indeed several of them, already exist and form the core of the aforementioned revolution in behavioral science. Psychology and anthropology are increasingly opening to them, and show corresponding signs of scientific reinvigoration. Sciences have always borrowed from one another. Why not sociology? Herein lies the possibility of our survival. The sad question is whether it may not be already too late, or whether we are not too hopelessly unprepared. If anthropology and psychology, unlike sociology, are moving toward a theoretical alliance with evolutionary biology, the feat is in part due to the fact that those disciplines, unlike sociology, have long comprised biological specialties (e.g., physical anthropology, primatology, physiological psychology, neuropsychology). They have a headstart that is hard, though not impossible, to bridge.

Nevertheless, however distressing our plight, it is best to accept it as a challenge. We have nothing to lose, and it may not be too late. It is in this spirit of challenge and hope that we address our colleagues and their students. Failure to rise to the occasion, we fear, amounts to conceding defeat and accepting as our only option the pursuit of those same self-defeating strategies that engendered the crisis in the first place.

Signs of the Crisis

At the end of World War II, sociology was a half-century old as an academic discipline and well into its second century as a recognized social science. The scientific revolution was about four centuries old, and had broken through such formidable barriers as relativity theory, quantum mechanics, and some of the basic chemistry of molecular biology. It was now poised to scrutinize the cosmic and the subatomic dimensions of the physical universe, on the one hand, and the properties of our minutest units of organic heredity, on the other. Thus in retrospect it would seem thoroughly preposterous to imagine a society of scholars being then reminded that no scientific progress was possible without an intimate linkage between theory and research, and that there is a substantial difference between mere chatter and scientific theory.

Mid-Century Wake-Up Calls

Yet, in 1948 Robert K. Merton, one of the most esteemed sociologists of the post-World War II era, imparted precisely such lessons. He warned that much of what passed for sociological theory consisted only of "general orientations towards data, suggesting types of variables which need somehow to be taken into account, rather than clear, verifiable statements of relationships between specified variables. We have many concepts," he continued, "but few confirmed theories; many points of view, but few theorems; many 'approaches' but few conclusions. Perhaps a shift in emphasis would be all to the good" (Merton 1948: 165). The causes of this affliction, according to Merton (1948: 165), were: (1) a disjunction between theory and method; (2) a tendency among theorists to perpetuate or ape the "sterile" "grand theories" of those often referred to as "the Masters" (e.g., Coser 1971); and (3) the opposite extreme of grand theorizing, namely the plethora of miscellaneous facts, amounting to "a marked dispersion of empirical inquiries." As the years went by, Merton (e.g., 1957, 1968: chaps. 4–5), like many others, saw little or no improvement in sociological practice. Accordingly, he (1957, 1968) proceeded to propose three major remedies. One stressed the mutual bearing of theory and research. A second was a call for "theories of the middle range" as an antidote both to raw empiricism and to the grand theories of times past. Finally, he provided a "codification," "theoretical orientation," or "paradigm" termed "functional analysis."

This last proposal took fire for a few years, in part because its elements had already been published and were fairly familiar to many sociologists and cultural anthropologists, though in varying forms and from varying perspectives (e.g., Durkheim 1912; Pareto 1916; Radcliffe-Brown 1922; Malinowski 1926; Davis and Moore 1945). The heart of Merton's functional analysis is the famous essay on "manifest and latent functions" (Merton 1957, 1968). A brief examination of the paradigm may be useful both as a means of noting an opportunity possibly wasted and as a means of perceiving likely flaws that invited the waste.

Merton's (1957: chap. 1—emphasis added) essay starts as follows: "Functional analysis is at once *the most promising* and possibly the least codified of contemporary orientations to problems of sociological interpretation." It then proceeds toward a critical analysis of basic "functional terms," at the heart of which are "function," defined as an "observable objective consequence," and certain "prevailing postulates," concluding with the paradigm for functional analysis, which "presents the hard core of concept, procedure and inference in functional analysis" (Merton 1957: 50f).

The apparent emphasis is on the distinction between manifest and latent functions, what Pareto (1916: section 2115, *passim*), whom Merton had studied at Harvard under the guidance of physiologist L. J. Henderson (1935), had termed "direct and incidental effects" (Lopreato 1965, 1980). In fact, the paradigm begins with "concepts of subjective dispositions (e.g., motives, purposes)." "At some point," the author (1957: 50) justly argues, "functional analysis invariably assumes or explicitly operates with some conception of the motivation of individuals involved in a social system."

Upon subjective dispositions follow "concepts of objective consequences" (functions, dysfunctions), which contain the distinction between manifest and latent functions, and a set of other conceptual tools and directions, which for convenience sake may be represented briefly with a series of questions: Function for whom? What, if any, are the functional prerequisites of systems? What are the functional alternatives? What are the mechanisms through which functions are fulfilled? Given systemic interdependence, what are "the structural constraints" on the units that can fulfill designated functions? And what are the functionalist paths to the analysis of dynamics and change?

In fairly quick order the general understanding of the paradigm narrowed considerably. It came to be viewed broadly as a tool for the study of functions. Moreover, functional analysis became a trivialization of causal analysis. That is, if functions are defined as "observable objective consequences," there is hardly any reason why they should not be termed just plain *effects* resulting from specifiable causes. Merton had endeavored, in part, to redirect our attention from the verbiage of the Founders' grand schemes, but there was no escaping the infatuation with new words for old concepts.

It would have been useful to know that a causal analysis does not exclude a functional analysis or, better still, to recognize that the latter is a particular species of the former. It is also an inextricable part of *system analysis*. Most of us in sociology have never quite understood the special demands of system analysis and hence the fact that a proper functional analysis, as various scholars have shown (e.g., Nagel 1961: chap. 14; Hempel 1968), requires careful specification of the system under study and of the *goal state* of the system toward which given system components make particular contributions.

This sad state of affairs was encouraged by Merton himself. His famous essay on "social structure and anomie" (Merton 1957: chap. 4), for example, was intended to refute explanations of "deviant behavior" that allegedly emphasized "biological tendencies." In their place Merton (1957: 132—emphasis in the original) offered a "sociological perspective" whose "primary aim is to discern how some *social structures exert a definite pressure upon certain persons in the society to engage in nonconforming rather than conforming conduct*." The upshot of this goal is summarized in the "typology of modes of individual adaptation" (Merton 1957: 140) in view of the "disjunction" (inherent in the "American Dream") between enjoined lofty "goals" and unequally distributed "means" necessary for their achievement. Merton's emphasis is on the adaptation, that is, *function*, termed innovation. "This response," he (1957: 141) writes, "occurs when the individual has assimilated the cultural emphasis upon the goal without equally internalizing the institutional norms governing ways and means for its attainment."

But this is not, contrary to Merton's intention, functional analysis. Right or wrong, it is plain causal analysis. Innovation and other specified adaptations may at best be seen as *effects* of some cause(s), for example, the disjunction existing between the lofty goals of the American Dream and the gross inadequacy of "institutionalized" means of achievement existing in some social strata. It bears stressing that the idea of function derives from physiology, and, as Merton's own use of the term adaptation might have suggested, it refers unambiguously to an evolutionary concept. The basic idea may be rendered in simplified form as follows: Given an organism that has certain functional requirements, for example, the circulation of blood, in order to maintain a state that may be termed survival, the beating of the heart (a relatively persistent trait that coevolved with the rest of the organism) may be said to serve that requirement—it performs the function of helping the organism to survive (see, e.g., Hempel 1968: 188). Accordingly, to even begin to approximate a functional analysis, in conjunction with an inevitable causal analysis, Merton would have had to specify his system in terms of a set of variables, proceed to specify the American Dream as the system goal state, and conclude that, among other things, innovation, etc. had the function of perpetuating (or doing something to) the American Dream. It might have helped if Merton had more fully understood the biological foundation of the form of analysis he was seeking. But if this is asking too much of Merton, it is not asking too much of those who read him. Yet, the discipline paid no heed to the problem even when outside critics most assuredly did (e.g., Nagel 1961: chap. 14; Hempel 1968: 188).

What happened to functional analysis? Mostly, and for a while, the topic surrounded itself with a great deal of trifling debate. Moreover, lacking an understanding of the fundamentals of system analysis, sociologists came to consider functional analysis (or functionalism—indeed, various kinds of functionalism) as a special approach to sociological theorizing somehow invented, or at least perfected, by sociologists for their own very special and unique needs. Then the reaction set in. As early as 1959, Kingsley Davis (1959), then president of the American Sociological Association, could address his colleagues with a topic titled "The Myth of Functional Analysis as a Special Method in Sociology and Anthropology" (but see Turner and Maryanski 1979). A decade later at the latest, functionalism was gasping on its deathbed.

Indeed, already by the end of World War II, committed sociologists could not avoid alerting their colleagues to the fact that the promise of sociology was in jeopardy. In the same year of Merton's wake-up call, Edward Shils (1948), for example, wrote that, despite the large output of empirical studies and conceptual essays, there was a widespread degree of "bewilderment...about the rationale of sociology" accompanied by "the contemptuous and often ill-informed hostility of the other parts of the academic profession towards sociology" (Shils 1948: 3).

The concern was "not without justification." Sociology had "not yet ascended to the heights of science.... There is a vast disorder in sociology. There is little cumulative growth, relatively little deliberate concentration of effort on major problems; and those who demand a finished science or definitive answers are justified in their dissatisfaction" (Shils 1948: 4). Shils, however, remained hopeful, seeing "signs, here and there, of a turn in the right direction—in the selection of problems, in the formulation of hypotheses, and in the creation and application of techniques" (Shils 1948: 4).

Shils' most basic preoccupation was that sociological research all too frequently lacked any grounding in "explicit causal hypotheses" (Shils 1948: 26). Sociologists were skilled in the collection of vast quantities of descriptive material, but lacked the means to systematically "classify their raw data." As a result, they were forced to test their hypotheses "by very rough impressions rather than by rigorous proof" (Shils 1948: 44). The proper rigor "can be achieved only if observations are made to test hypotheses and *if hypotheses are fitted into a general system of propositions, internally consistent with one another*" (Shils 1948: 55—emphasis added). Unfortunately, this essential accomplishment has not come to pass.

Giants with Feeble Shoulders

For about a quarter of a century, beginning in the 1940s, two American scholars were in contention for theoretical supremacy. One was Talcott Parsons, R.K. Merton's intellectual kinsman. His sociological recipe bore the name of "structural functionalism." The other was George C. Homans, originally the foremost exponent of Vilfredo Pareto's (1916) general sociology (Homans and Curtis 1934; Homans 1950). His brand of sociology was widely known as "exchange theory" (for a useful collection of comparative analyses of these two scholars, see Turk and Simpson 1971).

George C. Homans. The very label of Homans' speciality, as a name for a general sociology, is an indication of sociological crisis. The fundamental assumption of exchange theory is that persons are engaged in networks of reciprocities. That is true enough, but even when explicated in some detail it is only a limited part of a much fuller story. Why are there varying degrees of faithfulness to rules? And why do we have reciprocity systems in the first place? These, and others, are crucial questions that Homans' (1961, 1974) work does not satisfactorily confront. Presented as general theory rather than as an aspect of it, it helped to fuel modifications and controversies that perpetuated the crisis while adding to its complexity (see, e.g., Blau 1964, among many others; and

Turner 1991: chaps. 14–16 for a brave attempt to make sense of exhange theory).

Whatever its defects, however, Homans' exchange theory contained valuable lessons. Pareto's old insistence that the fundamental focus of sociological theory must be on "the social molecules," namely on individuals as agents of behavior, became law in the work of Homans who, like Merton and Parsons, had learned Pareto at Harvard University from the physiologist Lawrence J. Henderson (1935). This methodological individualism transpires in the very title of his major work, *Social Behavior: Its Elementary Forms* (1961). As Homans put it succinctly in his 1964 presidential address to the American Sociological Association, this work involved "bringing men back in" (Homans 1964)—focusing on the properties of individual actors as contrasted to the tendency in structural functionalism to focus on structural properties. To strengthen his point, Homans (1967) wrote a basic book on the scientific method with the focus on social science.

Homans' work may well be judged by historians of twentieth-century social science as one of the closest approximations to a scientific sociological theory. It also set the stage for several renditions of exchange theory, as illustrated by P. Blau's 1964 *Exchange and Power in Social Life* and more recent contributions to what today is commonly called "rational choice theory" (e.g., Hechter 1987; Coleman 1990). In a language that is both eminently readable and on the whole falsifiable, Homans' work covers, inadequately but with a clear grasp of the fundamentals of scientific inquiry, many if not most of the elementary aspects of the human condition: reciprocity, power, authority, aggression, cooperation, conformity, dissent, leadership, innovation, status relationships, and some of the basic emotions. Unlike most sociologists, Homans was at pains to distinguish between variables, or "properties of nature" properly speaking (say, frequency or intensity), and more discriptive terms (e.g., social structure and role, among the more beloved darlings of the sociological vocabulary). By the same token, he was clearly aware that scientific propositions specify relationships between properties of nature, and are thus inherently quantitative in nature (Homans 1967).

Accordingly, Homans could rightly argue that, even assuming an abundance of discoveries in sociology, there was reason for concern about the future of the discipline. The job of a science is not merely discovery of facts. It is *discovery plus explanation*. Moreover, the basic aim of a science is to "deduce the largest variety of empirical findings from the smallest number of general propositions." Having achieved this "economy of thought," no longer does a science "face just one damn finding after another. It has acquired an organization" (Homans 1967: 27).

That was a breath of fresh air harking back to the Founders. Of course, in science there are different levels of theoretical organization. The organization that, for example, embraces Kepler's empirical laws contitutes a lower, less comprehensive level than that which surrounds Newton's law of universal gravitation. There are narrower and broader types of methodological individualism. Unfortunately, Homans chose the narrower, grounding his theory in the environmentalistic premises of B.F. Skinner's (e.g., 1938, 1953) behaviorism. The upshot of this denouement, to the extent that it influenced sociologists, was to help perpetuate two of our most debilitating deficiencies: (1) the assumption that the explanation of individuals' behavior lies in their past experiences, and (2) the failure, ironically, to honor his own cherished principle of economy of thought.

The following is one of Homans' (1961, 1967, 1974) most commonly applied general propositions: "The greater the value of a reward to a person, the more likely he is to take action to get that reward." Good enough, as a statement of central tendencies, whose worth Homans (1967: 20) is inclined to deride. But is it a general proposition? That depends on what is meant by "general." Economy of thought demands that we explain individuals' *tendency to value rewards*. That is a feat that Homans, shackled by behaviorist dogmas, did not even consider. By his own standards, therefore, his general proposition is not much of an explanatory proposition at all. It is more like a discovery, the sort of thing that, as he (1967) notes, we already have an excess of in sociology.

The fundamental flaw in Homans' Skinnerianism—and in exchange theory in general—was the perpetuation of Locke's *tabula rasa* assumption, namely the failure to understand that human beings cannot be conditioned to act outside of the potentials developed during the evolutionary history of our species. No doubt we behave as we do as a result of experience. The role of learning—or socialization, as sociologists prefer to say—cannot be denied. Without socialization we would not become human. But experience does not shape the development of behavior without guidance from innate predispositions. Thus we learn some things a great deal more easily than others, some more efficiently at certain stages of development than at others, and some not at all. Behaviorist theory focuses at best on the *how* of learned behavior—on the techniques of learning; it neglects the *why*, the *when*, and much of the *what* (for an excellent critique of the "standard social science model" in general, see Tooby and Cosmides 1992). Accordingly, the real error does not lie in the sociologist's emphasis on socialization. The focus is justified. The problem lies in the failure to recognize that learning is an evolved adaptation—that learning is "biased" in view of our species' evolutionary history (e.g., Lumsden and Wilson 1981). In short, learning is only a vague one-half of the whole story.

Talcott Parsons. The case of Talcott Parsons is far more complex. He was a much more prolific writer, but also much more repetitive, turgid, and perhaps harder to evaluate. Parsons' goal was nothing less than the integration of sociology, anthropology, psychology, and economics (Berger 1963: 184). This effort, though laudable in principle, must be judged a failure, in part because Parsons focused on emergent phenomena as the lynchpin of his analysis. Now, a focus on emergent properties of behavior in principle involves many exciting questions and eventually may yield rewarding answers. But science has barely begun to develop the tools necessary for the analysis of emergent phenemona in even the most elementary of "complex adaptive systems" (e.g., Waldrop 1992). In the hands of sociologists, like a Durkheim or a Parsons, the emphasis on emergence rarely if ever transcends the level of descriptive analogy, thereby encouraging a tremendously oversimplified and reified conception of human society (e.g., Machalek and Cohen 1991; Turner 1991: chaps. 2–3).

At the expense of omitting numerous details and various pathways along which Parsons proceeded, the focus of his writings may be viewed as an effort to develop a "general theory of action" (e.g., Parsons 1951; Parsons and Shils 1951). This work is organized around an elaborate conceptual scheme describing basic system functions (adaptation, goal attainment, integration, and latent pattern maintenance) allegedly operating at distinct, but mutally dependent, levels of analysis (the behavioral, personality, social, and cultural subsystems). In addition, each of these subsystems and the elements within them are so conceived that they too are amenable to the same sort of four-function assessment. This classification of the functional traits of several sequentially inclusive systems, subsystems, sub-subsystems, and so on has led one scholar to conclude that "Parsonian theory…is only a kind of parlor game in which one invents puzzle-boxes and then solves them, with each solution making possible a whole further set of puzzles" (Collins 1988: 60).

Inasmuch as Parsons intended to develop a theory to explain the functional quality of social systems, the Hobbesian problem of order

loomed large in his sociology. How are individuals motivated to behave in ways that are conducive to order and societal stability and survival? Parsons' answer was guided largely by Durkheim's ambiguous
dictum that the forces engendering conformity and commitment are
external to the individual. In his view (1951), societal stability and survival depend on the system's capacity to instill overarching "value orientations" in its members, commiting them to common attitudes, beliefs,
values. Normative consensus—especially regarding the distribution of
statuses, roles, and rewards—is thus alleged to be essential for the
maintenance of a stable social order. The assertion invites two fundamental objections that, taken together, partially reveal the inadequa-
cies of Parsons' effort.

First, by focusing on the social system as the crucial unit of analysis,
along with the attendant emphasis on societal prerequisites and functions, Parsons (e.g., 1964) ignores or minimizes the fact that societies
are a heterogeneous blend of individuals and groups often adhering to
divergent interests and values that are a real threat to social order. This
is a conventional complaint leveled against structural-functionalism in
general and Parsonian sociology in particular (e.g., Turk and Simpson
1971). The stricture is well-taken, and indicates that at a crucial point
in his analysis Parsons forgot at least one of the good lessons once
learned in Pareto's (1916) earlier version of system analysis, namely
that the basic units of analysis are men and women in the flesh with
often conflicting orientations to conformity.

Second, the causal priority that Parsons attached to the social system also led him to stumble over the closely related question concerning the sources of individual commitment to the social order. In this
context we confront Parsons' assessment of the relationship between
individual and society and the mysterious workings of its agents: socialization along with enigmatic sociocultural forces external to the
individual. Recall that in Parsons' scheme societal survival depends on
widespread commitment to certain value orientations. These are said
to be inculcated in individuals through the influence of parents, siblings, neighbors, peers, schools, churches, and so on (e.g., Parsons 1951:
chap. VI). At birth, individuals are portrayed as entering the world with
an array of needs (for food, warmth, protection, etc.). Over time, while
embedded in specific configurations of status and role relations, they
are said to successively employ five "cathetic-evaluative mechanisms"
("reinforcement-extinction, inhibition, substitution, imitation and identification") and, later in their development, two "cognitive mechanisms"

("discrimination and generalization") enabling them to incorporate the normative content of their environment (Parsons 1951: 209f). Value orientations are thereby pressed onto the raw mental map of individuals. But there is no answer in this scenario to a variety of basic questions. Why, for example, are individuals susceptible to reinforcement in the first place? Why do they inhibit certain desires, substitute others, or imitate and identify with those around them? We are told only that, though it is individuals who act, their motivations to act can be understood only in terms of the social systems they are a part of. The cart is placed firmly before the horse, as the following passage makes abundantly clear (Parsons 1951: 202–03—emphasis in the original):

> We may take for granted that motivation is *always* a process which goes on in one or more *individual* actors. We may speak of the "motivation" of a collectivity only in an elliptical sense of referring to certain *uniformities* in the motivations of its members, or to a certain *organization* of those motivations. But in order to select the relevant uniformities and patterns of organization, it is necessary to have criteria of relevance which are seldom if ever given in generalized knowledge of motivational process itself. It must be given in terms of mechanisms which involve, as part of their conceptualization, the specification of the types of consequences of alternative outcomes of the processes concerned which are significant to the social system. But in order to make this specification in turn we must be in a position to say in systematic terms what these consequences are. It is this circumstance which…gives the "structural" analysis of the social system a certain priority over its "dynamic" or motivational analysis. If we do not have the structural analysis we do not know where to begin dynamic conceptualization, because we are unable to judge the relevance of motivational processes and laws, above all to distinguish between mechanisms of personality and mechanisms of the social system.

Of course, to be able to judge the relevance of motivational processes and laws, one must look deep into time and be willing to open the door wide to modern psychology and the behavioral laws of human evolution. There is a difference between inability and unwillingness.

A more thorough critique of Parsons' sociology would have to delve much more deeply than is the case in the preceding comments. Fortunately, our basic intention is only to define a crisis in which his work participated. For this task, the fortunes of Parsons' work in subsequent sociological theorizing speak more clearly than any further analysis of ours possibly could. Parsons has disappeared almost entirely from the current scene. That is not exactly a surprise. Even a quarter of a century ago, at the peak of his fame, it would have been hard to predict that his success would be very notable today.

His critics were many, and by his own account (Parsons 1971) the quarrels were less a result of technical disagreements than of basic misunderstandings. But whose misunderstandings? And why so many? The criticisms suggested that it was Parsons himself who did not fully understand what he was producing. Either that or he had a naive conception of what science was all about and hence could only engage in complexly trite disquisitions.

One of the most telling statements on the state of Parsons' theory was provided by the philosopher of science Max Black (1961b: 268–88; but see also the other essays in Black's [1961a] collection, especially the critical exegeses by Edward C. Devereux, Jr. [1961: 1–63] and Robin M. Williams, Jr. [1961: 64–99]). Focusing on Parsons and Shils' (1951) *Toward a General Theory of Action*, Black (1961b: 279–80) was led to conclude that "the component concepts of Parsons' scheme are laymen's concepts in the thin disguise of a technical-sounding terminology." We quote below the core of Black's verdict.

> The following might be the result of trying to express Parsons' postulates in plain English:
> 1. "Whenever you do anything, you're trying to get something done."
> 2. "What you do depends upon what you want, how you look at things, and the position you find yourself in."
> 3. "You can't do anything without thinking and having feelings at the same time."
> 4. "Human life is one long set of choices."
> 5. "Choosing means taking what seems best for you or what others say is the right thing."
> 6. "When you deal with other people, you always have to take account of what they expect you to do."
> 7. "There's a lasting pattern to the way people behave."
> 8. "Families, business firms, and other groups of persons often behave surprisingly like persons."
>
> I think these aphorisms contain nearly all of the content of the Parsonian principles....

Black proceeded to offer a fundamental lesson about the nature of scientific discovery and explanation. We quote again:

> Perhaps this shows how close Parsons has remained to the wisdom of the *hoi polloi*. But one may wonder whether it is plausible for fundamental social theory to be so close to common sense. If the history of the development of the natural sciences is any guide, fundamental social theory will have to employ recondite notions, at a considerable remove from direct observation, in order to have any hope of providing an adequate framework for research. As Ernest Nagel [1952: 63] has said, the concepts of a comprehensive social theory "will have to be apparently remote from the familiar and obvious traits found in any one society; its articulation will involve the use of novel algorithmic techniques; and its applica-

tion to concrete materials will require special training of high order." Parsons' theory is far removed from these requirements.

Once upon a time in the history of science it was one thing to argue, for example, that the apple falls when it's ripe; that epitomizes the Parsonian, and the normal, depth of sociological theorizing. It was quite another to finally conceptualize the apple's fall in terms of a force, gravity, that is conditioned by such intervening variables as mass and distance. In *Principia Mathematica*, Newton tells of his extraordinary insight in 1666 that the force acting on the falling apple was the same force that acted on the "falling" or orbiting of the moon. No longer would scientific minds be ruled by concrete and immediate conceptions of the separation of earth and sky. Scientific prediction on a grand scale was born out of the organizing anchorage point provided by the law of universal gravitation. It was this law that made possible, for example, Halley's persuasive and correct prediction that, since a particular comet (Halley) had appeared in 1531, 1607, and 1682 (about every seventy-six years), it could also be expected to reappear, as it did, in 1758 (Trefil 1989: chaps. 1–2). Physical science proceeded to develop at vertiginous speed. Sociology will never get anywhere but farther out of the scientific course as long as it adheres to the banality that the fundamental cause of behavior resides exclusively in the immediate influence of culture and social structure.

The Crisis is an Open Secret

M. Black's verdict on the work of one who, some believed, was the Newton of sociology was an indictment of sociology in general. In fact, there has been a multiplicity of analogous, though perhaps kinder, indictments. Two years before Black's criticism, C. Wright Mills, one of the most eloquent voices within the profession itself, had taken whole pages of Parsons' language and reduced them into far more economical "in-other-words" (e.g., Mills 1959: chap. 2). Parsons' work was "drunk on syntax, blind to semantics" (Mills 1959: 34). Mills cried for "the sociological imagination." This implied a variety of scholarly virtues. In the "Age of Fact," on the one hand, and "Grand Theory," on the other, it referred especially to "a quality of mind that will help...to use information and to develop reason in order to achieve lucid summation of what is going on in the world and what may be happening within" ourselves (Mills 1959: 4). Further, the "sociological imagination enables us to grasp history and biography *and the relations between the two* within society" (Mills 1959: 6—emphasis added).

Speaking of social science in general, Mills (1959: 132—emphasis added) rightly argued that it "is properly about...the human variety, which consists of *all social worlds in which men have lived*, are living, and might live." Accordingly, he (1959: 6–7) could raise questions that were continuous both with the early promise of sociology and with modern behavioral science, for example: "Where does this society stand in human history? What are the mechanics by which it is changing?... What kinds of 'human nature' are revealed in the conduct and character we observe in this society in this period?" Given such alarm calls, one might have predicted some widespread concern, some serious scrutiny of our craft, and perhaps some mending of our ways. In fact, libraries have been bulging with the sociological wisdom of the *hoi polloi*. Fortunately they also contain respectable empirical studies and some realistic awareness of the affliction, although the latter is sometimes revealed by cheerleaders rather than by professionals intent on finding a remedy.

Several years ago, for example, *Perspectives*, the newsletter of the Theory Section of the American Sociological Association, published the following disheartening statement: "There is no longer a theoretical core [in sociology], such as Parsons provided in the bygone postwar era" (Gerstein and Sciulli 1987). The authors proceeded to point out trends toward alliances among other social sciences that underscored the increasing isolation of sociology. There are several points worth noting in the quoted verdict. First, it recognizes the crisis; in principle that is helpful. Second, it seems to be saying: C. Wright Mills, Max Black, Ernest Nagel, and like-minded critics all be damned!, when Parsons was around we did have a core. Third, the statement suggests a conception of theoretical cores that lays bare the great depth of the sociological crisis; do cores dissolve that easily! Had Parsons not died a few years ago, would we now have a core? Put otherwise: Copernicus, Galileo, and Newton died in 1543, 1642, and 1727, respectively; did the core provided by them for a scientific revolution disappear with their passing away? Surely cores are more than mere names. Most of what is termed sociological theory consists of names, labels, and an excess of verbiage on commonplace topics typically invested with one ideology or another. There has never been a core in sociology.

On the International Scene

But when no reliable standard exists to judge the state of an art, what is coreless assortment to one may very well appear as a unitary discipline to another, at least at a distance, though the more immediate view may also be chaotic. Around 1992, the editor of *Theory*, the newsletter of the Theory Section of the International Sociological Association, asked a European colleague to write "a short article on the current state of European social theory." The heart of the answer follows (Joas, n.d.: 1–2—circa 1992):

> There is simply no counterpart to American sociology in the sense of unitary European sociology. What we have is a mere juxtaposition of very different national traditions which are heterogeneous in themselves. France, for example, is in many intellectual respects like an island. The deeper sources of many German contributions are very distinctly German, in spite of all contact between American and German scholars.

Joas proceeds to state that in recent years the "scope of sociological theory has been narrowed" by complementary developments in philosophy and economics, which "play a much more important role in public discussion than does sociology"—in the case of economics through the increasing appeal of rational action models. One of the reasons for this situation, Joas continues, "may be that the most pressing problems of our age are not typical fields of interest for sociological traditions. This is true in the case of ecological problems, the origins of war, inequalities on the international level, and the transformation from Stalinism to capitalism and democracy."

So, add *irrelevance, isolation,* and *removal from reality* to the wisdom of the *hoi polloi.* As the Founders recognized, the fundamental sociological issues concern the vicissitudes of the evolution, present and current, of society and culture. Therefore, our most pressing problems are global in nature (e.g., Pareto 1916; Mills 1959; Horowitz 1993). They are global, in the vast majority of the cases, even when they appear to be strictly local, *simply because human nature is global.* So, for example, the findings of a study—a very good study—of "job training in U.S. organizations" (Knoke and Kalleberg 1994) is hardly of lasting relevance apart from, say, issues of technological innovation and the competition, at both the personal and the intersocietal levels, that innovation helps to engender. Likewise, the multitude of studies of racial affairs in the U.S. is of little significance if disconnected, for example, from the facts in Rwanda and Bosnia, to mention but two (seemingly disparate) cases.

With very few, and hardly influential exceptions, sociology has proven to be unregretfully inept on the global scene. Too many sociologists are obsessed with parochial problems typically proposed by personal experience and ideology (Cole 1994b: 148). Despite the extraordinarily intense focus on ethnic prejudice and conflict in American sociology, no one in sociology even imagined that, as part of the turmoil in Eastern Europe, the Balkan volcano would explode and the republics of the old Yugoslavia proceed to erupt in genocidal hostilities. Worse still, S.G. Meštrovic´ (1996: 203) has noted that not a single session at the 1995 meeting of the American Sociological Association was devoted to "the genocide that has been going on for the past five years in the Balkans and elsewhere in the world, nor to the difficulties experienced by Eastern Europe and Russia as they try to emulate Western liberal institutions." But there was a great abundance on gender and race in the program. It is humiliating to consider that Ronald Reagan, the *bête noire* of the typical sociologist in the 1980s, may have had a keener eye than sociologists on the dynamics of the Soviet empire. And yet we should have known. People despise capricious and violent masters. They deeply resent their poverty when great wealth is consumed conspicuously by the masters. And they certainly cherish the freedom to enhance their comfort according to their self-conceived merits. This and so much more is well-known about human beings—outside of sociology. How very little, if at all, is sociology interested in the current evolution of the former Eastern European nations, the various African nations, the Russian Federation, the China Mammoth, the intended European Union, or for that matter the changing political culture of the United States!

We are reminded of the many occasions when well-meaning colleagues in effect solve the worry about our crisis with the bromide that sociology is Social Critique, not a science. Others view social science as a whole as "public philosophy" (Bellah et al. 1985: 297). So relax, we are told; don't take our problems too seriously. There is, however, a little flaw in this dodge. Countless periodicals throughout the world perform social critique and popular philosophy functions far better than sociological *hoi polloi*. With our poorly written banalities, we cannot even begin to compete with the likes of the *New Republic* and *Foreign Affairs*, to name but two among numberless possible examples.

The pages of *Theory* are worth pursuing further because in recent years they have devoted much attention to the state of sociology—or, as we may more correctly say, to the state of the sociologies. Three major trends in the commentaries are observable. One is represented by what we may call the *diplomats*. An illustration is provided by the editors of *Sociology in Europe: In Search of Identity* (Nedelmann and Sztompka 1994). The diplomats recognize the crisis or lack of identity but proceed on the assumption that a strong faith and a quickly organized conference among heterogeneous points of view may very well solve the crisis after all. Unfortunately, Faith and science do not mix. Moreover, the very recognition that there is a *European* sociology containing sub-sociologies implicitly ridicules the lingering idea of sociology as a discipline conceived universally in the singular. It hardly helps to argue, as the editors do in their introduction, that the disharmony between sociologies stimulates scientific development. Tension by itself is not creative. Besides, development of what? German, Polish, French sociology?

Admired, even applauded, by the diplomats are, ironically, what we may loosely term the *regional realists*. An excellent representation of this faction is Richard Münch's (1994) essay published in the aforementioned collection on sociology in Europe. Title notwithstanding, this essay says little of value about the German contribution to European sociology. What it really does is to argue that as long as sociology remains addicted to the focus on cultural diversity and the assumption of cultural determinism, it can only add up to a peculiar mixture of national sociologies—a condition that has been noted often before (e.g., Aron 1965, I: 1–11).

But something worse inheres in the culturalist epistemology of this brand of sociological practice. Just as ethnocentrism leads peoples to battle one another, so national sociologies contend with one another, and their relative influence reflects to an extent the relative political and economic power of their respective nations. So, Münch clearly wishes to say, for a while after World War II, American sociology reigned supreme, though Americans had profited from absorbing the thought of earlier European scholars. But as the decades approached the end of the second millennium, American power waned and European, especially German, power waxed. Add the persisting superiority of European intellectual prowess, and who now in the United States can compete with the likes of Habermas and Luhmann? And some scholars, American as well as European, would include Derrida and Foucault in this cozy little circle. We do not share this assessment of relative worth.

The debate has involved a number of participants on both sides of the Atlantic. For instance, Jeffrey Alexander (1994), the American paladin in the battle, took issue with various points, real or imagined, in the

Münch essay. On the whole, his position seemed defensive, not entirely true to text, and a bit vacuous. Münch (1995: 2—emphasis added), in turn, reacted angrily, in part by demanding that Alexander read his other publications; in part also through a reinterpretation of what, by his own admission, were "some exaggerations." He then accused Alexander of having "written a pamphlet that *misrepresents and distorts my argument in such a fundamental way that the contrary to my intentions emerges.*" Such is the nature of many sociological debates. Sociologists either do not wish to carefully read one another or they are unable to. Either way it's bad business.

The third strain occupying the debating pages of *Theory* consists of a small number of scholars who recognize the crisis and say so publicly—and hopefully. We may call them the *pragmatists*. A couple of examples follow. Writing from Spain, J.E. Rodriquez-Ibanez (1997: 6–7) has recently lamented:

> The real thing is that sociology has dramatically lost reputational ground everywhere since the golden years of the fifties and sixties [nostalgia *assidue* for the phantom core]: as thinkers and leaders of public opinion we are superseded by philosophers and political scientists, and even as professionals of surveys, market prospects, human resources or management we are superseded by economists and social psychologists.

What to do? The situation is not "apocalyptic." "Our task is to follow" the tradition of the "great theoretical classics like *Suicide* or *The Protestant Ethic*," that is, build on "the shoulders of makers of plausible hypotheses such as Durkheim, Weber, Parsons or Merton." This is an astonishing invitation to retrace the path that has led to the present pickle. There is no glimpse in this practical scholar's analysis of the most crippling problem of sociology, namely its almost total isolation from the extraordinary revolution taking place in behavioral science under the aegis of neo-Darwinian theory.

Five years earlier, another pragmatist had been less patient with his tribe. The Swedish sociologist G. Therborn (n.d.: 1–2—circa 1992) cried bluntly: "What about taking ourselves seriously?" Why is it, he asks, that in our theory journals and at professional meetings the "ridiculous" is more common than the "sublime," "bombastic banalities" more frequent than "rigour and erudition," "sheer wooliness" less rare than "brilliance"? And why do "a significant number of serious sociologists accept this state of affairs?" The debate continues, but by now we get the idea. Ours is a form of paralysis.

A View from the Real World

The signs of the crisis are innumerable. In January 1978, *Footnotes*, the monthly newsletter of the American Sociological Association, initiated a series of articles and comments by sociologists in a variety of job settings. This first, titled "Is Sociology Relevant to the Real World? Yes but...," reported comments by a number of sociologists in nonacademic jobs. Some were cheerful or at least complacent. Most were not. Listed below are some of the latter:

- in "criminal justice, most of the thinking has been done and the policy made by lawyers";
- "most sociologists tend to be myopic...[and] to frame problem questions... with little regard to input from other disciplines";
- sociologists "don't do enough communicating. And when they do communicate they often sound like amateur politicians rather than skilled scientists";
- often the non-academic sociologist's form of communication consists of "telling someone how relevant [sociology] is rather than showing them how it can be relevant";
- "we sometimes bore the world with our truisms and platitudes rather than enlightening it with new ideas";
- "even reading the *New Republic*, I notice writers sneering at sociologists' language";
- "sociology is still perceived as 'soft.'"

Clearly, the practitioners sent by sociology into the real world to market its wares are by their own assessment poorly equipped to sell very much at all. In the meantime the real world will not go away, and sociology will be under ever greater pressure to prove its worth. After all, the university is a crucial institution of modern society and the value of its output necessarily receives periodic public scrutiny, especially in view of recurring fiscal crises.

In a recent article in the *New York Times Magazine* Louis Menand (1996) has directed attention to the crisis in graduate training in general and to that of graduate programs in the social sciences and the humanities in particular. It takes too long to get a Ph.D., and then the market fails to accommodate large percentages of applicants. The university was a great beneficiary of the cold war. Education budgets are now in serious trouble. As professors retire or depart for other reasons, budget lines leave with them. The fiscal crisis is serious, and will not vanish in the forseeable future. In such a context, is there any real justification for separate departments of anthropology, sociology, political science, even history? If push comes to shove, who is ready to bet on sociology to prevail? As we shall see, deans have a poor opinion of sociologists. Our intellectual and political clout on campuses is the lowest, in part because we are isolated and have few or no allies in other departments and colleges. Fiscal crises tend to prey on the weakest enterprises.

In an exceptionally frank and limpid statement on the fortunes of the discipline, Joan Huber (1995: 195) has offered the following remarks:

> My biases are those of a sociologist turned administrator. Especially in bad times, administrators tend to think like ecologists because they must deal with competition for a pie never big enough to go around. They must choose, in effect, between a semistarvation diet for everyone or the starving of weaker units in order to give stronger ones a chance to flourish. Cuts across the board may please feeble units, but they enrage strong ones and weaken the institution.

Professor Huber's logic and the realities it rests on give a lesson of profound, practical significance across a variety of fields and problems. Here at least, she also reveals sociologists at their very best. The diagnosis is impeccable. Accordingly, we should seek all available means to strengthen our credentials. As matters stand now, however, most sociologists may be expected to react by debating the wrong causes of our impotence or by settling down in apathetic if not virulent denial. Indeed, the denial came immediately in thoroughly postmodernist form and thus in part grounded in the claim that a scientific sociology is undemocratic or antidemocratic (Denzin 1997). Never mind administrators' realities. According to one of Huber's critics (Hill 1996: especially 230–33), there is "hypocritical incongruity" in her arguments; she is "hosting a puritanical witch hunt"; she and her "privileged club" are "deftly purveying exclusionary venom"; and they should be held "accountable for their pernicious, intolerant and increasingly shrill brand of antirationalist demagoguery." Oh Virtue, why art Thou so Unholy?

Or consider the reaction to a rather mild discussion of our difficulties carried several years ago by *Newsweek* (Kantrowitz 1992). The author begins by pointing to sociologists' dismay at the then recent recommendation by a faculty committee at Yale University, where the great W.G. Sumner held sway a century ago, that the sociology staff be slashed by some 40 percent as part of a broad cost-cutting plan. "Sociology has always had an image of being more liberal than the other social sciences," was the quoted reaction of a sociologist at another Ivy League school. The statement, true or otherwise, is hardly to the point, considering that sociology began its decline, from whatever height it had achieved, during the 1930s, precisely when American liberalism was at its peak, and proved itself most inept during the 1960s, a period of popular revolutionary fervor and widespread student sympathy for sociology.

The *Newsweek* article points to a number of problems and signs thereof, including the elimination, or threatened elimination, of some sociology departments; the heavy reduction of American students earning Bachelors of Arts in sociology between 1973 and 1989 (presumably from 35,996 to 14,393); and the grumbling of some members of the American Sociological Association at its annual meetings, where "the subjects are often trivial and...jargon has overtaken thought." The author further notes "a methodological division in the ranks," referring to the almost total lack of communication between "the quantifiers" and "the thinkers" (presumably the theorists).

The *Newsweek* author hypothesizes that sociology "may simply be a victim of its own success" and claims to quote a distinguished sociologist to the effect that "out of sociology has come a major proportion of the people who describe American life to the public." Sociologists have allegedly created social work, opinion polling, urban studies, market research, and, we may add, such other areas as criminal justice programs and much of the "theory" and methods taught in business schools and schools of communication. In principle, however, it is not clear why such fertility, if real, should be damaging to sociology. Philosophy has long played midwife to various disciplines and yet it keeps spawning, relatively free of academic difficulties. Indeed, Georg Simmel (1950), one of the more insightful sociologists at the turn of the century, would have had sociology be the basic social science, entrusted with the task of providing the theory of the "forms" wherein the substance of other social sciences would be studied. Nevertheless, as already noted, at present it is true that to an extent the crisis of sociology is an effect of the proliferation of academic and other programs of endeavor that specialize in more productive or practical types of sociologizing. They tread where we dare not, or do not know how. At the same time, sociology has no core to keep the offshoots from going too far astray.

"My own feeling," James Coleman, then president of the American Sociological Association, is allegedly quoted as saying in the *Newsweek* article, is that "it's extremely important for sociology to demonstrate its utility to society if it's going to be viable in the long run." We share that feeling. We shall also argue that at present sociology offers a shallow and distorted view of human nature that prevents it from understanding the real world and thus from the likelihood of demonstrating its utility to society.

And the Footnotes

The *Newsweek* article triggered off a lively debate in the "Open Forum" section of *Footnotes*, the official newsletter of the American Sociological Association. In the following comments we prefer not to refer to names, though our information is subject to easy verification. The participants are a good representation of the ASA. The first reaction may be found in the May 1992 issue. One writer is livid, and commits just about all the errors typical of sociologists in deep denial. His students, he reports with inflated pride, are hungry for sociology even at the ungodly hour of the first morning class. For him sociology is not only important. It is the salvation of all our ills. It shows that people pursue goals through the wrong strategies. "They...say they prefer peace to war" but would find peace "in the realm of technology." Or they foolishly turn to biology for the answer to the pregnant question, "Where do all these babies come from?" Or take the naive chemists who "got into the act and invented a simple pill that would stop the flow of babies." In short, never mind biology, chemistry, agronomy, the Supreme Court, and just about everything else. Without a shadow of a doubt, "all the world and national problems that concern us most have their solutions in the realm addressed by sociology: the ways we humans devise for living with each other," otherwise labeled "the structuring of political and economic systems, the nature of inequality, and so forth."

No hint is given as to how sociology can solve the social problems arising from such structuring, despite the fact that it is humans who devise it. Just the same, the author is absolutely certain that it is "social structure" that "holds the explanation" for our social problems. Unfortunately for this advocate, social structure is "something invisible" and thus the "importance of the sociological enterprise is sometimes difficult to see"— no matter that astrophysicists, for instance, do manage to find things that they cannot see. But see we must, for it is this "invisible realm that must be probed and understood if we are to create a truly humane and just society."

This untutored obsession with the "just society" is in some sense admirable, but it can hardly win sociologists much respect either in the scholarly community or in the population at large. One wonders how many of the students crowding in this professor's early morning course proceeded to become attorneys, physicians, businesspeople, politicians, soldiers, journalists, and so on—people far too clever, and far more practical, who sensed the wisdom of the *hoi polloi* in the first place and who never forgot the trained naiveté of the sociology professor.

In the same May 1992 issue of *Footnotes* another sociologist is far more scholarly in an attempt to show that the *Newsweek* article "greatly understated sociology's stature and vitality," but in the process he sounds a bit too much like a cheerleader. He recalls, for example, that one of our own "has played a leading role in the research battle against AIDS"; that "sociologists have led the way in refining survey research methods" (which have contributed little or nothing to the solution of the crisis); that another one of our own has played a role of "inspired leadership" at the National Institute on Aging; and so forth. Three months later, in the August 1992 issue of *Footnotes*, another sociologist both challenges and joins this optimism with an invitation to consider the publicity as beneficial to sociology but also to be more realistic about our difficulties. He briefly enumerates six problems facing sociology: "disciplinary fragmentation," "jargon," "too much success" ("Other disciplines have stolen our concepts and methods and we are left impoverished"), a lack of demonstrated "usefulness," "conservatism" in the era of "Reagan/Bush/Buchanan," and "unfulfilled promises" (the failure to deliver on "our utopian visions").

Much could be said about this interesting view of our crisis. We shall focus briefly on the alleged conservatism dominating American society. By this scholar's logic, we should have fared better as a science in the 1930s and 1960s. But that, as indicated by Merton's and Shils' lament and other signs of the crisis noted earlier in this chapter, is when our troubles began turning into our Furies. And what is meant by "conservatism" anyhow? Consider another *Footnotes* column, right next to the one that just above lists the problems facing sociology. Its author writes in support of a colleague's prior "objections concerning the questionnaire that Sociologists for Women in Society (SWS) inflict on candidates for ASA offices." "The questionnaire," justly states the writer, "is a study in the unbridled pursuit of single-issue politics, a disaster for a country or a learned association." Is the intellectual despotism of SWS "liberal"? Sociologists are a bit glib with such labels as "conservatism" and "liberalism." What does the ASA do with this sort of sociological politics? According to the same concerned author, it "has become and will remain little more than a conglomeration of contending interest groups, none of which give even lip service to the promotion of sociology as a discipline" (see also Simpson and Simpson 1994). This is a grave, somber indictment coming from a scholar who has devoted a lifetime searching earnestly for the key to a scientific sociology.

The debate about the status of sociology continues on a regular basis in *Footnotes* as well as in other media, both in the United States and abroad. So, for instance, one scholar finds an abundance of sociological "preconceptions and prejudices" about freedom in Great Britain (Marshland 1988). Another scholar (Coughlin 1992) notes "a sense of vulnerability" in her interviews with American sociologists. In a recent collection of essays on the state of sociology (Halliday and Janowitz 1992), the sense of disarray, lack of cohesion, and lack of any "clear image or demarcated terrain of work outside the university" transpire with a most disturbing reality. Even Randall Collins (1990), scholar and optimist, has had to write of a sociology that has "lost all coherence as a discipline." But it is hard not to keep the faith; this same expert is later inclined to see not one but "two core commitments" in sociology (Collins 1998: 4).

Some authors predict a resurgence of sociology. Others note the recent "dramatic decline" in sociology positions. Still others extol the virtues of sociology as the "queen" of the social sciences, mostly on the basis of "its pluralistic quality," and in the process commit gross blustery that can hardly endear us to other social scientists. It is hard not to agree that, as another scholar put it bluntly in the April 1993 number of *Footnotes*, we have brought our troubles on ourselves. Sociology teaches what by now is obvious to the typical student: "What we could and should be offering [instead] is a comparative analysis of social systems, one that provides a coherent view of the universe of social systems (past as well as present) and that encourages students to look at our society and its characteristics in this larger perspective." Of course, that is what anthropology does to a large extent (and history as well), and that is why anthropology is, relatively speaking, a thriving and modernizing science with intellectual and political connections to a variety of other disciplines, including literature, classics, history, biology, and even geology and physics, among others. Robin Fox (1994: xi–xiii), an excellent and impatient evolutionist, has written critically of anthropology but has also noted that "the unity of anthropology, its uniqueness among the social sciences, lies in its devotion to the study of the human species as a product of evolution." Indeed, a recent study

(Lieberman 1989) has found that even among cultural anthropologists 68 percent of the Ph.Ds. find it useful to their research to consider the "interaction of genes and environment." By contrast, sociologists are much less likely to see any relevance of genetic forces to their work (Sanderson and Ellis 1992).

The problem involves more than the content of our teaching. One study reported in *Footnotes* (February 1993) reveals that college deans have a dim view of our teaching skills. In response to this report, another participant in the *Footnotes* debate (May 1993) bravely remarks: "If sociologists, as well as deans" do not rate our teaching as "outstanding," "perhaps we have more than a public relations problem," the typical sociologist's diagnosis of our illness. This author proceeds to quote a colleague, a departmental chairperson, to the effect that "sociology is rapidly becoming nothing more than a series of ideological claims that do not merely fail to address the relevant evidence but claim the opposite of what the evidence suggests."

Little wonder that, with few exceptions—some of truly exceptional ability, who, however, are often tempted to go to law school rather than to graduate training in sociology—our majors are far from being the cream of the crop or even the plainly talented. It is less surprising still that, as is well known, our graduate students are deeply ambivalent about the craft of their choice, troubled by the uncertain relevance of sociological practice, and on the whole disoriented by the lack of any intellectual cohesion and any degree of theoretical leadership.

Running in Place

Sociology's ills are, thus, widely recognized by its practioners, though considerable disagreement exists regarding their nature, extent, and causes. Some see the difficulties as inherent in the complexity of our subject matter. Cultural diversity, according to this view, entails a commitment to cultural relativism that precludes the formulation of a uniform science of society. Still others perceive the crisis but respond with little more than hand-wringing. And then there are those who deny the reality of the crisis, bury their heads in the sand, and presume that all is well and good (a good approximation to this scenario may be found in the commentary on "A window on the discipline" symposium published in *Contemporary Sociology* [January 1998]).

In our view, the path that sociology is following is both steep and slippery. We keep running in place. We may recall that half a century ago R.K. Merton decried the breech existing between method and theory as well as a number of other even more basic shortcomings. Note now the leading article of a fairly recent issue of the *American Sociological Review*, the flagship of the American Sociological Association and arguably the foremost sociology journal in the world. In a brief and concise statement, Gerhard Lenski pointed out that sociological ("macrosociological") theories fall short on at least two important, broad criteria: (1) They are rarely falsifiable; (2) they "lack substantive conceptual links to established theories in other scientific disciplines." Our theories come and fairly quickly go not because they have been falsified but because "newer theories have come along and crowded them out of our limited span of attention." As a result, "theory has not advanced nearly so much as it has proliferated" (Lenski 1988: 165; see also, Davis 1994: 181; Rule 1994: 242–43).

For a solution to this state of affairs, Lenski suggests the pursuit of several desiderata. Two are embarrassingly basic: (1) define variables in an "operationally unambiguous manner" and (2) unambiguously specify relationships among and between variables (Lenski 1988: 166). Two others are more challenging. One requires "the development of multilayered theories," namely logically structured sets of propositions within each of which there is at least one "covering principle or covering law." The other calls for "the specification of constants," both biological and environmental. Thus a theory "should contain an explicit statement of assumptions about the nature of human nature (i.e., the relevant effects of our species' common genetic heritage on human action)" as well as such other environmental constants as "the peculiar geographical patterning of societal economic development in the world today" (Lenski 1988: 168–70).

So, half a century has gone by and we are still exhorting one another to define our concepts unambigously and to produce falsifiable theory. Could our troubles be more obvious? There is, however, a glimpse of something new today. Whereas Merton began his famous essay on social structure and anomie by denying the relevance of biological science to sociology, we now hear, as we did through the Founders, that sociological theories should contain explicit assumptions about biological constants. The next quarter of century will show, we believe, that the survival of sociology depends very much on whether the profession can cope with the extraordinary revolution now taking place in evolutionary biology, an alliance of disciplines that are increasingly becoming behavior-oriented. As already noted, rising numbers of psychologists and anthropologists are recognizing the revolution and making pertinent adjustments. Moreover, they are steadily elbowing us aside, and will swamp us if we fail to do likewise.

3

Why the Crisis: A Sketch

The description of a fact often holds excellent clues as to its causes. Hence, part of the answer to the problem faced in the present chapter lies in the preceding chapter. The same may be said with respect to some of our comments in chapter 1. Moreover, there is not always a clear-cut line of demarcation between causes and effects, so that, for example, denial of the crisis in sociology can be both cause and effect of the plight. Certainly, the causes of the crisis are various and complexly interwoven; and many scholars, both within and without the discipline, have written about them. Moreover, debate has intensified in recent years, and critics have underscored several problems, though with varying degrees of success or relevance to fundamentals (e.g., Turner 1989; Turner and Turner 1990; Horowitz 1993; Cole 1994a, 1994b; Davis 1994; Lipset 1994; Bleiberg Seperson 1995; Huber 1995; Wallace 1995; Ellis 1996). In the last analysis the problems of sociologists qua social *scientists* have to do with how seriously we take ourselves as *scientists*, which is to say how well we know and apply the fundamental requirements of scientific inquiry (e.g., Turner and Turner 1990).

So put, the issue unavoidably suggests a serious question: If the crisis is real and we do not take ourselves seriously as scientists, is it because of intrinsic incompetence (e.g., van den Berghe 1990) or an "unwillingness" that may inhere in an addiction to ideology (e.g., Lipset 1994; Simpson and Simpson 1994)? Or both (Horowitz 1993)? The two deficiencies are closely related, though in principle they are distinct if for no other reason because ingrained incompetence and ideological addiction are not equally susceptible to remedy. At any rate, they are both grave problems and may coexist in many sociologists. As we shall see, they imply a number of other disorders. One of the best statements on the double problem has been offered by I.L. Horowitz in a volume, *The Decomposition of Sociology*, that takes a thorough and

49

scholarly view of the historical context wherein sociology has developed and to which in various ways it has responded. Horowitz's (1993: 5) basic argument is that

> sociology, as a result of a special set of historical and current situations, and internal pulls no less than external pushes, has become so enmeshed in the politics of advocacy and the ideology of self-righteousness [and anti-statism] that it is simply unaware of, much less able to respond to, new conditions in the scientific as well as social environments in which it finds itself.

On what amounts to the problem of incompetence, one of the more compelling statements has been provided by evolutionists John Tooby and Leda Cosmides (1992). Unlike Horowitz (1993: 5) who thinks that "the condition of social science [though not of sociology] in America has never been healthier," Tooby and Cosmides fault the "Standard Social Science Model" (SSSM) as a whole (see also Duffy Hutcheson 1996), although they are perfectly aware that psychology and anthropology have of late been more adept than sociology at shedding the SSSM in favor of an evolutionary "new framework" termed the Integrated Causal Model (ICM). Without biological roots, Tooby and Cosmides (1992: 23) argue, the social sciences have for more than a century been adrift within "a babel of incommensurate technical lexicons. This is accompanied by a growing malaise, so that the single largest trend is toward rejecting the scientific enterprise as it applies to humans." This diagnosis is especially applicable to sociology.

The Irony of Grand Sweeps: The Legacy of the Founders

In chapter 1 we recognized the promise of early sociology and argued that we may have squandered the legacy inherited from the Founders. We also suggested that their bequeathal was a mixed bag of goods. The birth of sociology was marked with an irony. The fact is evident beginning with Auguste Comte (1875–1877). We have noted some constructive and promising aspects of his work. We may now add that it was tremendously overextended. Comte conceived of sociology as no less than the synthesis and the crown of all other sciences. This lordly reach was ludicrous and self-defeating even according to the most ecumenical of sociologists.

The irony in the birth of sociology lies in the general rule that the larger a poorly organized empire—intellectual as well as political— the easier are the assaults from the periphery and the greater the danger that the citadel itself will collapse (e.g., Olson 1982; Kennedy 1987). Much of what was comprised by early sociology has since scattered all over the intellectual landscape. Some has become common knowledge through the mass media of communication. More has entered the domains of history, anthropology, literature, drama, and philosophy, among other disciplines. The clearest evidence of the irony, however, lies in the fact that, as we have noted, sociology is being cannibalized by various other disciplines. If these developments continue, there is every danger that sociology will fold. The people who pay the salaries will want more than verbiage, correlations, ideology, and unremitting debate from sociology.

The great sociologists who came after Comte crashed brilliantly through rich and lush frontiers. But they never rid their craft of its imperial birthmark. Nor were they able to lay the groundwork for a universalizing and stalwart social discipline analogous to philosophy among the humanities. They are thus in part responsible, on the one hand, for the debilitating encroachments on our sector and, on the other, for a degree of internal fragmentation that only our innocent majors and the most naive of our graduate students are still able to ignore.

The Case of Émile Durkheim

Consider the enormous area of intellectual space covered by Durkheim's work (Alpert 1939; Lukes 1973). *The Division of Labor in Society* (1893), for instance, offers something for everyone: anthropologists, economists, and business students as well as sociologists, among others. So far, however, it is hard to assess its impact, and, as we have noted, it may be most productively amenable to the evolutionary analysis that is currently avoided. Other Durkheimian works have been too much within the realm of philosophy (e.g., Durkheim 1924b). Still others pertain to child psychology (Durkheim 1924a) and what has been termed evolutionary epistemology (e.g., Piaget 1970, 1976) where they have been developing steadily almost entirely without sociological participation. Durkheim's (1912) volume on "the simplest existing religion" has been more helpful to anthropologists, who until recent decades focused almost exclusively on preagrarian societies, than to sociologists, many of whom have never really grasped, or accepted, the logic of fundamentals in the first place. Nor have we been ready to cope heuristically with the Durkheimian corollary that a multidenominational country like the United States of America is really a multiplicity of societies.

Among Durkheim's major works, *Suicide* (1897) has received the most unqualified approval by sociologists. Yet, in the large literature that has surrounded this book, there is no agreement as to what it really says and as to how its argument may be properly put to a test. In the meantime, considerable progress toward a scientific grasp of suicide is being made in areas that Durkheim adamantly rejected as irrelevant to social facts, namely psychology and biology. Moreover, *Suicide* promotes, at least in part, the worst of the etiology practiced in sociological theorizing: structural analysis. Even assuming that suicide is a "social fact," as Durkheim claimed, it is *the individual* who commits the act. Hence, one would expect "integration," one of the two presumed causes of suicide, to be interpretable as a property of the individual, say, as a need of varying intensity. Yet, it is still viewed as a property of the famous Durkheimian unknown, "society," one of the most problematic terms in his sociology (e.g., Bellah 1973: Introduction; see also, e.g., Crippen 1987, 1988; Machalek and Cohen 1991).

Durkheim added substantially to sociology's irony and encouraged later sociologists to isolate themselves from the rest of the scientific community and to seek fundamental causes where only intervening variables could be found. This is the structural tradition of sociology wherein independent variables like social class, religion, and occupation necessarily beg the question. Sociologists theorize as physicists might reason if, somehow taking leave of their senses, they mistook the sign of the thing for the thing itself and argued, say, that the cause of artificial light in the library is the gadget that someone switches on. The electrical switch is a mere convenience, and can have an effect only in association with electrical energy. Indeed, it can be dispensed with altogether, although in the form of a dimmer it can modify the flow of energy. But never mistake the point: Without the energy, the switch is totally without relevance. Much of sociology, thanks in part to Durkheim, has become *the science of social switches*. Hence, it is mostly acausal, misguided, and necessarily ephemeral in its findings (e.g., van den Berghe 1990; Tooby and Cosmides 1992; Carey and Lopreato 1994; Crippen 1994a).

The Case of Max Weber

The most famous, and beloved, of sociologists is Max Weber. To have an allergy to this scholar, if we may borrow Braudel's (1979: 568) expression of aversion to Weber's (1904–1905) famous speculation in

The Protestant Ethic and the Spirit of Capitalism (*PESC*), is to be seriously flawed as far as many sociologists are concerned. We ask for
forebearance, for we are about to commit a sacrilege. The domain of
Weber's sociology is vast, comprising philosophy, ethics, economics,
religion, law, politics, the scientific method, and what has come to be
called complex organizations, among a prodigious array of other topics. We can certainly hold Weber in awe for such breadth of learning.
Unfortunately, however, his legacy has been more affliction than glory.
It has been a heavy load, and heavy loads too often overwhelm the
bearers. The enfeeblement is obvious, for universities include departments or schools of philosophy, theology, law, economics, political science, and, among many others, business administration (where "complex
organizations," for example, has been fairly thoroughly appropriated).

The celebrated *PESC* purports to demonstrate "the qualitative and
quantitative contribution" made by ascetic Protestantism to "the spirit
of modern capitalism." Curiously, for a scholar so widely acclaimed as
a historical sociologist, the argument is not adequately placed within a
historical setting, so that it is impossible to determine the stage that the
spirit of capitalism had reached at the time of Weber's focus (circa
mid-seventeenth century), and thus to understand clearly the contribution of the Protestant ethic. Nor does it offer any clues as to how it
might be subjected to an attempt at falsification.

His "confusing method of argument" (Braudel 1979: 568; see also
Tawney 1926; Zetterberg 1963) sets a poor example. For instance, Weber (1904–1905: 180) rightly noted that the Ethic was but one of the
"fundamental elements" that determined the further development of the
preexisting form of capitalism. Let us, then, say that his chosen task was
to assess the contribution of a given force, f_1, to X. We are left with f_2, f_3,
f_4...f_n, which together with f_1 determine our X. How now is it possible to
demonstrate the effect of f_1 on X without at the same time accounting for
f_2, f_3, f_4, etc.? In economics, presumably one of Weber's specialties, system analysis was already fairly well-developed in his own time (e.g.,
Pareto 1906), and he seemed to be aware of its implications. In the
"Author's Introduction" to the volume, for example, Weber (1904–1905:
31—emphasis added) noted that it "must be one of the tasks of sociological and historical investigation *first* to analyze *all* the influences and causal
relationships which can satisfactorily be explained in terms of reactions
to environmental conditions." Nevertheless, Weber (1904–1905: 180)
proceeded with a narrowly circumscribed analysis and concluded his argument by categorically asserting the effect of the Ethic (f_1) on modern

capitalism: "One of the fundamental elements of the spirit of modern capitalism...rational conduct on the basis of the idea of the calling, was born...from the spirit of Christian asceticism." There have been attempts recently to rehabilitate Weber's errors by reference to lectures (Weber 1923) on related topics published after his death (e.g., Collins 1980). But they merely compound the problem.

It is remarkable, further, that at the denouement of Weber's argument the focus on rationality and culture breaks down completely, so that the attempt to demonstrate the independent causal power of ideas turns into a failure. The articles of predestination in the Westminster Confession of 1647, a crucial document for Weber's thesis, stated not only that eternal destiny was a matter of God's "immutable purpose" reached even "before the foundation of the world" "without any foresight of faith or good works." They also declared that predestination rested in God's "secret counsel" or "the unsearchable counsel of His own will" (Weber 1904–1905: 100). "How was this doctrine borne," Weber (1904–1905: 109–10, emphasis added) rightly asks, "in an age to which the after-life was not only more important, but in many ways also more certain, than all the interests of life in this world? The question, *Am I one of the elect?*, must sooner or later have arisen for every believer and have forced all other interests into the background." In short, let God and the Doctrine say what they will, the believers were motivated by the irresistible, nonrational need to know their eternal fate. This stressful mental state has been termed the "denial of death" (Becker 1973), and there is good reason to believe that it is a cultural universal (Brandon 1962), rooted in a deeply embedded predisposition in the human psyche (Lopreato 1984: 274–81).

Presumably, early ascetic Protestants did succeed in resolving their stress. There were unintended consequences of the doctrine of predestination, and Weber, to the just delight of his admirers (e.g., Berger 1963: 38–39), was perfectly aware of them. What seems to have escaped him is the irony inherent in the most remarkable of such consequences. The resolution of the stress was effected with more than a dash of Darwinian logic, namely with the alleged conclusion that *wealth was a sign of grace*. In short, the moral and spiritual quandary ostensibly created by the tenet of predestination was alleviated not by religious ideas but by the appeal to one of the classical factors working at the service of genetic fitness: richness of material resources (Lopreato 1984: 93). The quest for certainty regarding one's spiritual fate thus became enmeshed in the very real world of the struggle for existence.

Beyond that, what kind of science could possibly have developed under Weber's (1904–1905; see also 1949) inspiration, when subsequent generations of sociologists were enjoined to somehow grasp *the meaning* (*verstehen*) that given facts have, or have had, for the people implicated in them? This crucial aspect of Weber's sociology must share responsibility for the excesses of subjectivist approaches currently fashionable in sociology despite, ironically, one of Weber's (1919) greatest contributions, namely his call for objective, dispassionate analysis. At any rate, reasoning by intuition or pure insight is a form of inquiry with which our colleagues in philosophy have millennia of experience to their advantage. Little wonder that so many current sociological "theorists" are eagerly aping the intuitions of ideologues in philosophy and literature who, in bitter disappointment for collapsed Utopias, are busy "deconstructing" everything in sight but ever quarreling about the very meaning and method(s) of deconstruction. We shall return to this topic.

The troublesome legacy of Weber's sociology is probably most evident in that aspect of his work that concerns one of the fundamental assumptions of economics, the most developed of the social sciences, namely rationality. In sociology it has produced little or nothing beyond an enormous lot of verbiage and bickering. In an international symposium on rationality, Nikolai Genov (1991) has noted that there are more than a dozen meanings (not types) of rationality in Weber's work. In principle, there is nothing deleterious in that. But sociologists are stuck in an ever-recurring debate as to what Weber meant by "it" and in the associated attempts to clarify what apparently resists clarification (e.g., Bunge 1987; Lash and Whimster 1987; Hindes 1988, 1991; Halfpenny 1991). The confusion on the subject produces marvelously strange creations. Thus, one of the main titles in the rationality literature represents man as "rational" and society as "irrational" (Barry and Hardin 1982). This is sociological metaphysics at its most curious. One wonders who society is here and how millions of pluses can somehow result in one enormous minus.

Of course, there are serious attempts to harness the theoretical value of rationality concepts. A case in point is the work of James Coleman (1990) in the area of so-called rational choice theory. But the sociologists' verdict on this effort again promises mere debate (e.g., Horowitz 1993; Wrong 1994: 197–201; Hill 1996: 235, among others). Moreover, rational choice theory makes demands for which there is no adequate sociological theory (see Coleman 1992 for a brief review of rational choice theory). Further, there is plentiful evidence that this perspective has already been effectively appropriated by economists as a part of their own expansion and can best be developed by them (e.g., Becker 1976, 1981; see also, Davis 1994: 181–82).

The upshot of sociology's birthmark is that the cannibalization of our subject matter has been extraordinarily easy work. It may become entirely destructive if sociologists persist in what James A. Davis (1994: 189) has termed their "doctrinaire denial of any biological influence on human behavior." Evolutionary biology is one of the rapidly expanding frontiers in behavioral science, and, as already noted, such disciplines as anthropology and psychology show notable signs of welcoming the evolutionary challenge with activities that reduce sociology's domain or suggest its superfluity. In principle, to conclude this section, the irony could have been glory rather than affliction. Philosophy, as already noted, has long been the matrix of a great array of daughter disciplines, including the natural sciences, and yet it is in good health and thriving in the academe. The potential ill effects of the irony, therefore, have been nourished by a variety of shortcomings evident in the subsequent development of sociology, and it is to some of these that we must now turn.

Disorientation and Fragmentation

The passing of the Founders has been accompanied by an ever-shifting variety of sociological orientations, theoretical perspectives, and a plethora of *isms* whose combined effect has been unbridled confusion, corrosive fragmentation, and a rampant feeling that we are getting nowhere and there we are likely to remain. Some of the best minds in sociology see little if any hope for sociology (e.g., Davis 1994: 185–87; Rule 1994: 250; Turner 1996: 200). According to I.L. Horowitz (1993: 5–6), current sociology "suffers an internal laceration"; and the irony is that it is not the State or any other external force that perpetrates the work of decomposition; it is rather the "resistance of fanatics" to "honest research" and to the *ideal* of *objectivity* in theory.

This diagnosis stands in sharp contrast to the expectations of an earlier era. Discussing in 1945 the prospects of systematic theory in sociology, Talcott Parsons (1954: 348–69) harangued the troops as follows:

> It is my judgment that a great opportunity exists. Things have gone far enough so that it seems likely that sociology, in the closest connection with its sister-sciences of psychology and anthropology, stands near the beginning of one of those important configurations of culture growth which Professor Kroeber has so illu-

minatingly analyzed.... I have no doubt whatever of the capacity of American sociologists in this respect.

What happened in subsequent decades made a mockery of this prognosis. Sociology is largely isolated. Sociologists ignore the findings of other social sciences and of other sociologists across the provinces. The sisters have become second cousins at best, and instead of culture growth there has been a ruinous inability to respond to new scientific challenges. Sad to say, Parsons' prognosis was wishful thinking. At about the same time, C.W. Mills (1959: 85–86) was warning against the "democratic theory of knowledge," according to which "all facts are created equal." Sociology has experienced an erratic movement in a multiplicity of disconnected directions.

A recent survey shows that about 18.5 percent of sociologists still have either a primary or a secondary commitment to functionalism, of the Parsonian and/or Mertonian variety (Sanderson and Ellis 1992), but that represents a significant recession. Accordingly, some sociologists think that the demise of functionalism signaled the onset of crisis that has invaded our ranks. We may recall the Gerstein and Sciulli (1987: 2) verdict that there "is no longer a theoretical core, such as Parsons provided in the bygone postwar era. Only its ghost: almost universal criticism, thematic or latent, of old 'structural-functionalism.' The center no longer holds." Little or nothing has changed since 1987.

Of course, a certain amount of diversity in sociological theorizing has always been present—and is in principle salutary. For example, while functionalism held sway, there were at least three other competing perspectives. One, exchange theory, has already been noted (e.g., Homans 1961, 1974; Blau 1964, among others). A second perspective, revolving chiefly around the work of the social philosopher George H. Mead (1934), has gone by the name of "symbolic interactionism." Of all sociological brands, this has been the most durable, in part because it is understood to underscore most emphatically the primacy of "symbolic systems" (culture) for an understanding of human behavior (e.g., Blumer 1981). The endurance of Meadean sociology may also owe to its focus on the small group (the family, the team, the peer group, the little community), wherein the social self is developed. Excessive cultural emphasis notwithstanding, it thus directs attention to basic social units and helps to maintain some welcome linkage to anthropology and psychology. But here, too, we may note a regretable neglect. No one who reads Mead's masterful *Mind, Self, and Society* (1934) can fail to be impressed by his explicit debt to Darwinian reasoning (Crippen 1987; Turner 1991: 372). And yet, scholars who claim to build upon Mead's work (e.g., Blumer 1969; Hewitt 1976) manage to easily ignore this vital aspect of it.

A third competitor of functionalism has been "conflict theory," and the relationship between the two deserves a special note for a variety of reasons. Predominant is the charge, leveled especially in the turbulent 1960s, that functionalism was inadequate to account for social change and conflict in society (e.g., Dahrendorf 1959; Gouldner 1970; Collins 1975). There was no real basis to such an indictment, which in large measure was an excessive reaction to Parsons' frequent and fuzzy use of "equilibrium," a concept widely misunderstood in sociology (Lopreato 1971), and perhaps worse, "consensus." For functionalists, consensus was in effect a result of what Pareto (1916: sections 1115–32) had termed the *need for conformity*. The problem that was inadequately grasped by Parsonians and critics alike is that this need varies in intensity among individuals and groups. Further, different groups tend to have different bases of conformity, with the result that a sort of paradox inheres in the need for conformity. On the one hand, the predisposition may in fact lead to conformity. On the other, it lends itself to enforcement upon those who would resist it and the expected result is conflict. Consensus and conflict are thus two sides of the same coin, as some sociologists (e.g., Pareto 1916; Simmel 1950) clearly recognized. No other debate in sociology epitomizes more clearly the tendency for complementary diversity to degenerate into gratuitous battles of words and rampant fragmentation.

On the current scene of theoretical perspectives, according to the Sanderson and Ellis (1992: tables 1–3) survey, conflict theory is the leader both as a first or primary choice of the respondents and as the primary-secondary combined preference. The latter is embraced by 28.4 percent of sociologists. Following it in descending order, with relative percentages in parentheses, are eclecticism (25.9), symbolic interactionism (25.3), functionalism (18.5), structuralism (17.3), Marxism (12.3), Weberianism (11.1), phenomenology-ethnomethodology (9.3), exchange-rational choice theory (6.8), sociobiology-evolutionism (3.7), atheoretical (4.9), and "other" (11.7). This residual category includes "feminism, behaviorism, Durkheimianism, historicism, materialism, pluralism, positivism, and ecology" (Sanderson and Ellis 1992: 33)—a veritable smorgasbord of disconnected and incoherent sociologies. The researchers have interpreted their data as revealing a high degree of theoretical fragmentation and have underscored the following findings: (1) "the respondents were highly antibiological in outlook"; (2) "political outlook was the best predictor of the respondents' theoretical outlooks, followed fairly closely by age."

That is no surprise. Sociologists have long been motivated by ideological agendas, and still interpret any opening to biology as a "conservative," and thus "bad," attempt to prove that all efforts toward desired changes are destined to fail. This, as we shall see, is an elementary misunderstanding. Evolutionary science may well be the best tool found so far for the discovery of mechanisms that can produce social change. The antibiology bias reveals ignorance of the logic of evolutionary analysis, especially in view of the extraordinary effects that environmental (or proximate) factors have been shown to have by evolutionary scientists. The point deserves special emphasis. According to Darwinian theory the evolution of any "phenotype" (behavioral, anatomical, etc.) is the resultant of the interplay between genetic information and environment, *culture included*. Darwinian knowledge is widespread among the sciences and is sometimes employed even in theoretical physics (e.g., Hawking 1988). By contrast, with few exceptions, in sociology there is at best gross misunderstanding of it. A.L. Stinchcombe (1994: 279), for example, places sociology among academically "precarious," "disintegrated disciplines," which include, among others, history, philosophy, *and* evolutionary biology. Believe it or not.

Postmodernism vs. Modernism

An inflation of labels is in itself a sign of fragmentation. When they are assertions for vacuous conceptions of theory, they shout the ominous scope of sociological poverty. J.A. Davis (1994: 188) finds a "weak immune system" in sociology. "Consequently, we have put up with an appalling amount of bunk...." Jack P. Gibbs (1994), among others, has pointed out that sociology has long been a fertile ground for movements that belittle the very idea of a scientific sociology: for example, liberating sociology, critical sociology, hermeneutics, "and all of the 'posts.'" That is the price of the failure to reach a consensus on the criteria appropriate for assessing the serviceability of theories. Gibbs proposes, among other useful tools, "social control" as the central notion of sociology and thus as a solution, however partial, of the sociological crisis. We adhere to the position that sociology cannot be a science without discovering, or borrowing, at least one general law or principle, but we applaud any scientifically informed effort to provide general sociological focus.

One of the post-isms missing in the Sanderson-Ellis findings is "postmodernism," despite the fact that for several years it has been conspicuous in sociological debates. Indeed, its development would seem to have taken place at such a rapid pace that we are now ready to move on to *After Postmodernism* (Simons and Billig 1994). Postmodernism has for years been offered as the principal antithesis to what many sociologists disparagingly call sociological theory. *Sociological Theory*, the theory-specialized journal of the American Sociological Association, has devoted much attention to a debate between postmodernists and their target of opprobrium: the "modernists." According to Alan Sica (1993: 17), a standard computer scan revealed a menu of 242 articles on postmodernism published between 1988 and 1992. Why, then, the absence of postmodernism in the 1992 Sanderson-Ellis report? One possible answer is that for many sociologists postmodernism is not just a sociological specialty but a synonym for sociology itself: *the new sociology* that rejects nearly all the sociology that came before it. Thus, many sociological specialties, for example, some branches of feminism, exist *within* postmodernism not along with it. The rise of postmodernism may be said to constitute the most unambiguous evidence of the sociological crisis.

Postmodernists have keen awareness of the crisis and sometimes refer to it euphemistically as "the end of sociological theory," to which they offer "the postmodern hope" as a substitute (e.g., Seidman 1991). Exhausted by the plethora of senseless sociologies, a multiplying number of sociologists, with some leadership from philosophers, litterateurs, and sundry European scholars, have in effect called for an end to what is for them, as for us, little more than mere babble. In the process they have entered an area of social, or perhaps more appropriately ethical, debate whose roots go back at least to the humanists of the Italian Renaissance though they are most transparent in the vicissitudes of the last two centuries. The key passwords are *modernity* and *postmodernity*. Surrounding these are issues of authenticity, identity, alienation, power, truth, individualism, reason, rationality, loss of freedom, self-fulfillment, moral ideals, and so forth. They are topics that may recall Karl Marx's alienation, Max Weber's (1904–1905) iron cage, Daniel Bell's (1976) cultural contradictions of capitalism, and, among others, Robert Bellah et al.'s (1991) insidious technologies of "the good society."

Within the philosophical-historical tradition, we are reminded of Alexis de Tocqueville's vulgar pleasures of democracy, Kierkegaard's passionless present age, Nietzsche's pathetic comfort, and more recently

Hannah Arendt's (1959) paradox of permanence, Christopher Lasch's (1989) minimal self, and Charles Taylor's (1989, 1991) struggle for moral ideals and significant horizons, among many others. These are topics of all ages, and the sociological participation in the debate is in principle much to be applauded. Unfortunately, the remedies of postmodernists only underscore, by the very clutter and fury of their verbiage, the chronic nature of the crisis.

Our reading of the debate reveals several grounds of discourse. There is, first, the recognition that the modern era, typically corresponding to the last two centuries, has introduced changes that have unsettled, in some respects radically, social institutions, moral orders, and not least the individual's capacity for self-identity, authenticity, and the sense of moral well-being. On this point there is fairly general agreement between the modernists and the postmodernists, although the nuances vary, and it is not always clear as to who is a modernist, or so is being represented in the literature, and who is a postmodernist, or so is being portrayed (e.g., Arendt 1959; Bell 1976; Bellah 1975; Bloom 1987; Derrida 1987; Habermas 1987; Bauman 1988; Spelman 1989; Giddens 1990; Denzin 1991; Borgmann 1992; Lash and Friedman 1992).

A second ground of discourse, closely related to the first, strongly reveals the personal-ideological response of postmodernists to the modern condition. As a review essay argues, "it's impossible not to read these assessments of PoMo as expressions of their authors' dailiness." Moreover (Sica 1993: 18):

> This, it seems to me, is the crux of the matter: the postmodern complaint(s) against modernity, as sloppily defined as both terms often are, turn(s) on matters foreign to ideas per se. That is, they reach far beyond the properly intellectual or analytical and into the arena of power, whether small-time (university life) or big-time (the culture industry's impact on civilization).

The intensity of personal reactions has led philosopher Charles Taylor (1991) to distinguish between "boosters" and "knockers." More important for us, the personal, affective, aspect of the contention is invariably cloaked in a debate as to what theory in sociology should be like. This is the third and most harmful ground of debate. The brief comments that follow will focus on it, and for convenience sake represent it mostly with an essay that appears to capture fairly closely the postmodernist view of the debate.

In the lead article of a symposium on postmodernism in *Sociological Theory*, Steven Seidman (1991: 131) states:

> Sociological theory has gone astray.... Its social and intellectual insularity accounts for the almost permanent sense of crisis and malaise that surrounds contemporary sociological theory. This distressing condition originates, in part, from its project: the quest for foundations and for a totalizing theory of society.

This refrain against foundations is now common in sociology. For example, F.H. Molotch (1994: 238), participating in the aforementioned symposium on "What's wrong with sociology?," writes: "If we could climb out of the science trap, we could acknowledge different modes and write in many voices." As if we weren't doing enough of that. Seidman's verdict is a mixed bag of truths, half-truths, and plain untruths. Many of us certainly think it true that sociological theory, indeed sociology in general, suffers grievously from insularity. Whether, however, it *has gone astray* is at best only a half-truth by the author's own accounting, which spares no one from the responsibility of creating the crisis: not even the Founders, for example, Durkheim, Weber, and Marx. So, it is not clear as to what we have strayed from. As to the quest for foundations, we only wish it were true. The indictment is baseless and underscores the roar of the sociological cacophony. As we have noted, other sociologists argue conversely that the basic problem with sociology lies precisely in our loss of faith in science, and in our failure to use general, abstract, and formal theory and thus "foundations" (e.g., Lenski 1988; Turner 1989, 1996; Turner and Turner 1990).

Some of Seidman's (1991: 133) specifics are far closer to the mark. "Instead of a concentrated, productive discourse focused on a limited set of problems that exhibits sustained elaboration, we find," he writes, "a dispersed, discursive clamoring that covers a wide assortment of ever-changing issues in a dazzling diversity of languages." And again (Seidman 1991: 133): "There is a virtual babble of different vocabularies addressing a heterogeneous cluster of changing disputes." For Seidman, the antidote to sociological theory—the solution—is "social theory," the postmodern hope. Behold the hope (Seidman 1991: 131–32):

> Social theories typically take the form of broad social narratives.... [aiming] not only to clarify an event or social configuration but also to shape its outcome—perhaps by legitimating one outcome or imbuing certain actors, actions and institutions with historical importance while attributing to other social forces malicious, demonic qualities.... Social theories... arise out of ongoing contemporary conflicts and aim to affect them.... They are typically evaluated in terms of their moral, social, and political significance.

Salem renascent! We can hardly derive hope from theories battling malicious, demonic forces. And yet. And yet writers of this ilk deserve some praise at least for being so perfectly open in their prejudices. How many sociologists, deep to their synapses in "moral intent," have the gall to explicitly reveal it?

In the last analysis, postmodernists appear to suffer from a grievous form of philosophical paranoia. Systematic knowledge is essentially evil. Thus: "Once the veil of epistemic privilege is torn away by postmodernists, science appears as a social force enmeshed in particular cultural and power struggles. The claim to truth, as Foucault has proposed, is inextricably an act of power—a will to form humanity. This epistemic suspicion is at the core of postmodernism" (Seidman 1991: 134–35).

An old phantom lingers behind this paranoia. Stripped of its mystery, it amounts to a gross misunderstanding of the nature of science itself. Science is alleged to be in the business of asserting *the* truth. In fact, the job of science is quite another. What science does is to look for regularities of behavior, and on that basis it then makes predictions about other sorts of likely behavior. If the predictions fail repeatedly to be *falsified*, they become part of knowledge, *for now*. Tomorrow the knowledge may change. Hence, scientific knowledge is hardly the same thing as truth. Nevertheless, it can hardly be denied that some truths are more truthful than others—or that they last longer. Postmodernists are addicted to the pluralistic assumption that facts are just a matter of opinion. On this issue, scientists occasionally lose their patience. Sociobiologist Richard Dawkins (1995: 31–32—emphasis added) has written as follows in a recent volume:

> There is a fashionable salon philosophy called cultural relativism which holds, *in its extreme form*, that science has no more claim to truth than tribal myth: science is just the mythology favored by our modern Western tribe. I once was provoked by an anthropologist colleague into putting the point starkly: Suppose there is a tribe, I said, who believe that the moon is an old calabash tossed into the sky, hanging only just out of reach above the treetops. Do you really claim that our scientific truth—that the moon is about a quarter million miles away and about a quarter the diameter of Earth—is no more true than the tribe's calabash? "Yes," the anthropologist said. "We are just brought up in a culture that sees the world in a scientific way. Neither way is more true than the other...." Western science, acting on good evidence that the moon orbits the Earth a quarter of a million miles away, using Western-designed computers and rockets, has succeeded in placing people on its surface. Tribal science, believing that the moon is just above the treetops, will never touch it outside of dreams.

"Sensible relativists" (i.e., those who merely claim that "you cannot understand a culture if you try to interpret its beliefs in terms of your own culture"), Dawkins (1995: 32n) continues, "should work harder at distancing themselves from the fatuous kind." Unfortunately, however, the latter kind appear to be gaining ground in contemporary sociology.

Of late, the muddle about the nature of science has been fueled by a New Age type of philosophy of science that derides the old notion that science proceeds systematically from observation to theory to prediction and finally to "verification." Astrophysicist James Trefil (1989: 41) relates an experience he had while attending a seminar delivered by a sociologist of science. Her topic was the reaction of the scientific community to the hypothesis that dinosaurs became extinct because of the impact on earth of an extraterrestrial body. She is alleged to have been very good on the details of the disputes with journal editors, phone calls to reporters by interested parties, and such other matters of a personal nature. But she never troubled herself to consider "the slow accumulation of supporting evidence" that had led many scientists to accept the hypothesis. Evidence was simply not of much importance to her. Finally, a frustrated paleontologist expressed the general disdain: "Is it really news to sociologists that evidence counts?" Of course, evidence does count among sociologists, but few of us can deny that debates on trivia too often become ends in themselves.

The literature on postmodernism is now very large (e.g., Ritzer 1997), and encompasses various strands of thought, perhaps especially deconstructionism. Equally enormous, however, is the crippling confusion that runs through it all. In a recent issue of the *American Sociological Review*, for example, S. Fuchs and S. Ward (1994a) address the question, "What is deconstruction, and where and when does it take place?" In the same issue then, Ben Agger (1994) argues that Fuchs and Ward "have got deconstruction wrong." Then it is Fuchs and Ward's (1994b) turn again with a rebuttal in which they state, among other things, that their critic "has nothing at all to say about the substance of our argument." Quarrels are common in science, and often solve important problems. In sociology, however, they too frequently become their own ends and typically reveal irreconcilable misunderstandings.

Denial and Mediocrity

One effect, ironically, is a tendency among some to deny that sociology is in any danger at all—or at any rate to be fairly comfortable with the state of the discipline (e.g., Meštrović 1996: 211; Collins 1998: 6). Other sociologists are in such deep denial that they become fervent cheerleaders of their troubled craft. Should we, for example, be inclined to take seriously presidential messages in the Spring-Summer and Fall issues of *The Southern Sociologist*, a publication of the Southern Sociological Society, we would be heartened to learn that "we should view sociology as a discipline which integrates knowledge from diverse sources. In short, in the study of human behavior sociology is at the center.... sociology is the core." Further, according to this sociological Pollyanna, "efforts that attempt to identify the particular theoretical concepts that make up the core of the discipline are intrinsically divisive, for they suggest that all other theoretical concepts are on the periphery of the discipline" (see also Gove 1995). Recall the "epistemic suspicion" that sociological theory, or "the claim to truth," is "an act of power—a will to form humanity." Here is another stark version of the postmodernist mentality and a misleading understanding of science. Not to accept that some concepts are more basic than others is truly an affliction that may kill the afflicted. Did disaster strike astronomy and physics when gravity became the central concept? Or did the core concepts of uniformitarianism in geology, natural selection in general biology, DNA in molecular biology, and system and equilibrium in chemistry doom those disciplines into divisiveness?

But as it turns out, the esteemed colleague is not averse to core concepts, after all. Indeed it is his "perception that the premise that sociology is *the* integrative discipline in the study of human social behavior is a concept" of far-reaching consequence (emphasis in the original). "And, if sociologists were to use this notion for *the unifying concept* [emphasis added], the issue of specifying the theoretical issues that make up the core of the discipline will not seem nearly as important, for it is the field of sociology that is the core."

Might other social scientists "see us as pretentious and/or contentious"? Not to worry, for "it is unlikely that this would be the case if what we say to other disciplines is that 'you have specialized knowledge that we need to draw on; can you help us?'" One is reminded of the delusion attributed to Auguste Comte, and wonder whether Comte himself would cry or laugh at our current illusions. Little wonder that, while other social sciences are forging edifying interdisciplinary alliances, sociology is moving toward a sort of quarantine. We, of course, value our colleague's optimism. But might it not do more harm than good?

As previously noted, a study reported under Open Forum in the February 1993 issue of *Footnotes* showed that (1) deans rank sociology low in teaching skills and (2) sociologists themselves frankly echo the deans' evaluations. Fortunately, then, denial is not universal. But where it does exist, it can reach truly frightful proportions. The October issue of the same publication published an attack on the above study by none other than the Academic Responsibilities and Freedom Committee of the Midwest Sociological Society. The good folks of the Freedom Committee were dismayed that *Footnotes* considered the critical findings "credible enough to publish." "The issue here," you see, "goes to the heart of academic freedom." "We do not feel," the free thinkers continued, "that the publication [of the damning article] was consistent with that objective." Little wonder that some sociologists speak of "left-wing fascists" (e.g., Horowitz 1993) or "a bunch of intellectual fascists" (Turner 1996: 193).

Fortunately, the same issue of *Footnotes* published also the response of the original authors, and it was devastating. Far more scholarly and genuinely devoted to their profession, they rebutted: "Instead of contributing to the task of strengthening sociology departments, [the "critics"] give readers a quick lesson in bad sociology and illustrate exactly the problem that we are attempting to bring to the attention of the discipline." Further: "Their comments exemplify some of the reasons that certain deans cite in justifying their low opinion of sociology."

The problems of sociology cannot be fantasized away. Better to confront them. The signs that they are real are superabundant. Consider the quality of the texts introducing students to sociology. With a few happy exceptions (e.g., Lenski et al. 1991; Sanderson 1991), they are "dry, dull, and lacking in...appeal to students" (Fabianic 1991). They are also written by teachers who brag about their "common sense" or "down-to-earth" approaches. Laden with the most pitiful jargon, their "concepts" are ill-defined to begin with, and then change in meaning from one page to another. Facts generally consist of a hodgepodge of commonsense, trivial, everyday knowledge when they are not disgraceful distortions. Theory consists of mere names and little summaries of many-times-over summaries of verbiage apparently meant for the functionally illiterate. Banalities, however, are graced by abundant and expensive color charts and photographs.

In recent years it has also become fashionable for textbook authors to take potshots at sociobiology. A typical example follows: "Human behavior, he [Edward O. Wilson] said, is no different from the behavior of cats, dogs, rats, bees, or mosquitoes—it has been bred into homo sapiens through evolutionary principles." Having read this specimen of tutored illiteracy, an honor student whose thesis one of us had the privilege of supervising, was visibly shocked. Conversation eventually got around to where she would like to go for her Ph.D. "I think," she said, after thinking a moment, "I've just decided to go to law school instead." Little surprise. That is where many of our brightest majors end up.

Our theory texts are a little more scholarly and some are excellent by many standards (e.g., Turner 1991; Turner et al. 1998). There are two major kinds of theory texts. One typically consists mostly of exegeses of "the classics." If they are to sell, as publishers cunningly hope, such interpretations are necessarily comfortably shallow in what they contain. Moreover, as one goes from the representation of a given theory in text X to its interpretation in text Y, one must wonder whether the two authors have read the same thing. The other type of theory text, the famous collection of readings, obviously avoids the problem of variably authored interpretations but encourages the often capricious rendition of the classroom instructor. Furthermore, the readings very rarely if ever even approximate a coherent whole in any sense of the expression. The result is generation after generation of students, at both undergraduate and graduate levels, who at best have learned a few names, a few terms, and a few catchy phrases.

Of late, moreover, there has been a major move away from the classics and other modernist theories toward postmodernist and kindred arguments, which while failing to improve on the content of the old are a definite regression in the hope they inspire. They come to the market with a veritable cascade of promises like "Controversies," "Reconsidered," and "Refocusing" in their titles. "The new stuff" is on the whole so far removed from what until recently passed for sociological theory that it is hard to avoid the feeling that sociology is disintegrating altogether. A recent collection, for instance, includes the following as sociological theorists: William James, John Maynard Keynes, Reinhold Niebuhr, Virginia Woolf, M.K. Gandhi, Mao Zedong, Simone de Beauvoir, Martin Luther King, Jr., Betty Friedan, Vaclav Havel, and George Kennan, among many others. Death by ingestion of stolen goods!

Sociologists with few exceptions are so out of touch with science and with what has been happening in the scientific disciplines of behavior that in some departments Theory is grouped with Qualitative Sociology in the specification of departmental specialties. The feeling is epidemic among professionals and students alike that theory is just something that somehow "we have to do" but nobody knows why, or what it is. As students so often put it, "I like sex roles" (or juvenile

delinquency, religion, etc.) "but I don't know any theory." Death by
ingestion? Death by self-banishment as well! If there is no theory in
courses on sex roles, family, delinquency, etc., where then is the beef!

The question, thus, rises as to the quality of our substantive courses,
say, the Family, which constitute the corpus of the sociological enterprise. In a recent report to the Council on Families in America, Norval
Glenn (1997) presents the results of his examination of twenty marriage and the family texts with publication dates of 1994, 1995, or early
1996. The evaluation had specific foci, such as adequacy for preparing
students to understand public debates about family issues and to make
decisions about their own family relations. But ultimately, these were
convenient reference points for a broader scholarly assessment of the
factual and theoretical quality of the texts. The results are depressing,
and have created a furor among interested parties. None of the books is
rated "excellent"; most are considered "poor or mediocre"; and two are
judged simply "unacceptable." The weaknesses include misrepresen-
tation of the literature, misstatement of facts, and faulty reasoning or
theorizing, among others. Underlying such faults, of course, are others—perhaps more revealing about the nature of sociology as an academic discipline. Nearly all contain "liberal or radical" biases that are
reflected in a number of deleterious ways. "Most of the books," for
instance, "are not explicitly anti-marriage, but overall they give a rather
negative image of marriage and pay little attention to theory or evidence about beneficial effects of marriage on individuals or society"
(Glenn 1997: 199). One can propose solutions, as Glenn tries to do. But
wisdom is as wise as it is wisely received. In the last analysis, the realization of solutions rests with such problems as the adequacy of the
authors' scholarship, the ability to aim at the maximum possible degree
of objectivity, the adequacy of general sociological theory, and not least
of all the gumption to accept the idea that the family is not only a universal social institution; ultimately it is also the result of a complex set
of biological forces, pertaining both to ontogeny and to evolution by
natural selection, that inform serious students of reproduction and the
family.

Political Correctness

As we have already noted, much of sociology is so enmeshed in the
politics of advocacy and the ideology of self-righteousness that it is
neither aware nor able to respond to new conditions in the scientific

world (Horowitz 1993: 5). This is a fair diagnosis, although we are less certain about Horowitz's related call (which we share, *as citizens*) for "democratic options." It is unlikely that the culture of past centuries was more democratic than current culture, and yet it spawned sociology. Science must be fiercely apolitical—fiercely because it takes great effort to even approximate the apolitical in the service of the scientific.

When science and politics are mixed, both activities may suffer. A case in point is provided by the American Sociological Association's adoption of a manifesto known as the "Seville Statement on Violence" drafted by an international team of scholars in May, 1986. The statement (for full text, see *Footnotes*, March 1991: 6) was intended "to challenge a number of alleged biological findings *that have been used*, even by some in our disciplines, *to justify* violence and war" (emphasis added). "*It is scientifically incorrect* to say that we have inherited a tendency to make war from our animal ancestors...that war or any other violent behaviour is genetically programmed into our human nature...that in the course of human evolution there has been a selection for aggressive behaviour more than for other kinds of behaviour... that humans have a 'violent brain'...[and] that war is caused by an 'instinct' or any single motivation" (emphasis in the original).

What are we to make of such a statement? Forget the sloppy conceptualization (the apparent conflation of aggressive proclivity, violent behavior, and warfare). Forget the slander—would anyone who endorsed this statement be prepared to name just one reputable scholar who has argued that biological evidence of aggressive behavior "justifies" acts of warfare? Or that war is caused by a single motivation? The apparent intent of the Seville proclamation is to stifle inquiries regarding the evolutionary bases of human aggression. It reveals an intent to bully and browbeat those who would inquire beyond received clichés. The evolutionary anthropologist Lionel Tiger (1990: 100) has aptly summarized the chilling implications of the Seville declarations: "If they are the starting point of a programme of investigation, they will doom it immediately; and if they are the endpoint, then they foreclose the possibility of new findings or new theories with which to interpret old findings."

In retrospect, Horowitz's democratic options sound very good, after all. Science thrives on the freedom of inquiry that democratic cultures are most likely to foster. Far too many sociologists are apologists of various narrow programs of political action. There is a heavy concentration of liberal-leftist reformers in sociology (Huber 1995: 201). "The hectoring, badgering tone of an Old Right has now found a home in the New Left" (Horowitz 1993: 23). A study of U.S. colleges and universities shows that in 1984 nearly 40 percent of the sociology faculty had a "left" or "liberal" identification. This figure represented a 6 percent decrease since 1969, roughly the peak of campus liberal activism, but there is reason to believe that what the Left lost in numbers was more than regained in fervor. This is perhaps why during the same period, the moderate-to-strong "conservative" identification grew (by reaction?) from 27.5 to 33.8 percent (Hamilton and Hargens 1993).

Political ideology certainly has played a crucial role in the vicissitudes of sociology. Indeed, sociologists have been reformers from the start (Cole 1994b; Lipset 1994; Turner 1996). But ideology in itself is not responsible for the growing crisis, at least not entirely. Often ideology is but a smoke screen for grievances powerful enough to motivate activism at the expense of scholarship. Such a tendency could be harnessed productively by theoretical leadership. It is because of the lack of leadership that sociology has become a magnet for intransigent apologists of feminism, gay rights, postmodernism, neo-Marxism, queer theory, rhetorical analysis, critical theory, and deconstructionism, among many other such "theories." This evolution has been facilitated by none other than the management of the American Sociological Association. In a detailed analysis of the ASA transformation, Simpson and Simpson (1994: 265) argue that "disciplinary interests have declined as new interests [e.g., sundry caucuses] have competed for organizational resources" and thus "weakened...the reproductive structure of the discipline." Hence: "What began as a righteous rebellion against benign neglect has now become an absolute ban against the spirit of inquiry as open-ended, color-blind, or gender-neutral" (Horowitz 1993: 35; see also, Horowitz 1968, 1970, 1977).

Political agendas give rise to ruinous deficits. They tend to produce superficially trained professors who resist intellectual challenges and demand little from their students beyond the ideologies and banalities that led them to sociology in the first place. The result is cultivated ignorance at the heart of which are the environmentalist dogma and a veritable phobia to the biological connection. Within this intellectual context, one of the most delectable sports is what Lewis M. Killian (1968) termed "intellectual lynchings." The executioners are frequently zealous feminists and their radical allies backed up by politically correct or terrified adminstrators. One of the most dangerous things one can do nowadays in sociology is to teach what just about every parent has discovered by the bassinet: that there are innate differences as well as similarities in average behavioral tendencies between males and females.

"There are taboos on certain topics, taboos which if broken lead to sanctions not primarily from administrators or the general public, but from one's own colleagues" (Coleman 1990–1991) and, we might add, from their students as well. Chief among the taboos today are those that concern questions of biology and of differences between the genders. In a related vein, Coleman (1991–1992: 17) writes elsewhere:

> Two years ago I received an award from the Sociology of Education section of the American Sociological Association. I took the occasion to remind the sociologists present that the person to whom they were making the award had earlier been harassed, vilified, and attacked by officers of the association, as well as by other social scientists—for precisely the same research that was now the cause of an award.

Those present had a hearty, self-congratulating laugh, and that was the end of any chance at self-scrutiny. Coleman had become a highly respected public figure, and that was good P.R. for sociology. Hence the award after all and hence, too, the (impulsive and transient) bonhomie of the audience.

Intellectual timidity is the cause of many self-inflicted casualties, one of which deserves brief comment here. Just as sociologists tolerate sloppy scholarship within their ranks, they impose few stringent expectations on their students. One result is that few professors nowadays have the courage to fail students who perform at substandard levels. Weak programs attract weak students whose increasing presence, in combination with low faculty expectations, further weakens whatever academic integrity is left in the discipline. Students with marginal academic skills drift into sociology programs in part because they view them as relatively obstacle-free paths toward a desired degree. Sociology departments appear to be only too happy to oblige.

But if it is true that sociology collects more than its share of mediocrity, it is equally true that it attracts and maintains a small minority of scholars whose intellectual worth is second to none. Our hope is that they will come forward very soon and go to battle. To a large extent, the future of sociology depends on the direction this minority will take in the next two or three decades. We are inclined to see a good concentration of such promising sociologists in the areas of demography and advanced statistics. It is another irony: whatever little theory may exist in sociology, here is where we are likely to find it. The conditions in favor of demographers and kindred types are various. As a group, they are more interested in "counting and measuring" than in ideologies. Moreover, given the focus on a small set of fundamental concepts, there is more theory, however modest, (e.g., Namboodiri 1988) in this type of activity than in the awful ramblings of so-called theorists. Further, demography is by definition a branch of evolutionary biology. Or, differently put, Darwinian theory is an eminently demographic type of scientific activity (e.g., Crippen 1994a: 319–23). Its basic orienting system, like that of demography, consists of birth, death, sex, and migration. We are not surprised, therefore, that studies of human demography increasingly are incorporating the tools of Darwinian science (e.g., Lopreato and Yu 1988; Vaupel 1988; Turke 1989; Olshansky et al. 1990; van den Berghe and Whitmeyer 1990; Weiss 1990; Low et al. 1992; Chisholm 1993; Sen 1993; Udry 1994; Carey and Lopreato 1995b; Whitmeyer 1997). If demography will enter the current of the present revolution in behavioral science, it will not only survive. It is also likely to absorb and modify for the better several areas of sociology, including sex roles and such other specialties as family, crime and delinquency, race and ethnicity, and problems of inequality, among others.

Bestriding Two Half-Truths

A fundamental cause of the sociological crisis transpires from the fact that too many sociologists adhere uncritically to the following methodological positions: (1) Human behavior is the result of *socialization*; (2) The causes of human behavior are to be found in *social structure*. There is an element of truth in both assertions. While human beings are born with certain behavioral propensities, the latter are developed through processes of socialization. Likewise, the degree to which socialization is an efficient means for the manifestation of innate tendencies may be mitigated or conversely intensified by structural, *intervening* variables. For instance, we are born with a tendency to conform and imitate, and the tendency is developed to varying degrees by family, church, school, and other socializing agents.

But we learn to conform because we are innately social beings. Should we be an inherently asocial animal, we would not be susceptible to mechanisms of socialization. Most persons readily grasp the lesson inherent in the old apothegm: You can't teach new tricks to an old dog. Likewise, sages have always recognized the role of heredity. According to one of Aesop's fables, a raven admired the whiteness of the swan and, thinking this was due to constant washing, changed environment, where he perished for want of food. Yet, most sociologists have difficulty with an even more compelling lesson. According to Aristotle's famous metaphor, there is immanence in what an acorn can become. It cannot, for example, yield a cherry tree. Human beings are the descendants of individuals who lived and thrived genetically in the small groups called clans. Imagine two clans at war with each other: one consisting of highly cooperative members; the other, of individuals who were more likely to disperse and run than to make common cause and fight. We may be reasonably certain that the more united society prevailed over the less compact one. Moreover, the more cooperative members were more likely to survive, reproduce, and convey their conformist propensities to future generations.

Our current populations are, therefore, loaded with cooperative people whose tendency to conform is a *hereditary* factor, although it is most assuredly developed within a social and socializing context. So, of course, we do tend to behave as we have been socialized to behave. Moreover, structural factors condition—mitigate or stimulate—the effect of socialization processes, say, on conformist tendencies. But the two together work in the first place because we are genetically constituted to be susceptible to pressures toward cooperation.

Left without an evolutionary linkage, the socialization and structural perspectives are half-truths at best. They induce "holistic fallacies," logical vacuities, sterile propositions, and emergent properties which, even if real, would be far too complex to grasp in view of our still rudimentary skills. They may also hide facts instead of revealing them. It is said, for example, that the cause of various "social pathologies" and depredations must be sought in society. But who, what is society? Are exploited women, for example, not members of society? Should they therefore blame themselves when they complain about their exploitation? The term "society" is excellent at hiding facts rather than revealing them. It is not society that penalizes women for aborting an unwanted child. It is particular people in the flesh who adhere to different standards of behavior and have the power, direct or indirect, to make life difficult for those who do not think as they do. By the same token, if the poor, the homeless, and other minorities go to jail for reasons they consider unfair, is it society that sends them there? Irreparably lost in this reified conception is the crucial fact that what we call society is a highly heterogeneous entity. In short, the excessive emphasis on socialization produces banalities. The associated and often contradictory reliance on structural variables mistakes intervening variables for causes, thus leading to very superficial explanations of facts instead of probing their deeper significance. This is a concoction for poor scientific nourishment and a chronic ailment.

This situation cannot endure. Developments in other behavioral sciences reveal that Darwinian theory is a "strong acid," or "universal solvent, capable of cutting right to the heart" of numberless problems (Dennett 1995: 521) and, in the process, dissolving the faulty Standard Social Science Model (Tooby and Cosmides 1992; Pinker 1994). Whether organized (i.e., academic) sociology will cope with these developments is the vital question. The signs are not especially encouraging. Little if any evidence suggests that our students (our intellectual replicas) are being prepared to deal with the demands created by the rapid changes currently underway in modern behavioral science. Will sociology thus be selected out of the population of academic enterprises, a victim of obsolete design? Or will sociologists come to recognize that, to do their jobs productively, they must take note and adapt to a transforming intellectual environment?

Dodging General Principles

Our most debilitating deficiency, a sort of synthesis of all the causes of our crisis, is the failure to establish at least one general law or principle (terms that we use interchangeably). Combined with this deficiency has been our inability or unwillingness to do as other aspiring disciplines have done, namely *borrow* it, with or without initial modification, from an established and related science—from what zoologist E.O. Wilson (1978b) has termed the anti-discipline.

There is almost general consensus that the establishment of general laws "on the basis of experience is a [crucial] function of science" (Braithwaite 1964: 9). Again, "the intellectual conquest and *ordering* of nature seems to form an essential part of scientific endeavor for many of those who participate in it" (Rose and Rose 1969: 217—emphasis added). Findings we have in abundance in sociology, probably more than even the most sanguine optimists ever suspected (e.g., Collins 1989). As Homans (1967: 105—emphasis added) noted over three decades ago, our failure has not been in discovering facts but in the job of *"organizing them theoretically*—showing how they follow under a variety of given conditions from a few general principles."

General laws or principles may be defined in various ways. The common denominator, for us, is that they are *causal statements whose in-*

ner logical program is large enough to encompass a variety of lower-order propositions and the relative discoveries indicated by these. We make no attempt to follow the methodological niceties of the philosopher of science. Our basic aim is to underscore the three fundamental functions of general laws, such as (1) *to instigate inquiry into unexplained areas*; (2) *to help discover new statements of theory specialized for given problems*; and (3) *to organize propositions and discoveries in relation to one another, thereby producing cumulative systematic knowledge.*

Associated with these basic functions are other important ones. Laws provide *logical directives for concept formation that is theoretically contextual in nature, rather than ad hoc.* A nomologically guided definition of concepts implies, further, *the nomological function of the operationalization of concepts.* It follows that one fundamental function of laws is *to provide a firm and logically adjudicated basis for intelligible and productive communication among interested parties.*

General laws further provide *the means wherewith to recognize a hierarchy of causation for any given phenomenon and thereby encourage a stepwise structuring of ancillary propositions according to their varying degrees of comprehensiveness or, conversely, specificity.* That is, laws in general and general laws in particular constitute focal points of discoveries and explanations that, taken together, constitute what are termed scientific theories. Within the context of any given theory, any given fact may be explained from various perspectives and with varying degrees of generality and logical integration. It is in this sense that scientists sometimes speak of *ultimate* (or *distal*) explanations (referring to the level of the law) and *proximate* (or *mediate*) explanations (referring to lower-order or intervening statements) (e.g., Machalek 1986; Low 1995). A fact is most thoroughly explained when it is explained at both ultimate and proximate levels. For example, a given case of ethnic conflict may be due, at one level, to competition for jobs between two nationality groups. At another, deeper, level, it is also due to the ethnocentric tendency that, as we shall see in chapter 9, was forged by natural selection during the evolution of clans in competition with one another. The difference between the two levels is that the second, unlike the first, is likely to apply to most if not all cases of ethnic conflict.

Some sociologists recognize the importance of nomological theorizing. But it is one thing to recognize it; it is quite another to detect and transcend the shackles that are inherent in the current culture of sociological inquiry. In his 1991 presidential address to the American Sociologial Association, Stanley Lieberson, for example, undertook to convey a number of lessons that are inextricably rooted in the problem of nomothetic inquiry. The basic point was stated as follows: "It is relatively easy to determine if evidence supports or does not support a given theory or conclusion, but a central problem in sociology is our inability to go beyond this and develop truly convincing evidence about a theory" (Lieberson 1992: 1). A number of suggestions ensue, for example, the exhortation to avoid "nonproductive assaults between sociologists" and, "more fundamentally" (still, in the 1990s!), to stop viewing theory "as one pole of a continuum with research on the other end." True to the spirit of basic scientific inquiry, the author (1992: 4) turns to two experts in the logic of theory formation (Woods and Walton 1982) to underscore his position that a theory performs a number of functions, crucial among which are: (1) "a systematic and orderly organization of what is already known of a given subject matter"; (2) the articulation and exposure of "underlying principles"; (3) the discovery of "new implications of those principles and new applications of them"; and (4) the utilization of "somewhat abstract and idealized concepts."

The rest of the paper, in many ways instructive and, for us, generative of new hope, addresses several problems in sociological research, all of which concern the evaluation of evidence and lead to the following conclusion: "The key is the development in social science of the epistemic term 'adequate evidence,'" as opposed to "conclusive" or "inconclusive" evidence (Lieberson 1992: 7). This reasoning, in turn, is embedded in the centerpiece of Lieberson's paper, namely the injunction to discard our "deterministic perspective" in favor of a "probabilistic social epistemology" (Lieberson 1992: 7–9). A pithy definition of this is offered in the paper's abstract as follows: "A probabilistic view of theory is proposed such that a theory may be correct even if there is negative evidence." In short, a theory, basically, should take the following form: If X, then Y *provided* that P, Q, R...also hold (see also Zetterberg 1963: chap. 4). The specification of "a given set of conditions" helps to "correctly describe" "the reality of social life" and will also free us "from assuming that negative evidence automatically means that a theory is wrong" (Lieberson 1992: 7).

Now, if sociologists still need to learn this much, it might as well be said, and we certainly admire the simplicity and elegance with which it was conveyed by Lieberson. On the other hand, it is a bit depressing to read for the nth time that the race in sociology has not yet begun. Equally troublesome is the fact that, having stated his conception of theory in the nomological terms of the logician, the author then proceeds in fair disregard of them. Gone, for example, is the promised emphasis on underlying principles and their new implications and applications. Where does the problem lie? We cannot hold Lieberson responsible for failing to uncover underlying principles as long as he remains within the long-trodden sociological path and those principles are simply not there, at least not yet, though we do wonder why there is still resistance to exploring a new trail with the help of our neighbors.

In this volume, we propose adoption of a general principle from sociobiology that is central to all evolutionary behavioral sciences. It may conveniently be stated as follows: *Organisms tend to behave in ways that maximize their inclusive fitness.* This law, sometimes referred to as the maximization principle, will represent a focal point of reasoning in the remainder of this volume. In the relevant literature it appears in various degrees of explicitness and under slightly varying expressions. Its fundamental message, however, is this: Whatever organisms, human beings included, may do—and they do engage in a near-infinity of behaviors—*in the last analysis*, and *with varying degrees of success*, they typically behave in ways that *tend to* favor their reproductive success and the reproductive success of their blood kin. Surrounding this principle is a growing number of ancillary propositions concerning sexual selection, parental investment, altruism, and so forth.

The principle is inherent in Darwin's theory of natural selection, which will be discussed in the next chapter. High sensitivity to it, however, is probably only some thirty years old (Hamilton 1964; Wilson 1975). The core of what is sometimes termed fitness theory, the principle has stimulated a rich program of research. The paragraph below provides a select list of phenomena that have been comprised under its logical umbrella and thus are at the *ultimate* level represented by it.

Social conflict, including ethnic and religious conflict; mating patterns, for example, polygamy and monogamy; induced abortion; infanticide; rape; male-female differences in mate preferences; male philandering; conflict of interests between the genders; generational conflict; socioeconomic inequality; dominance; differences in communication style and content between the genders; play activity; the ambiguity of fatherhood; mother-infant bonding; cooperation; altruism; victimization; child abuse; harems; despotism; intrafamily favoritism; favoritism in last wills and testaments; adoption of children; various aspects of morality; alliances; voluntary associations; mate guarding and male jealousy; deception, of self and others; socialization processes; friendship; sense of guilt; sense of distributive justice; incest, incest taboo, and incest avoidance; hypergyny; effect of hormones on emotions; hunting and fishing as sports; various aspects of criminal behavior—these are among a host of facts that have been shown to fall under the theoretical reach of the maximization principle. We need not add that they are eminently sociological subjects. We may stress, however, that they are currently being revisited and appropriated by psychologists, anthropologists, and zoologists.

In approaching the end of this chapter, we must note that not all sociologists think that general laws of the type called for here are possible in sociology. Others are entirely averse to them. Examples of the latter were encountered earlier in this chapter among postmodernists. Those who question or deny the possibility of laws in sociology tend to allege such problems as the following: (1) in the study of human behavior it is impossible to engage in controlled experimentation; (2) there is too much mutability in human society (e.g., Cole 1994b); (3) human behavior is too subjective. These and other objections have been effectively countered by excellent philosophers of science, and we shall not belabor the point. E. Nagel (1961: chap. 13), for instance, has shown that there is little that is unique to sociological science. Thus, on the alleged impossibility of controlled experimentation, he has reminded us that geology and embryology as well as astronomy are in the same boat with us; yet they have hardly been hindered by the alleged problem. As to mutability and subjectivity, physics, for example, has its meteorology and the Heisenberg Principle as well as Newtonian and relativity theories; it can hardly be considered impeded by insurmountable problems.

There is a third, far more congenial, position on the question of laws in sociology. Randall Collins (1989), for instance, has rejected the verdict that "sociology has made no lawful findings" and argued that "valid general principles exist in many areas" of sociology. We cheer Professor Collins' faith but cannot share his optimism. Consider the following candidate:

> The longer, more intensely, and more exclusively persons interact with each other, the more that they will identify with one another as a group, and the more pressure they will exert and feel for conformity to local patterns of behavior and belief, provided that they are not unequals in power or competitors for scarce resources. (Collins 1989: 124–25)

There are various problems with this sort of "general principle." For example, the proposition is intended as an idealization with two provisos. Idealizations are crucial in science (Lopreato and Alston 1970; Lopreato 1989a), but the validity of the provisos must be demonstrated, *and additional statements of theory discovered to account for departures from the idealized conditions, if they are to be serviceable.* In principle, then, Collins' statement could serve as a productive challenge, but to our knowledge it has had little or no issue. We must recall, further, that such terms as equality and power constitute old conceptual problems in sociology, and any statement comprising them necessarily suffers from their indefiniteness. The more fundamental problem with the proposition, however, is that it contains, or implies, no logical basis for a needed link between the terms *interact, identify, pressure, conformity, inequality,* and *competition for scarce resources.* This failure is tantamount to failing to specify why it is that the members of the group are assumed to aim at conformity. Conformity, an evolutionary scientist will argue, is in the last analysis "adaptive"—it confers reproductive advantages, among other things. Non-conformists tend to be weeded out by natural selection. This is the ultimate rationale. There is nothing corresponding to it in Collins' principle. To the extent, moreover, that Collins' proposition has any validity, it is predictable from the viewpoint of the evolutionary theory of cooperation and "altruism" (Trivers 1971, 1985: chap.15), which is, in turn, derivable from the maximization principle.

In conclusion, with little if any exception, sociology has become an amorphous mass of meaningless facts and hunches. Assuming it has scientific ambitions, its fundamental difficulty refers to its isolation from the established scientific enterprise and to the concomitant failure to either generate or borrow some focal general statement of theory— the theoretical "constant" that in practice frees the imagination. Why not borrow? The history of scientific development reveals that astronomy came of age not because of the validity of Copernicus' heliocentric theory but because both his blunders and his accuracies were clear enough to stimulate further developments; astronomy "made it" by leaning on mathematics. Physics came of age under the influence of astronomy and mathematics; chemistry under the aegis of physics; biology on the persuasion of geology and chemistry (for it was the emergence of genetics, a biochemical discipline, that made sense of the truly causal-explanatory variable in Darwin's *Origin,* namely "variation").

What is the fertilizing agent of sociology (and her sister disciplines)? What has prevented us from learning lessons from our most immediate natural science, evolutionary biology? We suspect that the answer lies in the failure to countenance the hypothesis that *Homo sapiens*, too, is an organism resulting from and subject to evolution by natural selection. Such a failure—among many a veritable biophobia—reflects a sociological corollary of the pre-Copernican fallacy of geocentrism, that is, *anthropocentrism* (Lopreato 1986; van den Berghe 1990). This zoophobic assumption at the dawn of the twenty-first century and in the age of the genome project leaves sociology so far removed from the revolution now exploding in behavioral science that we risk separation from the academia. In the next two chapters we shall provide some basic elements of modern evolutionary science. In subsequent chapters we shall then proceed to apply them to a select number of sociological problems.

Part 2

Elements of Evolutionary Theory

4

Darwin's Theory of Natural Selection

"Nothing in biology makes sense except in the light of evolution."
Few today would reject this verdict by one of the great architects of
modern evolutionary theory (Dobzhansky 1973). It is now sociologists'
turn to consider the possibility that *little in sociology makes lasting
sense except in the light of modern evolutionary theory*. For some 150
years a scientific revolution of enormous scope has been erupting with
ever increasing force at the interface of the social and the biological
sciences under the aegis of Darwin's theory of natural selection and the
science of population genetics. Most sociologists remain oblivious of
this fact, even in view of breakthroughs in such closely pertinent areas
as brain science, endocrinology, and human genetics, which clearly
reveal the dramatic import of evolutionary forces for the explanation of
human behavior.

The causes of our self-absorption are inherent in the causes of the
crisis, preeminently in a disciplinary history of fragmentation, in the
antiscientific posture taken by radical subjectivism, in the ready tolera-
tion of mediocrity, in the associated commitment to political correctness, in the exclusive focus on environmentalism, and, among others,
especially in our failure to apply a law-like form of theorizing. We may
now add another, more abstract and more encompassing at once. Scientific revolutions, like other radical transformations, are rarely welcome in their formative stage. Typically they meet with what Pareto
(1916: sections 1130–32) termed the sentiment of neophobia, which
tends to defend reigning customs and habits, although it inevitably
weakens when new knowledge shows that the old ways are grossly
inefficient if not altogether deleterious.

From another perspective, the course of revolutionary science re-
sembles a series of autocatalytic processes. The greater the stored knowledge, the greater the momentum of future developments feeding upon
it. But autocatalyses do not last forever; hence movement is rhythmic

in nature, revealing alternating syncopes and outbursts. The phenomenon is evident in the chronicles of scientific paradigms. Once established, these stimulate new discoveries that are inherent in their inner logic, for a while. Eventually, however, paradigms encounter anomalies, or problems for which existing theory provides no solutions. Syncopes set in. Again they may encourage neophobia and myopia, but again only for a while. Soon, discovery becomes extralinear, and what was previously puzzling is accommodated under new or more comprehensive paradigms (Kuhn 1962). Discovery again becomes explosive.

There is also a paradox in scientific revolutions. They infiltrate large expanses of reason, challenging old systems of thought and initially creating frail new disciplines "at the frontier"—the *terra incognita*. Hence, science ever wraps itself in systems of thought that tend to slow its progress or call its powers of arbitration into question. Aiding this resistance to scientific progress is, ironically, one of the most creative features of the human mind, namely the capacity for symbolization—a trait that includes abstracting from experience profound meanings that may then be elaborated to such a bewildering degree that they transcend falsifiable reality. Here then is the paradox: A mind that specializes in seeking the meaning of things inner and remote is a specialist also in constructing systems of causality that are pure fictions of the imagination. It follows that scientific progress may be most easily impeded there where the mind is at its imaginative best. The paradox has imprisoned sociology. Sociologists specialize in the search for symbolical representations, frequently mistaking in the process the wayward sign of the thing—the symbol—for the thing itself: for instance, ideologies of equality for equality itself. But it is fair to add that sociologists also deal with phenomena that in part constitute the extralinear stages of the current revolution in behavioral science. The fact would be a blessing if only the neophobia did not stifle its potential for creativity.

It is our position that sociology, like other social disciplines in varying degrees, constitutes the frontier—part of the *terra incognita*—of evolutionary biology, the family of natural sciences kindred in both substance and method to the aspirations of the social sciences. Hence, in order to survive in the next fifty years, sociology will have to make adjustments and somehow cope with the accelerating invasions by various branches of evolutionary biology. "Darwin," wrote T. Dobzhansky and his associates (1977: 495), "completed the Copernican revolution by drawing out for biology the ultimate conclusions of the notion of nature as a lawful system of matter in motion." We need not accept this hasty verdict of completion. The Copernican revolution is still in its infancy. What Darwin (and Wallace and Mendel and countless other scholars) did was to build bridges between the science of nature in its more remote phases to the science of nature in its more immediate human aspects. Darwinism broadly understood will prove itself to be the master key to the study of the social behavior of humans as well as other species. Movement in this direction is already quite notable, although large pockets of resistance are only too evident in social science. Too many sociologists, for example, lack knowledge of Darwinian theory, even when they are so bold as to challenge and reject it. But knowledge of its basics has become a fundamental necessity.

Natural Selection: A Powerful Metaphor

Darwin's fundamental idea is that species are mutable entities, thus in time often giving rise to new species. To varying degrees of explicitness, this insight is at least twenty-five centuries old. Among European peoples, it was seriously challenged by the doctrine of "the permanence of species" as special and separate creations only in the seventeenth and eighteenth centuries, when the latter idea became a basic tenet of natural history (Dobzhansky et al. 1977: 9). But faulty ideas run most quickly into trouble when they are expounded by scientists. Naturalists could hardly be expected to break this rule. Thus, the immensely creative nineteenth century resurrected the old evolutionary idea, giving it full expression and hosting a new series of intellectual outbursts.

Charles Darwin is credited with the paternity of this revolution in biology, though what is conveniently termed Darwinian theory really comprises contributions by a variety of scholars working into our own time in such areas as geology, botany, zoology, biogeography, entomology, and of course genetics, among many others. But his work does constitute the scaffolding for the entire architecture. Moreover, Darwin was well-suited for the role of promulgator. With the exception of genetics, which was officially born six years after his epoch-making *Origin* (Darwin 1859), he was conversant with all of the disciplines mentioned above. He was the quintessential synthesist endowed with an exceptionally methodic mind and a large body of field observations to serve it. Along with, but more so than Alfred Russel Wallace, he is the discoveror of the fundamental *mechanism* of evolution: natural selection. We have underscored an important concept. Evolution is quite different from mere change. It is one thing to have a conception of change and of a variety of factors that are causally related to it; that is the case with what sociologists call social evolutionism (Lopreato 1990). It is quite another to pinpoint a factor that *uniformly* underlies change in all relevant systems at all times and places. Transformation without a uniform mechanism is not evolution but mere change.

Darwin was convinced of the reality of evolution, what he termed "descent with modification," for some time before he became aware of its mechanism. Various factors nudged him toward the discovery of the mechanism, which will be defined presently. Three are especially noteworthy. First, geologists, preeminently William Smith and Sir Charles Lyell, had demonstrated that the history of the earth could be explained in terms of forces—for example, volcanic and oceanic activities—that acted uniformly throughout the ages. Lyell's "uniformitarianism" replaced faulty theories, for example "catastrophism," that relied on such questionable facts as the Great Flood. Given Lyell's theory, the fossil record could be taken, according to Darwin, as evidence of continuous change of biological organization across the lengthy span of geological time. This much was strong indication in favor of the hypothesis that the species were mutable, and most probably related to one another, rather than the result of divine and independent creation.

While doing field work during 1833–1836, Darwin witnessed an amazing richness and diversity of life, both in living and fossil form, in the Amazon forests and the rocky barrens of Patagonia, among other places around the world (Darwin 1902). All along, he sent specimens back to England, where they influenced the thinking of various scholars, with the result that by the time he returned home on October 2, 1836, at age twenty-seven, he had already achieved fame as a naturalist.

Darwin was especially struck by the subtle differences of anatomy and behavior that were observable across the geographic distribution of various types of animals and plants. As environmental conditions changed—for example, the availability of foodstuffs—so too changed the biological makeup of populations. This awareness became particularly poignant during a five-week visit to the Galápagos Islands, some 600 miles off the coast of Ecuador. Here Darwin became keenly aware of the differentiation of populations as he compared island species with manifestly related species on the mainland and as he moved from one island to another (Darwin 1902: chap. XVII). A sub-family of birds commonly known as Darwin's finches, for instance, are distributed discontinuously, some inhabiting particular islands or areas thereon while others may range over several islands. Altogether, Darwin's finches constitute four genera and fourteen species (Lack 1947; Weiner 1994), and yet all fourteen species are obviously related to one another, the differences in many cases being hardly noticeable to the untrained eye.

To Darwin, the finches represented a transparent case of evolutionary history. What could account for the observed similarities and differences existing between the various species? Chances are good that the island species originated on the mainland, and in the course of time enough "variations" (today we say genetic mutations) accumulated among the migrants' descendants to give rise to related but different species, that is, to new *genetically closed populations*. As the finches distributed themselves away from their original area and across the islands, they encountered different challenges or ecological pressures acting on their chances for survival and reproduction. And here is where *natural selection* comes in, though the idea did not dawn on Darwin until after his return to England. In response to given ecological pressures, some individual birds were better "adapted" than others (had more suitable variations) to survive the challenge, reproduce, and thereby convey their successful traits to their offspring.

For instance, assume the arrival on the islands of a mainland flock featuring some variation in beak structure. Assume next that in the gene pool of the flock there was some potential for change in the structure and function of beaks. Assume further that in a given area food was more easily procured by some birds—say, those with longer beaks—than by others. We may conclude that these had a better chance to survive and reproduce in that area. We have arrived at the concept of *natural selection*, which may conveniently though incompletely be viewed as *differential reproduction*. But we shall not be quite yet into the Darwinian logic until we specify several other justifiable assumptions. One, assume that there was an inherent tendency, up to a point, for certain beaks—say, the longer ones—to become even longer, *from one generation to another*. Two, assume *heritability* of traits, namely the fact that parents convey their genetic traits to their offspring. The result, as Darwin saw it, was evolution by natural selection over a given period of time. In time, the original species gave rise to a population loaded with birds endowed with longer beaks than those present in the original species.

We may also assume that, as the beaks were being modified across the generations, other secondary characteristics were developing that contributed to the process of "speciation": the emergence of new species from an old one. Further, some of the original migrants may have discovered an ecological niche that favored shorter beaks. These may have proven to be best suited, for instance, for gathering seeds rather than, say, catching insects or retrieving prey from within coiled leaves. Thus, in the course of time a part of the original flock modified (evolved) in another direction, say, toward specialized smaller beaks. In either case, according to Darwin, the drift was toward evolution, or modification by descent.

We have in effect conceptualized the evolution of two species of finches. Taking all fourteen species into account would have been a far more difficult task, but the basic logic would not have changed. Evolution would have been the resultant of the interaction between genetic potential for change in structure and function, on the one hand, and ecological factors, such as diversity in available foodstuffs, on the other. Students of Darwin's finches have illustrated the great diversity of their feeding habits associated with the variety of their beak shapes (Dobzhansky et al. 1977: 187; see also Lack 1947; Weiner 1994).

Darwin himself was at great pains to establish the principle of descent by modification and the equally crucial point that evolution was the joint product of heritable variations and environmental pressures. "The most striking and important fact for us," he (1859: 376–77) wrote in 1859, "is the affinity of the species which inhabit islands to those of the nearest mainland, without being actually the same.... the close affinity of most of these birds to American species is manifest in every character, in their habits, gestures and tones of voice." Darwin further remarked that in climate, geology, and conditions of life, the Galápagos and the South American coast diverged considerably. Conversely, in these respects and others, resemblance was considerably greater between the Galápagos and, say, the Cape Verde Islands. But "what an entire and absolute difference in their inhabitants! The inhabitants of the Cape Verde Islands are related to those of Africa, like those of the Galápagos to America. Facts such as these admit of no...explanation on the ordinary view of independent creation."

By now, then, the idea of descent through modification (evolution), as contrasted to independent and immutable creation, was firmly established in Darwin's mind. Missing still was a clear idea of the uniform mechanism of evolution, what was later termed natural selection. A crucial factor in Darwin's discovery of this mechanism was provided by one of the masters of early sociology, Thomas Robert Malthus. This scholar, the putative father of human demography, had argued in 1798 that population growth tends to outstrip the rate of increase in the resources needed for survival; hence, competition for really or virtually scarce resources was an inescapable fact of life. It was this idea that, on September 28, 1838 (Bowlby 1990: 223) suggested natural selection to Darwin (Dobzhansky et al. 1977: 97). Darwin reasoned that the Malthusian tendency toward an excess of population is a universal condition in the biotic world. And yet, most of the time, if not always, most species experience zero growth. Clearly not every individual survives long enough to reproduce. Darwin himself (1859: 75—emphasis added) reveals the sociological inspiration.

> Hence, as more individuals are produced than can possibly survive, there must in every case be a *struggle for existence*, either one individual with another of the same species, or with the individuals of distinct species, or with the physical conditions of life. *It is the doctrine of Malthus applied* with manifold force to the whole animal and vegetable kingdoms; for in this case there can be no artificial increase of food, and no prudential restraint from marriage.

The next question, of course, was whether success or failure in the struggle for existence was a matter of pure chance or was rather dependent to varying degrees on constitutional factors. While Darwin had no conception of genetics as this science is known today, he certainly was keen to the fact of "variations" among individuals whereby some were better adapted than others to meet the challenges of the environment—to survive and reproduce. And he even had a fair grasp of what he termed "the laws of heredity," rather well suggested by the facts of animal and plant breeding, namely "artificial selection." He therefore concluded: "This preservation of favourable individual differences and variations, and the destruction of those which are injurious, I have called *Natural Selection*" (Darwin 1859: 88—emphasis added).

We may now summarize the core of what is generally considered Darwin's theory as follows:

1. Reproduction within populations (e.g., species) takes place at a faster rate than the corresponding expansion of resources needed to sustain all their members.
2. As a result, populations must cope, most if not all of the time, with a scarcity of resources needed for survival.
3. Such scarcity causes, or stimulates, competition for resources within and between populations: the struggle for existence.
4. Some individuals in any given population are more successful than others in the struggle, and hence are more likely to reproduce.

5. Such differential reproductive success is in the last analysis due to different endowments of "variations" ("genes" or complexes thereof).

6. In short, some variations are better suited (adapted) than others for the competition; and the better suited they are, the more likely they are to be conveyed, through offspring and their descendants, to future generations.

7. This differential reproduction—that is, the preservation of favorable variations and the elimination of unfavorable ones—is termed *natural selection*.

8. The transformation of a species through the natural selection of variations was alleged by Darwin to lead to the "transmutation" of one species into another, or into others—to lead to descent with modification (evolution).

But does it? In raising this question we do not intend to argue against Darwin, let alone the stupendous richness of theory, in the form of clarification and elaboration, that has come to surround his epoch-making breakthrough. Our intention is to celebrate the promise of imperfections when these are taken as scholarly challenges. Theories need not be perfect, especially when they are first hatched. Stanley Lieberson (1992) was refreshingly correct. Nor do they need to be exactly what they claim to be. What is more important—and here is the crucible of scientific progress—is that a theory imply the way to rectification, elaboration, linkages to other theories. In this respect, Darwin's theory has been supremely successful. Nevertheless, Darwin's conception of evolution had several flaws, inevitable in view of the state of knowledge prevailing in 1838. In particular, there was no knowledge of how hereditary variations arose. As a result, according to E. Mayr (1982: 400— emphasis added), the "two essentially independent processes" of organic evolution—transformation and diversification—were conflated in Darwin's account. "Transformation deals with the 'vertical' (usually adaptive) component of change in time" and, in the language of today's evolutionists, refers primarily to changing gene *frequencies* in a breeding population. The process is, *in principle, unrelated to the introduction of genetic novelty and thus has little to do with "the multiplication of species nor, more broadly...[with] the origin of organic diversity."* As Mayr notes, Darwin "was aware of this difference...[but] did not sufficiently stress the far-reaching independence of these two components of evolution." Nor could he in the absence of genetic science.

In order to have evolution, three processes working concurrently are necessary: Natural Selection, Heredity, and Mutation *or variation as novelty* (Lewontin 1974; Dobzhansky et al. 1977: 5; Thompson 1989: 11). The latter is a process that modifies existing genetic matter (DNA) and thus introduces new DNA into the gene pool of a given species. It is absent in Darwin's work (Simpson 1949: chap. XVI), though he (1859: chap. II) did have an insightful if vague conception of "variations which seem to us in our ignorance to arise spontaneously." Without mutation, natural selection and heredity can together shuffle and reshuffle an existing gene pool, changing thereby the frequency of existing genes in it; but they add no new DNA, though they may subtract some. Thus, in the strictest sense, it is questionable whether Darwin's theory is a theory of evolution, though as a minimum it strongly implies it. Natural selection in itself does not entail the mutability of species (e.g., Thompson 1989: 7).

Of course, the science of genetics, born around 1865 out of experiments on cross-breeding by Gregor Mendel, was unknown to Darwin. Indeed, Mendel's laws of inheritance did not enter the domain of evolutionary theory until they were rediscovered in 1900. In the meantime, and up to the 1920s, Darwinians did good work demonstrating the reality of natural selection. On their part, most early geneticists focused on mutation and paid little attention to natural selection. It was not until around 1930, as we shall see in chapter 5, that Darwinian science and Mendelian science came together to form modern evolutionary biology: the Synthetic Theory, or the Modern Synthesis (Huxley 1942). Hence, depending on whether we take 1865 or 1900 as the benchmark, it took about thirty to sixty years for two obviously cognate disciplines to produce together a grand synthesis. That bespeaks a record of patient toil, great genius at work, and also a mentality that celebrated interdisciplinary linkages and alliances. The repercussions of the synthesis are now having accelerating resonance throughout the broad space of behavioral disciplines.

Another problem of sorts with Darwin's theory is that natural selection has never been an unequivocal conception. This difficulty may have played a part in the continuing alienation of much social science from evolutionary biology. Certainly, the fact that in a revised edition of *The Origin* Darwin equated natural selection with Spencer's "survival of the fittest," an ambiguous concept that had much to do with the rise of Social Darwinism, did not encourage social scientists to join the Darwinian revolution. In principle, the idea of natural selection would seem to be quite simple to understand. As already noted, it may conveniently be thought of, as it often is in biology, as differential reproduction, though Darwin's own emphasis was specifically on differential *survival*. In practice, however, its implications are legion, and require earnest attention. Moreover, there is an objectively confusing element in the concept. The problem lies in the fact that, while natural selection is almost generally understood as *the mechanism* or *cause* of evolution, its equation with cause is only a convenient metaphor. It often appears, for example, that evolutionary scholars view natural selection as something whose causal status in the biotic world is analogous to the force of gravity in physics. That is an improper view, though nevertheless a convenient and, for all intents and purposes, a harmless one. It is also widespread among Darwinian students whose scholarship is quite beyond reproach. Biopsychologists Martin Daly and Margo Wilson (1978: 5), for example, appear to view natural selection as "the mechanism that causes evolution." Bioanthropologist Donald Symons (1979: 9) understands natural selection as "the central explanatory principle of biology" and "by far the most important determinant of the course of evolution." Likewise, biologists Robert Trivers (1985: 9) and Richard D. Alexander (1990: 244) view natural selection, respectively, as "the causal agent behind evolutionary change" and "the principal guiding force of evolution." Philosopher of science Paul Thompson (1989: 6) writes of "the causal principle of natural selection." In their excellent essay on the psychological foundations of culture, Tooby and Cosmides (1992: 54–55—emphasis added) rightly argue that it is the set of adaptations that constitutes the mechanisms and "regulates our behavior— not natural selection directly." But then almost in the same breath they proceed to state: "Adaptations are the accumulated output of selection, and selection is the single significant anti-entropic or ordering *force* orchestrating functional organic design."

The tendency, then, is to place natural selection in the same class with such other mechanisms in science as gravity, chemical valence, the binding force of the atom, and, for us, the force of Mendelian mutation. But natural selection is in no sense a force. While the former are "causally energetic" concepts, natural selection is the *result* of *genetic* and *environmental* forces. As Dobzhansky and his associates (1977: 98—emphasis added) have correctly pointed out, natural selection is "a *consequence* of the 'struggle for life' or 'existence,'" thus suggesting that it is the elements making up the struggle that constitute the mechanisms. Nevertheless, they (1977: 18—emphasis added) also accept the assumption that "all biological organization, down to the level of molecules, has evolved as a result of natural selection *acting upon* genetic variation." We should note that Darwin himself was critical of a causal understanding of natural selection. Thus he (1859: 88—emphasis added) wrote:

Several writers have misapprehended or objected to the term Natural Selection. Some have even *imagined that natural selection induces variability*, whereas it implies only the preservation of such variations as arise and are beneficial to the being under its conditions of life.

Quite right. Natural selection is not an agent; it is a demographic process. Darwin may have taken a few false steps, but in the end genius rarely goes astray. By 1860, only months after the publication of *The Origin*, he regretted not having used the expression "natural preservation" instead of natural selection. And Alfred Russel Wallace, the co-discoverer of natural selection, was always concerned about the misconceptions that "Darwin's metaphor" gave rise to, and constantly pleaded with Darwin to make the change (Bowlby 1990: 338; see also F. Darwin 1885: 346; Darwin and Seward 1903: 267–71).

Several debates, none deleterious, have arisen around Darwinian theory. One is especially worth noting because it has occasioned some interest among sociologists (as well as creationists) and reinforced some of their misconceptions. It appears to have been initiated by paleontologists N. Eldredge and S. J. Gould (1972; see also, e.g., Stanley 1981; Eldredge 1985). Eldredge and Gould have proposed a theory of "punctuated equilibrium" that opposes Darwin's alleged "phyletic gradualism" with the argument that evolution is typically episodic and rapid—that populations or lineages split within relatively "rapid and episodic events of speciation." Such episodes punctuate "homeostatic equilibria," namely protracted periods of natural selection characterized by little or no mutation. The focus of this conception of evolution ("macroevolution") is on small populations split from larger ones and isolated from the latter by physical barriers, e.g., a mountainside that falls into a lake and traps small numbers away from the parental population. Under these circumstances, mutations or genetic errors in cellular replication, if retained, will spread rapidly, and new species are thus likely to emerge in relatively short periods of time—thousands, even fewer years, depending on the species—rather than the much lengthier periods that presumably were visualized categorically by Charles Darwin (see Stanley 1981: chap. VI for some examples from Lake Victoria, among other areas).

As paleontologists, Eldredge and Gould began with a consideration of the fossil record of human evolution and were led to argue that this record may be more complete than it has seemed. Specifically, the so-called gaps in the record (the famous "missing links") allegedly refer to cases of homeostatic equilibrium that were punctuated by occasional spurts of speciation. The subject is not central to the aims of this volume, and we are not inclined to dwell on it. However, we do wish to stress the point that, while the theory of punctuated equilibrium was intended to rectify an aspect of Darwinian theory, it was not meant to reject natural selection and most certainly not the theory of evolution as a whole.

Furthermore, punctuated equilibrium theory has not gone unchallenged. One of the most informative and cogent criticisms has been provided by Richard Dawkins (1986: chap. 9). "Eldredge and Gould," this author (1986: 251) writes in obvious pique, "don't whisper. They speak out, with eloquence and power!" And they unwittingly provide ammunition to antiscience specialists. Creationists, for instance, do not specialize in catching subtleties and react self- servingly with hallelujahs. Dawkins quotes the editor of *Biblical Creation* as follows: "it is undeniable that the credibility of our religious and scientific position has been greatly strengthened by the recent lapse in neo-Darwinian morale. And this is something we must exploit to the full."

Dawkins rightly argues that the focus on isolation and punctuation as factors of evolution has long been an integral part of neo-Darwinian theory (e.g., Mayr 1963). In fact, we may add, while Darwin certainly emphasized a "gradual" process of evolution ("*Natura non facit saltum*"—nature does not take leaps or jumps), he (1859: 106–7) also recognized "isolation" as "an important element in the modification of species." Moreover, many geneticists have long emphasized "stepwise mutational changes of large extent" (Huxley 1958: xii).

Dawkins argues, not without some justification, that punctuationists mistakenly emphasize the originality of their claims by relying on a rigid and naive conception of Darwinian gradualism. He makes his point with an interesting analogy. According to Exodus, the children of Israel took forty years to cross the desert and reach the promised land. Imagine two "gradualist" biblical historians concluding thereby that the Israelites traveled regularly a total of twenty-four yards a day. Absurd! Obviously there were times when they were not traveling at all. At other times, they may have taken detours. All along they traveled in fits and starts. What punctuationists are really opposed to, presumably, is not gradualism properly understood. They really object to "Darwin's alleged belief in the constancy of rates of evolution" (Dawkins 1986: 241). Accordingly, it turns out that the theory of punctuated equilibrium itself "is a gradualist theory, albeit it emphasizes long periods of stasis intervening between *relatively* short bursts of gradualistic evolution" (Dawkins 1986: 244—emphasis in the original).

Punctuationism does not, then, appear to be a major challenge to Darwin's theory. But what about the important fact that there are gaps in the fossil record? Dawkins is sanguine about this issue, and does not even bother to consider that future findings may close at least some of them. Indeed the gaps are exactly what we would expect from the viewpoint of an "orthodox neo-Darwinian theory of speciation." There is little or no doubt that isolation, for example through migration, has played a major role in evolution. Imagine, for instance, a small population living at the foot of a mountain. At some point, a part of it migrates—for any number of reasons, including conflicts over a shortage of resources—to the other side of the mountain. If contact between the two sub-populations ceases, in time the two groups may become two separate species, as apparently was the case, we may recall, among Darwin's finches. This is standard reasoning among students of evolution.

We should not leave this brief discussion of punctuated equilibrium theory without noting that, whatever its overall worth, because of it we now have keener awareness than ever before that speciation can be very rapid, in some cases occurring in the course of a mere few thousand if not hundred years even in highly advanced organisms, such as species of fish (e.g., Stanley 1981). (Of course in microorganisms, such as viruses, evolution can be far more rapid.) But it also bears noting that what for a while appeared as a major challenge to modern evolutionary theory has really turned out to be a minor, and in equivalent degrees useful, perturbation. That underscores the value of uniform mechanisms and nomological reasoning. Challenges may refine good theory. They rarely destroy it. Moreover, whatever the tempo of evolution, which is no doubt rhythmic in nature, all evolutionists of the organic world are in the last analysis interested in the forces that act on that world, occasioning the differential reproduction of DNA, including novel DNA, from generation to generation. That is, they are interested in the forces that produce differential *fitness* through the generations. This is a core concept of evolutionary science, and it is surrounded by a very rich body of facts and theory.

We close this section by noting that, while evolutionists with few exceptions have given natural selection the place of prime mechanism and causation, most if not all have also understood it, technically, as metaphor rather than as agent properly speaking. Hence, such an exceedingly common statement as "natural selection acts on" is just that, metaphor. More to the point, whether as error or ambiguity, it has not interfered with the astonishing progress of evolutionary science. The fact underscores the remarkable power of metaphors, as well as analogies among other heuristics, in the development of scientific inquiry (e.g., Pareto 1916; Lorenz 1974; Wilson 1984: 66, *passim*). The translation of metaphor into cause-mechanism may, however, have delayed, by way of hiding the full import of genetics, the eventual blossoming of the behavioral branch of evolutionary biology. If so, it may also have delayed the now irreversible rapprochement between evolutionary biology and the psychocultural disciplines (the so-called social sciences).

We may add that to an extent we too shall follow convention and, when need be, shall feel at liberty to treat natural selection as *the mechanism*, even cause, of evolution. Technically, however, the causes and mechanisms of evolution are aspects of genotype and environmental pressures, including behavior (see Sober 1984 for a thorough discussion of issues surrounding the natural selection concept). There is a crucial lesson in this fact, at least for sociologists and other recalcitrant social scientists. There are two fundamental orders of causes in evolution, and in behavior: one is genetic in nature; the other is environmental, and it includes the cultural. It follows that all talk of "biological determinism," which verges on the epidemic among sociologists, is sheer poppycock and reveals an intellectual lacuna that with the years has become a huge impediment to cross-disciplinary fertilization.

Sexual Selection

The struggle for existence may take various forms, and may be observable in various contexts. The members of a given population may, for example, have to struggle in the face of a dire scarcity of water, or may be in competition with members of another population for a given source of nourishment. In both cases, the ultimate result is a process of natural selection, that is, differential reproductive success. But, as has been suggested, Darwin was a little fuzzy about the meaning of natural selection. Strictly speaking, the above equation of natural selection with differential reproduction refers to a clarification that subsequent evolutionists have effected to better make sense of Darwin's theory. Darwin himself tended to focus on survival as *longevity* or, viewed from the reverse perspective, on *prereproductive* death. This view tended to underestimate the fact that what counts for evolution in the last analysis is the differential transmission of genetic matter through the generations. That concerns differential reproduction.

Darwin was aware of some limitations of his concept of natural selection. For example, it did not seem to adequately account "for the differences between the races of man" (Darwin 1871: 556). More broadly, given its focus on survivorship, natural selection did not help him to understand the evolution of certain peculiar "phenotypic" characteristics. Why, for instance, the splashy feathers of certain male birds? Why, across the various species, the pugnacity, the great horns, the displays, the mimicry, the special weapons, "the instrumental music," or, among endless other characters, the extraordinary beauty of the peacock's tail that, while attractive to the peahen, reduces motility and attracts the attention of the predator? In 1871 Darwin published a book on *The Descent of Man and Selection in Relation to Sex* in which he discussed in marvelous detail a great abundance of such "secondary sexual characters" across various classes of animals. The underlying message throughout the discussion is this: If certain traits enhance the bearer's ability to reproduce, they are likely to be favorably selected—to increase in frequency—in a given population even if they tend to act negatively on longevity. Darwin comprised this scenario under the label of *sexual selection.*

This concept has turned out to be a blessing for evolutionary science. As we shall see, it does not refer to a different type of selection. Rather, it concerns what is perhaps the foremost type of "struggle for [genetic] existence" once organisms reach the age of reproduction (Darwin 1871: 594). But the stress on *competition for reproductive mates* has struck the right chord and fueled a great deal of activity in the emerging sciences of evolution and behavior.

Darwin's (1859: 94) treatment of sexual selection initially appeared in *The Origin of Species*, where it was defined as follows:

> This form of selection depends, not on a struggle for existence in relation to other organic beings or to external conditions, but on a struggle between the individuals of one sex, generally the males, for the possession of the other sex. The result is not death to the unsuccessful competitor, but few or no offspring. Sexual selection is, therefore, less rigorous than natural selection. Generally, the most vigorous males, those which are best fitted for their places in nature, will have most progeny. But in many cases, victory depends not so much on general vigor, as on having special weapons, confined to the male sex.

We have reported this statement in order to again underscore the point that if evolutionists had been inclined to favor easy assaults over theoretical promise, however ill-couched, they could have argued *ad nauseam* about Darwin's meaning of sexual selection and its relation to natural selection. Why such a heavy focus on death in relation to natural selection when the crucial issue turns out to be the number of viable progeny? One can die *after* one has successfully produced offspring. Likewise, organisms sometimes die while competing for mates. By the same token, if the Darwinian bottom line is progeny, it is hardly proper to define sexual selection as less rigorous than natural selection. If anything (if the distinction between the two alleged types of selection were to hold), the reverse might be true, although in the state of nature death prior to reaching reproductive age is indeed extraordinarily frequent.

Nowadays, if sexual selection is viewed as selection at all, it is usually seen as a special case of natural selection, and while there has been some debate over the topic (see Mayr 1972 for a review), it has illuminated research instead of confusing it. Dobzhansky and his associates (1977: 118—emphasis added), for example, disposed of the issue simply as follows: "After all, Darwinian fitness is reproductive fitness.... Higher fitness may be achieved because of some advantage in the 'struggle for existence in relation to other organic beings or to external conditions'; it may also be achieved *because of greater proficiency in securing mates*." Sexual selection pertains to the struggle for genetic existence, not to selection, the process and end product of the struggle. Viewed as competition, sexual selection has become a very sharp tool among students of evolution and behavior, as we shall see in various contexts throughout this volume. It suggests that much animal behavior and appearance is adapted not so much to the problem of survival as to the task of securing adequate mates.

Darwin's later and much fuller discussion of sexual selection was eventually the proper catalyst for the more recent theoretical developments on the topic. His (1871:916) updated definition of sexual selection also provides various distinctions, as follows:

> Sexual selection depends on the success of certain individuals over others of the same sex, in relation to the propagation of the species; whilst natural selection depends on the success of both sexes, at all ages, in relation to the general conditions of life. The sexual struggle is of two kinds; in the one it is between individuals of the same sex, generally the males, in order to drive away or kill their rivals...whilst in the other, the struggle is likewise between the individuals of the same sex, in order to excite or charm those of the opposite sex, generally the females, which...select the more agreeable partners.

Evolutionists refer to the former type as *intrasexual selection* and distinguish between a male-male subtype and a female-female one, with emphasis, in accord with Darwin himself, on the former. The second type refers mostly to a form of male-male competition, too ("the power to charm the females"), but Darwin saw it as being occasioned by females' response to "charm," and therefore it has come to be known as *intersexual selection* or "female choice" (see, e.g., Cronin 1991: chaps. 8–10 for this topic).

In either case, the focus is on behavior (Trivers 1972: 137). It is our position in this volume that what is known as sociobiology ("evolutionary behavioral science," "biocultural science," "the study of evolution and behavior," etc.) is that stage and branch of evolutionary science that has made the study of behavior its central feature, thereby building a bridge, however frail it may still be, between evolutionary biology and the other disciplines of human behavior. It is thus evident why sexual selection has become such a crucial feature of evolutionary studies. It obliges to more fully retrieve the components of *behavior* in what for Darwin himself (1859: chap. 3) was *the basis* of natural selection: the struggle for existence. Sexual selection also directs attention to profound physio-anatomic differences between males and females and hence to a multiplicity of associated behavioral differences, as well as similarities, that may be expected to have evolved in the course of the evolution of a species, including *Homo sapiens*. Indeed, this focus has of late cast considerable light on why men and women are so unique, and uniquely rich, in so many aspects of their behavior and life in general. We shall return to this context especially in chapters 5 through 7. The next chapter will attempt a fuller view of theory for the study of evolution and behavior.

5

Elements of Evolutionary Behavioral Science

The discovery of natural selection is the foundation upon which marvelously rich theoretical systems have been built by scholars in the various branches of evolutionary science. As noted in the preceding chapter, a theory of evolution must account for mechanisms of variation, heredity, and selection. Moreover, as we have argued, the recent work on behavior and perhaps especially the current focus on sexual selection as competition strongly suggest that an encompassing theory of evolution must account for behavior mechanisms as well. Much has happened in evolutionary science in the last seventy years or so, specifically since the rise of the modern synthesis around 1930 (Huxley 1942), namely the marriage of Darwinian theory with genetic science. The present chapter will focus briefly on some of these developments especially insofar as they are strictly relevant to the current coming together of the biological and behavioral sciences. We begin with a brief comment on mechanisms of heredity because they have played a capital role in the development of evolutionary behavioral science.

The Modern Synthesis

The mechanisms of heredity were discovered by Gregor Mendel and described in 1866 in a paper on "experiments in plant hybridization." The paper contained the "fundamental theory of heredity, from which a whole new branch of science, genetics, would develop" (Dobzhansky et al. 1977: 482). On the basis of studies on the transmission of different traits (e.g., color of seeds) in the garden pea (*Pisum sativum*), Mendel stated two generalizations that were later termed the "principle of segregation" and the "principle of independent assortment." These are often referred to, respectively, as the First and Second Laws of Inheritance. They have numerous implications for evolutionary science. For our purposes they are particularly relevant to a level of selection referred to as *kin selection*. This is exceedingly important for evolutionary studies of behavior, and will be treated shortly in this chapter. Central to studies of kin selection is the "coefficient of relatedness" (r), which is a measure of genetic kindredness by descent. The context for this development is Mendel's theory of heredity.

The following are the basic elements of Mendel's theory, when generalized to species relying on diploid strategies of sex determination (i.e., species in which male and female each contribute to their offspring one-half of their complement of chromosomes). (1) For each feature in an organism (e.g., an aspect of eye color), there is a pair of genes, one from each parent; (2) each pair segregates at random during meiosis (the formation of sex cells, or gametes), and each gamete receives only one of the two genes; (3) each of the genes in the pair has a .50 probability of appearing in the gamete. It is this latter statement that underlies the proposition, common in many study contexts, that the parent-child $r = .50$.

Mendel's work was lost to scholars for some thirty-five years, but it was rediscovered about 1900. In the next three decades, genetic science made major strides, central to which was the focus on genetic mutation. Around 1930 Darwinian theory on the selective retention of variations and the Mendelian theory on "particulate" heredity and mutation were joined by a number of great minds into what is known as the synthetic theory, or the modern synthesis. The term synthesis indicates that evolutionary theory is in fact a family of interrelated theories and that the synthesis was both stimulated by, and was in turn a stimulant of, a number of disciplines, including population genetics, botany, zoology, physiology, anatomy, paleontology, physical anthropology, microbiology, biochemistry, entomology, biogeography, ecology and systematics, endocrinology, neurobiology, and developmental biology, among several others.

The modern synthesis is constituted by a number of theories of varying comprehensiveness. All rest on the general assumption that "all biological organization, down to the level of molecules, has evolved as a result of natural selection acting upon genetic variation" (Dobzhansky et al. 1977: 18—emphasis added). We reiterate the point here that, *stricto sensu*, natural selection is not an agent, and hence cannot act on genetic variation; the predicate "acts upon" must thus be understood as a convenient metaphor. What the synthesis assumption is intended to state is that organisms are subject to differential reproduction, that is, natural selection, while the genes themselves are subject to mutation (replacement, by error in replication, of old genes by new ones). Consequently, any given biological organization (e.g., a species, a family, an organ, and so forth down to a molecule) is ultimately the result of changes in genetic matter that have taken place in previous generations. The result, should it be due to mutation alone, would always be random; randomness, however, is checked and ordered by the demographic process of natural selection—by the selective retention of genetic changes.

It is not necessary, for our purposes, to attempt anything even approximating a sketch of the synthetic theory (but see Huxley 1942 and Dobzhansky et al. 1977 for two thorough and readable representations). E. Mayr's (1980: 1) widely known definition of it, reported below, is sufficiently instructive:

> The term "evolutionary synthesis" was introduced by Julian Huxley in *Evolution: The Modern Synthesis* (1942) to designate the general acceptance of two conclusions: gradual evolution can be explained in terms of small genetic changes ("mutations") and recombinations, and the ordering of this genetic variation by natural selection; and the observed evolutionary phenomena, particularly macroevolutionary processes and speciation, can be explained in a manner that is consistent with known genetic mechanisms.

Note that the causal role of evolutionary processes is attributed to genetic mechanisms, while an "ordering" function is reserved for natural selection. This view is much more faithful to the proper etiological structure of evolutionary science than what is sometimes encountered, as we have noted, in various conceptions of the respective roles of natural selection and genetic mechanisms. Mayr's conception is important for various reasons, not least of all because of its implicit suggestion that students of human behavior must learn to feel comfortable with the idea of *some degree* of genetic determination before they can enter the rapidly expanding range of the modern synthesis. The deed has been achieved in zoology almost fully and to an accelerating degree in psychology and anthropology as well. Sociology cannot afford to avoid participation:

> The resistance to new ideas, the role of terminologies, the failure of communication, the fusing together of disjunct pieces into new theories, the bridging of gaps between hierarchical levels, the role of generalizers, and many other phenomena are important not only for objective historiography but also for an understanding of the actual method of science. (Mayr 1980: 44)

One of the most productive feats of the modern synthesis, as it has continued to develop through the decades, has been to clarify the meaning of Darwin's natural selection. Recall Mayr's statement above that natural selection orders genetic variation. That amounts to saying that natural selection keeps a record, as it were, of differential reproductive success—differential fitness—in any given population of breeding organisms.

In Darwin's theory, "fitness" is an ambiguous concept, in large part because of the focus on the struggle for *survival* and thus on direct reproduction (sometimes referred to as Darwinian or classical fitness). This emphasis, as we shall presently see, made it difficult to reconcile certain facts with the theory. Preeminently, the reconciliation required recognition of the effect of kinship on selection. In social species kinship is very often a crucial factor in behavior, including reproductive behavior, and thus in selection and evolution. It is also the filter for some very interesting, and often surprising, observations of behavior. Numerous studies reveal, for example, that individuals of various species often engage in behavior that, instead of enhancing their survival, actually results in their death. A bird gives an alarm call to announce the presence of a predator and thereby singles itself out to the predator's attention. Among humans and many other species, parents sacrifice themselves, on specialized occasions, in defense of their children. Or consider the now famous case of the hymenoptera, an order of insects that includes bees, wasps, and ants, among other groupings of species. The majority of individuals do not reproduce—make no effort to reproduce. Instead, they invest their time and energy in the care of the nest. In short, they sacrifice their own reproductive potential to foster the reproductive success of their mother, the colony's queen. Such "altruism" technically escapes Darwin's theory, although he was not without clues as to how it might fit in it.

Kin Selection and Inclusive Fitness

An elegant solution to this problem was provided by William D. Hamilton (1964), and represents a landmark in the development of the modern synthesis. It also provided an important stimulus to the development of sociobiology, the "New Synthesis" (Wilson 1975), a new major stage in the modern synthesis that brings evolutionary biology closer to the social, perhaps better psychocultural, disciplines. Ants, for example, have a rather odd system of reproduction and sex determination known as haplodiploidy. The queen lays two kinds of eggs. One type, the majority, is diploid or fertilized; these, all female, develop into so-called workers. The other is haploid, or unfertilized, and yields the male drones. Drones, thus, have no father and carry only the genetic material inherited from the mother, that is, half of her genotype.

Let us now assume the common, though not always true, case where the queen of a hypothetical generation I is fertilized only by one male (the king or duke). What, to recall Mendel's work, will be the genetic relatedness (*r*) between any two pairs of her daughters (the workers)? Since one or more of them will be the next queen(s) (hypothetical generation II), the question goes to the heart of the matter on the issue of fitness. Mendel's work shows that each worker has inherited 50 percent of her mother's genes, and on the average she shares one half of that (25 percent) with each sister (for our purposes we need not worry about drones). Since workers are diploid, the other 50 percent has been inherited on the father's side. But recall that he derives from a haploid or unfertilized cell, and thus has only one half of the diploid complement of genes. It follows that all his daughters must have inherited *all of his genes*. In short, on the father's side, the sisters are genetically identical and share thereby 50 percent of their genes with one another. Add this 50 percent to the 25 percent that they have in common on the mother's side, and note Hamilton's discovery: If sisters were the result of a diploid, rather than a haplodiploid, system of reproduction (like us, for example), they would on average be related to one another by descent at the 50 percent level (25 percent on the mother's side plus 25 percent on the father's side). Being subject to a haplodiploid reproductive strategy (though they are themselves diploid), they hold in common 75, not 50, percent of their genes. Hamilton's crucial discovery is this: Sisters (the original queen's daughters) are more closely related to one another than they are to their mother. Moreover, on average they will share half of this *r*, or 37.5 percent of their genes, with their nieces, at least one of whom will be a queen. Note then: The *r* between the original queen and daughters is 50 percent. The *r* between queen and granddaughters is half of that: 25 percent. But the *r* between aunts and nieces (the queen's granddaughters) is 37.5 percent. The relevant coefficients of relatedness are shown in table 5.1, where they are compared to the corresponding coefficients for diploid organisms.

The upshot of Hamilton's work is that direct reproduction is not necessary in order to achieve fitness, and the problem posed by Darwin's theory disappears. In the case described here, functional sterility would appear to pay off handsomely in terms of indirect reproductive success. It would almost appear that it is genetically advantageous for workers

TABLE 5.1
Select Coefficients of Relatedness (r) in Species
Featuring Diploidy or Haplodiploidy

Kin Relation	Diploidy	Haplodiploidy
Mother-Daughter	.50	.50
Sister-Sister	.50	.75
Grandmother-Granddaughter	.25	.25
Aunt-Niece	.25	.375

to promote the reproductive success of their sisters instead of their own. But there is a paradox involved here that concerns, among other things, fitness comparisons between generations (i.e., mother and daughters). We need not go into it. It is, however, possible to say that, if there is some fitness loss associated with nonreproduction, the loss is probably compensated for, as we shall presently see, through "altruistic" behavior.

The haplodiploid system of reproduction and kin behavior suggests a broadened concept of fitness. The concept in question is *inclusive fitness*, which is to say that an organism's fitness comprises not only its direct reproductive success but also that portion that results from its contribution, in the form of assistance, to the reproductive success of its genetic relatives. Further, inclusive fitness implies a level (not a different kind—Hamilton 1964; Dawkins 1979) of natural selection that has been termed *kin selection*. The concept sensitizes to the fact that kin group behavior is a major means of natural selection.

Hamilton's work both broadened Darwin's concept of fitness and amended his emphasis on the organism as the unit of heredity. The gene is now explicitly recognized as the heritable unit on which natural selection is said to act. It is the selection of shared genes by descent that constitutes kin selection. Organisms come and go, and so do genes, though typically in far larger spans of time. But evolution concerns the coming and going of genes, the units of heredity, not of individuals. Thus, genes may be viewed as assemblers of bodies designed to behave in ways that are consistent, in varying degrees, with the intergenerational survival of their assemblers. In short, to use R. Dawkins' (1989) famous metaphor, organisms are "survival vehicles" of "selfish genes." At death, organisms persist, to the extent that they persist, only in the form of genes. It is, then, the differential survival of genes that constitutes the subject matter of Darwinian evolution.

Altruism: The Selfish Basis of Reciprocity

Nothing in evolutionary science has implicated genetics in the study of social behavior more effectively than Hamilton's work, the cornerstone of a large and increasing body of research and theorizing. Numberless species of animals, including ourselves, are very adept at helping their kin (e.g., Wilson 1971, 1975; Alexander 1971, 1987). Ants, for example, are not only diligent helpers of their mother and her young; if need be, they also sacrifice themselves on their behalf. Observations of this sort have introduced into evolutionary studies the perennial philosophical question: For whose benefit do individuals behave? This is the problem of *altruism*, a term coined by sociology's own Auguste Comte. The problem has never been solved by social thinkers. Most, having found human beings to be selfish, have proceeded to argue cavalierly that we should be altruistic. The solution of the problem has escaped social science and moral philosophy in large part because of the indefiniteness of the language employed. The discovery of inclusive fitness has gone a long way toward solving the problem. Altruism may now be defined by reference to the maximization principle as genetically "self-destructive behavior performed for the benefit of others" (Wilson 1975: 578). The definition is nomologically anchored and provides an unambiguous metric: the unit of heredity.

To return to Hamilton's (1964) work, having considered varying degrees of relatedness and varying degrees of mutual aid in his research, he was led to conclude that altruistic acts will be favored by natural selection when $k > 1/r$. That is, the probability of altruistic behavior increases (1) as the coefficient of relatedness (r) between benefactor and beneficiary increases, and (2) as the benefit accruing to the beneficiary exceeds the cost incurred by the benefactor (k). For example, the closer Mary is related to John and the lower John's cost of a good turn to Mary in comparison with the benefit reaped by Mary, the more likely is John to engage in the good turn. From this perspective it seems obvious enough that altruism and sociality itself are deeply intertwined with the genetics of kinship and self-interest. The implications of this discovery are numerous and transcend the topic of altruism or cooperation among clearly definable kin. The chapter on ethnicity will expand on this notion by arguing that the widespread phenomena of ethnic allegiance and ethnic conflict make inadequate sense apart from the logic of kin selection.

But here is an interesting issue: Why all the emphasis on kin or nepotistic altruism, especially in view of the estimate by geneticists that the degree of genetic similarity between any two members of our species is at least 90 percent before kinship is taken into account? Indeed, we all have read at one time or another that the human "genome" and the chimpanzee genome are related at something like the 98 percent level (e.g., Diamond 1992). So, why all this focus on kin altruism and 50 percent coefficients of relatedness? Aren't we all related at a higher level than that? In a sense the coefficients of relatedness are imposed upon us by Mendel's laws and the facts of meiosis, namely the halving of somatic cells when sex cells are produced. It is thus the recombination of sex cells into new organisms that leads evolutionists to speak of kinship by descent. In view of the fact that in many species one or both parents of a new organism reiterate the behavior of ancestors who devoted much of their life resources to the upbringing and well-being of their offspring—in view of that fact alone, we would be inclined to conclude, intuitively, that kinship by descent does matter: that it adds something to relatedness by virtue of conspecificity (belonging to the same species).

But there is also a far finer basis on which to answer the above questions (e.g., Dawkins 1986). It is important to note that nondescent estimates of genetic similarity take into account the genotype as a whole, namely all the gene-bearing loci on the various chromosomes. Kinship theory, conversely, holds that there are special loci that code for altruism, and it is these that are favored by kin selection. At these loci, kin by descent are more closely related than mere conspecifics. Hamilton's work showed that this is the case in each generation. If, for example, we divide a given individual's genotype into a part that is shared with the parents on the basis of conspecificity and another part that is shared with them by virtue of descent or consanguinity, the latter may be expected to endure through the generations and to be more determinative than the former of kin-related behavior in every generation.

Altruism, however, is not limited to relations between members of kinship groups. Social scientists are very keen to this fact (e.g., Mauss 1925; Malinowski 1935; Homans 1961, 1974; Blau 1964; Gouldner 1973; Allison 1992). They have not, however, produced a theory on the phenomenon that can claim two very crucial features: general acceptance and linkage to an established nomological context. One such theory has been provided by zoologist Robert Trivers (1971), as we noted in the earlier discussion of Durkheim's work on solidarity. Trivers has expanded kin selection theory to encompass reciprocally beneficent behaviors between individuals unrelated by descent, indeed even between members of different species. A good example of the latter is provided by the phenomenon of cleaning symbiosis among fish (Trivers 1971). In this case, members of certain species need the fish counterpart of a dentist to rid them of the ectoparasites living in their mouth and gills. Members of other species, including at least six species of shrimp, need a meal. In some instances, the latter have been observed to take up rather permanent cleaning stations, while the clients have, in turn, been observed to wait in queue in order to obtain service.

Wherever we observe frequent interaction, we often observe also this form of exchange for mutual benefit. Trivers (1971) has proposed that the evolution of what he terms *reciprocal altruism* may be thought of as a function of three major conditions: (1) a large number of situations in which given individuals can be of mutual help; (2) repeated interaction in a small group; and (3) fairly symmetrical (nondominant) exposure to situations inviting mutual aid. These conditions may be elaborated into six sociological parameters: (a) longevity; (b) low migration rate; (c) mutual dependence, for example against predators; (d) prolonged parental care; (e) a weak dominance order; and (f) exposure to combat situations.

Trivers' theory proceeds to consider that, wherever there are systems of reciprocity, some participants may be expected to obey the rules better than others. In short, there are "cheaters" in our midst—some "gross," and these are subject to relatively easy deletion by natural selection; others "subtle," and these are harder to detect and hence to delete through aggression or avoidance. Nevertheless, precisely because reciprocal altruism is vulnerable to cheating, its evolution was probably quickly followed by the evolution of a defense system consisting of various psychological adaptations: moralistic aggression, a sense of justice, gratitude, sympathy, friendship, guilt, and so forth. More recently it has been cogently argued that "the human mind must include inferential procedures that make one very good at detecting cheating on social contracts" (Cosmides 1989). Cosmides and Tooby (1989) have also shown that at least in clanlike societies (our ancestors) natural selection favored the frequency of genes that maintained the vitality of reciprocal altruism (see also Machalek and Cohen 1991).

One thing must be stressed about altruism theory in general. At least as used by zoologists, it is a theory in which altruism is a misnomer; it really concerns selfishness or self-interest. Thus, in practicing nepotistic altruism, one acts in favor of one's own evolutionary fitness. Likewise, consciously or more likely unconsciously, when we engage in systems of reciprocal altruism within the broader social context we typically expect to receive in return at least as much as we gave, and preferably more. It makes sense, therefore, to read in B. Malinowski (1926: 173), for example, that among the Trobriand Islanders even "within the nearest kinship group, rivalries, dissensions, the keenest egotism flourish and dominate indeed the whole trend of kinship relations." Altruism is typically selfishness by another name. The literature on this topic is now so large that it constitutes a "field" in its own right (see Allison 1992 and de Vos and Zeggelink 1997 for brief useful reviews as well as attempts at complementary developments).

David Barash (1979: 167-68) has tackled a particularly challenging case to show the human tendency toward self-serving altruism, namely the apparent exception of Japanese kamikazes during World War II. These were pilots who flew their airplanes into American warships and thus committed suicide in favor of the general Japanese population. Barash points to a number of self-serving factors underlying the self-immolation. Kamikazes were promised eternal life and were thus enabled to weaken their sense of self-destruction. They also reaped more mundane rewards. For instance, as volunteers they received national acclaim and privileges that may have included fitness-enhancing activities prior to self-sacrifice. Moreover, they were often of low status both socioeconomically and as pilots, and their families' status was enhanced as a result of their willingness to self-destruct. In the latter case, we must be reminded of kin selection and inclusive fitness.

The New Synthesis: A Leap into the Study of Behavior

Evolutionary studies of behavior, especially if placed in the human arena, tend to leave social scientists incredulous if not altogether ill-humored. We have Culture to blame. The discovery of culture as a technical term in the nineteenth century was both glory and affliction. It was essential to the emergence of a science of human behavior, for culture is unmistakably one side of the coin that features biology on the reverse. It was not long, however, before neophobia and myopia led students of culture to vandalize the other side of the coin without realizing that in the process they would damage their own side as well. Despite the participation, in varying degrees, by nineteenth-century sociologists and anthropologists in the rise of evolutionary theory, culture soon came to attain almost hypnotic powers. Thus it was that just as naturalists and geneticists were adding a dimension of enormous breadth and ramifications to the Copernican revolution, sociologists proceeded to get mired in one of the most debilitating redundancies of intellectual history: what amounts to saying that culture is the cause of culture (for evolutionary critiques of cultural determinism, see, e.g., Flinn and Alexander 1982; Lopreato 1989b; Crippen 1992; Tooby and Cosmides 1992).

That, too, was an evolutionary fact of sorts; the times were good for intellectual parochialism and an effervescence of the eminently human adaptation termed self-deception (e.g., Trivers 1985: chap. 16). The millenary social and political orders were collapsing, and the old vile subservience of man and woman to masters and institutions was breaking down in step with them. The making of a great nation with humble masses who were bred on the axiom of the sanctity of the individual encouraged a frame of mind in which all was an effect of free will. For homo americanus, and gradually for those who came to move in their sociological orbit, one of the most preposterous ideas had to be, and to a considerable degree remains, that human fate is the result of anything but the willful cultural manipulation of the human condition.

In the meantime, the revolution in the biological sciences was rapidly fracturing the assumption of uninhibited cultural determinism. Not that biological evolutionists saw no role for culture in the study of human behavior. After all, as already stressed, their position has always been that *evolution is the resultant of the interaction of genotypes* (the genetic endowments of organisms) *and environmental pressures*, which most assuredly include culture in the case of human beings (e.g., Simpson 1949; Wilson 1975; Alexander 1979; Symons 1979; Barash 1982: 29-31). But this stance has never really been widely understood outside of biological science. Besides, it carries a message that is perhaps too much of a challenge: We may not know the effects of culture apart from the effects of its inseparable companion, the genotype (e.g., Kimura 1992).

When, therefore, Edward O. Wilson (1975) published his monumental treatise, an extraordinarily creative synthesis of those developments in the modern synthesis that auspiciously pointed in the direction of the social and humane disciplines, its reception was reminiscent of what had welcomed Darwin's own path-breaking work nearly 120 years earlier (e.g., Caplan 1978; Gregory et al. 1978; Ruse 1979). "Sociobiology" is what Wilson, using a term apparently coined around 1946, termed the "new synthesis." The label was intended not only to underscore the contributions of disciplines that had either emerged within the modern synthesis or had been energized by it but also to motivate the social sciences to partake of the modern synthesis and to enrich it in turn (Wilson 1975: chaps. 1, 27).

We shall later examine briefly some of the controversy—some still alive, most now faded away—surrounding human sociobiology or off-shoots of it. Our preference, however, is to focus on achievements and promise. There is much to cheer about in this blooming perspective on human behavior. From a methodological viewpoint, particularly remarkable perhaps is the view from a distance that sociobiology enjoins upon social scientists. Carrying Darwin's own challenge far into the citadels of the psychocultural disciplines, the various disciplines that constitute the new synthesis are casting new light on many aspects of human behavior and at the same time suggesting refinement and law-like organization of a large array of findings about human behavior. We shall encounter some of them in part 3. Here we turn to several crucial tools of evolutionary theory, including again sexual selection, that in the past twenty to thirty years have achieved great prominence in behavioral science.

Anisogamy, Parental Investment, and Sexual Selection

Few if any mothers are unaware that boys and girls "are just different." The genders are driven by different endocrine systems. By comparison to girls, boys tend to develop aggressive, combative, exploitative, in short particularly selfish tendencies as they approach sexual maturity. Truth to tell, in the logic of evolutionary science, there is no reason why females who are subject to such behavior should not experience some discomfort and reasonable resentment. Male aggression is costly to females, and yet there is a sense in which it can be said, as we shall presently see, that "boys are to girls as dirt is to gold" (Lopreato 1984: 324).

It is little wonder, then, that from time to time in the history of human society we observe protest movements that currently bear the label of "feminism," the most recent variants of which have become a vociferous part of sociological practice (e.g., Sanday 1981; Smith 1987; Epstein 1988; Hubbard 1990). Something good may come of them, but for the time being certain strains have added greatly to the sociological crisis by exhorting political correctness at the expense of scholarly research and concomitantly spreading false rumors about the motives of those who prefer scientific to political correctness.

Of course, there are various brands of feminism, but one may reasonably speak of core assumptions that most have shared. These have been discussed by Tooby and Cosmides (1992), among others, as part of their analysis of the standard sociocultural model. The basic message, for reasons that do honor neither to scholarship nor to femaleness, is that such remarkable differences as exist between men and women are simply the result of differential socialization, specifically the effect of traditional patriarchal training for different roles. The heavy emphasis on socialization is not only, in itself, wrong and counterproductive. It is also embarassingly deficient in common sense. Consider that, strictly speaking, it assumes not only that, if children were socialized in sex-neutral ways, they would grow up to behave, as adults, in sex-neutral ways. It also implies the inconceivable, namely that if boys were trained to behave like girls, and girls like boys, as adults the two sexes would in effect switch "gender roles." We shall return to these matters in more detail, especially in chapters 6 and 7.

There is, among countless similarities, a fundamental difference between males and females that is the basis of numberless implications for the proper understanding of human behavior along sex lines. *Anisogamy*, the name given to it, technically refers to the difference in size and structure between male and female gametes. Male gametes (sperm) are minute, and their value lies only in the genes that they convey. Being miniscule, they are also numerous and, among sexually mature individuals, produced in huge quantities almost continuously after the onset of puberty. In principle, a male could father thousands of offspring. By contrast, female gametes (eggs) are much larger and far fewer. Once fertilized, they are for a period of time also responsible for the nutrition of the developing embryo. Moreover, they (oocytes) are produced once in a lifetime, early *in utero*, and are thus subject to daily and protracted wear and tear, so that by the time of the menarche the typical woman may look forward to releasing no more than 400 mature eggs (ovulations), only a very small number of which can be promoted into offspring. Women bear the cost of pregnancy, the cost of nursing, and at least during the children's tender years, most of the cost of protection and guardianship as well. Accordingly, in the typical case, each fertilized egg represents a huge chunk of the precious twenty-five to thirty years of reproductive vitality.

By comparison, while few men will plead guilty to the fact, they contribute very little. They don't get pregnant. They suffer no nausea. They don't risk their life at the birth of a child, and thereafter for months.

They are free to "toil" and be "breadwinners," a fact whose value has always been greatly exaggerated. Even so, if they are the breadwinners, their wives, if "unemployed," have their hands full with the young, and must also keep house and prepare the meals. That is considered by many to be a two-job profession. If they also earn their bread outside the home, as many do nowadays, and as they did in agricultural society and earlier, they may end up with two jobs and then some (e.g., Hochschild with Machung 1989). When we further consider such facts as abandonment, divorce, and the high percentage of fathers who nowadays refuse or fail to provide even legally prescribed child support, the level of relative paternal investment is on average truly puny to behold.

It is not our intention to condemn men, nor to glorify women. To a large extent, the above facts, and numberless others associated with them, are facts of the differential parental investment (Trivers 1972) inherent in the physio-anatomic condition of anisogamy. The two sexes are by nature endowed with different reproductive strategies, and from this difference arise various behavioral tendencies. On an earlier occasion, the point was expanded into what was termed the *law of anisogamy*: "The two sexes are endowed with differing reproductive strategies, and their behaviors reflect that difference in direct proportion to their relevance to it" (Lopreato 1992: 1998). There is thus another sociological irony here, for it is students of sex roles, most of whom are adamantly opposed to evolutionary theory, who would stand to profit most from the use of evolutionary science.

The basic implications of anisogamy have been drawn by Robert Trivers (1972) in a seminal paper focused on "relative parental investment." They constitute a rich number of inferences that are at the core of a large and growing area of research and theorizing, some of which will be treated at some length in chapters 6 and 7. We are interested here in drawing only some of the very basics that constitute average male and female behavioral profiles in our species.

Females are the descendants of other females who, within the limitations imposed by their life conditions (e.g., sex ratio and personal attractiveness), tended to be discriminating, choosy, or "coy" in their sexuality and preference for a mate (Trivers 1972: 165-72). Those who behaved otherwise were less likely to mate with males who were relatively good co-providers and protectors of the young. This is not to say that there have not been, or there are not now, relatively carefree women. But being the sex that invests more in reproduction, they are also the sex that, in the ultimate sense, profits less if at all from indiscriminate mating. Mating for women has always been far riskier than for men. A mistake—for example, mating with a "loser," one who will contribute nothing to the well-being of the offspring—may well consume years of a woman's life when gestation and the nurturing of the offspring are factored in. As noted above, given the relatively limited female reproductive cycle (typically twenty-five to thirty years), each offspring constitutes a major portion of its mother's reproductive potential. There is, thus, no escaping the conclusion that on average women, more than men, have been selected to prefer mates who are in fact, or show promise of becoming, relatively rich in the resources needed to help raise healthy and reproductively viable offspring. Chapter 6 in particular will provide empirical evidence in support of this proposition (e.g., Buss 1989, 1994a, 1994b).

The implications of differential parental investment (DPI) for males are in numerous respects quite different. Men are endowed with an almost limitless capacity for reproduction, and yet must compete for scarce and discriminating resources. Women are men's ultimate limiting resource. The consequences are numberless—many of them having to do with male jealousy, aggressive behavior, violence, and various sorts of "power games." We shall encounter specific examples in subsequent chapters. Here we may emphasize the general point in Trivers' (1972: 140) own words:

> Individuals of the sex investing less will compete among themselves to breed with members of the sex investing more, since an individual of the former can increase its reproductive success by investing successfully in the offspring of several members of the limiting sex.

But there is a sort of catch-22 in this type of "game." The greater the competition in a population, the greater the probability of failure. In many species a large percentage of males never reproduce. A few, the dominant males, do most of the siring. That is, sexual selection is greater among males (Bateman 1948) who, as Darwin noted, are driven into mutual competition "to charm" the females. Hence the widespread observation that, in most species, male reproductive success varies more than female reproductive success (e.g., Trivers 1972: 138). Hence, too, as we shall see, the widespread phenomena of polygyny and hypergyny in human history. One result of this combination of facts is not just domination of women by men but also domination of men by men with the aid of women.

The reader will have noted in the passage just quoted that DPI and sexual selection are closely linked. Therefore, we now return to the problem of sexual selection (as competition for mates) and again quote Robert Trivers (1972: 141—emphasis in the original): "*What governs the operation of sexual selection is the relative parental investment of the sexes in their offspring.*" That is, DPI is viewed as the cause of sexual selection. This is where theory stands, and there is hardly anything of great consequence amiss with it. We are, however, inclined toward a slight modification. It may be useful to draw a deeper distinction between *initial* parental investment and *subsequent* parental investment than that made by R. Trivers (1972: 145-46). The former is inherent in the ancient fact of *anisogamy*, and it is this initial differential that, with some possible exceptions—for example, species that like most fish practice external fertilization—is also the cause of subsequent differential investment. It is the relatively enormous value of the egg that governs what is sometimes referred to as the "maternal instinct," with all the expenditure of a mother's care that this implies. Likewise, the relative abundance of cheaply produced sperm controls a subsequent paternal investment that, in the typical case, is far inferior to the maternal investment.

If this reasoning is correct—and we reiterate the point that Trivers' conceptualization has been extraordinarily productive—it follows that, in the strictest sense, what in the last analysis governs sexual selection is not the relative parental investment of the sexes in their offspring but the physio-anatomic, and thus prior, fact of anisogamy. Consequently, we understand both DPI and sexual selection as interwoven by-products of this basic sex difference: anisogamy (Lopreato 1992).

The conception of DPI and sexual selection in cause-and-effect terms disallows the systemic relationship that typifies evolutionary etiology, indeed scientific causation in general. In fact, the two mechanisms inherent in anisogamy may at times exchange causal role. While DPI often governs sexual selection, the reverse can also be true. For example, the philanderer who is successful in sexual selection and sires many offspring does so in part because he invests little in previous offspring. Parental investment here governs sexual selection. But it is also true that the more offspring he sires—the more successful he is in sexual selection—the less further parental investment he is capable of making. Sexual selection now reacts on parental investment. There is a relation of mutual dependence between DPI and sexual selection.

The Fitness Principle

Well-established scientific paradigms are constituted by a variety of interlocking theories. These, in turn, are sets of related propositions that are held together by at least one principle or law. Sometimes, the theories are empirically cognate and logically homologous enough to be tied together by a comprehensive general principle. That, for example, was the case with so-called Newtonian theories in view of the law of universal gravitation. In biology, the analogue of the gravitation law is considered to be natural selection, which, as we have seen, some scholars sometimes refer to as a principle as well as *the* cause and mechanism of evolution. There are various ways in which to think of natural selection as a general principle. One, previously encountered, refers to the general assumption of the modern synthesis, which Dobzhansky and his associates (1977: 18) stated as follows: "All biological organization, down to the level of molecules, has evolved as a result of natural selection acting upon genetic variation."

So put, the principle says nothing explicitly about behavior. And yet something about behavior is implied by virtue of the fact that, as was noted by Darwin himself, natural selection is a consequence of the struggle for existence. The moment the struggle is introduced in the reasoning, natural selection unavoidably implies a statement of capital importance about behavior at the organismic level of organization. The implication is that at any given time, in any given population, individuals are descendants of organisms that were reproductively successful in the struggle—of organisms that behaved more adaptively than others.

If to this reasoning we add Hamilton's (1964) work on kin selection, we can fairly readily grasp the logic whereby evolutionists view organisms as being so programmed as, *on average*, to behave adaptively for themselves and, in varying degrees, for their recognizable genetic kin as well. But, of course, there are genetic variations among individuals. Moreover, the environment of today may pose challenges that are different from those confronted by the ancestors. Traits that once encouraged adaptive behaviors—such as the enjoyment of sweet, salty, or fatty foods—may induce today behaviors that are maladaptive. As stated by S.B. Eaton and his associates (1988: 5), the "discordance between our current life-style and the one in which we evolved has promoted the chronic and deadly 'diseases of civilization': the heart attacks, strokes, cancer, diabetes, emphysema, hypertension, cirrhosis, and like illnesses that cause 75 percent of all mortality in the United States and other industrialized nations." Further, the logic of natural selection demands that we expect some organisms to behave more adaptively than others. If there were no such differentiation there would be no natural selection. It is essentially this train of thought that in recent decades has led the way toward a general principle of evolutionary *behavioral* science. Under this principle, "the central principle of sociobiology" (Barash 1982: 41), can be subsumed other statements of behavioral theory, such as those that pertain to altruism, parental investment, and sexual selection. Various names are given to this principle. A common one (Schulman 1978) is the maximization or fitness principle, and this can be conveniently stated as follows: *Organisms tend to behave so as to maximize their inclusive fitness.*

The proposition is stated in stochastic terms because, as implied above, it addresses the varying frequency and intensity of fitness-enhancing behavior among individuals constituting a breeding population. There may be some ambiguity in the proposition as far as some students of behavior are concerned, but it may be fairly interpreted as follows. Given the Malthusian problem—real or virtual scarcity of needed resources—individuals have evolved to behave, consciously or otherwise, in ways whose *irreducible result* is to enhance, *in varying degrees*, the probability of conveying, directly or through kin selection, the maximum possible proportion of their genotype to at least the immediate future generations. In short, the maximization principle may be rephrased to state, with less temptation for unnecessary debate, that *natural selection has favored behaviors that promote inclusive fitness.*

As the science of evolution and behavior develops, this principle will no doubt undergo some improvements. Statements of theory are typically valid in view of certain specified conditions. For instance, falling bodies accelerate at uniform speed *provided* that they fall in a vacuum. Thus, improvement will likely take the form of reducing the probabilistic nature of the principle by appending to it modifying conditions. An attempt of sorts in this direction has been made as follows, and can no doubt be much improved upon:

> Organisms are predisposed to behave so as to maximize their inclusive fitness, but this predisposition [may be negatively] conditioned by the quest for creature comforts, by self-deception, and by the [at least partial] autonomization of phenotype (e.g., behavior) from genotype. (Lopreato 1989a: 129)

In keeping with the strategy of theoretical idealizations (e.g., Nagel 1961; Lopreato and Alston 1970), this proposition incorporates some of the possible conditions that to an in-principle specifiable extent inhibit the maximization tendency. A complementary, and possibly more effective though more difficult, technique might be to specify the conditions that enhance, rather than inhibit, the tendency.

A number of considerations should be kept in mind about the maximization principle. First, it does not state that all behavior is adaptive (or contributes positively to genetic fitness). Second, it does not imply that what is adaptive today is necessarily adaptive tomorrow. Today, for example, craftiness in bargaining may fetch some valuable resources; tomorrow a few years in jail, a setting that hardly encourages reproductive activity. Third, what is adaptive for X may very well be maladaptive for Y. A fight for dominance, for example, may fetch honor and rich rewards to the winner and nothing but humiliation and poor health to the loser. Finally (but further clarifications would be possible) "adaptiveness" is always a *variable* (any given behavior is more or less adaptive) and always *relative* (e.g., a modest cache of food may be far more important to an individual of modest means than to one endowed with enormous resources).

What, we may now ask, are the theoretical bases of the maximization principle? One, as already noted, refers to the Malthusian-Darwinian problem, namely the scarcity of resources (viewed both objectively and subjectively) in any given population and the associated competition for them that results in varying degrees of reproductive success. From the competition and its result we infer a fitness maximization tendency as an ultimate strategy. A second basis is suggested by the fundamental biochemical property of the cell: self-replication. Accordingly, we may infer that organisms are so constituted as to act *as if* their ultimate mission in life were to perpetuate their cells, or more precisely the units of heredity therein, the genes. The inference is encapsulated in the ingenious assertion that organisms are the genes' "survival machines" (Dawkins 1989). A third basis refers to the numberless observations across the multiplicity of animal taxa indicating that organisms direct much of their behavior toward enhancing the probability of their direct or indirect reproductive success. Recall Hamilton's discovery of extraordinary fitness-enhancing behavior among the hymenoptera, where it appeared to be almost entirely absent. As for humans, we can summarize a great many classes of fitness-enhancing behavior by underscoring the fact that upon departing from the earthly scene, rarely do we leave our wealth to others than our own blood kin (e.g., Clignet 1992). And this points to a fourth, and theoretically more compelling, basis of the principle. The path-breaking work on altruism, parental investment, sexual selection, and various other aspects of evolutionary behavioral science (e.g., Shepher 1983; Thornhill and Thornhill 1983; Buss 1989, 1994a, 1994b) constitutes plentiful and powerful proof of the fitness principle. They all point to behavior that fits its logic. Indeed, they may all be considered corollaries of theory wherein the maximization principle is the central law.

A clarification is now in order concerning the empirical focus of the maximization principle. Why the insistence on *fitness*? Is fitness the overwhelming aim of human beings? Probably not. But it is not aims, whatever is meant by this term, that we are concerned with. What we are dealing with is a metric that, across the eons of time and the variety of organisms, assesses the final result of lifecycle activities. In short, the answer to our question is that degrees of fitness constitute the bottom line, *the irreducible result*, of the various types of activity observable at all times in all species. This focus does not fit neatly the mold in which we human beings experience our life. We are not overtly obsessed with fitness self-enhancement. It is necessary, therefore, to stress the point that the principle does not assume conscious awareness of the fitness consequences of behavior. Nor does it deny the importance of the great variety of human activities as possible ends in themselves as far as the consciousness of the actor is concerned. Like the physicist who causally loads the behaviors of bodies in motion with the bottom line known as gravitational force, the evolutionist underscores the results of behaviors in terms of the ultimate measure of survival, namely reproductive success or fitness. This is a time-honored technique of scientific inquiry. General principles are broad perspectives that causally organize and tie together large bodies of facts and their respective, unique, or domain-specific explanations on the basis of an irreducible metric. They are the grand marshals of systematic, cumulative knowledge. This point, as we have seen, is not always understood in sociology.

Human Nature

The fitness principle represents a major contribution of the sociobiologists to the modern synthesis. It is also playing a fundamental role in the evolutionary study of behavior. To say that organisms are so constituted that in varying degrees of success they behave so as to maximize their inclusive fitness is to instigate the following highly fruitful question: Do they behave in such a fashion *by chance alone or because they are under the pressure of directive tendencies*? If evolution were the result of genetic mutation alone, the answer would have to appeal to chance alone; mutations are random occurrences. But here is another perspective on the genius of Charles Darwin: Such random events and the behavioral potentials associated with them are ordered and constructed by natural selection into adaptive mechanisms, that is, "systems of properties...to solve the specific problems posed by the regularities of the physical, chemical, developmental, ecological, demographic, social, and informational environments...during the course of a species' or population's evolution" (Tooby and Cosmides 1992: 62). Given the basic message of natural selection—that is, that some organisms behave more adaptively than others—this definition of adaptation or adaptive mechanism may be represented also as follows: "any structure, physiological process, or behavioral pattern that makes an organism more fit to survive and to reproduce in comparison with other members of the same species" (Wilson 1975: 577). It follows that the answer to our query above necessarily favors the directive tendencies, what have been termed behavioral predispositions or psychological adaptations. In short, the fitness principle is the core principle of the expanding theory of human nature. It is its logic and the logic of the primary theory surrounding it—for example, kin selection, sexual selection, altruism, parental investment—that guide research toward the discovery of adaptations applicable to various sorts of behavioral contexts: reciprocity and exchange systems, forms of competition for dominance in hierarchy systems, the choice of reproductive mates, sexual jealousy, courtship and marriage patterns, the "battle" of the sexes and of the generations, ethnic encounters, and a great multitude of others.

One point deserves the utmost emphasis: The fitness principle should in no way be construed to represent an all-encompassing, general purpose, self-sufficient statement of theory. Like all other general principles, it performs certain crucial functions. Two are worth stressing here: (1) *to direct discovery of lower-order, domain-specific explanatory tools typically referred to as adaptations—that is, to guide the discovery of the sub-mechanisms that function as its specialized tools*; (2) *to organize and classify these into a logical and hierarchical whole, that is, into a logically structured theory of human nature.* That is the way of nomologically driven science. As we shall see in the next section, one sometimes encounters objections to the principle presumably on the basis that there are a large number of domain-specific adaptations (e.g., Symons 1992; Tooby and Cosmides 1992: especially 54–55). We have no objection to this, perhaps unnecessary, complaint. But the point is not how many. *It is, rather, what logical structure they, few or many, will take in view of some general statement of theory.*

The adaptations that are, and will continue to be, comprised under the general principle may conveniently be divided into two major types. One is of a *species-wide nature*; that is, it refers to innate tendencies that *in varying degrees* (Wilson 1975: 19-21) are common to the human species as a whole. For example, the tendencies to engage in co-operative behavior and to avoid incestuous relations are probably general to all "normal" human beings, though they may oscillate in their force depending on time, place, and to some extent perhaps gender as well (e.g., Shepher 1983).

The second major type of adaptations results from the fact of anisogamy and the neuroendocrinology that is necessarily associated with it. In short, this second class of adaptations accounts for the fact that there are remarkable behavioral differences as well as similarities along sex lines (e.g., Trivers 1972; Wilson 1975; Symons 1979; Kimura 1992; Buss 1994b). Successful work in this area of sex-specialized adaptations has been proceeding at considerable speed, to a large extent because of the heuristic payload of such tools as differential parental investment and sexual selection (behind which, we inevitably find, explicitly or implicitly, the appeal of last resort: the fitness principle). The remainder of this volume is intended as a modest contribution to the developing theory of human nature as it applies to a variety of social contexts.

A Note on an Instructive but Receding Debate

There has been debate over the applicability of evolutionary theory to human behavior, but in recent years it has become less acrimonious. The new synthesis is fairly firmly established. A number of factors have favored this development. One has been the discovery of genes and their products that have remarkable implications for human behavior. Most pertain most directly to medicine and pharmacology, but they have important implications for social behavior as well. A second factor has been the recognition by specialists in the philosophy of biological science that the new synthesis—the study of evolution and behavior—represents an extension of the modern synthesis, and as such its fate is logically and securely tied to it (e.g., Ruse 1979; Thompson 1989; Holcomb 1993). Third, on the whole there has been rising awareness that the debate over human sociobiology is reminiscent of the debate in the sixteenth through the seventeenth centuries over the Copernican revolution and of the debate, a little later, over Darwinian theory (Ruse 1979: 4). There may be an inevitability in this recurrence of theses and antitheses, perhaps due to the apparent fact that scientific debates are frequently based far more on underlying metaphysical issues than on fact and logical structure (e.g., Kuhn 1957).

At any rate, if there are imperfections in the evolutionary approach to the study of behavior, they are part of the natural history of science in general. For instance, there are no credible debunkers today of the modern synthesis. Yet, E. Mayr (1980: 3) could write just a few years ago: "The very few books on evolution written by authors who were firm adherents to neo-Darwinism (such as Haldane 1932) had various shortcomings" (see also Holcomb 1993: especially 184-86). Science is ever an imperfect approximation to phenomena. But it is still the best one because one approximation invites a closer one.

The debate over human sociobiology can be divided into two major categories, and both give strong signs of dying out. One comprises those who actually practice sociobiology, though sometimes by another name, for example, the evolutionary psychologists and those whom these have termed Darwinian anthropologists or human sociobiologists, among other labels. The encounter has produced some strange but on the whole beneficial quarrels. The other category pertains to those who have seen little or nothing that is of value in human sociobiology: the naysayers. We turn briefly to the latter first. In past years, they made great noise, but it is fair to say that only the echoes now remain.

The Naysayers

In general, human sociobiology has been accused of *biological determinism* and the related problems of *reductionism, overadaptationism,* and *nonfalsifiability.* The charge of biological determinism can be illustrated by reference to S.J. Gould's (1978) discussion of the case of elderly Eskimos who sometimes sacrifice themselves instead of burdening the kin group on long and dangerous voyages. Gould considers first the sociobiological explanation of the fact, which calls into action kin selection and inclusive fitness. "Grandparents with altruist genes," he notes, "increase their own fitness by their sacrifice, for they insure the survival of close relatives sharing their genes." Such an explanation, he adds, is "scarcely conclusive since an eminently simple, nongenetic explanation also exists." The crucial portion of his "nongenetic" explanation follows: "Families with no tradition for sacrifice do not survive for many generations." The reader will be surprised to note that a scholar of Gould's credentials would bury the logic of natural selection under the vague notion of "tradition" even as he implicitly asserts it: families lacking such a tradition *do not survive* (for a fuller discussion of Gould's contorted position see Lopreato 1984: 24-27; Degler 1991: 283; Dennett 1995: chap. 10).

The problem of determinism is closely related to the problem of reductionism. *Methodological reductionism*—that is, the subsuming of less comprehensive explanations under more general ones *for the sole purpose of economy and/or logical organization of the less comprehensive explanations*—has played a critical role in the history of scientific development (e.g., Popper 1961; Mach 1974; Wilson 1978b). Science may be viewed "as a minimal problem consisting of the completest presentment of facts with the least possible expenditure of thought" (Mach 1974). As D. Thiessen (1996: especially chap. 7) has argued, the reductionist path gives no comfort to the traveler but, like it or not, that is the way to comprehensive explanation. We must, however, emphasize our oft-repeated point: General laws (economy of explanation) do not deny detail of explanation; they partly sacrifice it *in themselves* for purposes of systematic, logical, economic organization of related explanatory contexts *while leaving the discrete elements of these contexts the amplitude to account for detail.*

On the question of falsifiability, the two most ardent critics of human sociobiology have joined forces as follows: "We would not object so strenuously to the adaptationist program if its invocation, in any particular case, could lead in principle to its rejection for want of evidence" (Gould and Lewontin 1979: 587). These authors assert in effect that sociobiologists will have it by hook or by crook, for "the rejection of one adaptive story usually leads to its replacement by another... without proper confirmation" (Gould and Lewontin 1979: 587-88).

Aside from the fact that many sociobiological explanations have firmly stood their ground, this sort of attack is hardly compelling. It is analogous to accusing, say, astronomers for trying one hypothesis after another in their attempts to explain the recent shower of massive matter on the planet Jupiter, all of which were rooted in Newtonian laws. The hypotheses tested by evolutionary students of behavior must in the last analysis be consonant with the logic of natural selection and fitness theory. And they are. Moreover, as Holcomb (1993: 90-93) points out, the Gould-Lewontin charge of nonfalsifiability, though seemingly intended to appeal to the Popperian standard, in fact makes poor use of it. Contrary to those esteemed authors and other critics on this issue (e.g., Kitcher 1985), for Popper, and for scientists in general, confirmation, or rejection, is neither sufficient nor necessary for scientific reasoning—at least not at any given time. Much of Newtonian theory took centuries to "confirm." Much of Einsteinian theory is still to be "confirmed," or falsified. The presence of Pluto in the solar system was never falsified, and was not confirmed until thirty years after it was hypothesized (for a critique of Gould and Lewontin as well as Kitcher, see, for example, Wilson 1986; Alexander 1988; Holcomb 1993: 90-98; Dennett 1995).

As to the remaining criticism of the alleged adaptationist program (e.g., Lewontin 1979), it is hard not to be a bit mystified by it. The problem seems to have been started by Darwin himself (1859: 90—emphasis modified), as follows:

> It may metaphorically be said that natural selection is daily and hourly scrutinizing, throughout the world, the slightest variations; *rejecting those that are bad, preserving and adding up all that are good*; silently and insensibly working, *whenever and wherever opportunity offers, at the improvement of each organic being* in relation to its organic and inorganic conditions of life.

Lewontin's (1979: 6—emphasis in original) charge follows:

> I call that approach to evolutionary studies which assumes without further proof that all aspects of the morphology, physiology, and behavior of organisms are adaptive optimal solutions to problems *the adaptationist program*.... Sociobiology is one manifestation of the adaptationist program, concentrating on the behavioral aspect of the phenotype.

If the attribution were valid, the criticism would be justified. But it is only a strawman, a shallow accusation that evolutionists do not understand the logic of natural selection.

How could anyone who has not taken leave of his or her senses hold, for example, that women who subject their children to stepfathers' abuse behave adaptively? How could sociobiologists make the alleged error when adaptation has been defined as "any structure, physiological process, or behavioral pattern that makes an organism more fit to survive and to reproduce *in comparison with other members of the same species*" (Wilson 1975: 577)? We note, again, that the assumption of differential adaptiveness (of morphology, physiology, and behavior) is demanded by the very logic of natural selection. Natural selection could hardly preserve certain traits and discard others if they were not unequally adaptive. David P. Barash (1982: chap. 4), who has written an excellent text on sociobiology, has also devoted an entire chapter to thirteen obstacles to adaptive behavior.

To the degree that sociologists have participated in the debate about sociobiology, the stance typically taken parrots the naysayers' complaints, especially the alleged errors of determinism and reductionism. Additional, and equally unwarranted, concerns include claims that sociobiology is flawed by teleology and tautology, and/or that it is nothing more than a veil behind which lurks the evil of an unregenerate Social Darwinism (e.g., Freese 1994). Such remarkably naive complaints still surface on occasion in both textbooks and professional journals, despite the fact that they have been countered time and again in various venues of scholarly, including sociological, discourse (e.g., Wilson 1978a, 1978b; Lopreato 1984; Alexander 1988; van den Berghe 1990; Holcomb 1993; Carey and Lopreato 1994; Crippen 1994b; Nielsen 1994).

An In-House Debate

As has often happened in the history of science, especially when new frontiers are being charted, a quarrel of sorts has developed among evolutionary students of human behavior. Some "evolutionary psychologists" claim that "Darwinian anthropologists" (DA) (or "Darwinian Social Scientists" [DSS] or just plain sociobiologists), who are typically more closely allied with zoologists, misuse the Darwinian adaptationist program (e.g., Cosmides 1989; Cosmides and Tooby 1989; Symons 1989, 1990, 1992; Tooby and Cosmides 1989, 1990, 1992). A brief summary of the psychologists' position is conveniently provided by Donald Symons (1992), and may be briefly represented as follows:

1. "In short...human beings, like all other organisms, have been designed by selection to strive for *specific* goals, not the *general* goal of reproduction-maximizing. There can be no such thing as a generalized reproduction-maximizer mechanism because there is no general, universally effective way to maximize reproduction" (Symons 1992: 139—emphasis in original).

2. The specific goals are said to "comprise many, domain-specific, specialized mechanisms" (or adaptations), as contrasted to the one "domain-general" mechanism of "inclusive fitness maximizer," or at best "a few domain-general, unspecialized mechanisms" that are allegedly claimed by the sociobiologists (Symons 1992: 142).

3. Darwinism "illuminates human behavior only insofar as it illuminates the adaptations that constitute the machinery of behavior. In other words, the link between Darwinian theory and behavior is psychology"

(Symons 1992: 139). Natural selection designed adaptations, not, except for such cases as walking and smiling, "behavior per se" (Symons 1992: 150).

4. "To claim that a trait is an adaptation is...to make a claim about the *past*," for, as evolutionary biologists unanimously agree, adaptation refers to something produced in the past by natural selection (Symons 1992: 140—emphasis in original). Thus, as others put it, "the past explains the present" (Tooby and Cosmides 1990).

5. Moreover, with regard to the past, "the brain/mind mechanisms that collectively constitute human nature were designed by natural selection in the EEA [environment of evolutionary adaptation]...[hence] they must be described *solely* in terms of the phenomena that existed in the EEA; but the kinds of data that can be used to evaluate evolutionary hypotheses are potentially limitless, and evolutionarily novel phenomena can be just as informative as phenomena that existed in the EEA, or more so" (Symons 1992: 144—emphasis added).

6. The EEA refers to the Pleistocene epoch of our hunter-gatherer ancestors (namely the part of the quaternary period that comprises the last 2.5 million years, up to approximately 5,000 B.P. [Dobzhansky et al. 1977: 316]).

7. The significance of the EEA with respect to adaptations cannot be overemphasized. Hence, Leda Cosmides (1989: 194n) puts it starkly as follows: "Our species spent 99% of its evolutionary history as Pleistocene hunter-gatherers.... Thus, our cognitive mechanisms should be adapted to the hunter-gatherer mode of life, and not to the twentieth century industrialized world."

8. It follows that DSS are not "genuinely Darwinian." Their central, faulty, "hypothesis is that 'evolved behavioral tendencies' cause human 'behavior to assume the form that maximizes inclusive fitness'" (Symons 1992: 146).

This argument, represented here only in *nuce*, is not without merit. However, there are various problems with it, and the opposition has been quite vigorous, particularly on the part of the distinguished zoologist Richard D. Alexander (e.g., 1990; see also Irons 1990; Turke 1990a, 1990b; Betzig 1993b; D.S. Wilson 1994).

We—and all we know—agree with the evolutionary psychologists' argument that a theory of human nature will have to account for many domain-specific adaptations. Work with which we are particularly familiar has in fact followed this approach. Thus, an initial classification of twenty-three "innate mechanisms" or "behavioral predispositions"

(Lopreato 1984: 105, *passim*) is then explicated into a large number of sub-mechanisms. The "urge to victimize" (Lopreato 1984: 129-41), for example, has various domain-specific expressions depending on various contexts: socioeconomic, ethnic, educational, religious, health-medical, moral-legal, and so forth. The psychologists' critique is better suited to the learning-theory practice of pre-evolutionary, behaviorist psychology, as sometimes transpires from the critics themselves (e.g., Tooby and Cosmides 1992: 29), than it is with respect to the DSS. As Alexander (1990: 256-58—emphasis in original) points out, the psychologists' argument is not new, for "virtually every evolutionary biologist or evolution-minded social scientist already adheres to some such position, and, moreover, would also expect the existence of a *hierarchy* of such mechanisms becoming *increasingly* specific with respect to environmental domains." The assertion that DSS are satisfied with the assumption of a generalized reproduction-maximizer mistakes the logic of science as well as the strategy of DSS's work.

The real point, as we have already noted, is not how many adaptations there are in the human brain, although the question of numbers is not unimportant. The crucial point concerns *the logical form that a theory of human nature will take in view of some organizing general principle*. General theories typically take treelike formations, namely *hierarchies* of differentially comprehensive or, conversely, differentially specific explanatory statements. One of the fundamental heuristics of evolutionary theory is taxonomy. The implications of *taxonomy* cannot escape any serious student of evolution and behavior.

It bears reiterating the point that, if properly understood, the fitness principle is but a focal point of the developing theory of human nature that serves various functions, two of which are basic. (1) Along with other tools, for example, sexual selection, it guides the quest for the elements (adaptations) that must enter the theory; (2) it provides the anchorage point for a logical structuring of those elements. Some evolutionary psychologists give the impression of ignoring the role of general principles in scientific inquiry or, perhaps worse, of mistaking statements of general principles for statements of uncatechized fact.

On the other hand, we must hasten to note, perhaps with some irony, that one of the fundamental virtues of the evolutionary psychologists lies precisely in the fact that much of their research puts into practice a deductive, theorematic approach to the discovery of adaptations. The fact is illustrated with particular clarity by the work on human mating strategies. One evolutionary psychologist, for instance, sets out from sexual selection and parental investment to propose a cogent "theory of human sexual strategies" consisting of nine general hypotheses and various operationalized predictions pertaining to each (Buss 1994b; see also Buss 1994a). We shall have occasion to return to this area. This same scholar, who in some contexts appears to join other psychologists in rejecting the importance of the fitness principle, does not hesitate to argue that "sexual-strategies theory holds that patterns in mating behavior exist because they are evolutionarily advantageous" (Buss 1994b: 238). Like it or not, that is to say that they obey the fitness principle—which is to say that, however many the strategies, they are anchored to a general principle.

The "many adaptations" hypothesized by the psychologists rarely if ever fail to point toward a general fitness principle. Indeed, it could hardly be otherwise. As Alexander (1990: 243) has noted, evolutionary biology stipulates, by virtue of both fact and logic, that organisms are reproductive or survival vehicles. The fitness principle merely explicates this stipulation. Moreover, it does so with considerable caution. Symons (1992: 146), like many other evolutionary psychologists, categorically attributes to the opposition "the hypothesis that human beings are reproduction (or inclusive fitness) maximizers." Careless statements to this effect are indeed present in the literature, though typically for the convenience of avoiding excessive reiteration. But as noted repeatedly above, Darwinian evolutionists understand the fitness principle in stochastic terms. Thus, according to Alexander (1990: 242), adaptations, Darwinian algorithms, or "adaptive specializations," as Rozin (1976) termed them more than two decades ago, "have been designed by natural selection as mechanisms whereby the organism *tends to* maximize its inclusive fitness (Hamilton 1964) in the environments of history." As we have repeatedly argued, any departure from this *relative and variable* conception of the fitness quest is a serious departure from the "winnowing" logic of natural selection itself, and can only lead to error and unnecessary debate.

The argument over whether evolutionists should emphasize psychological adaptations or behavior is simply misguided. There is certainly a sense in which it may be said that a certain primacy is by necessity due to the adaptations in the human brain-mind; they are closer to the genes. This is what Symons (1992: 139) apparently intends to say in stating that "the link between Darwinian theory and behavior is psychology." But this is not a useful way to resolve the problem in question; it sounds too much like a quarrel over turf. The point is: *How shall we go about discovering those adaptations?* Obviously in whatever ways turn out to be useful. Cross-cultural comparisons, for instance, may be productive because cross-cultural similarities might suggest homology (e.g., Lopreato 1984; Brown 1991). P. W. Turke (1990a), among others, has clearly shown that knowledge of the contexts in which people express their behavior offers crucial information on the nature of adaptations. The same may be said of the great wealth of cross-species comparisons, which, we should note, evolutionary psychologists seem to belittle in view of their emphasis on the Pleistocene.

Approaches that focus on behavior are essentially inductive in nature. Science has never failed to find induction useful, especially early in the development of a discipline. And scientists are certainly delighted when they can also proceed toward discovery on the basis of deduction from existing theory. Both are necessary. P.W. Turke's (1990b) injunction, "Just do it!" is felicitously conceived (see also Alexander 1990; Irons 1990).

Evolutionary psychologists seem to deny the utility of a pragmatic mixture of the deductive and the inductive methods. The proof is in their extreme emphasis on the assumption that to say X is an adaptation is "to make a claim about the *past*." The "brain/mind mechanisms that collectively constitute human nature were designed by natural selection in the EEA...[hence] they must be described *solely* in terms of the phenomena that existed in the EEA," although present-day data can be quite informative (Symons 1992: 144—second emphasis added). Propriety of qualification aside (it's either "solely" or it's not), this posture creates problems instead of solving them. As noted, the EEA refers to the Pleistocene (2.5 million—5,000 years B.P.). Here is the pickle. We need data to test hypotheses from established theory. Can we recreate the conditions of the Pleistocene? Why not use data wherever *and whenever* we find them—which is, as noted above (e.g., Buss 1994a, 1994b), what evolutionary psychologists themselves have in fact been doing all along?

Is it true that "our cognitive mechanisms should be adapted to the hunter-gatherer mode of life [99 percent of our evolutionary history], and not to the twentieth century," as Cosmides has asserted above? We do not know for sure, and may never know. Perhaps today's *Homo sapiens* exists in a state of evolutionary chaos or void. In part, however, the answer depends on what is meant by adaptation. In zoology, as we have noted (e.g., Darwin 1859; Simpson 1949; Wilson 1975; Dobzhansky et al. 1977), adaptation invariably implies (variable) fitness. Moreover, there is a fair measure of the adaptiveness of cognitive mechanisms for recent times. As late as 10,000 years B.P. the human population probably amounted to about 10,000,000 souls. As recently as 300-400 years ago, it had not reached one billion. Today we number approximately six billion. That would seem to be proof enough of our being adapted to current conditions—always relatively speaking. In addition, we seem to be perfectly capable of creating, in the midst of the megasociety, the facsimiles of times long gone by. For example, we practice what is in effect the tribal warfare of yesteryear in the form of endless ethnic conflicts (e.g., Pareto 1916; van den Berghe 1981; Tönnesmann 1987). Or if we no longer go on the warpath in small groups of warriors, we go to the stadium or the arena as "Tigers" to compete with "Bears." There is "a generalizing tendency" in the human brain—and in the many adaptations lodged therein (Lopreato 1984: 306-10). That is most probably why analogy is such an extraordinarily productive tool of science (e.g., Lorenz 1974). As E.O. Wilson (1984: 60) puts it, the "mind specializes on analogy and metaphor, on a sweeping together of chaotic sensory experience into workable categories labeled by words and stacked into hierarchies for quick recovery. To a considerable degree science consists in [organizing] the maximum amount of information with the minimum expenditure of energy." The generalizing tendency helps to account for cross-temporal adaptations. No doubt, moreover, there are adaptations at work today that hark back to times all along the Pleistocene era—*or even earlier*. We still seek today relationships, among other things, that to varying degrees of success satisfy our gene-driven goals: the entirety of our emotional system and the fundamental aim of life itself. Yes, the past is prelude. And the future of social science belongs to evolutionary scientists.

Part 3

Select Adaptations
and Applications

6

Fundamentals of Sex Differences

We have made and tried to support a variety of claims. Very broadly viewed, they may be briefly summed up as follows. First, the crisis in sociology is primarily a function of sociologists' inability to discover at least one general principle from which a series of logically ordered hypotheses could be derived and around which a potentially rich array of facts could be organized. Second, this shortcoming can be alleviated to some degree by selectively applying certain principles inherent in the expansion of the modern synthesis toward the behavioral sciences. Together, these—natural selection, kin selection, the fitness principle, reciprocity, sexual selection, differential parental investment and confidence, and, among others, a host of domain-specific psychologcial adaptations—constitute the foundations of a theory of human nature and behavior that is taking shape in the evolutionary behavioral sciences. As previously noted, this theory is two-pronged. It points, on the one hand, to *species-wide* features and, on the other, toward *sex-specialized* ones. The former are relevant to a wide array of subjects, including various aspects of economic, political, and ethnic behavior (e.g., van den Berghe 1981; Frank 1988; Masters 1989), the organization of family life (e.g., van den Berghe 1979), and, among others, even the expression of religious and aesthetic beliefs and behaviors (e.g., Reynolds and Tanner 1983; Eibl-Eibesfeldt 1989: chap. 9). Chapters 8 and 9 will be devoted to select topics within this context. The second set—sex-specialized features—refers to individual differences along sex lines. They are the focus of the present chapter and the next. We thus enter a variety of topics that have long fascinated sociologists and, more recently, have captured the imagination of feminist theorists.

In a great many respects, men and women behave in similar ways. But in various other regards they behave and treat each other differently. For instance, they exhibit measurable differences in aspects of sensation, cognition, and emotion. They have unequal access to economic and political resources. They are universally held to different standards of sexual behavior, the more severe restrictions typically being imposed on females. They participate differently in reproduction and child rearing. And, among other things, they rely on distinctive strategies for attracting and selecting mates. In sum, there "has been no [known] human society that has not distinguished the sexes, by their anatomies and by their behavior" (Barash 1979: 46).

There is reasonable consensus among social scientitsts regarding these facts. It is upon entering the level of explanation that we encounter a peck of troubles. Most sociologists and many other social scientists attribute them almost solely, if not exclusively, to environmental influences (e.g., Collins 1975; Connell 1987; Epstein 1988). Their argument typically takes the following form. Men and women are born with the same potentials. But ancient and persisting *patriarchal* arrangements inhibit women's access to power, status, and other valued resources. Women are socialized to be passive and subordinate whereas men are taught to behave aggressively and to achieve dominance. Hence, so-called gender or sex roles are the effects of discrimination and must accordingly be explained in terms of cultural causes.

Evolutionists emphatically agree that differential socialization affects the expression and persistence of sex differences, but they argue that socialization informs only part of the whole story; increasingly, scholars in various fields have been exploring deeper, and *complementary*, sources of the variation. Their findings indicate that many sex-differentiated behaviors are deeply rooted in evolved aspects of human nature. The evidence covers numerous areas, for example, sex differences in aggressive potential and the care of the young (Maccoby and Jacklin 1974; Konner 1982; Brown 1991; Udry 1994); techniques of mate attraction, pair-bond formation, and parenting (van den Berghe 1979; Buss 1989, 1994a, 1994b; Ridley 1993; Wright 1994; Walsh 1995); and the division of household and market labor (Brown 1970; Maryanski and Turner 1992), among many others (Murdock 1937). Such sex differences, while overlapping and expressed with variable intensity across time and space, are nevertheless ubiquitous. This universality cannot be taken as a given. It is a fundamental problem of science that begs for an explanation. In short, even assuming that patriarchy is the culprit discovered by environmentalists, it is incumbent upon students of human behavior to try to explain the rise of patriarchy in the first place. The rationale is plain enough: If patriarchy turns out to be the effect of deeper causes, it is hardly justifiable to treat it as the primary cause.

It is worth noting that such logic did not escape many early sociologists, including especially women sociologists (e.g., Eliza Burt Gamble 1894; Lester Frank Ward 1883, 1903; Lydia Commander 1909; Charlotte Perkins Gilman 1911). They explicitly relied on Darwin's thesis of sexual selection to explain various types of sex-differentiated behaviors. Interestingly, as historian C.N. Degler (1991: chap. 5) has observed, these scholars also argued that Darwin's reasoning was amenable to the view that women were both physically and morally superior to men. Women's longer life expectancy and their greater capacity for sympathy, for example, were explained as straightforward consequences of sexual selection pressures operating over the course of our species' evolutionary history.

Feminism and Biology

Over the past quarter-century, sociological explanations of sex differences have been increasingly dominated by self-proclaimed feminist writers. The label encompasses a vast and growing literature representing a range of diverse epistemic and ideological styles, thus defying easy summary. As one well-informed and sympathetic scholar has remarked, "the differences between [feminist] lines of thought have become more distinct, the conceptual and political differences greater. Current theories of gender are not converging. Rather, they present incompatible accounts of issues" (Connell 1987: 38). This is no surprise. In part, the condition mirrors the fragmented nature of sociology as a whole. Nevertheless, despite the great diversity of feminist literature, there is one issue on which it reveals nearly universal agreement: It is necessary to reject any attempt to explain sex differences even partly in terms of biological factors.

Feminism and Patriarchy

The feminist aversion to biology takes several forms. For instance, among a few it is tempered with an agreeable dose of scholarly caution. For many others the rejection is grounded only in the polemics of victimization or grievances, many of which have real bases but are nevertheless poor bedfellows of scholarly reasoning. In view of the diversity of feminist thinking, the remarks that follow will be directed especially to its more radical brands, in part because of their influence, in part also because their claims are utterly preposterous. Feminist scholarship today is dominated by those whom philosopher Christine Hoff Sommers (1994: 51) has labeled "gender feminists," writers who "are convinced they are in the vanguard of a conceptual revolution of historic proportions...predicated on the 'discovery' of the sex/gender system." The alleged discovery of the "sex/gender system" (Rubin 1975), what others have termed the "matrix of domination" (Collins 1991) or the "relations of ruling" (Smith 1990), has been touted by some "second wave" feminists as equivalent in intellectual import to the revolutions generated by Copernicus, Darwin, and Freud (e.g., Heilbrun 1983), to the Renaissance (e.g., Lerner 1988), and to the influence of the *philosophes* of the French Enlightenment (e.g., Bernard 1987).

Accordingly, as far as gender feminists at least are concerned, the idea of a crisis in sociology is plainly preposterous. For example, the previously noted June 1994 symposium on "What's Wrong with Sociology?," published in *Sociological Forum*, has been severely criticized. Feminist Scholars in Sociology (a self-described "collective of researchers and scholars at the University of Colorado interested in exploring and sharing feminist theory and methodology") have rejected the concerns regarding excessive fragmentation, incoherence, politicization, and antiscience biases expressed by several contributors to the symposium. For these Feminist Scholars, the presumed signs of the crisis in sociology are "actually what's right" with the discipline (Fitzgerald et al. 1995: 494). They see sociology today as "an exciting, dynamic, and challenging discipline." Its "boundaries are being shifted [by] postmodernists, scholars in race and ethnicity, and queer and feminist theorists, among others, [who] have broadened the debate and expanded our understanding of society" (Fitzgerald et al. 1995: 493). They also applaud the increasing influence of "marginalized scholarship," which contributes to the "transformational" project of feminist research that, among other things, "challenges the assumptions of biological theories of gender and opens the doors for a social constructionist approach" (Fitzgerald et al. 1995: 496).

This conception of an epoch-making scholarly revolution is a stupefying case of self-delusion. The Faithful confuse social movements with scholarly progress. Various factors drive the wishful thinking, including the aversion to the "modernist canon," the addiction to cultural relativism/pluralism, and the horror of biological theory. Permeating them all, however, is the erroneous assumption of patriarchy or male dominance as a "socially constructed" phenomenon. The error belies poor scholarship nourished by a bit of paranoia.

Feminists define patriarchy in various ways. On the whole, however, they view it as a condition whereby "men hold power in all important institutions in society and...women are deprived of access to such power" (Lerner 1986: 29). Patriarchy is thus a reason for grievances, and one can hardly deny that many of them are only too well-founded. In a nutshell, women's contributions to society—not to mention its very foundation, the family—have always been at least equal to those of their brothers; and, if anything, this is a conservative assessment. Yet, they have been discriminated against and abused in countless ways (although at home they have sometimes been quite capable of turning the tables around).

On the question of male dominance there is rather general consensus. Sarah Blaffer Hrdy (1997: 7), for example, has noted that, while frequently "viewed as antagonists, a Marxist, a feminist, and a sociobiologist concur that men seek to control women, and to a lesser extent, they concur on why patriarchal systems...emerge: a perceived need by males to control female sexuality."

Radical feminists and sociobiologists, however, part ways at the point where the question of range of explanation necessarily arises. In many feminist accounts, patriarchy is said to have emerged around the third millenium B.C. (e.g., Lerner 1986). In short, like creationists, feminists ignore our species' evolution and tend to think of human history in terms of a few thousand years. By contrast, evolutionists argue that patriarchy, or male dominance, is with few if any exceptions a mammalian phenomenon, and therefore far more ancient. Thus, several women scholars (e.g., Gowaty 1992; Smuts 1995; Hrdy 1997), among others, have argued that "an evolutionary perspective pushes the search for patriarchy's origins back in time by millions of years by asking an additional question: *Why* should males seek to control females?" (Hrdy 1997: 8—emphasis in original). In keeping with Darwinian logic, they "assume that the *ultimate* goal of male domination is reproductive success, and they identify sexual selection...rather than male desire for power as the engine driving the system" of patriarchy (Hrdy 1997: 7—emphasis added).

The irony is that the specific dynamics that almost certainly produced patriarchy include female complicity with domineering males against less aggressive ones. As chapters 4 and 5 suggested, there has been a great deal of sexual selection, or male-male competition for mates, in human evolutionary history. In this competition, dominance has been achieved by certain males in part by virtue of female preference for them (female choice). So, the pickle that feminists (and ourselves among many other people) find so distasteful not only turns out to have been seasoned without the influence of culture, although once culture arose it made it even more tartish. It is also true that our female ancestors had a hand in the preparation. And that is why, ultimately, many women throughout the world continue to participate in the perpetuation of male dominance by having a strong prefernce for hypergynous mating. It is difficult for feminist thinkers to come to grips with this basic point. But ideology is a poor substitute for dispassionate reasoning.

Essentialism and Biological Determinism

Gender feminists claim that "there is no *essential* femaleness or maleness" (Lorber 1994: 25—emphasis in original). To claim otherwise allegedly invites serious and politically malevolent errors. Hence, assertions of "essential" or "invariant" differences are portrayed as tools of oppression designed to legitimate male dominance and to treat sex differences "as natural and inevitable consequences of the intrinsic biological nature of women and men" (Bem 1993: 2).

To our knowledge, no one claims that all differences between the sexes are biological inevitabilities. The claim is rather that, given the sex difference in basic reproductive strategy, certain other differences necessarily follow, *in varying degrees*. A cardinal axiom of evolutionary theory is that organisms feature trait variations, including various average differences within sex as well as between the sexes. The misconception is related to another error in reasoning. Feminists frequently insist that evolutionary accounts are based on a naive biological determinism, namely the assumption that the differences between the sexes are not susceptible to environmental influence. This gross distortion is apparently necessary to undergird an undisguised political agenda. Sociologist Ann Oakley (1997: 44—emphasis in original), for example, complains that if the study of sex differences is "returned to the domain of the apparently 'natural,' a *political* response is ruled out. Natural [i.e., essential or invariant] differences cannot provide the organizing topic for revolution. Revolutionary agendas need differences attributable to preventable causes." Revolution, then, is the aim, and the cadre for the revolution are being trained especially in "women's studies programs" with more than a tinge of totalitarian doctrine. "The strategies of faculty members in these programs," as Daphne Patai (1998: A56) has noted, "have included policing insensitive language, championing research methods deemed congenial to women (such as qualitative over quantitative methods), and conducting classes as if they were therapy sessions."

Politics asides, the irony is that neo-Darwinian science has no peer precisely on the question of mechanisms of change, and hence of possibly preventable causes. If we recall the interaction principle, it becomes immediately evident that evolutionary etiology is perfectly systemic in nature. The point may be illustrated by reference to animal behavior, where presumably culture plays no role. Male dominance of females is nearly universal among mammals, including the primate order. But its intensity varies from one species to another as well as in conjunction with various intra-specific conditions. For instance, Bonobos (*Pan paniscus*), more commonly known as pygmy chimpanzees, feature behaviors among females that successfully mitigate if they do not entirely cancel male dominance. Two major factors combine to produce this outcome. One is sociological in nature; strong ties among females lessen the males' ability to dominate them. The other refers to a more nearly ultimate cause reflected in an unusual feature of this species' sexual behavior. Female alliances are apparently established and maintained to a large extent on the basis of mutually satisfying sexual stimulation (de Waal 1989, 1995; Parish 1996). Organization can indeed be a powerful factor of behavioral modification. And the point need not be merely asserted. It is an integral aspect of a firmly established theory of behavior.

Gender feminists almost invariably represent sociobiology as caricature. E.O. Wilson, for example, presumably argues that male dominance, polygyny, and sex differences in temperament are the exclusive result of the human "*desire* to pass on their genes" (Epstein 1988: 47—emphasis in original). Why sociologists license and apparently ratify this sort of travesty is a bit mystifying. As we have repeatedly seen, Darwinian theory necessarily emphasizes that phenotypic traits are the product of genetic information interacting with environmental pressures. An example from E.O. Wilson's work, the favorite whipping boy of gender feminists, will illustrate the point, again. In discussing cross-cultural universals in the sex-differentiated division of labor, E.O. Wilson (1978a: 132) notes that, even in times and places far removed from our ancestral environments, the differentiation may still be rooted in "a slight biological component." Thus, "at birth the twig is already bent a little bit—what are we to make of that? It suggests that the universal existence of sexual division of labor is not entirely an accident of cultural evolution. But it also supports the conventional view that the enormous variation among societies in the degree of that division is due to cultural evolution." One can scarcely imagine a clearer statement of the systemic nature of evolutionary science and a better appreciation of cultural causation.

To an extent, the senseless errors among feminist sociologists derive from an excessive reliance on the polemical critiques of sociobiology offered by feminist biologists such as Ruth Bleier (1984), Ruth Hubbard (1990), and Anne Fausto-Sterling (1992). These authors have great difficulty reconciling evolutionary explanations of behavior with their own political sensitivities. Bleier (1984: 17—emphasis in original), for example, applauds the sober and insightful manner in which Darwinian theory accounts for the evolution of physical traits in organisms. But she takes sociobiologists to task for "assuming that *behaviors* also evolve in similar ways." This is merely a "premise" or a "conjecture" because all evolutionists (including sociobiologists, as she admits) "agree that it is not possible to link any specific behavior with any specific gene or genetic configuration," though she herself affirms that "all behavior… reflects at least some component of gene action."

But whether it is possible to link behaviors to genes is a question of scientific curiosity and effort, not one of dogma. In fact the question is currently being answered in numerous laboratories participating in the human DNA mapping project funded by the U.S. National Institutes of Health, among other agencies. Furthermore, sociobiologists are led to assume some indirect genetic action behind certain kinds of behavior, especially those closely linked to reproduction, by the simple fact that genes are the matter of evolution. Strictly speaking, however, they need not rely on genetic demonstration, though that may be the eventual goal. As we have seen, the theory of natural selection and various theoretical tools comprised under its umbrella—for example, sexual selection and differential parental investment—are very productive of falsifiable predictions. This is the nature of the scientific game: science reduces to the better known.

The real problem is that critics do not wish to learn the rules of the game because these do not suit their prejudices. It is easy work, therefore, to superficially review differential parental investment theory, for example, and then allege that it is employed to justify the prejudices of "upper/middle class white male North American and English scientists" (Bleier 1984: 21). Such males are then condemned for their presumed commitment to the "sexual double standard." Evolutionists, like social scientists and ordinary folks, do write on such double-standard topics as female "coyness" and male aggressiveness in mating tactics; male preferences for younger, physically attractive mates; female preferences for slightly older, resource-rich mates; and sex differences in response to partner infidelity, among others. Whether they are committed to the double standard is certainly an interesting question. We rather suspect that people in general find it difficult to give up privileges. This is a legitimate subject of *study*. Another legitimate subject of study concerns the question whether the double standard is a purely cultural artifact. Proper view of patriarchy aside, evolutionists necessarily hypothesize that, if phenotype is the resultant of genotype-environment interaction, culture and biology are likely to be partners in the mischief. Bleier will not countenance this possibility. Despite her admission that all behaviors reflect some genetic component, she (1984: 25—emphasis added) offers the following complaint about evolutionary explanation: "There is no suggestion that the double standard could have social origins *independent of genes*, that it may be but one more reflection of the economic and political domination of men over women in 'countless' patriarchal societies." There is disorientation in this kind of reasoning because the goal here is political, and it is clearly manifested by Bleier's (1984: 15–16) assault on E.O. Wilson's work. This scholar's sociobiology is portrayed as "a particularly dramatic contemporary version of biological determinist theories of human behavior" and a "particularly good example of bad science...[providing] 'scientific' support for a dominant political ideology that opposes every goal and issue raised by the women's movement."

Bleier, Hubbard, and Fausto-Sterling have become the darlings of feminist social scientists, often in ways that might even be astounding to themselves. According to sociologist Judith Lorber (1994: 46), for instance, "a purely biological substrate [of gender] cannot be isolated because human physiology is socially constructed and gendered." One wonders whether members of the medical profession are aware of this extraordinary discovery.

Social Constructionism Run Amok

Feminist accounts of sex-differentiated behavior typically begin with what by now has become dogma among most social scientists: the distinction between sex and gender. The former is intended to refer only to essentially insignificant anatomical and physiological traits, while the latter is typically portrayed as a social-psychological (i.e., behavioral) and/or cultural construct that is independent of sex. By so sharply divorcing gender and gender differences from their biological bases, it becomes possible to make all kinds of astonishing pronouncements. "Whatever genes, hormones, and biological evolution contribute to human social institutions," remarks J. Lorber (1994: 25), "is materially as well as qualitatively transformed by social practice.... Genders, therefore, are not attached to a biological substratum." And neither, presumably, is sex. "Another interesting twist to the sex-gender argument is provided by recent historical and sociological work showing that cultural construction applies also to sex. This means that the essential distinction between sex and gender collapses" (Oakley 1997: 48). Cases of hermaphroditism, for example, are said to demonstrate that "*sex* is socially and culturally constructed rather than a straightforward statement of biological 'facts'" (West and Fenstermaker 1996: 368—emphasis in original). Moreover, these writers condemn those who treat male and female categories as "natural, normal characteristics," for they provide "tacit legitimation of the distinctive and unequal fates of women and men within the social order" (West and Fenstermaker 1996: 370).

The political complaint thus rises insistently to the fore. Factual statements of difference are represented as moral justifications for inequality. Gendered norms are alleged to give rise to and legitimate "hegemonic masculinity" and an "emphasized femininity" (Connell 1987) that preserve a sociocultural *status quo* in which men are free to oppress women. One fall-out of such ideological posturing and angst is a distortion of facts, as Sommers (1994) has noted, for example, the promotion of wildly exaggerated estimates of instances of domestic violence, sexual harassment, eating disorders, and other such abuses of women in American society. Many scholars of this ilk are "experts" on the family, and thus teach courses in which our students are overtly or furtively taught to distrust marriage (where "marital rape" is alleged to be rampant), to exalt the single lifestyle, and to consider the virtues of gay and lesbian marriages, *inter alia* (see, e.g., Glenn's 1997 critique of recent Marriage and Family texts).

Sociology is comfortable home to feminist theorists who are devoted to an antiscientific, radically subjectivist, narrowly parochial, and politically charged enterprise. In their lectures as well as their writings, they preach obscurantist lessons. Summarizing a widespread line of thought, a feminist sociologist has recently written approvingly that the rejection of such dualisms as man/woman, analysis/empathy, thought/emotion, mind/body, and "objectivity/subjectivity" leads to the rejection of "the possibility of universal principles" (Rogers 1998: 71). "As postmodernist theorists (among others) emphasize, virtually no social categories approach uniformity. Instead, they mask diversity unless we theorists take care to articulate all the differences gathered together under terms like Women, Mothers, Lesbians, Chicanas, or Widows" (Rogers 1998: 5). This posture bespeaks an intellectual pathology of enormous proportions. As a discipline we are descending into a "swamp" of "exclusive devotion" to "correct politics," and "crude caricatures of society" (Horowitz 1993: 16–17). Fortunately, many sociologists reject the invitation to the swamp, but they are also intimidated by the artful weapons of the sociological vandals.

As we approach the end of this section, we should emphasize that this brief critique of feminist theorizing is by no means intended as an indictment of feminist scholars in general, in or out of sociology. A considerable and growing number of scholars with explicitly feminist sensibilities have made important contributions to the evolutionary understanding of sex differences, human and otherwise. This book owes a substantial debt to them, as our references have shown and will continue to show. For the most part, such scholars are anthropologists, psychologists, and several sorts of zoologists. Their work even illustrates that there is no necessary antagonism between evolutionary analyses of sex-differentiated behavior and many of the political goals of feminism (Arnhart 1992; Liesen 1995).

Some feminist sociologists, too, have attempted to improve the quality of feminist theorizing. J. Chafetz (1984: 3), for example, has argued that many attempts to construct sociological theories of gender are couched in "emotion-laden but unclear terms [such as patriarchy], combined with a heavily normative approach to the topic of sex inequality," a characteristic that "results in a maximum of rhetoric but a minimum of clear insight." Some fifteen years ago, Alice Rossi took the occasion of her presidential address to the American Sociological Association to remind her colleagues of an incontrovertible truth: that in certain fundamental ways men and women behave differently and in accord with their specialized biological natures: "Gender differentiation is not simply a function of socialization, capitalist production, or patriarchy. It is grounded in a sex dimorphism.... Theories that neglect these characteristics of sex and gender carry a high risk of eventual irrelevance against mounting evidence of sexual dimorphism from the biological and neurosciences" (Rossi 1984: 1). Unfortunately, Rossi failed to inspire other sociologists to follow her lead. In fact, they remember her best for the controversy she generated among feminists who viewed her earlier (Rossi 1977) invitation to biosocial analysis as plainly heretical (e.g., Gross et al. 1979).

Differences in the Brain

In human conception each parent contributes twenty-three chromosomes that pair and endow offspring with the normal complement of forty-six. One pair is especially relevant to the biology of sex-typical development and behavior. To this pair, mothers can contribute only an X chromosome; by contrast, fathers contribute either an X or a Y version. Sexual differentiation is "determined by a gene situated on the Y chromosome. The gene is named *testis-determining factor* or *TDF*.... If you have a Y chromosome you have a TDF gene and you develop as a male. If you do not have a Y chromosome you do not have this gene and you develop as a female" (LeVay 1993:18—emphasis in original).

The details of how the TDF gene operates are not fully understood. Research, however, continues to shed light on its wondrous workings (Marx 1995), and at least in broad outlines a plausible scenario has been proposed. "A set of genes common to both sexes drives the initial development of the gonad. At some point prior to the morphological differentiation into testis or ovary, one of these genes...commands the TDF gene to be turned on. If the embryo is a male, the TDF gene is present and is accordingly turned on, that is, the protein that it codes is synthesized. If the embryo is female, the TDF gene is absent and so the command falls on deaf ears" (LeVay 1993: 21). The TDF gene, thus, affects only the development of gonadal tissue, but the effect is critical. The development of embryonic testes or ovaries sets the stage for the production of sex steroids or sex hormones—androgens, estrogens, and progestins—that play crucial roles in the entire process of sex differentiation throughout the life course of the mammalian organism.

Crucial for our purpose here is the manner in which prenatal releases of sex steroids are associated with the sex-differentiated organization of certain features of brain anatomy. The lifetime effects of embryonic exposure to sex hormones are termed "organizational because they appear to alter brain function permanently during a critical period. Administering the same hormones at later stages has no such effect. The hormonal effects are not limited to sexual or reproductive behavior: they appear to extend to all known behaviors in which males and females differ" (Kimura 1992: 121). The relationships among gene, gonadal development, prenatal and postnatal hormone releases, brain organization, and behavior are complex, interdependent, and only dimly illuminated as yet. Nevertheless, feminist denials notwithstanding (e.g., Fausto-Sterling 1992: 11–12, chap. 8), there is compelling evidence that, as Doreen Kimura (1992: 119) has noted, boys and girls enter the world with "differently wired brains" and these differences in brain architechture "make it almost impossible to evaluate the effects of experience independent of physiological predisposition."

Some Differences in Brain Anatomy

At least three such differences appear to be significant for sociology and the behavioral sciences in general. First, the processing of information across the left and right hemispheres of the cerebral cortex seems to operate somewhat differently for men and women. For example, several speech functions are processed by males largely in the left hemisphere while visio-spatial and emotional functions are processed primarily in the right hemisphere. Among women, corresponding processing is more diffuse, involving greater communication across hemispheres (e.g., McGlone 1980; Kimura and Harshman 1984). In one of the early studies, S. Witelson (1978) exposed subjects to emotionally charged visual cues that were channeled into either the right or the left hemisphere by limiting their display to either the left-hand or the right-hand field of vision. Women generally recognized and responded to the emotional content of the cues transmitted to either hemisphere; in contrast, men were likely to recognize the cues only when they were channeled to the right hemisphere.

These differences in "lateralization" may be linked to a second feature of brain differentiation. The corpus callosum—the bundle of nerve fibers that connects the left and right sides—has been observed by some researchers to be thicker and more bulbous in women than in men, suggesting greater opportunities for the exchange of information across hemispheres (de Lacoste-Utamsing and Holloway 1982; Allen et al. 1991). Tentative evidence suggests that the difference is observable as early as the twenty-sixth week of fetal development (de Lacoste-Utamsing and Woodward 1982). Further, there is some evidence that the anterior commisure, a more ancient connection between the two hemispheres, is somewhat larger in women than in men (Allen and Gorski 1991). These findings have not gone unchallenged. Some researchers report no observable sex differences in the size of the two neural structures. Comparisons, however, should be made in relative terms. For example, LeVay found no significant sex difference in the size of the corpus callosum, but he also noted that on average women's brains are smaller than men's brains. In fact, "the corpus callosum occupies a larger fraction of the entire brain volume in women than in men, suggesting that the two cerebral hemispheres are more richly interconnected in women" (LeVay 1993: 102). Whether, however, there are behavioral effects of these possible sex differences in the size of the corpus callosum and the anterior commisure is as yet an unanswered question. Nevertheless, brain structure is not likely to be divorced from the structure of behavior.

A third and far more telling feature of sex-differentiated brain anatomy concerns the hypothalamus (e.g., Konner 1982; Kimura 1992; LeVay 1993: chap. 10), a principal component of the limbic system that plays a prominent role in the expression of the emotions as well as sexual activity (MacLean 1973). Research on the hypothalamus dates back nearly fifty years. Experiments on male and female rats, for example, have revealed the former to have a greater number of synaptic connections in the so-called preoptic area of the anterior hypothalamus, and the difference was shown to be associated with varying levels of circulating testosterone in neonates (Raisman and Field 1973). Castration of male neonates inhibited the development of this distinctively male pattern; correspondingly, injecting testosterone in female neonates stimulated the development of the male anatomical structure. The results "gave real credence to the possibility that the frequently observed preadolescent gender differences in aggressiveness were as biological in origin as the more easily comprehended postadolescent ones" (Konner 1982: 122). Further research on mouse hypothalamic tissue demonstrated convincingly the role of testosterone in accelerating the growth of neuronal connections (Toran-Allerand 1976; Gorski et al. 1980).

A similar dimorphism has been observed in the human brain. Specifically, certain nuclei of the anterior hypothalamus are reportedly larger in men than in women (Allen et al. 1989). It is well-documented that these regions of the hypothalamus govern, to a large degree, typical male and female sexual behavior in mammals—for example, mounting in males and lordosis in females (LeVay 1993: chap. 9). In addition, it is known that sex hormones concentrate most highly and bind most effectively in the hypothalamus and other regions of the limbic system, "exactly where [evolutionary] theory would like them to be. That is, concentrations occur in brain regions that play an important role in courtship, sex, maternal behavior, and violence—just the behaviors [on] which the sexes most differ and the ones most subject to influence by testosterone, estradiol, and progesterone" (Konner 1982: 117). Some caution, however, is in order. The mechanisms connecting the hypothalamus to other brain regions, in particular the cerebral cortex, are still inadequately understood. Determining the extent to which sex-differentiated features of the hypothalamus participate in the expression of male- and female-typical behavior must await more conclusive investigation. That these brain differences play some role, however, can hardly be doubted. At any rate, it behooves behavioral scientists to be curious and inquisitive about them.

Differences in Sensation, Cognition, and Emotion

As noted, the gene-gonad-hormone linkages that guide the early development of the sex-differentiated brain represent the organizational effects of sex hormones on brain anatomy (Kimura 1992; LeVay 1993). The prenatal releases of androgens, estrogens, and progestins prime the pump, as it were, establishing the architectural backdrop for sex variations in sensitivity to the action of sex hormones and neurotransmitters on certain regions of the brain throughout the remainder of the individual's life. Thus, we may reasonably entertain the hypothesis that male and female brains are prepared by a history of hormonal influences to operate differently, and that these differences express themselves in certain mental traits. For convenience, we shall focus below on select aspects of sensation, cognition, and emotion (see table 6.1).

On average, males and females experience the world differently from the time of birth. Infant girls, for example, smile more, and this trait endures to maturity; they pay more attention to sights and sounds; and, among other things, they are more likely to stay close to their mother's side. Women have more acute auditory sensitivity, and are more readily affected by annoying sounds, such as dripping faucets (Garai and Scheinfeld 1968; McGuiness 1976). Their vision is sharper in poorly lit environments and more sensitive to the red end of the color spectrum, whereas men see better in brightly illuminated conditions and have more keenly developed depth perception (McGuiness 1976). Furthermore, women appear to have a more finely developed sense of taste

TABLE 6.1
**Average Sex Differences in Select Aspects of Sensation,
Cognition, and Emotion**

Mental Domain	Average Male Tendencies	Average Female Tendencies
Sensation		
	Less acute hearing	More acute hearing
	Better vision in brightly lit environs	Better vision in poorly lit environs
	More sensitive to salty flavor	More sensitive to bitter flavor
	Less acute sense of smell	More acute sense of smell
	Less sensitive to sharp pain	More sensitive to sharp pain
	Less able to endure lengthy discomfort	Better able to endure lengthy discomfort
Cognition		
	Keener spatial abilities	Lesser spatial abilities
	Better higher-mathematical skills	Poorer higher-mathematical skills
	Greater aptitude for navigation	Lower aptitude for navigation
	Better target-directed motor skills	Poorer target-directed motor skills
	Poorer perceptual speed skills	Superior perceptual speed skills
	Less adept at arithmetic calculation	Superior arithmetic skills
	Poorer verbal skills	Superior verbal fluency
	Poorer visual memory	Superior visual memory
	Less able to carry a tune	Better able to carry a tune
	Poorer precision motor skills	Superior precision motor skills
	Less short-term memory capacity	More short-term memory capacity
Emotion		
	More aggressive	Less aggressive
	Less nurturant	More nurturant
	More apt to express "sexual jealousy"	Less apt to express "sexual jealousy"
	Less apt to express "emotional jealousy"	More apt to express "emotional jealousy"

Note: Table constructed on the basis of information from various sources cited in the text.

and to better appreciate the delicate interplay of flavors—which suggests that "great" male chefs should make room. Women moreover are more averse to bitter flavors, favoring sweeter consumables, while men are more sensitive to saltiness (Garai and Scheinfeld 1968). Women of all ages have a more acute sense of smell. In particular, they are keenly alert and attracted to musk-like scents often emitted by men, a sensitivity that appears to intensify with the approach of ovulation (Reinisch 1974). We may add, to the likely dismay of the boys, that while women are more sensitive to sharp pain, they exhibit greater ability to endure periods of lengthy physical discomfort (Restak 1979).

Do such differences have any evolutionary significance? Given the different selection pressures faced by males and females in our species' evolution, the likelihood is high. Women's greater tolerance of lengthy discomfort has every appearance of being an adaptation to the demands of their reproductive biology. The menstrual cycle, lengthy pregnancies, the rigors of childbirth, postpartum infections, and the soreness and strains associated with prolonged periods of nursing—these and other facets of women's reproductive physiology most likely favored the selection of relatively spartan female organisms. Or consider women's greater auditory sensitivity. The ability to hear a child wimpering in the night or in general to detect its cry would have helped our ancestral mothers to protect their heavy investment in their offspring. On the other side of the coin, men seem better able to cope with sharp pains like those attending cuts, scrapes, strained muscles and joints, blows to the body, and the like. These traits are consistent with the sexual selection and physical challenges facing our male ancestors: long hunting excursions, working with sharpened tools, and, among others, the recurring instances of interpersonal feuding and intergroup warfare.

As table 6.1 indicates, there is a fairly large array of cognitive sex differences. Men exhibit greater spatial skills, for example the ability to mentally rotate three dimensional objects and to solve maze puzzles, conditions that may be related to a greater aptitude for "mathematical reasoning" and navigating a mapped route. The differences in mathematical reasoning appear to be most pronounced at the higher ranges of the distribution. Women, however, have superior skills in "mathematical calculation" and in perceptual speed, for example, the ability to match objects by reference to common dimensions—such as identifying words that begin with the same letter (Benbow and Stanley 1980, 1983; Sanders et al. 1982; Hedges and Nowell 1995).

Men display greater accuracy in throwing objects at a target or in tracking and intercepting objects in flight. In contrast, women have superior precision motor skills, for example, a greater facility on tasks requiring manual dexterity (Kimura 1992), suggesting, one would suppose, that people would be better served by the availability of a much larger percentage of women surgeons. Females also display superior verbal abilities or "ideational fluency." They more efficiently acquire vocabulary, grammatical, and speaking skills; they learn to read more quickly; and they have fewer speech and/or reading disorders (Maccoby and Jacklin 1974; Harris 1978; Corballis and Beale 1983; McGuiness 1985). Better still, brain scientists have found that women recover better than men from strokes in the left side of the brain, where speech centers are concentrated. This advantage may be one consequence of the more richly interconnected female brain. Functional magnetic resonance imaging has even revealed that the two sexes use different parts of the brain while thinking and solving problems (Kimura 1992). Women also have better visual memory, for example, landscape and location recognition (e.g., Eals and Silverman 1994; James and Kimura 1997; McBurney et al. 1997), and superior short-term memory capacity (Buffery and Gray 1975; Hutt 1975). Moreover, they are better able to carry a tune in the correct key and with proper pitch (Garai and Scheinfeld 1968; McGuiness 1985).

Neuropsychologist Doreen Kimura (1992) has summarized findings of this sort in an exceedingly informative *Scientific American* essay. On most of these measures, average differences in male and female scores mask to various degrees overlapping sex-segregated frequency distributions; on others, however, both the average differences and the measures of dispersion reveal quite noticeable differences (Kimura 1992: 120). Kimura concludes her account with insightful remarks about their evolutionary significance, remarks that are worth quoting at some length:

> It seems clear that the sex differences in cognitive patterns arose because they proved evolutionarily advantageous.... For the thousands of years during which our brain characteristics evolved, humans lived in relatively small groups of hunter-gatherers.... Men were responsible for hunting large game, which often required long-distance travel. They were also responsible for defending the group against predators and enemies and for the shaping and use of tools. Women most probably gathered food near the camp, tended the home, prepared food and clothing, and cared for children. Such specializations would put different selection pressures on men and women. Men would require long-distance route-finding ability so they could recognize a geographic array from varying orientations. They would also need targeting skills. Women would require short-range navigation, perhaps using landmarks, fine-motor capabilities carried on within circumscribed space, and perceptual discrimination sensitive to small changes in the environment or in children's appearance or behavior. (Kimura 1992: 125; see also McBurney et al. 1997)

There are also important sex differences in emotional traits relevant to mate choice, competition for mates, and, among others, the nurturance of offspring. Women are more inclined than men toward a nurturing mood, especially in the presence of small children (e.g., Maccoby and Jacklin 1974; Konner 1982; Walsh 1995). The tendency is readily predictable from the law of anisogamy and parental investment theory. At the birth of a child, a mother has already made a substantial investment. She has expended significant time, energy, and resources during nine months of pregnancy and in the recurring menses before that. These investments then call forth relatively intense efforts to insure the survival of the child, often including a lengthy period of nursing and other care. The father's contribution can be considerable, too, but on average it does not compare favorably. In fact, evolutionary pressures acting on males have wrought an emotional system that in some respects is the antithesis of a nurturing tendency (e.g., Wrangham and Peterson 1996). This too is partly explicable in terms of distinctive reproductive interests. As noted, access to scarce and valuable mates has been the chief factor facing male reproductive potential, and has contributed to relatively greater variation in male reproductive success. In short, the evolution of males has taken place under intense sexual selection pressures—often severe rivalries for mates. Across human societies, even today, various forms of posturing and display, dueling and fighting, and fiercely competitive sports testify to a strong male propensity toward aggression and the material rewards that this may afford (e.g., Murdock 1967; Chagnon 1979, 1983).

The sex difference on aggression is one of the more thoroughly documented aspects of the human emotional system (Maccoby and Jacklin 1974; Whiting and Whiting 1975; Walsh 1995), probably encompassing our species' entire vertebrate heritage (Barash 1982: 348-49). Male-male competition for access to females is a widespread animal characteristic, although it exhibits variable intensity across species (and even a reversal in a few). At a hormonal level of analysis, the greater male tendency toward aggressive behavior is almost certainly related to higher average levels of testosterone acting on the limbic system, in particular the hypothalamus and the amygdala. "For instance, injection of testosterone lowers the threshold for firing nerve fibers in the *stria terminalis*," a channel through which signals are transmitted from the amygdala to the hypothalamus. "As such in all likelihood it mediates an excitatory influence of the limbic system...on...aggressive behavior. This finding gives substance to the action of testosterone on behavior. It is one thing to say that the hormone probably influences... aggression by acting on the brain; it is quite another to find a major nerve bundle deep in the brain, likely to be involved in...aggression, that can fire more easily when testosterone acts on it than when it does not" (Konner 1982: 117).

Male aggression may be seen as a set of basically mammalian adaptations installed ultimately in accordance with the fitness principle. Among our chimpanzee cousins, for example, males are more quickly than females aroused to aggression that leads to physical assaults. Very frequently, the context of these conflicts is male-male competition for mates, position in the dominance order, food, and other crucial resources (de Waal 1982; Goodall 1986a). Closer to home, preadolescent boys engage more often than girls in rough and tumble play, and young men are the more apt to pick fights, engage in violent crimes, and even maim and kill their kind (Archer 1994; Wrangham and Peterson 1996). Are there elements of socialization in such behavior? Very probably. But again, can we be taught to do that which is not in our nature to do? Socialization can only intensify or conversely mitigate a behavioral predisposition.

There are multiple implications of sex differences on what may be viewed as the nurturing-aggressive continuum. In sexual relationships, for example, men are more likely than women to express insecurity, suspicion, and jealousy. Moreover, as we shall see, on average men and women are susceptible to jealousy in different ways. From the standpoint of the individual's ultimate evolutionary interests, a pair-bond represents a relationship that, while in some measure based on mutual benefit, is also clearly asymmetrical; women obtain valuable survival and emotional resources from men; in return, men gain access to a scarce reproductive resource. Accordingly, fitness theory predicts that women will be more vigilant than men for threats against the resources needed for their children, such as the possibility that their mates will channel resources to other women and offspring. Men, conversely, are expected to be more alert to the threat of infidelity and thus to the danger of being put in a position to invest in children fathered by other men.

Paternal uncertainty has been a crucial evolutionary pressure on men. Mothers know without question that their children are their own. Not so with fathers, precisely because of sexual selection, and thus man-man "predation" and the associated female attraction to resource-rich or dominant men. The threat of cuckoldry, and thereby investing maladaptively, inevitably lurks in the neural background of a man's relationship with his mate. This is the deeply rooted cause of male jealousy, although we may expect it to be susceptible to some cultural conditioning. Findings from a cross-cultural study, for example, reveal that cultural patterns fostering heavy male investment in wife's children are common only where mating patterns foster high paternal confidence. "These results support the hypothesis that culturally defined paternal investment patterns vary with a biological variable, paternal confidence" (Gaulin and Schlegel 1980: 308).

Indeed, the predictive powers of evolutionary theory can be startling. For instance, if paternal uncertainty is a factor in men's family behavior, we would also expect to find differences between the two sets of grandparents in their attentiveness to grandchildren. Grandparents are merely a generation away from the focal point. Further, keeping in mind the fact of differential parental investment, we should be able to make successful predictions about differential solicitude toward grandchildren along the sex lines of grandparents. This is precisely the kind of study reported by H.A. Euler and B. Weitzel (1996). These scholars have found in a sample of 603 cases that the maternal grandmother was "the most caring" toward grandchildren. Contrary to prevalent stereotype, she was followed by the maternal grandfather. Paternal grandmother and paternal grandfather then followed in this order (see also, relatedly, Littlefield and Rushton 1986). Along the same lines, matrilineal aunts and uncles appear to be more attentive to their nieces and nephews than their patrilineal counterparts (Gaulin et al. 1997). Considerations of this nature may be used to help explain the widely documented fact that in many preagrarian societies, a mother's brother often assumed many paternal duties. Especially in societies featuring high rates of divorce and/or sexual promiscuity, a maternal uncle may have greater confidence in his genetic relatedness to his nieces and nephews than in his relatedness to his wife's children (Dawkins 1989: 106, 296–97).

Variations in parental confidence underlie in part sex differences in the expressions of jealousy. For example, when presented with evidence (or simulations) of their spouses' infidelity, women are more likely to respond with sadness and/or fear of emotional abandonment, whereas men are more likely to report feelings of anger (Shettel-Neuber et al. 1978). Similarly, women are more apt to respond jealously to the prospect of their mate's devoting time and emotional resources to a potential competitor, whereas men are more moved to jealousy when their mate is sexually involved with another man (e.g., Buss et al. 1992; Wiederman and Allgeier 1993; Buss 1994a).

Feminist theorists almost invariably attribute such differences to aspects of male domination and the "manipulative morality" associated with patriarchal social structures. Hence, "moral standards or rules do not appear to reflect evolved behavioral propensities. Rather, they reflect self-interest" (Paul et al. 1996: 315). On the face of it, this sort of reasoning seems to be antithetical to the evolutionary perspective. In fact, it is just vacuous. What are motivations rooted in self-interest if not evolved behavioral propensities? The aversion to biology can reach truly astonishing levels. Imagine the American Sociological Association conferring an award to a student for delivering a paper that "logically and empirically demonstrated that emotions are social"! No doubt. And the antipodes have fallen into the abyss.

Developmental Anomalies

The process of sex differentiation in the brain is extraordinarily fine-tuned and complex. Perhaps for this reason, there are times when nature "errs"; the typical path of development goes astray, giving rise to various deviations from the norm. These, too, shed light on the question of sex-typical behavior (e.g., Konner 1982; Moir and Jessel 1989; Walsh 1995). Turner's Syndrome (TS), for example, affects females who commonly have only one X chromosome, although they may possess a damaged second. As a result, TS females have atrophied or abnormally functioning ovaries (LeVay 1993: 22). They are sterile; they lack secondary sexual characteristics, such as a "female appearance"; and they exhibit deficiencies in right-hemisphere brain function. They are also unusually passive and "coy"; nurturing and submissive; "phlegmatic, compliant, equable, and accepting" (Downey et al. 1989). Thus, though deficient in the typically feminine physique, TS women exhibit behavior that may be aptly described as "hyper-feminine."

A different kind of hyper-femininity occurs in males with androgen-insensitivity syndrome (AIS). Grounded in a sex-linked recessive gene, AIS desensitizes neural tissue to the effect of male sex steroids during embryonic development. The result is genotypic males (XY) who develop along a markedly feminine pathway. AIS individuals possess undescended testes that produce normal amounts of testosterone; however, because their neural receptors are insensitive to this steroid, normal male development is short-circuited. At the same time, the release of testosterone inhibits the development of internal female reproductive organs, although normal external female sexual traits (clitoris, labia, vagina) are present (Money et al. 1985). These individuals are hyper-feminine in several respects. One study reports that they score lower on visuo-spatial tasks than do their male and female relatives (Imperato-McGinley et al. 1991). As children they play "primarily with dolls and other girls' toys," and they daydream about future lives as wives, home-makers, and mothers. As they grow older, they have "a positive and genuine interest in infant care," despite their sterility. In fact, when they rear adopted children, they prove to be "good mothers." They al-most invariably report themselves to be fully content with the female role, to prefer feminine clothing, and to have a strong interest in per-sonal adornment. They also tend to describe their sexual practices as "conservative" and "passive" (Money and Ehrhardt 1972: 111–12).

To an extent, the obverse of AIS is the condition of congenital adre-nal hyperplasia. CAH can afflict both males and females, and stems from a genetic flaw that disables the mechanisms allowing the adrenal cortex to synthesize cortisol, a stress hormone. CAH individuals se-crete unusually large doses of testosterone. In males, one effect is an earlier than average appearance of the secondary sex characteristics. Females exhibit more pronounced consequences, amounting to some masculinization of the genitalia (e.g., an enlarged clitoris and labia fu-sion) and brain anatomy. In both sexes, behavior is more male-oriented. CAH young girls, for example, are described as more tomboyish; they report less interest in doing "girl things" (e.g., babysitting or playing with dolls); and, as they grow older, they are less interested in getting married and raising a family (Dittman et al. 1991; Nass and Baker 1991; Berenbaum and Hines 1992).

There are various sexual anomalies. The last to be noted here poses particular difficulties for researchers who insist that maleness and fe-maleness are exclusively the product of gendered socialization and cul-tural experiences. The condition in question is known as 5 alpha-reductase deficiency, and stems from a recessive gene that ap-pears in some small, intermarrying human populations. It has been es-pecially well-studied in three rural villages in the Dominican Republic (Imperato-McGinley et al. 1979). The enzyme that gives name to the condition is essential for synthesizing dihydrotestosterone (DHT). In male embryos, DHT is responsible for masculinizing the external geni-talia but plays no role in the masculinization of the brain, that is, in sensitizing neural receptors to the later action of male sex steroids and in lateralizing brain anatomy. Lacking the enzyme for processing DHT, these individuals have, from birth to the onset of puberty, every external appearance of being females. In fact they are socialized to behave as girls. But at puberty, surprising anatomical developments take place. Copious amounts of testosterone are released. The testes descend. What was thought to be a clitoris enlarges into a penis, and all other typical features of male secondary sex characteristics emerge. And, because the fetal brain was unaffected by the condition, and developed in accordance with the process of masculinization, the escalation of androgen levels at puberty causes these "girls" to exhibit behaviors typical of boys.

Close study of the developmental histories of eighteen such individuals found that, despite some twelve years of socialization as girls, all but one successfully made the transition to manhood. The transition was not always easy; nevertheless, researchers concluded that "environmental or sociocultural factors are not solely responsible for the formation of a male-gender identity"; in fact, "it appears that the extent of androgen exposure of the brain in utero during the early postnatal period and at puberty has more effect in determining male-gender identity than does sex of rearing" (Imperato-McGinley et al. 1979: 1236).

This brief review of developmental anomalies only hints at the complex relations existing among genetic information, hormonal influences, anatomical development, and sex differences in behavior. Nevertheless, the evidence strongly suggests that "gendered" aspects of social behavior depend upon much more than merely the influence of patriarchy or other aspects of the sociocultural environment. However much socialization may condition sex-typical behavior, the fact remains that an individual's sex and sex-related behaviors are fundamentally biological phenomena which no amount of cultural conditioning is likely to override entirely.

The variable design features of male and female brains underlie variations in average psychological adaptations that serve the varying fitness interests of men and women. Precisely how the whole apparatus regulates sex-typical behavior is not yet fully understood. As better information appears, it may be expected to specify mechanisms of enormous complexity. But we need not wait for that day to recognize that, on average and across sociocultural environments, men and women behave differently especially, as the law of anisogamy states, when behavior is linked to reproductive strategies. Differential mating strategies commonly employed by men and women bear directly on their reproductive interests. And it is here that we observe some of the better documented differences between the sexes. The irony—and the great risk—is that they concern eminently sociological topics that are being given away, self-destructively, by sociologists themselves.

Mating Strategies

"Beauty is in the eye of the beholder." Moreover, there is reason to believe that, just as men and women possess different brains, they have different eyes as well. For the plain fact is that, on average, men and women are attentive to distinctive sets of traits in their mutual assessment of attractiveness. To some degree, sexual attraction tends toward what behavior geneticists call "assortative mating" (Karlin 1969; Wright 1969; Crow and Kimura 1970). This phenomenon, whereby "like attracts like," is well-documented, and involves any number of social and physical characteristics (e.g., Thiessen and Gregg 1980; Collins and Coltrane 1991; Diamond 1992: chap. 5, 375–76). Of special interest to us are the widespread and enduring differences in mating strategies.

The two sexes enter the mating market with distinctive assets and debits and, driven by ancient strategies, seek to strike the best available bargain, weighing the strengths and weaknesses of prospective mates against each other and their own as well. "Women should be selected for rating men in large part by the reproductively relevant resources these control" (Lopreato 1984: 328). Accordingly, women are more inclined than men to value evidence of a mate's resource holding potential and his willingness to invest in their offspring. Men, by contrast, have a greater bias toward physically attractive mates. Cross-cultural studies of sexual behavior in hundreds of primarily non-Western and nonurban societies reveal this recurrent theme. Women more than men emphasize status characteristics of prospective mates, while men, more than women, value aspects of physical appearance (Ford and Beach 1951; Gregersen 1982). This is a rich and growing area of study (e.g., Symons 1979; Diamond 1992; Ellis 1992; Ridley 1993; Buss 1994a, 1994b; Wright 1994).

How Many Sex Partners?

On average, men are more promiscuous than women. For example, young American men indicate preferences for a larger number of sex partners over a range of specified time periods. When asked to enumerate their ideal number of sex partners over the next six months, they report an average preference for about three partners, in contrast to the women's average of one. Over the course of their lifetime, the average ideal number of partners for men is about eighteen, whereas for women the corresponding figure is only four or five partners (Buss and Schmidt 1993: 210–12). Such responses, along with related evidence, buttress the claim that the "human species can...be said to be pair-bonding with a significant polygynous option and tendency" (Konner 1982: 274).

Differences in stated preferences dovetail with reported differences in actual sexual behavior. According to a recent national survey of American adults, for example, 5.1 percent of men reported five or more sexual partners during the past year; the corresponding percentage for women was 1.7. For the past five years, 7.5 percent of men reported having had eleven or more partners, in contrast to 1.8 percent for women. Asked about the number of sexual partners since reaching eighteen years of age, 16.6 percent of men reported over 20 partners, while only 3.2 percent of women matched such wealth of experience (Laumann et al. 1994: 177–79; see also Klassen et al. 1989; Turner et al. 1989). This sex difference is revealed even by studies of sexual fantasies. A recent study of 307 American college students inquired as follows: "Considering your sexual fantasies throughout the course of your life, do you think that in your imagination you have had sexual encounters with over 1,000 different people?" Four times as many men (32 percent) responded affirmatively to the question as did women (8 percent) (Ellis and Symons 1990: Table 1).

Clearly, men value quantity. The fact, like others accompanying it, is predictable from the condition of anisogamy, and hence from sexual selection and parental investment theory. Males are bearers of countless sex cells and, correspondingly, are under more hormonal pressure to seek sexual opportunities. For example, more than six times as many American men (21.3 percent) as women (3.4 percent) report that they lost their virginity to someone with whom they were not well-acquainted, including strangers and prostitutes (Laumann et al. 1994: 329). Another study emphatically underscores the sex difference in question. On an American college campus, research-prompted (and attractive) males and females approached opposite-sex strangers and remarked: "I have been noticing you around campus. I find you very attractive." They then randomly asked one of three questions: "Would you go out with me tonight?" "Would you come over to my apartment tonight?" "Would you go to bed with me tonight?" Among the women, about one-half agreed to a date, only 6 percent agreed to visit the man's apartment, and *none* consented to the unadorned request for sex. Among men, about the same percentage agreed to a date with the interviewer. But, in marked contrast to women, nearly 70 percent agreed to visit her apartment, and even more, about 75 percent, agreed to have sex with her (Clark and Hatfield 1989; see also Buss and Schmidt 1993: 210–12; Bailey et al. 1994). Of course such facts jibe nicely with the assumption of patriarchy and its corollary, the socially constructed sexual double standard. There is, however, a slight problem with the assumption. As we have seen, the facts also accord with evolutionary forces that account for patriarchy in the first place, so that the facts may be taken as descriptive of a patriarchal system, not as effects of it in itself.

We should note here that Americans are not unique in the above respects, a fact that underscores the necessity not to take patriarchy as given. In a sample of 853 pre-industrial societies, polygyny was the preferred or accepted practice in 83.5 percent of them (Murdock 1967). One must be careful, of course, to distinguish what is acceptable in principle from what is common in practice. Marriages in nearly all societies are most commonly monogamous. Although men may harbor a polygynous tendency, sexual selection and hypergyny in themselves suggest that the inclination is subject to formidable control. Other factors, too, govern it to a considerable extent. Among the !Kung, for example, one observer (Lee 1984: 79) notes that polygyny "is allowed and men desire it," but the wives in general oppose it. !Kung women prefer mates who are able and willing to commit emotional and material resources exclusively to them and their offspring. The polygynous inclinations of !Kung men are thus thwarted by the monogamous preferences of women, as both evolutionary theory and feminist theory would predict, with a difference. If women check, they do not checkmate. Of 131 married !Kung men studied by Lee (1984), seven practiced polygyny. These were regarded as especially skilled in the healing arts, a competence that conferred unusually high prestige. Another researcher estimates that, at any given time, about 5 percent of !Kung marriages are polygynous (Shostak 1981). Similarly, about 15 percent of men among the Aka pygmies are estimated to have multiple wives (Hewlett 1988). It must be noted, however, that these percentage variations in themselves may be misleading. Far more significant is information that is less readily obtainable, namely the percentage of women who willingly participate in polygynous arrangements.

The polygynous tendency is subject to restraint in view of various conditions. Where, for example, great wealth and power are concentrated in the hands of relatively few males, the tendency is both intense and uncommon. In part aided by female choice, the mighty easily deprive many among the mass of men. In turn, greater variation in male status may stimulate competition among women to attract high-status men (Hooks and Green 1993), but these may be numerous enough to check polygyny to varying extents. At any rate, it "appears that when resources and custom permit, men tend toward polygyny, and when any factor (e.g. health, resources) makes some men much better mates than others, women too can profit reproductively from polygyny" (Low 1988a: 122; see also Josephson 1993). Polygyny and hypergyny are complementary strategies (Dickemann 1979a, 1979b; Betzig 1986, 1988, 1993a).

The fitness benefits accruing to polygamous males have been amply documented across a range of societal types (e.g., for horticultural societies: Chagnon 1979, 1980, 1983; Chagnon et al. 1979; for pastoralist societies: Borgehoff Mulder 1988; Cronk 1991; and for a wide variety of agrarian societies: Dickemann 1979a, 1979b; Jeffrey 1979; Hartung 1982; Mealey 1985; Betzig 1986, 1993a; Hrdy 1990; Smuts 1995). We may add that polygyny and hypergyny are ancient evolutionary phenomena that concern not only the family institution but the entire institutional framework. In chapter 8, for example, we shall see that they are among the fundamentals of human stratification systems.

The very rare instances of polyandry are also amenable to explanation along the lines of fitness theory. Where resources are extremely scarce, one man may be unable to support a wife and her children. This condition appears to underlie polyandrous practices observed in some Tibetan communities (van den Berghe 1979; Crook and Crook 1988). Although diminishing in frequency over the past fifty years, owing to improved economic opportunities for men, a not uncommon marital practice involves two brothers eking out a rough existence by herding yaks in desolate ecosystems and sharing one wife. The wife and offspring are thereby in an improved position to obtain the needed resources for survival. But the arrangement is not ideal for either man. Junior husbands would prefer to acquire sufficient resources to enable them to establish an independent union. Nevertheless, sharing one wife is better, from the vantage point of the co-husbands' fitness interests, than having no wife at all. As a minimum, fraternal co-husbands practice kin selection. They may be reasonably certain that their parental efforts are directed toward their nieces and nephews if not toward their own progeny. Polyandry and kin selection go together.

TABLE 6.2
Select Types of Sex Variations in Partner Preferences

Trait Domain	Male Preferences	Female Preferences
Personality		
	Highly value intelligence	Highly value intelligence
	Highly value kindness	Highly value kindness
	Value emotional stability less	Value emotional stability more
	Value sexual faithfulness more	Value sexual faithfulness less
	Value emotional faithfulness less	Value emotional faithfulness more
Physical Characteristics		
	Value younger mates	Value moderately older mates
	Value average height and weight	Value above average height and weight
	Value physical appearance more	Value physical appearance less
	Value clear complexion more	Value clear complexion less
	Value symmetrical face more	Value symmetrical face less
	Value firm muscle tone more	Value firm muscle tone less
Social Status		
	Less attentive to mate's social status	More attentive to mate's social status
	Less attentive to financial prospects	More attentive to financial prospects
	Less attentive to prestige markers	More attentive to prestige markers

Note: Table constructed on the basis of information from various sources cited in the text.

Desirable Personality Characteristics

Among the many characteristics that men and women value in a prospective mate (see table 6.2), intelligence and kindness rank very high (Buss 1989, 1994a, 1994b). On average, more intelligent partners are more adept at securing resources, planning for the future, and, among other things, evaluating the costs and benefits of various courses of action concerning household problems. Kind people are likely to treat their mates and offspring with respect and love. Beyond these and some other general similarities, certain personality features appear to be differentially valued by men and women. Women, more than men, stress signs of a mate's love and emotional commitment, his ability and willingness to express affection and compassion (Howard et al. 1987). These facts are consistent with women's heavier investment in offspring and the related desire to secure the resources necessary for successful child rearing. We might predict, therefore, that they are more likely than men to demand some evidence of emotional commitment prior to escalating relationships to the sexual level. The statement is supported by a variety of facts, some previously encountered. American women, for example, are twice as likely as men (roughly 50 percent vs. 25 percent) to report feelings of affection for their first sexual partner (Laumann et al. 1994: 329); and, unlike men, they almost never lose their virginity with a stranger. Women are also favorably impressed by men who reveal good paternal features, such as playfulness with small children (Remoff 1984; Buss and Barnes 1986).

Men's attention is captured by rather different traits. Especially when considering a possible long-term partner, men appear to be alert to the promise of fidelity. As previously noted, paternal uncertainty figures as a major force in the male reproductive psychology. Thus, men may be expected to be keen to cues that enhance paternal confidence. It follows that, while males typically reveal a readiness for "sexual conquest," they may, ironically, be most attracted to those who foil such lustful haste.

Cues are by definition subtle and thus vulnerable to mechanisms of deception. But some cues, such as perservering signs of love and affection, are more reliable than others. A willingness to marry, for example, is a fair measure of a woman's likely fidelity. Chastity is an even better cue, and in many human societies evidence of premarital chastity appears to be taken as a sign of a woman's future fidelity. A cross-cultural study by D. Buss (1989) shows that men value chastity in prospective long-term mates more highly than women do; on this point the sex difference is most pronounced in less economically developed societies. Nevertheless, where a sex difference is found, it is always in the expected direction—men value chastity in a bride more than women value chastity in a groom (see also van den Berghe 1979; Daly and Wilson 1983).

The premium placed on premarital chastity makes good evolutionary sense from the male's point of view, at least in view of expected male monogamy, where paternal investment is relatively high. Moreover, past behavior is likely to be considered a reliable predictor of future behavior. A young woman who is promiscuous prior to marriage stands a chance of being viewed as a poor marriage risk in comparison to a "good girl." Recent developments seem, however, to have weakened men's stress on female chastity. In industrial societies, for instance, men do not appear to place a very high value on virgin brides. Many changes have undermined to a degree the traditional male stress on female chastity, and in this context we find an excellent illustration of the interaction principle. Changes in sociocultural conditions—for example, the development of reliable contraceptive technologies and improved economic opportunities for women—interact with the fitness maximization tendency to modify male mating strategies. Given modern conditions, men who desire to find a wife must often control their longstanding preference for a virgin bride. The alternative might be no wife at all. The feminist focus on culture, we reiterate, is not entirely misguided; it is just excessive and myopic. It is sexual fidelity, not sexual history, that is, and must be, the primary concern of modern men. In a recent survey of American men, "faithfulness and sexual loyalty emerged as the most highly valued traits" in a prospective mate (Buss 1994a: 69). Does this psychology solve the ancient problem of paternal uncertainty? Probably not, but then that is the lot of the courting sex, and his brain is not inflexible, though it is not a slave to culture, either.

Men's preferences for chaste and faithful mates varies somewhat depending on whether the search is for short-term or long-term mates. Traits deemed to be attractive in prospective wives—for example, wanting a commitment, lacking extensive sexual experience, exhibiting signs of faithfulness and chastity—are de-emphasized by men seeking a more casual sexual relationship (Buss and Schmidt 1993: 213, 217). Indeed, given the ancient polygynous whisper, men may even be expected to value some evidence of promiscuity in short-term mates; it facilitates philandering at little or no cost to the philanderer. When men, however, are considering long-term mates, the focus shifts toward personality traits that may enhance potential paternal confidence, among other things.

The Relative Appeal of Physical and Status Cues

Women on average prefer to marry men who are somewhat older, usually about three years their senior (Harrison and Saeed 1977; Buss 1989; Bailey et al. 1994). The fact may indicate that women perceive age as a proxy for access to resources. Above average size and strength as well as signs of good health are also valued highly. In human evolution, a man's physical prowess has most probably signaled greater than average ability to secure food and safe haven. On the whole, we may hypothesize, the size of the male has long been an indicator of his power and status. On this issue, female psychology does not appear to have changed much. The evidence is strong that in industrial societies above average height is correlated with higher status in men (Gillis 1982; Handwerker and Crosbie 1982). In addition, women tend to find tall men particularly appealing (e.g., Beigel 1954; Graziano et al. 1978; Gillis and Avis 1980), and they are also attracted to men who exhibit various nonverbal signs of social dominance (Sadalla et al. 1987).

The emphasis on physical characteristics in potential mates is even stronger among men, though in different directions. They prefer women who are younger than they are, and apparently the fact has deep evolutionary roots. In his description of sexual behavior among the Trobriand Islanders, for example, Malinowski (1929: 524) noted that sexual intercourse with an old woman was regarded by men as "indecorous, ludicrous, and unaesthetic." Indeed, the bias has every appearance of being a human universal (Buss 1989), though to a lesser degree than Malinowski's language might suggest. A woman's fecundity peaks a few years after her menarche; thereafter it declines steadily. Hence, given fitness theory, the preference for younger women is ultimately consistent with men's reproductive interests. Variations in the preferred age-gap over the course of the male life cycle bear on this point. As men grow older, the desired age difference increases. Young men— say, those in their twenties—typically prefer to marry women who are about three years younger; men in their thirties have a preference for women who are about five years younger; and men in their fifties prefer women who are ten to twenty years younger than themselves (Kenrick and Keefe 1992; Buss 1994a: 52). The opportunities to act on these preferences are only heightened, as we shall see in the next chapter, by such factors as increased contact between men and women in the work place and by the increasing frequency of casual sex in industrial society.

The male desire for physically attractive mates is manifested in a variety of contexts (e.g., Jones and Hill 1993; Singh 1993a, 1993b, 1993c; Thornhill and Gangestad 1993). One of the most common in modern society concerns personals advertisements in newspapers and magazines. An example from the "In Search Of" (ISO) section of the *Washingtonian*, a monthly magazine geared toward upscale adults in the metropolitan region of the District of Columbia, illustrates the point:

ATTRACTIVE AND ADVENTUROUS SWM [Single White Male], 34, tall, fit & handsome, financially secure, sincere & warmhearted with a wide variety of interests seeking SWF [Single White Female], 21–30, attractive, intelligent & passionate to share friendship/relationship leading to happy marriage & children. Please enclose photo (April 1997: 176).

The advertisement reveals a crucial theme of the human mating song. As we have emphasized, men trade heavily on their resource assets in exchange for younger, physically attractive women. Conversely, young and attractive women succeed more frequently than their less attractive competitors in marrying high-status men (Elder 1969; Taylor and Glenn 1976; Udry and Eckland 1984). Moreover, men and women seem to have a keen discernment of what potential mates appreciate. According to samples of American college students and newlyweds, young men are especially apt to brag about and/or display their resources (e.g., expensive cars and stereos, spending money freely, career success, etc.). By contrast, young women are more likely to enhance their physical and youthful appearance by wearing make-up, perfume, and stylish clothes; dieting to improve their figures; sunbathing; and the like (Buss 1988).

For purposes of illustration, we again quote an advertisement placed in the *Washingtonian*. By no means intended as representative of the types of ads found in this publication, it nevertheless suggests vividly the emphasis of the typical case.

STRIKING REFINED STUDENT ISO MILLIONAIRE BENEFACTOR: A Gorgeous Trophy, graceful, coquettish, brilliant, gourmet, athletic, French WF [White Female], 25, with discriminating taste and groomed to perfection with a pampered SVELTE BODY. I have beautiful flowing hair and silky soft skin. I am a savvy, cautious, struggling student with Beverly Hills taste. ISO a dapper, debonair, loyal and EXTREMELY GENEROUS 50+ WM [White Male], D&D [Disease and Drug] FREE to be my MENTOR and best friend. I am the perfect escort, companion and confidante. We deserve the best in life. Let's travel to exotic ports and I will dazzle you with my mind and my beauty. Possible LTR [Lifetime Romance]. Send business card and photo. Serious responses only please (April 1997: 171).

Such scenarios illustrate rather eloquently the sex-differentiated reproductive strategies. As D. Thiessen and his associates (1993) have put it, "lonely hearts advertisements reflect sexually dimorphic mating strategies." Social psychological studies reveal that women express a strong concern for the man's status at all levels of romantic involvement, and this focus escalates along with increasing degrees of prospective emotional commitment (Townsend and Levy 1990a).

There are, of course, variations across societies. Women's desire for men with high resource-holding potential or good financial prospects is less pronounced in economically more developed societies, although even there men and women follow the general rule fairly closely. In light of such findings, many social scientists argue that as women gain greater educational, occupational, and economic opportunities, this sex difference may diminish, or perhaps even disappear (e.g., Coombs and Kenkel 1966; Rosenblatt 1974; Murstein 1980; Dion 1981). But there is contrary evidence (Buss and Schmidt 1993) on this so-called structural powerlessness hypothesis. For example, the medical profession in the U.S. affords women outstanding opportunities for high earnings and economic independence (Baker 1996). And yet, female medical students express a strong desire for a marriage partner who has earnings and occupational prestige greater than or at least equal to their own (Townsend 1989). Again, there is an irony here for gender feminists and perhaps for women in industrial societies in general. They may understandably object to the persistence of male domination. But women's mating strategies encourage men to continue striving for high rank, the very thing that makes them especially attractive to women.

In closing, we have touched upon only a few of the many facts and clues that, taken together, point to the evolutionary foundations of basic sex differences in behavior. Discoveries in various fields—for example, neuroanatomy, endocrinology, psychiatry, and neuropsychology—reveal differences in the structure and functioning of male and female brains and corresponding differences in aspects of human sensation, cognition, and emotion. In addition, evidence from ethnography, social psychology, and comparative sociology forcefully suggests that universal sex differences in mating strategies and related behavioral predispositions are closely connected with these underlying differences in brain anatomy and physiology. Further, these disparities are amenable to partial but fundamental explanation in terms of a variety of psychological adaptations and the various features of fitness theory. Such tools facilitate the organization of information and a more complete explanation of it. They, along with an abundance of supporting facts, also challenge core assumptions harbored by many sociologists, especially those who advocate extreme feminist perspectives.

7

An Uneasy Alliance

In the absence of a deeply historical, evolutionary perspective, the sociology of "sex roles" will continue to stray very far from a productive grasp of subject matter. Radical feminist theorists in particular will necessarily settle on banalities about "gendered social space" and the fantasy of a "revolution for themselves." While they recognize what evolutionists metaphorically term the battle of the sexes (Dawkins 1989: chap. 9), they are busy condemning "the enemy" instead of trying to understand the profound causes of the battle and thereby contribute with scholarly policy toward its mitigation. One is reminded of the medicine men of old who sweated endless hours in vain attempts to expel with incantations the evil spirit that had possessed the diseased body.

In fact, for many radical feminists science is not about explaining phenomena. "Feminism," writes one of them (Haraway 1988: 589–90), "loves another science: the sciences and politics of interpretation, translation, stuttering, and the partly understood. Feminism…is about a critical vision consequent upon a critical position in inhomogenous [sic] gendered social space." From this perspective, statements of explanation, writes another such author (Rogers 1998: 7), must respond to "healing," "liberatory," and "revolutionary criteria."

Bent on revolution, one writer reviews the "Soviet solution" to the woman question and is led to conclude that in the last analysis it went the way of "most capitalist countries, by reinforcing the gendered division of labor that communist ideology originally questioned"(Lorber 1994: 270). She next delves into the Chinese case and notes that, while communist ideology was auspicious for women's rights, reality again went awry, producing widespread poverty, serfdom, prostitution: "Few women emerged as leaders for women's issues after the revolution…. Even young women who had not been tainted by sexual immorality were vilified" (Lorber 1994: 275). Quoting M.B. Young (1989: 241), she immediately adds: "Iron girls were unwomanly, unmarriageable, unattractive, in short, 'false boys.'" In due course, this author (Lorber 1994: 277—emphasis added) takes notice of China's one-child policy and indignantly complains: "The result is that Chinese girls, because of the continuing *cultural* preference for boys, are now disappearing by the millions—aborted, killed in infancy...," and so forth. We share the indignation. But why this "cultural" preference for boys? How do we know that the preference is unqualifiedly cultural? Might it not help to inquire about the evolutionary logic for sex preferences in children and how such preferences vary according to several factors, including the socioeconomic status of the parents (e.g., Trivers and Willard 1973; Dickemann 1979a, 1979b; Cronk 1991)?

"For women, all revolutions have failed" (Lorber 1994: 277). This is the final and convincing verdict. Hence, by now, one would hope that this proponent of women's rights has caught on to something—that she is ready to consider stubborn causes of stubborn facts and thus to propose realistic remedies. But the hope is quickly dashed. After the litany of revolutionary failures to improve women's rights, she (1994: 280–81) is driven to ask: "What would it take for feminists to become significant players in a revolution?" The answer was presumably suggested by Antonio Gramsci. Before a group can win "government power," the famous revolutionary argued, it must already have exercised leadership. Accordingly, our esteemed colleague (1994: 281—emphasis added) offers the following prescription: "Rather than waiting for the next societal breakdown, feminists could start a revolution *for themselves* by developing the organizations, programs, and leadership for a state that is truly gender-neutral." Never mind the logic of this gender-neutral revolution for themselves. But how about naiveté? This revolution is quite unlikely to happen, and there are a couple of good reasons for our pessimism. One, the vast majority of women do not want—are not constituted—to march to the extreme beat of a feminist drum; ironically, the masses are better attuned to social realities. Two, men would strenuously resist such a revolution, whatever may be meant by it in the first place. This vision of a gender-neutral society represents a fantasy no less ludicrous than Marx's conception of a classless society.

Conflicts of interests between men and women are deep-rooted, but they also constitute a tenacious complementarity. The sexes are programmed to cooperate even as they are constituted to compete. The drama of our daily lives revolves around efforts to reconcile the conflicts and coincidences of such interests. Man and Woman are unsure actors on this stage, and too often their efforts fail. Whatever the immediate cause—disagreements regarding child rearing practices, household finances, activities in the market, and so forth—one party typically gains an advantage over the other. Exploitation is one of the main themes of the drama; and men, given the ancient effects of sexual selection, tend to be the more aggressive players in the contest. Male exploitation, expressed in varying degrees of intensity, is a universal fact (Goldberg 1973; Smuts 1995; Hrdy 1997), though it is not necessarily an unmitigated blessing for men. Suffice it to note that, contrary to popular wisdom, the male is the more frail organism and across the life cycle is more readily susceptible to disease, trauma, and death (e.g., Trivers 1985: chap. 12; Carey and Lopreato 1995a).

Exploitation is not exempt from mitigating factors. But sex-related asymmetries of power and privilege are evident in numberless arenas of the social life: the labor market, community affairs, the court of law, household labor, even the house of God, among endless other contexts. Sociologists have been keen to these facts, and their inquiries have not been for naught. Rarely, however, have they penetrated the surface of proximate and often fleeting cultural correlates. In this chapter we shall explore several topics that illustrate how the two sexes are sometimes at odds with each other. For the most part, the focus will be on industrial society, for this has been of the greatest interest to sociologists. On each subject there is an extensive literature in sociology alone. Our goal cannot be a thorough review. In keeping with the aims of the volume as a whole, we limit ourselves to analysis sufficient to reveal behavioral uniformities that reflect the action of sex-differentiated psychological adaptations as well as various aspects of culture and socialization.

Marriage, Divorce, and Remarriage

Perhaps the principal act of the human drama focuses on the complex game surrounding the marriage contract. The energies invested and the tactics adopted to attract and secure a partner are associated with some of the more intense instances of joy and disappointment in our daily lives. As a cultural invention, marriage typically sets rules that to a degree defy the forces inherent in anisogamy, differential parental investment, and sexual selection. As a result, marriage constitutes a complex and potentially fragile relationship. While the pair-bond often lasts many years, even a lifetime, either or both parties may occasionally participate in extramarital liasons and eventually may even leave the union altogether. The inclination to cheat, cut the knot, and remarry is lively. Moreover, since men typically make the lesser parental investment, they are the more likely to cheat—and thus to intensify already latent discord.

Marriage

A major preoccupation of social scientists in recent years has been to explain the recent decline in marriage rates in Western industrial societies, especially in the U.S. The factors involved in this trend appear to be numerous (Easterlin 1987; Cherlin 1992), though among its more immediate correlates are an increase in the age at first marriage and an increasing rate of cohabitation among young adults. Nevertheless, 80–95 percent of adults in industrial societies marry at least once (Ahlburg and DeVita 1992; Goode 1993). Marriage is a universal institution, and there is reason to think that in most cases the partners enter the contract motivated by love, affection, and every intention to practice the strictest loyalty. And yet there are probably few contexts in the human condition where the influence of ancient biological forces is more overwhelming. Rule of monogamy notwithstanding, polygamy often asserts itself through various devices, preeminently extramarital affairs and of course divorce followed by remarriage. And for reasons noted in chapters 5 and 6, the polygamous tendency is predictably more powerful among men than among women.

Sociologists are quick to emphasize the adverse consequences of the polygynous tendency on women. Cheating husbands all too often abscond, leaving their wives to fend for themselves and their children. It bears noting, however, that some men pay a steep price for their sex's polygynous inclination, both in terms of emotional well-being and in terms of the organism's ultimate evolutionary currency. For example, fewer men than women ever marry. This pattern is uniform across industrial societies (Goode 1993), and appears to be even more pronounced in primitive and more traditional societies (e.g., Dickemann 1979a, 1979b; Irons 1979; Betzig 1986). Hence, unqualified claims regarding male exploitation and polygamy must sound rather curious to those men who never find a marriageable mate.

The advent of socially imposed monogamy and, in more recent centuries, the expansion of the middle classes may have enabled men to compete for mates on a fairly level playing field (e.g., Vining 1986).

But how level is it? A study of French-Canadian men, for example, has revealed strong positive correlations "between [men's] social status and a measure of mating success that would translate directly into reproductive success were it not for contraception" (Pérusse 1993: 277). In short, the higher a man's status (i.e., level of educational attainment, occupational prestige, and income), the greater the number of reported sex partners and the greater the frequency of "coital acts." By relying on this measure of "mating success" (number of partners rather than number of offspring), Pérusse was able to demonstrate the persistence of an evolutionarily relevant payoff associated with male high status and, at least inferentially, of the hypergynous tendency in industrial societies as well.

Men exploit their partners, apparently to a greater degree than women exploit theirs. For example, they are more likely than women to report instances of their own adultery; and they are much more likely to report multiple adulteries. A 1992 survey of sexual behavior in the U.S. reveals that these patterns apply across age cohorts (Laumann et al. 1994). Among those born between 1933 and 1942 (thus encompassing a cohort of women who had aged through their childbearing years), nearly 23 percent of men, but only 8 percent of women, reported adulterous behavior during their first (and, for some, only) marriage. In the same age group, men (17.6 percent) were far more likely than women (1.3 percent) to report multiple extramarital affairs. Roughly similar patterns held in the cohorts born in 1943–1952, 1953–1962, and 1963–1974. There is some evidence in these facts that as age of respondents decreases, both the incidence of infidelity and the sex difference on it also decrease. Does this narrowing gap suggest that, as a result of expanding opportunities for women, men may be becoming more sensitive to their partners' interests and/or that women may be becoming more equally promiscuous? Both are possibilities. It should be noted, however, that younger respondents had been married for fewer years and, thus, had had less time or opportunity to seek warmth in another's nest. Moreover, despite the fact that in the youngest age cohort (18–29 years old) men and women were almost equally likely to report one adulterous liason (10 percent for young men; 7 percent for young women), men (5.6 percent) were still over three times more likely than women (1.8 percent) to have engaged in multiple liasons (Laumann et al. 1994: 208; cited figures adapted from table 5.9A).

The facts of sex relations can easily call forth the deepest emotions, and at a personal level it is hard not to welcome some feminist grievances. Consider that, while men are more likely to cheat on their spouses, it is the infidelities of wives, often only concocted, that more commonly result in formal charges of adultery. These are also more frequently met with severe punishment and/or divorce (Betzig 1989). A cross-cultural and historical study of adultery law reveals that almost generally adultery is a crime whose victim is the husband (Daly et al. 1982). The same study shows that in a city like Detroit male sexual jealousy is the leading cause of "social conflict homicides."

Sociologists typically attribute such abuses to a culturally prescribed sexual double standard. Again, this position cannot be rejected outright. It errs only to the extent that it represents half of the equation. The other half ultimately refers to a variety of evolutionary forces, for example, *paternal uncertainty*, that in the first place explain what is taken as given by sociologists, namely the double standard. As we noted in chapter 6, women know without fail that their offspring are their own. Thus their maternal investment unquestionably serves their fitness interests. Given concealed ovulation and internal fertilization, the same cannot be said of men. Male jealousy, an emotional response underlying many instances of brutal and baseless abuse of women, may be viewed as a psychological adaptation "designed" to reduce the probability of cuckoldry. The costs of male cuckoldry, after all, are severely recorded by natural selection, which is to say that living men are descendants of jealous men. A betrayed wife, on the other hand, risks loss of her mate's affection and resources, but her fitness interests are not threatened to the same degree by his cheating, at least not unless it threatens the lives of her offspring. Little wonder, as we noted in chapter 6, that women fear emotional desertion more than infidelity, whereas the reverse is true of men. The sexes thus appear to behave in accordance with evolutionary predictions in various ways. For example, prior to the advent of "no fault" divorce laws and the subsequent rapid rise in divorce rates, nearly twice as many American men (51 percent) as women (27 percent) cited their spouses' extramarital sexual activity as having "major significance" in their decision to divorce (Kinsey et al. 1953: 445, table 125). Ironically, sociologist Lenore Weitzman (1985) reports that no-fault divorce laws, instituted largely in response to feminist demand, have greatly benefited men economically while impoverishing their former spouses. Weitzman's study has been criticized for exaggerating this differential effect (Peterson 1996); nevertheless, the reanalysis of her data confirms the direction and the essential validity of her basic finding.

Divorce

Divorce rates in nearly all industrial societies have risen sharply over the past forty years, especially in the U.S. where divorces per 1,000 married women increased over 1,500 percent between 1960 (1.3) and 1988 (21.0) (Goode 1993: 139; see also Ahlburg and DeVita 1992; Cherlin 1992). Moreover, researchers estimate that 40–64 percent of all marriages taking place in 1985 will end in divorce or separation (Castro Martin and Bumpass 1989; Cherlin 1992; Goode 1993). Corresponding divorce rates for the same period are considerably lower in other industrial societies, ranging from 4.4 in Switzerland to 12.7 in England and Wales. But they are still considerable, and have increased dramatically in nearly all industrial societies (Goode 1993).

According to some studies (e.g., Glick 1992), the median duration of marriages ending in divorce in industrial societies is about seven years, coinciding with the famous "itch" (e.g., Glick 1992). According to evolutionary anthropologist Helen Fisher (1989), however, cross-national evidence on the modal duration of marriages reveals that divorces most commonly cluster at about the fourth year; "despite the varying traditions for marrying, the myriad worldwide opinions about divorce, and the diverse procedures for parting, men and women desert each other in a roughly common pattern." Marriage reveals a *"cross-cultural pattern of decay"* (Fisher 1992: 111–12—emphasis in original). Moreover, Fisher argues that this pattern suggests a reproductive strategy that is deeply embedded in our evolutionary heritage. Four years corresponds awfully closely to the length of time that forager mothers typically devoted to the intense nurturing of each child. It is not unreasonable to speculate, therefore, that selection pressures on our remote ancestors encouraged reproductive pair-bonds to remain together for about the length of time that was needed to nurture one child to relative independence. Once a child was weaned and able to carry on with some independence within the extended kin group, the pair's freedom to go their separate ways increased—or so the enduring tenuousness of young marriages would suggest.

Various factors are commonly cited by sociologists and others as underlying the trend toward higher divorce rates. They include changes in divorce law; physical and emotional abuse; discrepant backgrounds; increasing educational and occupational opportunities for women, presumably liberating them from economic reliance on men; and changing norms, which have lessened the stigma of the divorce (e.g., Heaton et al. 1985; Ahlburg and DeVita 1992). Some researchers emphasize more general factors: for example, the weakening of social integration in industrial societies (White 1990; Goode 1993). Thoroughly Durkheimian in flavor, the latter proposes that as societies grow in size and complexity, the social bonds between individuals and their groups—families, communities, societies—are necessarily loosened. Living in fragmented communities, people find it difficult to perceive the links between their self-interest and the interests of the larger group. As a result, selfish motives rise to the fore, while duty, loyalty, and commitment to social ties and community traditions are undermined. Inevitably, marriage bonds get caught up in this diffuse breakdown. Another set of factors concerns changes in women's presence in the labor market. A "more promising line of inquiry centers on the changes in women's roles" (Cherlin 1992: 48). After reviewing evidence regarding changing attitudes, changing laws, increasing availability of contraceptive technologies, and other alleged factors, Cherlin (1992: 62) concludes that the critical factor underlying recent "trends in marriage, divorce, and childbearing" appears to be "an increase over time in the proportion of married women who work outside the home."

Such facts and arguments afford a golden opportunity to stress the necessity of theoretical cooperation between sociology and evolutionary science. The explanatory appeal to constants—for example, natural selection and its ancillary statements of theory—is ill-suited to explain rhythmic phenomena within short spans of time, such as rises and falls in marriage and divorce rates. These are perturbations demanding inquiry into immediate, proximate dynamics. This tactic has been the sociological specialization. But the story and the science will be awfully fickle if the result fails to reveal regularities that transcend the ups and downs of time—regularities that respond to predictions feasible from more deeply historical viewpoints. Accordingly, to reiterate once again a basic point, it is not so much that sociological explanations are erroneous. It is rather that they are a bit myopic; they sacrifice the more comprehensive and logically structured explanation in favor of often fleeting details.

Let us grant, for example, that in recent times modern society has lost intensity of integration and that, once disintegrating factors were released, these could hardly have failed to have effects on family facts, including divorce rates. But why the loss of integration in the first place? Is it not possible that its alleged effects are in fact indications of vulnerabilities in the social contracts, including marriage, that constitute societal integration? The question of what is cause and what is effect now becomes awfully murky. Indeed, what seems to be effect may well be cause. To an extent, the enormity of the complexity can be reduced if we can make successful predictions from an established general principle.

Suppose we focus on age in relation to the inclination to file for divorce. The facts show that women are more likely than men to petition for divorce, and this tendency is "inversely proportional to their age. Indeed, virtually all of the divorces granted before age 20 [are] initiated by women" (Buckle et al. 1996: 367–68, fig. 2). These findings are concordant with evolutionary theory. Specifically, the theory of differentiatal parental investment predicts that the younger the wife, the more adaptive it is for her, given cause, to seek a divorce. Her reproductive potential varies inversely with age. If the husband turns out to be nonreproductive or otherwise a "loser," she does not have many years left to undo her mistake by changing husbands. The reproductive strategy of the male is quite different. His reproductive potential lasts a much longer time. Hence, theory predicts, and Buckle et al. (1996) confirm, that divorces initiated by males increase as their age increases, that is, as their chances of remarrying with much younger women increase.

In a related vein, if, as we have seen, divorce rates in industrial society have risen sharply in recent decades, we should be able to successfully predict that they have escalated most sharply among the youngest couples, on the assumption that divorce is at least in part a result of error in mating strategy. We are reasoning now without regard to gender. Divorce makes most sense, in evolutionary terms, when possible errors of mismatch can be most easily rectified with the least risk of loss in fitness success (e.g., Fisher 1992: 112–14). Indeed, the facts show that in the U.S., for example, the divorce rate per 1,000 married women in the period 1970–1987 was highest among couples aged 15–24, and had the steepest rise in this same age group (Glick 1992: 1192, fig. 2).

To return to the question of reduced societal integration, we may not be able to explain with any certainty this historical transformation but, in view of the two examples given just above, we certainly are in a position to argue that, once the disintegration was set off, certain effects followed that respond to predictions from evolutionary theory. This perspective, moreover, suggests that there has been an interplay between sociocultural changes and changes in divorce rates. The precipitating factors may very well be most easily grasped in sociocultural terms, for example in terms of technological innovations that had repercussions for the fabric of the sociocultural system. But such innovations cannot be conceived exclusively in terms of, say, extensions of preexisting science and technology. They are also mental phenomena rooted in neurobiological properties (e.g., Pareto 1916: especially sections 972–75; Findlay and Lumsden 1988; Lopreato 1988). Further, the loosening of the marriage bond cannot be attributed exclusively to sociocultural factors. Like it or not, ultimately marriage is a reproductive contract; it has certainly evolved out of a reproductive alliance. If, therefore, it has weakened in keeping with an enfeeblement of the overall social contract, it is hard to escape the conclusion that it is fundamentally a precarious bond in the first place. The biology-culture interplay cannot be avoided without the risk of initiating chains of explanations that are rooted in a theoretical vacuum: for example, the weakening of social integration.

It bears stressing that sociological research often supports this biocultural perspective, although, with rare exceptions, only by unintended implication. For instance, several years ago, L. Margolin and L. White (1987) published an informative study on the differential role of physical attractiveness in marriage. Early in the report, the authors note: "Gender stereotypes suggest that males place more importance on the physical appearance of their sexual partners than females do" (Margolin and White 1987: 21). Noting, too, that men generally prefer mates who are younger and that this preferred age difference increases as men grow older, these scholars (1987: 22) add: "It is difficult to account for this preference for younger women by any means other than the importance which males place on the youthful good looks of their partners." They proceed to review research on the topic and even consider, in passing, the possibility that underlying biological factors may participate in the expression of these sex differences. But it is not hard to see where their preferences lie. Thus "the sociocultural perspective takes as its starting point the belief that people do not respond to their world in some automatic, predetermined way." Rather, "people's sexual preferences result from an elaborate normative superstructure that informs perceptions and gives meaning to the things we do." In short, to understand the problem in question "we must examine the cultural prescriptions and meanings associated with gender role behavior" (Margolin and White 1987: 22).

The report provides considerable evidence from previous research that "beautiful women...trade their looks for economic status in cross-gender relationships" and that "as couples age, husbands are more likely than wives to lose sexual interest in their spouses" (Margolin and White 1987: 22–23). All told, their own data analysis adds to this body of facts by demonstrating, however exploratively, that the "declining physical attractiveness of their partner affects marital sexuality more for men than women" (Margolin and White 1987: 26).

The unanswered question is why the differential? The Margolin-White study, which we have chosen at random from a fairly large set of admirable sociological reports, is only inches away from a productive linkage to the current revolution in behavioral science. And this is one source of our lingering hope for a durable and vigorous sociological future. It would be unthinkable to deny that the normative superstructure bears in various ways on sexual behavior. But however great this effect, the Margolin-White findings are easily predictable from evolutionary theory, for example, sexual selection and parental investment. What is especially interesting is that the effect is not even greater, and that most probably underscores the importance of cultural factors. We have already provided the relevance of such evolutionary theory on several occasions. Sexual selection implies a male philandering tendency, that is, a polygynous inclination, just as it implies a female tendency toward hypergyny associated with greater loyalty to the union in the nest.

So, it is erroneous and wasteful to tie the male's greater emphasis on physical appearance to "gender stereotypes." On the other hand, while it seems reasonable to view women as inclined to trade their good looks for economic status, it is erroneous to attribute such behavior to cultural prescriptions. This is a maimed explanation, for it leaves the existence of such cultural prescriptions unexplained. They cannot have emerged *ex nihilo*. What are sociologists afraid of? Consider that the findings here in question not only cry to be linked to a powerful, well-established, interdisciplinary theory. They also belong to a large and growing class of explained discoveries about male-female relations, for example, courtship rituals, age difference at first marriage, differential rates of marriage and remarriage, differential relations to children, differential rates of infidelity, variety of sex partners, and a huge number of other observations, including such a seemingly far removed fact as child abuse by stepfathers. This is systematic, cumulative, nomologically anchored knowledge. There is no longer any need for incoherence in sociology.

One of the more attractive proximate explanations of rising divorce rates takes into account the increased participation of women in the labor force. S.J. South and K.M. Lloyd (1995: 33—emphasis in original; see also Cherlin 1992: 48), for example, have been led to state that "women's labor force participation may increase *married men's* propensity to seek a divorce by increasing the probability that men will find a more attractive alternative to their current wife." The authors suggest that women's labor force participation increases (1) rates of social interaction and (2) the age at which women marry, "thereby expanding the pool of unmarried women, and thus the supply of alternative spouses available to married men." All of this "anchors the study of marital dissolution in…social structure" (South and Lloyd 1995: 33).

As our argument in chapter 3 suggested, we are now back to the "science of social switches." Left unaddressed are the forces that social-structural switches modulate. But despite this formidable sociological hurdle, and the possibility that some feminists will view the study as yet another case of "blaming the victim," the South-Lloyd study is representative of the best that today's sociological research has to offer. The reason for this judgment lies not only in the high quality of attention to methodological desiderata but also in the fact that, like the Margolin-White study, this one could very easily have been executed from a thoroughly evolutionary perspective, and thus have achieved a far more complete explanation.

As it is, the researchers merely pierce the surface of their correlations. Moreover, they miss at least one intriguing sex difference showing up in the data. Their broader claim is that "the risk of marital disruption is greater when *either* husbands or wives encounter a relatively sizable quantity of alternatives to their current spouse" (South and Lloyd 1995: 31—emphasis added). But surely this sex-neutral prediction is a slip of the tongue, so to speak. All one needs to consider, to see the error, is that prior to the *increased* women's participation in the labor force, women encountered quite a "sizable quantity of alternatives to their current spouse." And yet, divorce rates were then lower. The increasing presence of women in the workplace, however, has altered especially the mating habits of *men*. This sex-differentiated outcome cannot be grasped by reference to a sex-neutral prediction. But such sociological predictions are hard to avoid in the absence of a nomological anchor. Remember: on average and ultimately, women have less to gain from promiscuous behavior, and thus are *less likely* than men to be tempted by whatever quantity of alternatives.

South and Lloyd's findings in fact are much more compatible with predictions derived from sexual selection theory than with social structure, whatever is meant by the term. While powerfully motivated to enter into pair-bond relationships, men and women nevertheless remain alert to other sexual opportunities, although, as Darwin (1871) noted, sexual competition is more intense among males, and thus their alertness may also be expected to be more acute. The indications are numberless, and the South-Lloyd study adds to them. They are nowhere more evident, however, than in the noted tendency toward polygyny, on the one hand, and hypergyny, on the other. Married men's likely attraction to younger, unmarried women encountered at work, or elsewhere, is an established fact. The same applies to young women who are attracted to older, more established men. But there is a major difference between a fact uncovered by sociologists and the same fact discovered by evolutionists. The former turn to intervening variables (the switches) for explanation and thereby remain in the age of alchemy. The latter anchor their findings to underlying and relatively constant forces represented by general principles, thereby contributing to systematic, cumulative knowledge. T. Bereczkei and A. Csanaky (1996: 17–35), for example, report from Hungary that, *as predicted from theory*, not only do males prefer younger mates, while females fancy high-status males; marriages of this sort are more adaptive; that is, they produce more surviving children, they are more stable, and they promote higher "marriage quality."

Remarriage

Divorce is frequently followed by remarriage, though in keeping with declines in marriage rates, the rate of remarriage has also declined, especially in European nations. A single person need not live a lonely life, and marriages are no longer reliable enough to justify one's further emotional commitments. "Having experienced this uncertainty, both men and women divorcés are more reluctant to try marriage soon, or even again" (Goode 1993: 35–36). Nevertheless, remarriage is still with us, and several sex differences about it are worth noting. In sharp contrast to sex differences in marriage rates, men are much more likely than women to remarry (Glick 1992: 1195) and to do it quickly. A study of faculty and staff at the State University of New York at Albany showed that, among the previously divorced, three-quarters of the males but only one-half of the females had remarried at least once (Buckle et al. 1996: 370). High-status men are also more likely to remarry than are low-status men, whereas status appears to have little or no effect on the chances of female remarriage.

The key factors governing these sex differences are the value of male resources and women's reproductive value as reflected by age and marital status. With some exceptions, divorced women are older than their single counterparts and thus less attractive as prospective marital partners. As a sociologist points out, "women lose value in the marriage market relative to men with each year of age after thirty, and this difference is accelerated in their late thirties and early forties" (Goode 1993: 37; see also Glick 1992: 1193, fig. 3). This observation accords with predictions from sexual selection theory, although one could quibble about the specified ages. The reproductive value of women is highest in their late teens and early twenties. And if they terminate a marriage as mothers, their chances of remarriage are reduced even further (Ahlburg and DeVita 1992; Goode 1993). The Buckle et al. (1996) study shows that only 45 percent of females with children remarried, compared to over 60 percent among the childless. The corresponding figures for males were 67 percent and 83 percent, respectively. In fact, the larger the brood, the lower the chance of female remarriage—a pattern that did not hold for males. Moreover, when divorcés remarry, men are much more likely than women to find mates who are considerably younger than their former spouses, and who have not been previously married. On their part, women more frequently remarry with men who are close to their own age and who have been divorced themselves (Buckle et al. 1996).

The different manner in which these factors affect remarriage prospects are strikingly consistent with predictions derived from fitness theory. Female fertility is much more age-dependent than is the case for males. With increasing age, at least up to a point, men commonly enjoy increased earnings and other markers of high status. Hence, they are in a better position to attract younger mates who, more than men, have evolved to cherish a mate's capacity to provision. Richness of resources satisfies both ultimate ends and proximate ones, for example, a comfortable life style. Finally, women's chances of remarriage are more adversely affected by the presence of children; divorcées are more likely to retain custody of dependent children, and prospective mates may be expected to factor in the real costs of stepparenting. Material resources that are channeled to stepchildren are necessarily costs incurred by one's own offspring, past or future.

Again, these trends and sex differences in marriage, divorce, and remarriage, as well as the sex differences in mating strategies reviewed in the previous chapter, are typically viewed by sociologists as mere signs of the now famous cultural double standard (e.g., Millet 1970;

Collins 1975; Epstein 1988). The male desire for multiple and physically attractive partners, the greater popular acceptance of men's dating younger women, the greater remarriage facility of divorced men, the greater restrictions on the expression of female sexuality—these and related factors are often taken as evidence of an invidious and culturally determined asymmetry. And we, again, could hardly quarrel against an hypothesis of cultural input in the sexual double standard. Our argument is against exclusively cultural explanations, which not only fail to be justified in their own terms; they are also rejected by extensive evidence indicating that these universal sociocultural features are grafted onto a fundamental and sex-differentiated biological substrate. Let "culturologists" inform themselves of evolutionary theory and *demonstrate* that it is irrelevant to their subject matter; we shall be the first to convert to their new science.

Cohabitation

The increase in age at first marriage and the declining marriage rates have been accompanied by sharp increases in cohabitation, at least in industrial societies and especially among young adults. The following comments will focus largely on the U.S., a country that reveals trends with typical saliency. Estimates from various sources, including the U.S. National Survey of Families and Households, indicate that cohabitation in the U.S. has become a way of life. By the late 1980s, about one-half of Americans in their late twenties and early thirties had had a cohabitation experience (Bumpass and Sweet 1989). The phenomenon apparently represents a recent trend. In 1970, only about 89,000 unmarried couples under age forty-five were cohabiting, whereas twenty years later the corresponding figure had climbed to about 2,263,000 (Saluter 1991). While this form of pair-bonding is slightly overrepresented among blacks and the less educated, it is widespread among virtually all segments of American society (Rindfuss and VandenHeuvel 1990: 703). Comparable findings are available from other industrial societies, for example, Canada (White 1987), France (Cherlin 1981), and Australia (Khoo 1987). The pattern appears to be most diffuse in Sweden, where in recent decades nearly all adults have been in at least one cohabiting union prior to marriage (Cherlin 1981; Popenoe 1987; Lindquist Forsberg and Tullberg 1995).

The pertinent literature is quite considerable, and there are various attempts to explain cohabitation and determine its significance by reference to the institution of marriage. According to R.R. Rindfuss and A. VandenHeuvel (1990: 705—emphasis added), cohabitation is "generally viewed in one of two ways in the literature: as *an alternative form of marriage* without the usual legal sanctions; or as *the last stage in the courtship process*, a type of alternative engagement." The second view is presumably the more common (e.g., Gwartney-Gibbs 1986; White 1987; Riche 1988; Schoen and Weinick 1993).

In fact, the evidence, as we understand it, comes closer to supporting the first view, referred to by some scholars as "the looser bond" (e.g., Schoen and Weinick 1993). An analysis of data from the 1972 National Longitudinal Study of High School Seniors and follow-up interviews in 1973, 1974, 1976, 1979, and 1986 has revealed that in many respects cohabitors resemble single individuals far more closely than they compare to married people. For example, cohabiting partners were much less likely than childless married couples to have parenting plans within two years (Rindfuss and VandenHeuvel 1990: 709, table 1). They were also enrolled in school in larger numbers, had lower rates of home ownership, and were more heavily dependent on their parents for financial support. More important, a very large number of cohabitors identified themselves as single persons by reporting that they lived alone or with parents or other relatives (Rindfuss and VandenHeuvel 1990: 720, table 10).

If the facts on cohabitation are rich, the same unfortunately cannot be said of the quality of explanatory efforts directed at it. On the whole, this aspect of the problem can again be represented by the work of Rindfuss and VandenHeuvel (1990: 704, 721–23), according to whom "cohabitation may be but another step in the long-term rise of individualism relative to the decline of the institutions of marriage and family." Little wonder, then, that "cohabiting unions are of relatively short duration," and are far more frequently terminated by separation than by marriage.

Again, an unqualified rejection of this view would be inappropriate. The rise in cohabitation is almost certainly associated with a number of changes in the sociocultural environment that may be said to reflect the ideology of individualism. They include the enhanced economic independence of young women, readier access to contraceptive techniques, legalization of abortion or relaxation of pertinent laws, a moderation of sanctions against sexual activity outside marriage, and, among other developments, an increase in the geographic mobility of the young in view of changing educational practices and labor market requirements (e.g., Cherlin 1981; Popenoe 1988; Goode 1993). But to place the increase of cohabitation within a sea of other sociocultural and psychological changes hardly amounts to explaining it. The effort begs a number of questions. One is of capital importance, and underscores the utility of evolutionary perspectives, especially on a topic that is so intimately related to reproductive, that is, sexual, behavior. We have repeatedly stressed the facts of differential reproductive strategies between the sexes and the male tendency to exploit females. Accordingly, it is necessary to ask now (1) whether there are any basic, reproductively relevant, differences between males and females in the respective expectations they have of cohabitation and (2) whether the two sexes derive differential costs and benefits from the cohabiting union.

The answer to the first question is unequivocal. In cohabitation, too, the two sexes pursue different reproductive strategies, in keeping with the rule that male sexual pleasure "happens quickly and impulsively, female pleasure more slowly and with circumspection" (Tiger 1992: 149). Females are more likely than males to view the bond as a precursor to marriage. Conversely, males are more inclined to use it for immediate and temporary gratification, sexual and perhaps emotional as well (e.g., Arafat and Yorburg 1973). Scholars who are intent on understanding cohabitation as a loose bond are prone to downplay this difference. Rindfuss and VandenHeuvel (1990: 711–12), for instance, conclude that neither females nor males are generally inclined to view cohabitation "as a final courtship stage preceding marriage." But as they themselves note, in two of the four comparison years, females were "significantly more likely than males to plan marriage" within the next twelve months. Moreover, in no year was this finding reversed, and in 1976 the difference in question was quite large (28 percent for males versus 44 percent for females). It is little wonder that young American males aged fifteen to forty-four are more favorably disposed toward a cohabiting union than their female counterparts (London 1991). It follows that the debate whether cohabitation is a precursor to marriage or a looser bond is at least partially misguided. The available data indicate that marriage is more commonly on the minds of women, whereas temporary gratification is more typical of the men. In short, the debate on the general significance of cohabitation is to an extent vitiated by the unknown but contaminating role that is played in it by this difference between male and female motivations.

Who pays the bill? The second question is more problematic but not entirely unmanageable. There are both costs and benefits associated with cohabitation, as with marriage and any other type of relationship.

Modern society imposes a protracted period of economic dependence on its young, for example, through the demands for higher education made by industry, government, and the institutions of higher learning themselves. In short, there is an institutional bias toward delayed marriage. At the same time, the delay corresponds to the period of life that in our species' history has been marked by the greatest frequency of sexual activity. Moreover, in some areas and segments of society—for example, "the truly disadvantaged" of the American inner city—marriageable men are in scarce supply for one reason or another, including a lack of jobs and an exceedingly aggressive legal system (e.g., Wilson 1987). It follows that loose, temporary pair-bonds satisfy sexual and emotional needs that are perfectly normal among young but unmarried adults in modern society. These are among the benefits of cohabitation for both males and females.

There are costs, too, and on average these can be predicted to be higher for women. Since the male is the more polygamous sex, we may predict that, more frequently than his partner, he will cheat while in the cohabiting union and use the union as a temporary arrangement; that is, he exploits his partner's sexual resources during the years of her highest reproductive value. Various findings support these predictions. For instance, a survey of young American adults born in 1953–1962, a cohort that has participated keenly in the sharp rise in cohabitation rates, shows that cohabiting men report more frequent infidelities than their partners (Laumann et al. 1994: 209). Again, the Rindfuss-VandenHeuvel (1990: 711–12) findings noted above showed that cohabiting males were less likely than their partners to contemplate marriage anytime soon. Moreover, for never-married women, there is compelling evidence that cohabitation is *normatively childless* (Bachrach 1987: 635), although 1982 data from the National Center for Health Statistics "clearly show that cohabitation contributes to an increased risk of pregnancy by increasing frequency of sexual intercourse" (Bachrach 1987: 635). There is reason to suppose that pregnancy in cohabitation may increase the chances of marriage. But this is not necessarily a blessing for the woman and her offspring. Marriages between previously cohabiting couples are more rather than less fragile (e.g., Bumpass and Sweet 1989; but cf. Teachman and Polonko 1990). The difference can be dramatic. A study from Sweden, for example, shows that women who had cohabited prior to marriage had a marriage dissolution rate that was 80 percent higher than the corresponding figure for those who had not cohabited (Bennett et al. 1988).

Cohabitation thus contributes to the widespread phenomenon of female-headed households, perhaps in very considerable proportions, and we should recall that absent fathers frequently fail to pay child support even when it has been legally mandated. Mostly, however, cohabitation contributes to the tendency to postpone marriage, and, as we have seen, the reproductive value and attractiveness of women decrease as they leave behind their most fertile years. The delay in age at first marriage is almost certainly involved in the growing trend since the 1960s and 1970s toward first births to women over age thirty (Rindfuss et al. 1988). At the same time, the proportion of women remaining permanently childless may also be increasing (Thornton and Freedman 1983). No doubt, some bills are difficult to apportion. The present one is one of those. On balance, however, cohabitation appears to do greater harm to the reproductive, emotional, and possibly economic well-being of women than to that of men. The statement is suggested by evolutionary theory, specifically by the typical female reproductive strategy that is hypothesized by parental investment theory. Coyness or, as Tiger (1992: 149) stated above, circumspection is the defining characteristic of the evolved female strategy. Cohabitation tends to circumvent this adaptive feature. To the extent that cohabitation is culturally instigated, it may be possible to conclude that when culture is at odds with biology it may create more problems than are normally recognized.

Parenting: Who Cares More?

Any male-female comparison must ultimately lead back to the fundamental difference between the sexes, namely anisogamy and thus differential parental investment, including the nurturing of the young. In this latter respect, the fit between fact and theory is as close as can be. There is a marked sex difference in parenting, and it is universal. In all known societies, child care is the primary responsibility of mothers (e.g., Murdock 1967; van den Berghe 1979; Maryanski and Turner 1992). Many sociologists, gender feminists in particular, are predictably uncomfortable with this evolutionary fact and declare it culturally constructed. Thus: "Women's sense of caring and responsibility for others is...the *result*, not the cause, of gendered parenting.... Through their practiced skill at picking up the cues of the needs of others, women are *psychologically coopted into wanting to be good mothers*" (Lorber 1994: 169—second emphasis added). Can women be such dupes? We hold that the vast majority of them somehow know far more science and have far more common sense than those who would presume to teach them the "right" gender roles.

There is good reason to suppose that men, too, wish to be good fathers. After all, their fitness interests, if nothing else, demand some degree of attentiveness to the direct vehicles of their genetic survival. However, anisogamy and differential parental investment, in conjunction with paternal uncertainty, necessarily predict that—however attentive, loving, and nurturing fathers may be—on average mothers will best them on all counts. The facts are consistent with the prediction, despite a growing literature on the emergence of new styles of fathering in industrial societies (e.g., Coltrane 1996). For convenience sake, we may speak of two schools of thought on this topic. One heralds the advent of the "New Father" during the second half of the present century; the other, perhaps more skeptical about the malleability of the male nature, is more inclined to see the new father as "technically present but functionally absent" (LaRossa 1988: 454–55; for a good review of the debate, see Cutts 1994).

The new father is depicted as having become more personally and emotionally involved in the day-to-day rearing of his children. Indeed, so radical has been the allegedly recent change in the role of the father that he may be viewed as androgynous or "unmasculine"—"expressive and intimate…with his children" (Rotundo 1985: 17). Some studies have shown a major narrowing of the gap between mother and father in their relative involvement with, or nurturing of, the children. One team of researchers has written, for instance, that when the comparison is between spouses who are both employed full-time, the difference in the number of waking hours spent at home is nominal (Booth and Edwards 1980: 451).

The emergence of new styles of fathering, the argument goes, could hardly have failed to take place in view of various other changes in society, including especially the rise in female participation in the paid labor force, with the attendant increase in the "instrumental" nature of the mother's role at the expense of her "expressive" role (e.g., Amato 1989; Coltrane 1996). One observer has claimed that the rise of the women's movement "has led to a new set of ideals of manhood and womanhood that minimize the difference between the sexes. In this new view, women and men are seen as fundamentally alike with qualities such as rationality, nurturance, and assertiveness distributed randomly across the boundaries of gender" (Rotundo 1985: 16). Moreover, the new father has brought benefits for all concerned:

happier husbands and wives and above all better adjusted children (e.g., Pruett 1993).

Not so, argues the opposition, and their findings are compelling. More than one fourth of all U.S. births in 1990 were the children of unmarried women, representing "a five-fold increase in 30 years." Moreover, "one half of all children...can expect to live in such households before they turn 18." Further, one half of single mothers' children live in poverty, compared with 8 percent of those from two-parent families (Louv 1993: 54–55). One major cause of this pitiful condition is the failure of more than one half of absent fathers to comply with legally mandated child support payments (Furstenberg 1988: 202). Legal obligations aside, about two-thirds of children living in fatherless homes receive no paternal support whatsoever (Furstenberg and Condran 1988).

The idea of the new, involved father may thus be an "illusion" (Backett 1987). Proponents of the new-father thesis have essentially mistaken ideology for behavior; the "culture of fatherhood" has changed much faster than the "conduct of fatherhood" (LaRossa 1988: 451–52). What we really have is "the technically present but functionally absent father," namely a father who on one "level of consciousness" feels the tug of cultural prescriptions, while on another does "not find the idea all that attractive" (LaRossa 1988: 454).

We may recognize two major strands in the debate against the thesis of the new father. Some scholars point out that the new father is not there at all, and hence may be less desirable than the old kind of father, say, the disciplinarian of traditional society (e.g., Louv 1993). Others argue that, even assuming that the new father is physically present, he tends to be only peripherally involved in child care (e.g., Backett 1987; LaRossa 1988). As we shall see, both perspectives are more theoretically plausible than the alternative, and roughly for the same reason.

To a considerable extent, the new-father thesis is vitiated by conceptual confusion. What, for example, is meant by the "involved" father? Michael Lamb (1987: 8) has accordingly proposed three dimensions of involvement: engagement, accessibility, and responsibility. The first refers to "the time spent in actual one-on-one interaction with the child." Accessibility refers to a less intense degree of interaction; for instance the father is really predisposed to do X, for example, work, but is "available" to do Y, for example, play with the child. Finally, responsibility concerns the ability and willingness to primarily attend to the child's "welfare and care." As may be expected, mothers beat fathers on all three dimensions by a considerable stretch, especially on responsibility. Fathers fare best on engagement. On the whole, findings reveal that "mother-child interaction is dominated by caretaking whereas father-child interaction is dominated by play" (LaRossa 1988: 453).

These facts speak loudly and are consistent with predictions derived from the theory of differential parental investment. Natural selection has forged a sex-differentiated brain along with associated neuro-endocrinal equipment that inclines toward more intense nurturing in women than in men. Sociocultural constraints may modify and variously shape these basic sex differences, but they cannot be expected to eliminate them entirely, at least not in terms of the time horizons in which we are accustomed to think. Additional support for this point of view may be found in the evidence regarding male abandonment of parental responsibilities and step-parenting.

The theory of differential parental investment predicts that divorced fathers will be inclined to reduce their economic and emotional investments in their offspring. Leaving the mother to be in charge of the children's needs, thereby releasing at least some resources to invest in offspring with other mates, constitutes behavior that accords with the male's ancient reproductive strategy. Such behavior has been amply verified by social scientists themselves without, however, clear knowledge of its root-causes (Weitzman 1981, 1985; Meyer and Bartfeld 1996). Based on a review of studies from several nations, W.J. Goode (1993: 340— emphasis in original) summarizes the general trends as follows:

1) The number of needy one-parent families continues to grow; 2) Most are mother-headed; 3) The amounts that courts *order* ex-husbands to pay for child support are less than half the costs of rearing a child; but 4) The amounts they *actually* pay are still less, for most pay irregularly, and a substantial minority do not pay at all. In some ways the most striking finding is that there is little or no correlation between the father's income and what is actually paid, and in some countries (for example, Australia) research has actually revealed a negative correlation. That is, even if we accept the guess that very poor fathers can pay only little or nothing, at present the delinquents are mostly fathers who *can* pay.

We wonder: What must happen before sociologists ponder the fact that this sort of behavior is not a result of socialization? Indeed, in recent decades, across industrial societies, even government agencies have increasingly intervened, with mixed success, to remedy these widespread instances of paternal neglect (Cherlin 1992; Goode 1993). At any rate, to the extent that public policies are required to coerce fathers to "do the right thing," claims regarding the emergence of the new father must be viewed with a strong dose of skepticism.

The situation is further complicated when the matter of stepchildren is entered into the mix. Divorced men sometimes remarry and father additional children. They may also find themselves in households with children from one or more previous marriages where they are expected to invest economic and emotional resources in such children. In view of the finiteness of material resources alone, the men's own children and their mothers necessarily suffer some loss. But, as some studies of divorced males in America suggest, remarried men are to an extent involved in an extensive system of "child-swapping" whereby paternal obligations are determined in part by place of residence—men tend to engage in fathering behavior toward children with whom they live, natural parents or not (Furstenberg and Spanier 1984; Furstenberg 1987, 1988).

This phenomenon is not hugely different from many other systems of indirect reciprocity, the Social Security Administration, for example (Gouldner 1970). What we are observing is fairly in keeping with Durkheim's treatment of cooperative arrangements under conditions of organic solidarity. From an evolutionary perspective (e.g., Trivers 1971), another way of saying the same thing is that as kin altruism diminishes in significance as motive for cooperation in the megasociety, non-kin reciprocal altruism rises to the fore. As the expression "child-swapping" implies, biological fathers and stepfathers are to an extent engaged in indirect relationships guided by the rule: I'll care for your child and you'll care for mine. To a degree, therefore, the cost of divorce is compensated for. But only to a degree, for fitness theory predicts, and studies show, that in "blended families" one's biological children are favored to stepchildren by both men and women (MacDonald and DeMaris 1996).

In fact that is a conservative way of putting it. There is strong evidence that stepchildren are at far greater risk of abuse, including sexual molestation (e.g., Finkelhor 1980; Russell 1984) and fatal physical assault, than are natural children; and the principal abusers are stepfathers (Wilson and Daly 1987; Daly and Wilson 1988: chap. 4). In dramatic correspondence to evolutionary theory, furthermore, those most susceptible to abuse are the very young, namely those who make the greatest investment demands on the mother and hence interfere most directly with the more enduring reproductive interests of stepfathers. Stepchildren younger than four years are forty times more likely to be abused when compared to their counterparts living in households where both natural parents are present. Conventional sociological explanations emphasize "role ambiguity" or "role strain" as the chief culprit (Cherlin 1978; Kompara 1980; Giles-Sims 1984). One scholar remarks that the institutions of industrial societies offer "little guidance to...remarried adults...and to their children as to how they should manage their unfamiliar and complex family lives" (Cherlin 1992: 84). Of course, such factors may very well contribute to instances of stepchild abuse, but they cannot tell the whole story. Strain and ambiguity, after all, are not the monopoly of blended families. Moreover, the inverse relationship between child's age and stepfather's violence speaks volumes. Nor is it a uniquely human phenomenon, being rather fairly common among other mammals (e.g., Schaller 1972; Hrdy 1977). Ultimately, as Daly and Wilson (1988: chap. 4; see also Wilson and Daly 1987) point out, stepchildren enter as costs rather than as benefits in the reproductive strategies of stepparents; and age of child is quite relevant to the reproductive strategy of stepfathers.

The sex-difference uniformities that we have been discussing in this chapter—differences in marriage, divorce, remarriage, cohabitation, and parenting—are consistent with predictions derived from evolutionary theory. Given the intimate link between these patterns of behavior and sex differences in fitness interests, focusing on these observations is a bit like "shooting fish in a barrel." What, therefore, if we turn attention away from behaviors that have such a direct and obvious bearing on relative reproductive success? Can we still find evidence of sex-specialized adaptations and behaviors?

Division of Labor in the Household

Simone de Beauvoir (1952) compared the drudgery of housework to the torture endured by Sisyphus. What is cleaned gets dirty and must be cleaned again—and then again, again, and again. For many, few if any tasks are at once more tedious and less satisfying than domestic chores. The greatest share of such burdens falls, as always, on the shoulders of women in all human societies (Murdock 1937; Maryanski and Turner 1992). But the magnitude of the load varies in view of several factors, especially variations in female control of economic resources. For example, in forager societies, where women have contributed substantial means of subsistence, men appear to have participated fairly actively in domestic labor, including child care, though still not to the same extent as their wives (Leibowitz 1978). In horticultural societies, where women's labor in the garden plot produces the greater share of daily necessities, the male contribution to household labor is even greater. For instance, while women remain children's primary caretakers, their husbands sometimes maintain distinct "men's houses" where they care for many of their own domestic needs (Friedl 1975). Facts are quite different in pastoral and agrarian societies; here men control almost entirely the production and distribution of goods, and "the subordination of women reaches its highest degree" (O'Kelly 1980).

Roughly similar patterns seem to hold in present-day society. In the less developed countries women are heavily subordinate to men economically, and commonly perform at least 90 percent of household tasks. By contrast, in the more developed nations women have greater opportunities to generate income, and they are responsible for at least three-fifths of household chores (*Peter's Atlas of the World* 1990). This is a marked difference, but note that everywhere women still perform a disproportionate share of the household labor.

Recent trends in Western industrial societies suggest that, depending on perspective, the disparity between men's and women's contribution continues to diminish. In the U.S., for example, between 1965 and 1985 the average time that married men invested in household chores rose from 4.5 hours per week to 11.1 hours, while married women reduced their average time investment from 31.6 hours per week to 22.4 hours (Robinson 1988). Accordingly, women have managed to be less occupied in such activities as cooking, doing the dishes, house cleaning, laundry, gardening, caring for pets, and paying the bills. But this reduction is only partly a function of increased assistance from the husbands. In part it reflects the increasing number of hours spent by women in the paid labor force, the introduction of various labor-saving devices, and the trend toward a smaller household, among other factors. Moreover, the above estimates of time allocated to household chores do not include time spent on child care activities. When this factor is taken into account, the disparity in household labor between husbands and wives remains high (e.g., South and Spitze 1994: 341, table 3).

What accounts for such a tenacity of sex differences? Several sociological explanations have been proposed, though none has achieved wide acceptance. For convenience sake, we may group them into two broad classes: those that emphasize *differential resource contribution* and those that focus on *differential cultural conditioning*. Resource contribution explanations assume that husbands and wives bring their respective economic and social resources to bear on explicit or implicit negotiations regarding who will perform how much housework. The party who brings or is likely to bring more resources is presumably the party better able to limit time and effort required by housework. One of the earliest extended statements of this perspective was presented by R.O. Blood and D.M. Wolfe (1960) in their volume on *Husbands & Wives*, and its essential elements resemble aspects of exchange theory later outlined by such scholars as G.C. Homans (1961) and P.M. Blau (1964). The household is portrayed as a social organization primarily built around a sort of contract whereby husband and wife cooperatively blend their respective resources to rear children. In 1960 these authors could fairly easily claim that the husband "spends most of his time at work," earning the economic resources on which the family depends, while women's "lives tend to be centered in the home, in bearing and rearing children, entertaining and visiting" (Blood and Wolfe 1960: 80). To an extent, this picture reflected an American ideal symbolized in so many fictional households portrayed on television; its focus on "man the provider, woman the homemaker and caregiver" must appear rather quaint to today's reader.

More recently, the resource contribution model has been upgraded in *A Treatise on the Family* by the economist and Nobel Prize winner G.S. Becker (1981). Especially interesting from our point of view is Becker's explicit debt to evolutionary theorizing. He reasons that the allocation of household chores is principally a function of the cooperative exchange of economic, domestic, and *reproductive resources* between men and women: "Women have traditionally relied on men for provision of food, shelter, and protection, and men have traditionally relied on women for the bearing and rearing of children and the maintenance of the home.... The *biological differences* between men and women in the production and care of children, and the specialized investments in market and household skills that reinforce the biological differences, explain why the institution of marriage has been important in all societies" (Becker 1981: 27–28—emphasis added).

This is a far cry from the typical sociological position, most apparent, as we shall presently see, in the hypothesis of *differential cultural conditioning*, according to which "family roles are socially constructed beliefs" about who should do what and how much (Kamo 1992: 671; see also, e.g., Lorber 1994: chap. 8). Indeed, Becker's reasoning appears to irritate the sensitivities of the pure cultural sociologist (e.g., Coltrane 1996: 155–58). Nevertheless, several stubborn facts buttress the basic claims of the resource contribution model. For example, the higher the husband's income relative to his wife's, the less likely he is to share household chores (Eriksen et al. 1979; Model 1981; Ross 1987). In short, women appear to trade their ability to tend to the home in exchange for the rich resources that higher status men can provide. In addition, wives of rich husbands have the luxury of opting out of the labor force entirely and focusing their time and energy on household management. From the reverse perspective, we may note that men are more apt to engage in household tasks and child care activities when their wives participate in the paid labor force (Gecas 1976; Walker and Woods 1976; Duncan and Duncan 1978; Huber and Spitze 1981). Nevertheless, their contribution remains relatively paltry. Hence, some scholars justifiably write of a working wife's household duties as a "second shift" (Hochschild with Machung 1989).

The second class of explanations concerning relative contribution to household labor—what we have termed *differential cultural conditioning*—emphasizes features of the cultural environment that incline men and women to acquiesce to the demands of sex-role *stereotypes*, namely that the husband is breadwinner and king of the castle, while his mate is the dutiful housewife and loving mother. We may distinguish at least two variants in this context. First, the *differential socialization hypothesis* argues that imitation of and instruction by adults encourage boys and girls to adopt stereotyped behaviors. Patterns of upbringing presumably teach the young that women are passive, demure, nurturant creatures while men are assertive, adventuresome, and authoritative. The acceptance of these "stereotypes" allegedly translates into behaviors that result in a sex-differentiated distribution of household chores, especially when it comes to matters of child care (e.g., Goldscheider and Waite 1991).

Why these alleged stereotypes should be cultural universals is not a question that interests many sociologists. Like the findings from neuroendocrinology, the question is apparently more nuisance than anything else. After all, both nuisances would require attempts at hard work and serious demonstration, whereas the appeal to socialization rests so comfortably with ideology. Fortunately, some sociologists are, on rare occasions, nudged toward recognition of the universal and an effort to explain it. J. Chafetz (1984), for instance, argues that the universality of male dominance must be rooted in a universal feature of the human existence. The key clue, in her view, is that nowhere do women specialize in "productive/public sector roles." Their specialty lies in "reproductive/private sphere activities." It is women who "carry babies in their bodies and lactate, which circumscribes their physical mobility."

Today, of course, the demands of pregnancy can be reduced by lowering fertility rates, and the strains of child care can be alleviated by bottle-feeding and by reliance on nonparental care providers. But Chafetz rightly notes that these options have not commonly been available to women throughout our species' lengthy existence. Thus, "most *societies find it more efficient* if women also do the bulk of the caretaking of young children who are no longer nursing. That is, *on the basis of expediency*, the nurturance role is typically extended beyond the biologically based phenomenon of breast-feeding," resulting in women's close proximity to the home and to the children. This sequence of "expediencies" allegedly explains why women are more commonly expected to specialize in domestic chores and also to be content with less than a fair share of a society's valued resources (Chafetz 1984: 21–22—emphasis added).

Part of this analysis is indeed a welcome improvement. Another part represents an unfortunate case of fair promise gone astray. If the effect of reproductive biology is recognized, why not follow through with the theory addressed to it? After all, explanation of the universality, in rhythmic degrees, of sex-differentiated adaptations and behaviors, *especially in the nest*, is readily available and spreading rapidly in modern behavioral science. Furthermore, it makes provision for effects of the sociocultural environment. If, for example, a sex-differentiated division of labor simply refuses to go away, societies may indeed find expediency in the persistence and hence contribute through various means to the perpetuation of the differentiation. What kind of theory, by contrast, is represented by the teleological appeal to "expediency"? Why shoot in the dark when there is good illumination? Everything we know shows that, given anisogamy, such a differentiation has long been a natural part of human evolution, with or without expediency.

A second variant of the *differential conditioning* explanation proposes that much if not all social interaction between men and women involves "doing gender" (e.g., West and Zimmerman 1987). The division of household tasks is thereby viewed in typically postmodernist fashion as but one instance of an "everyday enactment of dominance, submission, and other behaviors symbolically linked to gender" (South and Spitze 1994: 329; see also Hartmann 1981; Berk 1985; Shelton and John 1993). An especially animated version of this view states that "the allocation of most unpaid domestic work and nurturance to women has signficant economic and social benefits for men and is exploitive of women's time and energy.... The arrangement may seem natural, but *it is the result* of the systematic deprivation of married women's rights to control their own property, profits, and wages" (Lorber 1994: 175—emphasis added).

The emphasis on sex-differentiated power relations is in itself appropriate, but the appeal to rights in effect rests the case in the obsession with patriarchy and thus merely labels rather than explains the inequality in household labor. As we have seen, the universality of patriarchy, like the universality of gendered socialization, must be viewed first and foremost as an *explanandum* before it can be considered seriously as a possible, proximate, *explanans*. It is hardly sufficient to assert that these universal "patterns...are human inventions and are produced through social interaction" (Lorber 1994: 124). In fact, they are more than human inventions, as chapter 8 will indicate by reference to primatology. At any rate, social interaction is not likely to produce fundamental patterns without rules. What, then, are the rules? And where do they come from, ideology aside?

In chapter 6 we provided a brief evolutionary theory of patriarchy. In a related and more extended vein, evolutionary biologist and feminist Barbara Smuts (1995: 10–20; see also Hrdy 1997) has discussed cogent hypotheses about the phenomenon. For example, for reasons not fully known, but consistent with the behavior of most higher primates, the hunting and gathering society of the hominid past practiced female exogamy. Hence, women were compelled to weaken, and perhaps even sever, their ties with kith and kin. As a result, they became heavily dependent on the patronage of their mate and his relatives. Men, by contrast, remained in close proximity to their kin and allies, and were accordingly in a better position to cement lifelong alliances grounded in kin selection and reciprocity.

Male dominance over women was later reinforced with the advent of the agricultural revolution and animal husbandry. Men gained greater control of resources needed for survival and reproduction, and this development increased also their power over women. Moreover, the evolution of agriculture introduced an "economic surplus"—and with it great inequality in male wealth and power. The surplus, in turn, stimulated ruling-class parasitism and warfare, and while some men lost power, limb, and life as a result, a few others gained great wealth and domination over large populations and great expanses of territory. The subjugation of women increased in step with such developments. Nothing shows this fact more clearly than the oft-noted rise of the harems maintained by powerful men (Betzig 1986).

It is also Smuts' (1995: 18) contention that in "pursuing their material and reproductive interests, women often engage in behaviors that promote male resource control and male control over female sexuality. Thus, women as well as men contribute to the perpetuation of patriarchy." But the key feature of this scholar's account is that the basic forces underlying patriarchy predate the emergence of the human species, a fact that undermines the more simplistic treatments of the topic so freely offered by many sociologists.

The adaptive significance of many human patterns, including sex roles in the family, very probably lies in evolutionary developments that hark back to the distant past, and are still observable today in the few remaining small groups of hunters and gatherers. In these societies, the division of labor between the sexes is quite marked (e.g., Katz and Konner 1981), and seems to reflect conditions that existed along the entire hominid line. For some two million years, the primary male responsibilities were hunting game, defense of the group, the production of weapons, and the training of pubescent boys for introduction into manhood. By contrast, in large part constrained by their reproductive physiology and underlying neuroendocrinal adaptations, females specialized in gathering food in the vicinity of the campsite, tending the home, and discharging the extraordinarily complex role of caring for the young.

In concluding this section, we may reasonably assert that women in general have some reason to complain. Certainly their talents have traditionally been hidden or smothered altogether. It is equally true that for deeply evolutionary causes maintaining and raising a family has failed to receive the appropriate recognition and retribution. But if we are what we are, women are not entirely blameless for the plight that, especially in recent decades, men and women have created for themselves and one another. Suppose we return briefly to the parenting question. There is some compelling evidence that, while mothers claim they want their husbands to be more involved with the offspring, they are too often likely to consider them incompetent, and even tend to guard jealously their own domestic power. One study shows, for instance, that despite stress and exhaustion, only 42 percent of working women wanted their husbands to increase their child care, and only 36 percent wanted to have men do more of the housework (Pruett 1987: 244). Mothers have further been found to inhibit the father-child relationship, for example by assuming in effect that they know what that relationship should be like (e.g., Backett 1987; Pruett 1993). They often organize "the times when the father and child could be available to one another" and not infrequently display considerable "possessiveness" (Backett 1987: 83, 85).

Male exploitation in the nuptial bond? There is little doubt about it, especially insofar as economic and labor aspects of the union are concerned. But there are also powerful emotions invested in parenting. On this score there is reason to believe that, today like yesterday, men sometimes get the short end of the stick. Consider, for example, that Father's Day pales in significance by comparison to Mother's Day. And while it is true that some fathers shirk their duties, even despite judicial responsibilities, it is also undeniable that others are deeply committed to their children, and struggle against many obstacles arising from occupational demands, not to mention occasional maternal animus, to perform their paternal role.

Gender in the Workplace

If sex roles have changed in recent decades, the results can perhaps be best observed in the workplace, where political and legal measures are likely to have the greatest effect and where social relations and behaviors are farthest removed from our species' ancestral environment. Traditionally, women and men have differed significantly in occupational orientations, rates of labor force participation, levels of earnings, and, among other things, the degree of authority exercised on the job. Have there been significant changes in recent times? What, for instance, is the situation today in a country like the United States, where the women's movement has been one of the major political causes of recent decades? We are asking a question rooted in an exceedingly rich topic, and can concentrate on only some of the most basic facts.

Sex differences in occupational participation have narrowed to some degree since the early 1960s. A fair indicator of this development is the extent to which women have been investing in higher education. Female high school graduates who nowadays attend college and earn undergraduate degrees outnumber their brothers. Similarly, women are increasingly attracted to academic specialties that traditionally have been male-dominated, for example, business, law, architecture, medicine, and engineering. Additionally, between 1960 and 1994, the proportion of women earning graduate or other advanced degrees rose sharply, especially in such fields as business, law, medicine, and dentistry. Time and effort may not yet have wrought the whole potential of such changes, and it is not certain they ever will. Despite these trends, for instance, the choice of a college major remains strongly gender-typed, with women continuing to dominate such specialties as home economics, library science, elementary education, and nursing (Bianchi and Spain 1996).

Such findings provide strong clues as to what we might be able to predict about sex differences in various occupational categories. Between 1970 and 1995, the percentage of managerial positions occupied by American women increased from 19 percent to 43 percent. An overall portrait of this shift is offered by D. Spain and S.M. Bianchi (1996) who have calculated an index of occupational dissimilarity to estimate the percentage of persons in the labor force who would have to change occupation in order to achieve parity between the sexes. Between 1970 and 1990, the index value declined from 68 to 53, which is to say that there was a noteworthy change toward gender parity. Some of this change probably resulted from broad transformations in the American occupational structure, such as the decline in the number of manufacturing jobs and the corresponding expansion of the service sector. But Spain and Bianchi have estimated that about 75 percent of the shift toward less occupational inequality was due to a real diminution of sex segregation in the workplace.

Other researchers, however, are not so sanguine. Today there are more female than male professionals in the United States, but women are heavily concentrated in the "semiprofessions," for example, nursing, school teaching, and library science, whereas men are better represented in medicine, law, and engineering. Furthermore, within the more prestigious occupations, women are more likely than men to be engaged at the lower end of the internal prestige scale. Women lawyers, for example, are more likely than men to work in government jobs and research, where salaries are relatively modest, than in the more handsomely rewarded specialties, such as litigation (Reskin and Roos 1990). Again, as women enter occupations that were once male-dominated, it is not uncommon for salaries and wages to stagnate, as has apparently happened in such occupations as editors, insurance adjusters, pharmacists, public relations specialists, and real estate agents (Reskin and Roos 1990).

When we focus on wage differentials in general, a commonly cited finding is that, up to about two decades ago, women in the U.S. labor force had been earning only about 60 percent of men's wages over the past half-century. Since 1980, however, the gap has steadily diminished so that in the mid-1990s women earn about 72 percent of male wages and salaries (Jacobs and Steinberg 1990; Phelan 1994; Ross and Mirowsky 1996). Fairly similar trends toward a lower disparity in earnings have been reported for other industrial nations (e.g., Rosenfeld and Kalleberg 1990; Mueller et al. 1994; Western 1994; Sorensen and Trappe 1995). The earnings gap has varied across nations, clearly indicating that environmental factors play an important role in sex-differentiated affairs. In the 1980s, for example, women in Australia were at 80 percent parity with men, whereas the corresponding figure for Japan was only 47 percent (Kalleberg and Rosenfeld 1990—report referred to in Reskin 1992: 2257).

The Causes, Real or Alleged

To explain such patterns of persistence and change, sociologists and others commonly emphasize one of three approaches. First, as can be expected, they most often posit the effects of differential socialization. The argument points to the various ways in which boys and girls learn sex-typical aspirations and behaviors through imitation of parental behavior, game playing, and exposure to role models in school, books, magazines, television, and movies. Certain tasks are said to be culturally defined as feminine, others as masculine. Through repeated exposure to such influences, sex stereotypes are instilled and past inequalities are thereby culturally reproduced.

But as we have repeatedly noted, there is a crucial deficiency in the differential socialization hypothesis. It fails to address the cross-cultural universality (e.g, Williams and Best 1982; Brown 1991) and persistence of "sex-stereotyped" roles (e.g., Judd and Park 1993; Feingold 1994; Eagly 1995; Lueptow et al. 1995). Why, for instance, are boys still more inclined, or encouraged, to adopt more assertive strategies (consistent with the ancient striving for high status), while girls are steered toward the more passive and nurturing strategies typical of our ancestral mothers? If sociologists cannot stomach Darwin, it may help them to turn at least to the great writers to grasp natural laws. "The law tradition makes," according to Euripides in *The Bacchae* (895–98), "is the law of nature."

Are "gender stereotypes" really stereotypes? The term typically implies a reference to group characteristics that are somehow untrue, or at the very least exaggerated, and that are employed to justify patterns of dominance and submission. A recent study reported by sociologist L.B.

Lueptow and his associates (1995) poses a serious challenge to this conventional sociological wisdom. These researchers assess data collected between 1974 and 1991 from students enrolled in introductory sociology courses at a large midwestern university in the U.S. They reason that, if gender stereotypes are primarily the product of socialization influences, changes in perceptions and related self-ratings should be detectable in view of the changes in sex-role attitudes and, to a lesser extent, sex-role behavior that have taken place since the early 1970s. The time span of their data coverage is well-suited to test the hypothesis: "Youths in the modal age group in the 1974 survey experienced their childhood socialization well *before* the significant changes began to occur. The 1991 respondents were born and experienced their entire socialization *after* the changes in traditional sex roles had commenced and intensified" (Lueptow et al. 1995: 518—emphasis in original).

Despite these changing cultural contexts, the researchers find that gender stereotypes on various personality traits, even on the basis of self-ratings, have remained remarkably stable. There is even some evidence of increased stereotypical responses. Over the time period reviewed, the traits commonly scored as most masculine included competitive, authoritative, adventurous, aggressive, and ambitious, while the following were least accentuated: obedient, affectionate, romantic, talkative, and sympathetic. The very reverse was true for perceived feminine traits (Lueptow et al. 1995: 519, table 2). This evidence, especially in combination with similar time-series results and corresponding cross-cultural findings, suggests that at least some so-called stereotypes are not stereotypes at all, but "reflect the perceptions of real personality differences between women and men, based to some undetermined degree on innate differences between the sexes" (Lueptow et al. 1995: 526). The findings are compelling, not only for what they have to say about the likely origins of sex-specialized adaptations, but also for the way the study illustrates how sociologists can effectively employ neo-Darwinian logic to improve their craft.

A second attempt at explaining sex differences in the workplace dips into the tool-kit of neoclassical economics, especially with respect to earnings. These are alleged to be a function of an individual's investment in "human capital." Particular jobs require particular skills. Skills, in turn, are developed through formal education, on the job training, and work experience. The greater the level of human capital investment demanded by an occupational category, the greater the earnings. We shall encounter an earlier version of this argument in chapter 8 in connection with the Davis-Moore (1945) theory of social stratification. At any rate, proponents of the human capital model typically explain that women, for various reasons, invest less than men in schooling and job training; that they are more inclined to take part-time as opposed to full-time jobs; that they less frequently take advantage of opportunities for continued training; and that they are more likely to enter, exit, and reenter the labor market, taking time out to have and rear children, interrupting thereby their career trajectories (Blau and Ferber 1992).

This view allegedly explains a considerable portion of the sex variance in earnings in industrial societies, and it has had some success in accounting for the recent declining disparity in earnings between the sexes (O'Neill and Polachek 1992; Wellington 1994; Tam 1997). A recent survey of American physicians illustrates the case (Baker 1996). Male physicians on average earn about 40 percent more than their female colleagues. The difference is particularly evident among older doctors. But for those under forty-five years of age with two to nine years of experience, the sex difference in earnings vanishes after controlling for the effects of specialty, practice setting (e.g., clinic, hospital, private practice, etc.), and number of hours worked per week. In fact, with similar statistical controls, females specializing in general or family practice have earnings that are slightly higher than those of their male colleagues.

This "rational choice" type of reasoning contributes useful findings and strongly implies biocultural interaction. Interrupted occupation due to maternal leave, for example, refers to a set of both ultimate and proximate factors at work. However, like its prior alternative, it does leave certain fundamental questions unanswered. Why, for example, are wages depressed even when women enter a given occupation with similar skills or human capital investment and persist in it without interruption? Sex differences in this context are frequently discussed in terms of differential expectations, desires, or demands somehow connected with family life. But the bases of these differentials are never explicitly addressed (e.g., Blau and Ferber 1992).

The third effort at explaining sex differences in earnings and other work-related rewards takes a presumably more structural approach. Since human capital explanations leave some portion of the sex variance in earnings unexplained, it is necessary, "structuralists" argue, to examine the operation of institutional barriers that may adversely affect women's earnings (e.g., England et al. 1994). In particular, the emphasis falls on the persisting effects of sex segregation in the workplace.

As we have already noted, occupational sex segregation has diminished in recent years, but it has not vanished. Many studies have long reported that, in female-dominated occupations, earnings are depressed (Treiman and Terrell 1975; Sawhill 1976; Ferber and Lowry 1976; Rytina 1981) and advancement opportunities are severely limited (Wolf and Rosenfeld 1978; Rosenfeld and Sorensen 1979; Roos 1985). In fact, the percentage of women employed in particular occupations and the degree to which these emphasize "nurturing" skills are correlated with lower earnings for both men and women, though more for women than for men (England et al. 1994; Kilbourne, England, and Beron 1994; Kilbourne, England, Farkas, Beron, and Weir 1994).

Other measures of workplace sex segregation reveal analogous findings. Women tend to be concentrated in marginal or peripheral industries, such as child care facilities or fast food enterprises, that typically yield lower earnings (Bibb and Form 1977; Beck et al. 1980; Bridges 1980). In addition, sex segregation by firm and occupational rank appears to limit women's earnings and authority (Talbert and Bose 1977; Sorensen and Trappe 1995). They are more likely than men to be employed in small firms characterized by labor-intensive production and lower levels of unionization, profits, and wages (England and Browne 1992). Moreover, while in recent years women have been represented in the ranks of management in increasing numbers, they tend to be concentrated at middle-management positions and remain underrepresented by far at the top of decision-making hierarchies.

These sorts of findings are taken as proof that sex differences in earnings and occupational status reveal a "gendered workplace." Hence, "the persistence of gender hierarchy" in industrial societies is said to be the outcome of "interactional processes that are largely taken for granted" (Ridgeway 1997: 218). The assumed processes allegedly concern the "presumed difference" between the sexes which reflects *only* "the cultural rules that organize interaction" in ways that give rise to "gender stereotypes" and inequality (Ridgeway 1997: 221, 219). As we have often pointed out, this type of reasoning is vacuous. It mistakes the label of the phenomenon for its explanation. The cultural rules cannot be taken as given. They too require explanation. Where did they come from? On what basis did they arise? Are they epiphenomena or, as gender feminists typically seem to imply, the result of deep-rooted male conspiracy? This is easy scholarship. The poorest of metaphysicians did much better with anchorless assumptions and unrestrained intuition.

As we have previously argued, what such "doing gender" hypotheses treat as cause is itself, at least in part, but another effect of causes that too many sociologists have an irrational aversion to. Is it likely that women are concentrated in so-called nurturing professions entirely for exogenous causes? Have they failed to crack the "glass ceiling" fully because of prejudice? And if so, why the persisting prejudice? Might the observed outcomes not reflect in part choices that women make as they struggle to balance the demands of job with the primeval specialization in family roles? In short, might there not be more deep-seated forces at work?

The evidence regarding persisting sex differences in socialization, occupational orientations, educational training, and career preferences, and how these differences are related to women's rewards and curtailed career opportunities, corresponds fairly closely to expectations derived from evolutionary theory, with its emphasis on the interplay between evolved predispositions and environmental influences. As noted in the preceding chapter, men and women exhibit *average* differences in aspects of sensation, cognition, and emotion. Such differences appear to be the evolved product of sex-differentiated features of brain anatomy and function. If, for instance, men are more assertive and women more conciliatory in the workplace, the evidence suggests that it is so not merely because they have been so socialized or because their verbal behavior is constrained by the everyday enactment of gendered power relations. They behave differently *in part* because in crucial ways they are equipped with brains that are wired to function differently. It may also suggest that greater assertiveness contributes to greater success in certain areas of the job market. Sex-differentiated socialization, strategies of human capital investment, and cultural constraints certainly play a role in shaping the differences between the sexes in the workplace. But such sociocultural influences are proximate, intervening factors that amplify or constrain more deep-seated forces. This view of the subject may offend sociological sensitivities, but it is no longer possible to avoid it and still survive, given the changing approach to human behavior in today's universities and research labs.

Occupational options in industrial societies, of course, are considerably more numerous and diverse than those faced by our forager ancestors. And yet, despite the enormity of change in the opportunity structure, women continue to gravitate in disproportionate numbers to the so-called nurturing professions. School teachers, nurses, daycare providers, and other occupations that emphasize care-giving skills remain overwhelmingly dominated by women. That such jobs are also poorly rewarded relative to the training undergone by those who fill them is a blameworthy residue of past environments. It may also indicate a huge irony in human, perhaps especially male psychology. We share other organisms' "obsession" for reproduction; yet we are particularly stingy in our rewards to our mothers and our nurses. But perhaps there is hope yet. The remarkable rate at which women have improved their economic and occupational status in industrial societies in recent years is telling proof that evolutionary adaptations are subject to considerable modification in the face of changing environmental pressures. Relevant sociological research could contribute a great deal to the how and what of such modification.

Nor is it surprising that recent trends in industrial societies indicate a narrowing of disparities between men and women in terms of occupational orientations and opportunities, rates of labor force participation, earnings, and authority. The gap can be filled still further. If women are innately better than men at ideational fluency and dexterity skills, then it is time to wonder, in company with our feminist colleagues, why there are not, say, more revered professors, famous attorneys, and perhaps especially surgeons, who in medical schools do little to encourage, and much to discourage, young women from their rich and highly honored specialization. Our evolution, we wish to stress, sets certain limits, but the range of the limits is broad, and men's tendency to dominate can be attenuated. Indeed it can be neutralized, as it often has been, by traits that are more subtle and in principle more efficient. Above all, the point is to treat facts and their causes with the tutored respect due to them. If "truth sets us free," and truth resides in falsifiable, established science, it is self-defeating for sociologists to seem strangely averse to both the search for truth and the joy of freedom.

8

Fundamentals of Social Stratification

Much of the subject matter noted in the previous two chapters is part of what sociologists term gender or sex stratification (e.g., Collins 1975; Huber and Spitze 1983; Reskin 1988; Chafetz 1990; Grusky 1994). As we have seen, a primary goal of writers in this area has been to document both past and present inequality, specifically the "victimization" of women by men (e.g., Tuchman 1992: 696–97). In this respect, gender stratification studies have followed the practice of much of sociology in general and of the broader studies of social stratification in particular. On the whole, sociologists have been more inclined to describe and denounce patterns of inequality than to seek general explanations of them. Engaged in "moral education," they "strongly suggest that there is a good; and it is operationally determined by the maximization of equality" (Horowitz 1993: 214–15).

There is mounting evidence, however, that inequality and dominance systems may be natural phemenona of social orders. As sociologist G. Simmel (1950: 183) noted, even when authority, for example, seems to "crush" us, "it is not based only on coercion or cumpulsion to yield to it." Dominance orders appear to perform basic functions, such as establishing a Hobbesian order of access to scarce resources (e.g., Durkheim 1897: 246–54; van den Berghe 1974). Accordingly, enumeration and denunciation of inequalities deserve to be accompanied by explanation, if for no other reason because without adequate understanding of causes, desired changes have little or no chance of realization. It seems hard to imagine an effective social engineering in the absence of a "social physics."

Our principal aim in this chapter is to seek out the fundamental causes of stratification systems. The focus on fundamentals is prescribed by the evolutionary perspective we have adopted and, not without some irony, by consideration of the forbidding variety and complexity that stratification systems have taken in time and place. We have no quarrel

with particular studies and historically circumscribed theories of stratification beyond the fact that they fall short of the necessary general
focus. By the same token, their relevance to our general goal is problematic, and we feel no obligation to engage in lengthy but ultimately
fruitless reviews. We hold, moreover, that general stratification dynamics
are most easily discovered in relatively simple social systems, such as
"primitive" human societies and the troops of our primate cousins. Further, given this focus, in what follows we shall use interchangeably
such concepts as social stratification, social hierarchy, and dominance
order, with a preference for the latter, largely because it is widely and
productively used among primatologists and other evolutionary scholars. In following this path, we shall avoid various sociological debates
that at one time or another have become ends in themselves, only to
eventually die out and leave in their wake nothing but mental fatigue,
disorientation, and above all a sense that nothing in sociology can be
resolved.

An instructive illustration of fruitless debate is provided by the old
but still engaging (e.g., Scott 1996) quarrel over one of "the most ambiguous sets of concepts" in sociology (Turner 1984: 144). Should sociologists, for example, study "social strata," apparently preferred by
most American scholars (e.g., Parsons 1954; Hodge 1981), or should
they study "class structures," as presumably preferred by most European scholars? The former tend to view inequalities along a continuum
of partly discrete socioeconomic categories, whereas the latter allege
to study social classes, namely historically discrete interest groups in
actual or virtual conflict with each other for economic and political
power (e.g., Dahrendorf 1959). For the Americans, inequality typically
expresses itself in complex and varied forms that deserve description
(and denunciation). For their European colleagues, the more proper
goal would be to grasp the historical emergence of given strata (capri-
ciously termed by them classes), such as the bourgeoisie, the prole-
tariat, and the "new middle class." The effect has been a considerable
literature of "moral preachings" and "concept mongering" that has contributed little or nothing to our understanding of social stratification
(Turner 1984: 145).

We must underscore the fact that today we are no closer to a general,
and generally accepted, theory of stratification than we were fifty or
more years ago. A close examination of two recent texts, for example,
reveals unequivocally the same exegeses and the same reviews of debates that have informed the profession for the past half century (Scott

1996; Hurst 1998). Lacking a firm basis for constructive theorizing and communication, we tend to fall back on the fine-tooled academic game: taking issue with real or presumed banal points; faulting the use of given variables; quarreling over sampling and measurement; attacking one another's open or implicit ideology. The result is a periodic recurrence of old debates, typically in slightly varied language, plus an immense repertoire of facts from particular times and places, most of which are welcomed by skepticism, sometimes even acrimonious rejection.

Highlights of Existing Stratification Theory

It is fair to note, however, that although they have never gained widespread acceptance, three theories have held sway at one time or another, and are still, singly or jointly, part of the sociological vocabulary among select members of the discipline. They are the work, respectively, of Karl Marx (and his lifelong collaborator Friedrich Engels); Max Weber, considered by many the foremost theorist as well as a rectifier of Marx's failures; and Kingsley Davis and Wilbert E. Moore (1945—updated somewhat in Davis 1948: chap. 14). The present section gives a brief account of these three efforts. We should first add that several other scholars have endeavored still other alternatives (e.g., Dahrendorf 1959; Lenski 1966; Giddens 1973; Collins 1975; Turner 1984). But, while for a time influential in some circles, their efforts have not succeeded in productively redirecting sociological attention. The basic problem, from our viewpoint, is that, while they may have addressed some basic aspects of human nature, and thus implied some fundamentals (e.g., Lenski 1966: chap. 23; Turner 1984: chaps. 5–6), they have avoided the deeply evolutionary perspective that is essential to cogently explain an ancient phenomenon. Moreover, these tentative bows to concepts of human nature are vitiated by a captivation with "societal interests," which are impossible to reconcile with the methodological individualism of scientific practice. Further, the fundamentals of what sociologists term social stratification do not begin with human society; they are primeval aspects of social species in general.

Karl Marx's Theory of Class Conflict

Marx's theory fails in various respects, though it also contains some useful elements. Probably more than any other, it underscores a preoccupation that, while useful to illuminate aspects of the current times, shuts the door on the past that the present is rooted in. Below is the core of his own summary of his achievement (Marx 1859).

> The general conclusion at which I arrived and which, once obtained, served to guide me in my studies, may be summarized as follows. In the social production which men carry on they enter into definite relations that are indispensable and independent of their will; these relations of production correspond to a definite stage of development of their material powers of production. The sum total of these relations of production constitutes the economic structure of society—the real foundation on which rise legal and political superstructures and to which correspond definite forms of social consciousness. The mode of production in material life determines the general character of the social, political and spiritual processes of life. It is not the consciousness of men that determines their existence, but, on the contrary, their social existence determines their consciousness. At a certain stage of their development, the material forces of production in society come into conflict with the existing relations of production, or—what is but a legal expression of the same thing—with the property relations within which they had been at work. From forms of development of the forces of production, these relations turn into their fetters. Then comes the period of social revolution. With the change of the economic foundation the entire immense superstructure is more or less rapidly transformed.... The bourgeois relations of production are the last antagonistic form of the social process of production—antagonistic not in the sense of individual antagonism, but of one arising from conditions surrounding the life of individuals in society; at the same time the productive forces developing in the womb of bourgeois society create the material conditions for the solution of that antagonism. The social foundation constitutes, therefore, the closing chapter of the prehistoric stage of human society.

We have already had occasion to recognize promising aspects of Marx's work. We should now underscore, first, the importance of Marx's focus on the economic structure of society, for it is here that are located the scarce resources needed for survival and reproduction. Whether, however, the mode of production "determines the general...processes of life" is a questionable assertion. Far deeper and far more ancient forces are implicated in the evolution of human behavior. Marx's thinking on this score was excessively shaped by his reaction against the neo-Hegeleans who were alleged to argue that "the consciousness of men determines their existence" (Marx and Engels 1845–1846).

Second, having focused on the production and distribution of economic resources, Marx was in a position to understand, perhaps better than most other students of political economy, the basic human facts of selfishness and *exploitation*—a form of *cheating* that involves appropriating resources acquired or produced by others. Unfortunately, he burdened these fundamental properties of dominance orders with all sorts of metaphysical camouflage. Hence, the focus falls not on the individual actor but on "class action"—and thus on class exploitation. Individuals appear only as passive pawns of historical processes "independent of their will," despite Marx's (1844: 130) prior warning "to avoid postulating 'society' [or "class"] once again as an abstraction confronting the individual." Having so oversimplified the nature of exploitation, it was of course far easier to get rid of it by speculative fiat than to grasp its persistent causes. In the famous *Theses on Feuerbach*, he (1845) could thus urge with unrestrained ideology: "The philosophers have only interpreted the world, in various ways; the point, however, is to change it." From this viewpoint it was not difficult to misconceive human nature and the societal dynamics of his own time, commiting thereby what is perhaps his least justifiable error:

> If the proletariat during its contest with the bourgeoisie...makes itself the ruling class, and, as such, sweeps away by force the old conditions of production, then it will, along with these conditions, have swept away the conditions for the existence of class antagonisms and classes generally, and will thereby have abolished its own supremacy as a class. (Marx and Engels 1848: 29)

Marx became so concerned with what ought to be rather than with what was that a radical transformation of human nature became a sort of theorem of his great work. No more selfishness, no more exploitation, no more action by the motive force (class struggle) of evolution as he had understood it to be working prior to the proletarian revolution. "From each according to his ability, to each according to his needs" was to be the practical reciprocity rule of the classless (communist) society. He simply failed to understand the deep causes of exploitation and the related point that the class structure is *only apparently* driven by collective interests.

Third, the above strictures notwithstanding, Marx's class is to an extent a serviceable concept. Exploitation, or cheating, may be expected to provoke conflict, and where there are struggles there are typically alliances (or classes) as well. But as Max Weber was soon to grasp more clearly, the undercurrent of alliances is the quest for *individual* power. By the same token, such alliances reveal human irony in its rawest form. They are most likely to be forged between individuals who implicitly or explicitly are in competition with each other for dominance, and are already within close reach of their coveted goal. A study of social conflict in Italy, for instance, shows that those who are most likely to challenge established authority are those who are in close proximity to it (Lopreato 1968; see also de Waal 1982: chap. 2). A general theory of dominance orders will, further, have to include recognition that, as Spencer (1876–1886) and Lenski (1966: 32), among others, put it, people are unequally endowed with the innate attributes necessary to succeed in the struggle for desirable resources, just as they are only too often privileged by social inheritance as well as other social connections.

Fourth, the concept of class is useful for another important reason. While so-called class action is almost certainly driven by selfish, individualistic forces, which become evident after it has been consummated (e.g., Djilas 1957; Gouldner 1982; Hill and Frank 1986), the concept at least sensitizes to the *appearance* of collective action which in turn helps to sharpen sensitivity to periodic episodes of massive movements. Besides, individuals, selfish or not, do often pursue their goals as members of groups, which viewed organizationally are examples of social systems. Accordingly, Marx's work rightly draws attention to the fact that stress is a fundamental property of systems, and reaches the breaking point under specifiable conditions. In short, Marx's understanding of class consciousness helps to pinpoint degrees of stress in social systems. When pointing to revolution, it indicates maximum stress and thus maximum probability of system disruption and a restructuring of an existing dominance order.

Fifth, and for brevity's sake finally, perhaps the major deficiency in Marx's theory lies in its focus on a tiny segment of human history, namely industrial society or at best agrarian society, where property relations are relatively well developed. On this restriction, we may call on F. Engels (1888: 4—emphasis added) himself to bear witness: "the whole history of mankind (*since the dissolution of primitive tribal society*, holding land in common ownership) has been a history of class struggles, contests between exploiting and exploited, ruling and oppressed classes." Marx's work, therefore, could not even begin to be a general explanation of inequality—of class or otherwise. It referred to only a very recent frame in a long sequence of scenes in the human drama. Moreover, to the extent that Marx considered the lessons deriving from ethnography, he made poor use of them. While the division of labor, for him a crucial complement of the emergence of classes, was certainly less developed in tribal than in industrial society, it hardly featured "primitive communism," as his alter ego Engels put it—certainly not in the Marxist sense of equitable distribution of resources. As we shall see, preindustrial and preagrarian societies were exploitative in more ways than one.

Max Weber's Tri-Dimensional Theory

Max Weber's theory of stratification may in part be viewed as an attack on Marx's position that class struggles constitute the fundamental mechanism of post-tribal societies. While Weber, too, failed to produce a general theory, his contribution is in some respects richer and also more kindred to an evolutionary perspective. According to this scholar (1921–1922, II: 926–27), in addition to the *economic order* of society—"the way in which economic goods and services are distributed"—and thus to classes holding "economic power," there are a *social order* and a *legal order*. The first refers to "the way in which social honor is distributed in a community between typical groups participating in this distribution," and features "status groups." The latter, less clearly defined, may be conveniently viewed as the distribution of "political power" in any associational setting; it yields "parties."

These distinctions have several useful implications. Weber grants competition and conflict a broader and deeper role in social relations and societal development. The picture begins with his treatment of classes themselves, of which he sees various kinds (e.g., acquisition classes, social classes, middle classes), all of which flowing from his treatment of the major type, namely "property classes" (Weber 1921–1922, I: 301–07, II: 926–39). Logically, however, property classes can be "positively privileged" (composed of owners) or "negatively privileged" (comprising non-owners). Having granted Marx this basic dichotomy, Weber (1921–1922, II: 928), however, argues that within each type there are numerous, and historically persisting, classes differentiated "on the one hand, according to the kind of property that is usable for returns; and, on the other hand, according to the kind of services that can be offered in the market." Marx had a fairly detailed view of the class structure in specific historical settings—for example, France in the middle of the nineteenth century (Marx 1850)—but saw it moving toward consolidation into two opposing camps in his own time. By contrast, Weber detected such a plethora of classes and class interests that the Marxist revolutionary dichotomization appeared only as a mere logical possibility at best.

This view of a multiplicity of possible bases of conflict was further enhanced by Weber's conception of the status order. Status groups are differentiated in terms of "social honor" and "may be connected with any quality shared by a plurality": education, taste, occupation, membership in given associations, ethnicity, family lineage, even fashion

(Weber 1921–1922, I: 305–06, II: 932). Status groups are in principle nearly infinite in number. Moreover, from the viewpoint of a theory of society-wide conflict there is a telling irony about them. Unlike classes, they do feature consciousness of kind, and thereby stimulate sentiments of common identity and of mutual obligation. But they are also *exclusive*. Their presence in society signifies narrowness of views and interests, in short a kind of obstinate tribalism—the anachronistic feature of complex society that shows the action of kin selection and nepotism gone hypertrophic (Pareto 1916; van den Berghe 1981; Lopreato 1984; Reynolds et al. 1987). Accordingly, as we shall see in chapter 9, Weber's theory of stratification can help toward a deeper understanding of problems of ethnicity as well.

Weber further understood that, while class and status stratification coexisted and expressed complementary features of human society, the two featured varying saliency in view of rhythmic technological transformations. Thus (Weber 1921–1922, II: 938):

> When the bases of the acquisition and distribution of goods are relatively stable, stratification by status is favored. Every technological repercussion and economic transformation threatens stratification by status and pushes the class situation into the foreground. Epochs and countries in which the naked class situation is of predominant significance are regularly the periods of technical and economic transformations. And every slowing down of the change in economic stratification leads, in due course, to the growth of status structures and makes for a resuscitation of the important role of social honor.

Finally, Weber's focus on clannishness is underscored by his discussion of the legal order, wherein parties are principal agents in competition. From this perspective, human beings are viewed as manifestly power-seeking animals. The acquisition of power, "legal" or otherwise, facilitates the acquisition and/or maintenance of class and often status resources and privileges. Parties, moreover, must be broadly understood as *alliances* that may arise in numberless contexts. "In principle, parties may exist in a social club as well as in a state" (Weber 1921–1922, II: 938). They are constituted by individuals, few or many in number, who make common cause, typically for limited periods of time, to realize their own will and interests. They are in sociology the counterpart of what primatologist Frans de Waal (1982: chap. 2) has termed "open coalitions" (temporary alliances of self-interested individuals). Like classes and status groups, they tend to add to fragmentation in society rather than to the simplification of conflict camps conceived by Marx as necessary to revolution.

In conclusion of this brief discussion, Weber's work contains some evolutionary undertones, which may be associated with aspects of kin selection and sexual selection, but these appear in misleading contexts. On the whole, the general output is essentially descriptive and historically circumscribed. Hence, it fails to show the way to a general theory of stratification. Typically, Weber on stratification is used by sociologists in one or a combination of three ways: (1) to belittle Marx's work; (2) to use or abuse some of his basic concepts (especially status and power); and (3) to underscore, though rarely to demonstrate, the fact that social stratification is multidimensional, and hence its proper study would require a fairly complex taxonomy as a basis (e.g., Scott 1996). In these respects, the Weberian literature is enormous. Unfortunately it is also amorphous, laden with improbable debates, and on the whole a microcosm of the crisis that defines sociology in general.

The Functionalist Theory of Kingsley Davis and Wilbert E. Moore

The so-called functionalist theory of stratification (Davis and Moore 1945) is the only sociological attempt known to us to focus on the "universal necessity which calls forth stratification in any social system" (Davis and Moore 1945: 242). The effort is also structured in fairly economic fashion, so that it is possible to represent the core of its logical structure in the following series of propositions.

1. Any society faces the functional necessity of "placing and motivating individuals in the social structure."
2. Societies must (a) motivate "the proper individuals" (presumably those with talents appropriate to their future positions) to train for those positions and (b) motivate these same individuals to perform (effectively), once they have completed their apprenticeship.
3. Positions vary in terms of: (a) *agreeableness*; (b) "*special talents or training*"; and (c) "*functional importance*" to "societal survival."
4. It follows that "inevitably" any society must have: (a) a set of differential rewards as inducements and (b) a mechanism for the distribution of those rewards.
5. Rewards come in three major types: (a) "the things that contribute to sustenance and comfort"; (b) "the things that contribute to humor and diversion"; and (c) "the things that contribute to ego expansion." All three are of roughly equal "importance" and "must be dispensed differentially according to positions."
6. If the rewards "must be unequal, then the society must be stratified, because that is precisely what stratification means."

7.   "Social inequality is thus an unconsciously evolved device by which
     societies ["no matter how simple or complex"] insure that the most im-
     portant positions are conscientiously filled by the most qualified persons."

8.   Two factors determine the relative rank, and thus rewards, of different
     positions: (a) "differential functional importance" to societal survival
     and (b) "differential scarcity of personnel" for given positions.

9.   "In general" the greater the functional importance of a given position
     and the greater the scarcity of personnel (due to requirements of "train-
     ing or talent"), the better the rewards and the higher the rank accruing to
     that position.

10. The two determinants are complementary, but scarcity of personnel bears
     the greater power to modify the action of its complement. Thus, while
     societies "must see that less essential positions do not compete success-
     fully with more essential ones," they need not reward positions accord-
     ing to their high functional importance if they are "easily filled." On the
     other hand, if they are both highly important and hard to fill, the rewards
     must also be high. In short, functional importance is "a necessary but
     not a sufficient cause of high rank being assigned to a position."

11. Finally, differences between one system of stratification and another are
     "attributable to whatever factors affect the two determinants of differen-
     tial reward": functional importance and scarcity of personnel. They may
     be varied and numerous. The authors make a slight effort to account for
     some variations; but their focus is, justifiably, on the fundamental prob-
     lem, that is, on the explanation of the universality of stratification systems.

Whether they have succeeded in this aim is another matter. Our verdict is negative, and accords in part with the controversy that for over
half a century has surrounded the theory. One common criticism concerns the difficulty of defining and assessing the functional importance
of positions for societal survival (e.g., Tumin 1953), a problem that the
authors themselves recognized and inadequately tried to solve (Davis
and Moore 1945: 224n; Davis 1948: chap. 14, 1953: 395). Another
widespread criticism addresses the apparent failure of the authors to
recognize that, once a system of stratification has emerged, those reaping the high rewards have also the power to monopolize them to a considerable extent. As G.C. Homans (1967: 67) succinctly put it, it is not
"society" but people in the flesh "who confer rewards upon one another. Some of them, moreover, are...in a position to take them—and
this is one reason why they are important."

To the extent that the Davis-Moore theory may have any scientific
utility at all, it must be understood as a "theoretical idealization" (Lopreato
and Alston 1970). The following rendition illustrates the point: "A person's
social position, as defined in terms of the rewards attendant upon his

occupational activities, is determined by the contribution made by those activities to a desired state X (integration, prosperity, or the like) of that person's society...*provided that* (1) free competition in the labor market exists and (2) the supply of personnel for given occupations meets exactly the demand for it" (Lopreato and Hazelrigg 1972: 109).

In the inimitable fashion of sociologists, the critics have provided ample fodder for debate but almost no attempts to test or clarify crucial aspects of the theory (but see Huaco 1963; Stinchcombe 1963). Without exception, all criticisms and all the results of the few attempts at testing the theory have concluded that the major difficulty is rooted in the vague concept of functional importance, thus rendering the theory unfalsifiable. The theory also features a confusing admixture of structural (e.g., societal survival) and psychological variables (e.g., motivation) that properly guided research rejects according to the demands of methodological individualism. Thus, in one of the few tests of the theory the conclusion was reached, on the basis of interview data, that it is actual human beings who necessarily define the functional importance of given positions; else, they would be unable to bestow the "correct" rewards upon one another. "And so it happens that a strictly societal variable turns out to be really a psychological one—or at least, it can be legitimately conceptualized in psychological terms" (Lopreato and Hazelrigg 1972: 104; see also Lopreato and Lewis 1963).

Statements of society as agent, of societal needs, and of societal survival create more problems than they solve; they invariably nudge the mind into the realm of metaphysics and unleash mere intuitionism. But again, with a proper view of system analysis, it is possible to improve our understanding of them. On the meaning of societal survival, for example, one clue was provided by Davis himself (1953: 395). Attempting to clarify functional importance, he noted that in wartime first priority in the allocation of resources in a given society goes to war-related industries (and personnel). Societal survival in this context equates with winning the war, the goal state of the system at war. But it is also true that the achievement of the goal state equates in the last analysis with the survival of individuals, or at least with a reduced risk to their life and hence ultimately to their fitness. Military conquest typically entails pillage, rape, devastation. If organisms are predisposed to so behave as to safeguard their genetic fitness, it follows that they may also be expected to grant sizable rewards to those who help them avoid the enemy's fury. On the whole, however, the emphasis on societal survival is just misleading. What does the concept really refer to? When, if ever, does a society cease to survive? Was the USSR a society? Has it ceased to survive? Or has it changed? In what sense? Sociologists seem addicted to societal or system needs, and this problem tends to vitiate even the best efforts at theorizing (e.g., Lenski 1966: chap. 2).

The fundamental virtue of the Davis-Moore theory is that it does make a deliberate effort at grasping first principles, and thus the general etiology of stratification systems, however erroneously. Failure, moreover, is not a vice. It can be a powerful invitation to future success. At any rate, it may be properly said that, whatever the alleged causes of stratification, what we invariably observe from its perspective is: *scarcity of resources, competition for them, differential success*, and of course differential power or *exploitation*. These are essentially Malthusian ideas that have been best nurtured, ironically, by Charles Darwin and the participants in the extraordinary revolution triggered by him.

When all is said and done, the Davis-Moore theory contains aspects of these basics, though rather poorly treated. But it has little or nothing to say about the evolution of systems of inequality. The fairest verdict is that it represents a mixture of supply-demand economic mechanisms and the implicit psychologies associated thereto (Lopreato and Lewis 1963). Accordingly, its flaws are similar to those of exchange theory, rational-choice theory, and human capital theory encountered in previous chapters. It also seems to assume a fairly advanced division of labor, again reflecting the sociologist's obsession with complex societies of very recent times. But if we wish to explain the fundamental facts of stratification we must look farther back into our history and to simpler social conditions. The irony is that the necessity of peeling away accretions in order to grasp fundamentals is known in sociology, though rarely if ever practiced. Marx himself (1867: 8—emphasis added), for example, wrote in the preface to the first edition of *Capital*: "The physicist either observes physical phenomena where they occur in their most typical form and *most free from disturbing influence* or, whenever possible, he makes experiments under conditions that assure the occurrence of the phenomenon in its normality." Likewise, Durkheim (1912: 20) argued, somewhat more to the point:

> Every time that we undertake to explain something human, taken at a given moment in history—be it a religious belief...or an economic system—it is necessary to commence by going back to its most primitive and simple form.... causes are proportionately more easily observable as the societies where they are observed are less complicated.

As already noted, our own focus is on the most elementary systems of stratification. These may be found among primate societies and the preagrarian peoples of hunting and gathering society, whose history goes back millions of years. The clan societies of our own times are not perfect representatives of the more ancient forms, but they may be very suggestive of them. In the 1930s, the anthropologist Lévi-Strauss (1944) was startled to find that even a very "simple" people like the Nambikuara Indians of Brazil had chiefs and leaders. Lévi-Strauss noted that leaders were favored with prestige, which they enjoyed "for its own sake." But chiefs enjoyed something else, too, and that will be important to our explanation of stratification. They exploited their subordinates in various ways, and reproductive females were "leadership's prize and instrument."

Keen to the crucial importance of differential access to reproductive activities, another anthropologist has argued that in the world's "so-called 'egalitarian' societies not all men are in fact equal"—in a fundamental sense. "Polygyny is widespread in the tribal world and has probably characterized human mating and reproduction for the greater fraction of our species' history" (Chagnon 1979: 375). According to Chagnon, exploitation begins with life's most basic activity: reproduction. Evidence accumulating from various lines of inquiry make it very difficult to quarrel with this proposition.

Dominance Orders among Primates

The Davis-Moore assumption of unavoidable stratification is compelling from an evolutionary perspective. If dominance orders were not inevitable, a number of relevant predictions that we can make would be easily falsified. For example, dominance orders are universal in human society. Moreover, attempts at "destratification" are destined to fail. Further, evolutionary forces of stratification, such as sexual selection, are represented at the ontogenetic level, for example in the endocrine system. Again, in their fundamentals, human dominance orders bear a significant resemblance to those observable among our close relatives, the primates. Each of these predictions is falsifiable but is not likely to be falsified anytime soon.

We turn first to the last proposition, namely to the world of our close relatives, about which there is a literature so vast, and growing rapidly, that we can barely touch on it. We begin with a definition. In evolutionary terms, *a dominance order may be conveniently defined as a social*

*arrangement wherein individuals and/or aggregates thereof compete
for and achieve unequal access to scarce resources, e.g., mates, food,
nesting sites, and "other objects promoting survivorship and reproductive success"* (Wilson 1975: 11; see also Dunbar 1988: 206–8).

Primate dominance orders, like their human counterparts, are highly
variable in form and fluidity (for excellent reviews, see Chance and
Jolly 1970; Wilson 1975: 282–97; Smuts 1987; Walters and Seyfarth
1987; Dunbar 1988; Ellis 1995). The complexity of these social structures is affected by a host of environmental, historical, experiential,
and genetic factors. Nonetheless, inspection of the literature, especially
among Old World monkeys and the anthropoids, reveals several common denominators that recall human facts.

Generally, the dominance order features an oligarchy, at the center
of which is a male, often referred to as the alpha male in the literature.
In sociology, this observation corresponds very closely to one emphasized by so-called elite theorists (e.g., Pareto 1902–1903, 1916; Michels
1914; Mosca 1939). "The most striking feature of social behavior in
the troop [of Japanese macaques] is the fact that a few males dominate
all the other animals" (Eaton 1976: 97). The alpha is the *primus inter
pares* in terms of the privileges that accrue to domination. Studies of
vervet monkeys, among others, reveal that rank among adult males is
largely a function of certain indicators of "intrinsic power" (Datta 1983),
that is, relative age, size, strength, and other determinants of "fighting
ability" (Cheney and Seyfarth 1990: 33). But of nearly equal, and in
some cases even greater, significance is an individual's "extrinsic power"
stemming from his alliance with others (Harcourt and de Waal 1992).
Frequently, the coalition also governs who is victorious in contests designed to determine dominance in the troop (e.g., DeVore 1965b). A
broad view of facts, therefore, indicates that primate "politics forms a
part of the endless struggle for existence" (Vänhanen 1992), and political parties are not uniquely human phenomena (Low 1992). Among
sociologists, Max Weber, as we have seen, came close to recognizing
this fact by defining parties as coalitions of few or many self-interested, power-driven individuals.

The privileges of dominant individuals, almost always male, are
many, and typically include priority of access to food and females in
estrus even in the relatively egalitarian societies of chimpanzees (e.g.,
de Waal 1982, 1989; Goodall 1986a). This elite exploitation is observable in both natural and contrived settings (e.g., DeVore 1965a). For
example, when the distribution of food resources was experimentally

reduced in a laboratory-housed group of bonnet macaques, overall levels of aggressive and submissive behaviors increased, and the monkeys obtained access to the food supply in order of their dominance status in the group (Boccia *et al.* 1988; de Waal 1989: 123–27).

Paradoxically it would seem, the same result is often observable when there is an abundance of resources. Jane Goodall (1986a: 334–36) notes from the wild that a number of ecological and social factors affect the probability that a chimpanzee will be aggressive in a given situation. Food scarcity is associated with diminished levels of aggression owing to the fact that, in the wild, troop members disperse across a wide territory. It is when food is abundant—for example, in the presence of substantial stands of fruiting trees or the availability of meat—that individuals congregate and competition intensifies. The observation recalls the stratification effects of the agricultural revolution in the history of our own species (e.g., Lenski 1966). The revolution, and hence the rise of an "economic surplus," was quickly followed by an arousal of aggression—internal and external—and thus by the rise of parasitic ruling classes, the brutal conquest of weaker societies, and other features associated with the rise of agrarian stratification systems, such as slavery and the harem. At any rate, "dominance is a means to an end, a proximate goal that provides an animal with priority of access to resources that are of crucial long-term importance in terms of reproduction" (Dunbar 1988: 207). Whenever environmental conditions stimulate competition, the quest for dominance may be expected to intensify.

Dominants are ever on the alert to defend their status and privileges. Their techniques are various. Sometimes they display aggressively, causing fear and momentary disarray in the troop. A reading of de Waal's dramatic description of the dominant male's return to his troop, after a brief absence, conveys lessons that may recall human military parades, midnight raids, and analogous activities of political intimidation (Kertzer 1988). Yeroen, the alpha in question, showed up like a rhinoceros run amok. When the furor subsided, the subordinates hastened to seek conciliation by offering him gifts, kissing his feet or some other part of his body, and among other things by "bobbing," which in chimpanzees is a series of deep, deferential bows. Pacified, or reassured that his status was unchallenged, Yeroen eventually relaxed and allowed himself to be groomed (de Waal 1989). At the same time, the troop's attention was intensely focused on him, much as when human beings are collected in wonderment at a coronation, or listen in awe to a political speech.

Dominance among primates, as among humans, is not lacking in certain trappings of humility. Chimpanzee leaders have especially clever political policies. For example, they spend a great deal of social time with the adult females, the masses, who constitute their main power base. Indeed, the ruling male is secure only as long as he has their support. When females no longer have reason to support him, he is apparently left helplessly to his own devices (de Waal 1982; Goodall 1986a). The phenomenon appears to be widespread among primate species. M.J. Raleigh and M.T. McGuire (1989) showed for captive vervet monkeys, for example, that females, especially the alpha female, had the strongest influence on which male would become dominant. Predictably, alpha males and aspirants to alpha status conspicuously court favor with adult females and their offspring. They frequently kiss the young and spend considerable time playing with them. Of course, they are especially attentive to the children of dominant females, and hence help to socialize such youngsters in the ways of dominant individuals. Above all perhaps, alpha males intervene in fights, typically in favor of the weaker parties, thereby solidifying support among favored subordinates and to an extent undermining the rise of challengers to their status. The strategy amounts to a clear instance of the divide-and-conquer technique so common in human politics (de Waal 1982: chap. 2).

Like the human ruling elite (e.g., Michels 1914; Pareto 1916; Mosca 1939; Mills 1956), the primate coalition is a fairly stable ruling body. With some exceptions (e.g., Goodall 1971; Hrdy 1977), only another coalition has the best chance of overthrowing it. The stakes are high and the tendency to form counter-coalitions is strong. Moreover, primate revolutions appear to have a greater probability of success than in human societies. One reason is that, although such factors as alliances, systems of reciprocity, and cunning play a large role in achieving and maintaining a dominant status (Goodall 1986a: 418–22), the successful use of brute force against the leader of an existing coalition tends to break up his coalition.

In chimpanzees, as in many other primate species, the challenge may begin with a form of civil disobedience. For example, the challenger refuses to greet the alpha male. The latter may be reaching the ripe old age of thirty or so, when downfalls are common. If the ruling coalition is unsteady, challenges will tend to accumulate in the face of decreasing resistance. As the challenger's confidence rises, he may be able to deliver a major blow, such as mating in defiance of the reigning male. Fights multiply, and eventually the challenger may draw blood. Frans de Waal (1982: chap. 2) shows how debilitating such an event is, causing the followers to lose confidence in the protective powers of their leader and hence to shift their allegiance.

This scenario bears considerable resemblance to the human case. Civil disobedience often spreads and weakens the rulers' resolve to use adequate or measured force in self-defense. A period of instability and realignment ensues. The challenger may succeed in his maneuver or he may be out-maneuvered by a disgruntled member of the existing coalition. In either case, violent overthrows are not uncommonly followed by conflicts within the ranks of the revolutionary vanguard, often featuring cases of "betrayal" and even reigns of terror (e.g., Marx and Engels 1848; Pareto 1916; Brinton 1938; Davies 1962). Likewise F. de Waal (1982) shows that chimp Luit unseats ruling Yeroen with the help of Nikkie only to lose the ensuing struggle to Nikkie himself and eventually to be murdered in the bargain (de Waal 1986). In general, however, peacemaking among chimpanzees is easier and quicker than among humans, thanks in part to the greater fluidity of their dominance orders and to the mediating powers of the females. Soon after a new coalition is formed, the old ruler typically makes peace and learns to cope with his rapidly descending social status.

There are numerous other primate parallels to the human case. For instance, among chimpanzees as well as various other primates, a position of dominance is rarely if ever reached upon attaining full body growth. Alpha males generally reach their lofty position in their mature adult years, a good eight to ten years into adulthood in macaques and chimpanzees, among others (e.g., Eaton 1976; de Waal 1982; Goodall 1986a; Walters and Seyfarth 1987). Gerontocracies are fairly widespread in the primate order.

Primate oligarchs and/or oligarchies perform basic social functions that correspond closely to the basic functions of human governments. A primary one is to defend the troop against external enemies, or at any rate to organize and lead the defense. Another is to direct the movement of the troop or otherwise lead the collective planning of troop life. But, as in human society, perhaps the most crucial social function is to maintain internal order. Studies show that the removal of dominant individuals sharply increases aggression in the lower ranks (Tokuda and Jensen 1968; Mazur 1973; Eaton 1976; de Waal 1989). In some cases, the order function is delegated to the lieutenants. Eaton's (1976: 102) study of Japanese macaques showed, for example, that the maintenance of order in the troop was the principal role of "subleader males," namely individuals who call to mind such functionaries as judges or even directors of state security, police officers, attorneys general, and the like.

Like human beings, many primate species practice a form of expulsion or ostracism. Rejection may be severe. In some primate troops, subdominant adolescent males, for example, are driven to the periphery by high-ranking adult males—an action that, according to K. Kawanaka (1984) seems to be the "the sociological equivalent of going into exile." Ostracism undermines one's opportunities for reproduction as well one's access to resources necessary to good health and longevity (Lancaster 1986), though the phenomenon appears poorly developed among our closest cousins, the chimpanzees (Goodall 1986b). Human beings are much richer in techniques of social rejection, humor being probably one of the most common and effective (Alexander 1986). But, in contrast to our primate cousins, we also have gossip mongers, stockades, jails, and firing squads, among other techniques, with which to humiliate or eliminate entirely unwanted individuals and even entire groups.

These observations suggest that, from one vantage point dominance orders may be termed systems of *social control* (Gibbs 1994), whereby the potential intractability of the masses is prevented from having free reign (e.g., Durkheim 1897: 246–54; Goodall 1986a; Eaton 1976; de Waal 1989; Bernstein and Ehardt 1985). Thus, while competition creates dominance orders, these in turn tend to regulate competition. Émile Durkheim explicitly recognized this aspect of dominance orders. For example, in the discussion of anomic suicide, he argued that human needs are in principle unlimited and thus inextinguishable; hence an external regulatory force is required to control this potentially "morbid" tendency. "As a matter of fact," Durkheim (1897: 249) went on to argue, "at every moment of history there is a dim perception, in the moral consciousness of societies, of the respective value of different social services, the relative reward due to each, and the consequent degree of comfort appropriate on the average to workers in each occupation" (see also Davis and Moore 1945). This insight suggests how both profound and misleading social theory can be, and thus how informative an interspecific approach may be. The primate evidence shows that self-accommodation to one's status may have very little to do with "moral consciousness" and much more to do with a case of who can get away with what (Gibbs 1994). Hence, dominance orders may also be viewed as evolutionary mechanisms that help sustain systems of reciprocity wherein a degree of cheating, often gross, is allowed to those who take on the job of enforcing the rules. Whatever else they do, leaders of social systems cheat. They use reciprocal systems to their immediate and ultimate advantage. We may add, by reference to Trivers' theory of reciprocal altruism, treated in chapter 5, that if a dominance order of low salience was a condition fostering the evolution of reciprocity, in the course of time it achieved a high profile and facilitated the practice of gross cheating or exploitation.

Order systems rest to a degree on some division of labor. Some scholars have observed fairly complex dominance orders in primate societies. Eaton (1976: 102), for example, writes of a role specialization among Japanese macaques that is "largely determined by class membership." The classes include the "leader class," the "subleader class," the "adult females," the "juveniles," and a "peripheral class." Moreover, where there is status differentiation, there is also likely to be a tendency toward status inheritance. The phenomenon, far from being unique to human systems, is fairly widespread in primate societies. Reviews of primate evidence indicate that daughters and subadult sons of dominant females have a fair chance of perpetuating their mothers' status (Willhoite 1975; Dunbar 1988; Cheney and Seyfarth 1990). Starting early in life, the young engage in repeated play-fights in which the help of mother, other kin, and dominant individuals is crucial in determining the outcome (Kawai 1958; Smith and Smith 1988). Status inheritance is more probable among females, significantly the sex that, as Darwin noted, is less susceptible to sexual selection (Goodall 1986a; Cheney and Seyfarth 1990).

Nevertheless, there appears to be a greater equality of opportunity in the societies of our close relatives than in many human societies, and thus more social mobility. Several scholars, for example, have shown that early advantages are not necessarily decisive in determining adult status either in natal or in non-natal troops (Koford 1963; Walters and Seyfarth 1987). But in general we are reminded of parallels in the nepotistic and political networks of human society: for example, the "connections" often required to clerk in high offices and to gain admission to military academies. Some scholars have remarked that these parallels are "something more than a fortuitous analogy" (Willhoite 1975: 274; see also Jolly 1972: 260).

Finally, it seems fairly clear that we know more about the social position of non-human females than about their human counterparts (Smuts 1987). As previously noted, in many primate species, adult females represent the main constituency of the top leaders. To a large extent, then, the stability of their social orders and the tenor of social relations in general are dependent on female behavior (Small 1992; Hooks and Green 1993; Wrangham 1997). Although some scholars prefer to speak of two dominance orders—one male, the other female (e.g., Goodall 1986a)—many adult females occupy a fairly high position in the overall dominance order (e.g., de Waal 1982, 1989; Goodall 1986a; Raleigh and McGuire 1989). The fact results in part from their high reproductive value, apparently better appreciated by apes and monkeys than by their civilized cousins. For example, in contrast to humans, other male primates appear to be less aggressive toward their females. Male chimpanzees do not use their canines in aggressive behavior toward females and the young, while they have fewer qualms about using them against one another (de Waal 1982: chap. 2). In part, too, the relatively high status of females may rest in the fact that they are excellent at cultivating male allies and have coalitions of their own as well (Smuts 1985; Goodall 1986a; Hooks and Green 1993).

Once female chimpanzees have "voted" for their leader, they are often second to none except him in importance; and it is not infrequent that two or more females combine to put the leader himself to rout, at least temporarily. When Luit started challenging Yeroen in the group studied by de Waal (1982), females showed little or no deference toward him; and Luit's helper, Nikkie, was long without the honor of the females' greetings. Moreover, in at least one species, the Bonobos (*Pan paniscus*), it appears that society is both female-centered and female-regulated, in large part apparently because of the readiness of females to engage in mutual erotic stimulation and thereby to cement female alliances (de Waal 1989, 1995; Parish 1996).

The social superiority of adult females to subdominant males is not unique to chimpanzees. Eaton (1976) reports for Japanese macaques, for example, that adult females rank in status just below the alpha male and the few subleader males of the troop, at the bottom of which are the other, more numerous males. There are, of course, advantages to high status, for females as well as males. Saroj Datta's (1988) study of free-ranging rhesus monkeys, one of the best for female rank, lists the following benefits associated with high rank: better food and drink, early breeding, higher fertility, and enhanced survival of offspring (see also Dunbar and Dunbar 1977; Whitten 1983; Cheney and Seyfarth 1990; Hooks and Green 1993; Pusey et al. 1997).

In conclusion of this section, we are keenly aware of the fact that most human societies are far more populous than other primate societies and, because of this fact alone if none other, human social organization, of which dominance orders constitute a central part, is far more complex than any that can be found among other primate species. Nevertheless, we have observed enough fundamental facts to suggest that dominance orders have ancient evolutionary roots. Among such facts, the following probably constitute a very conservative estimate of what may properly be labeled *common denominators*:

1. Dominance orders are universal in primate society.
2. The apex of the formation typically consists of a coalition, what political sociologists have termed an oligarchy, at the center of which is a dominant male (the alpha).
3. The members of the coalition and the alpha in particular profit from various sorts of privileges, which from the viewpoint of political sociology constitute elite exploitation.
4. Privileges are maintained through a variety of techniques, including aggressive displays, courting the good will of subordinates, and the ostracism of maturing young males, among other uses of force and cunning.
5. Coercion and/or deception plays a major role in acquiring and maintaining positions of dominance.
6. Dominance orders are characterized by a considerable degree of stability, though less than that enjoyed by human ruling classes.
7. The alpha position is normally reached several years after attaining adulthood, suggesting that gerontocracy is a natural phenomenon.
8. The ruling coalition, or the alpha alone, performs basic functions: defense of the group, guidance of the group activities, and maintenance of internal order.
9. Dominance orders may thus be said to be, in part, systems of social control. But being in a position to maintain order reduces the leader's obligations of reciprocity. To put it otherwise, a fundamental privilege of the leader is to cheat with relative impunity in the system of reciprocal altruism.
10. Status inheritance is common and is best observable in several species through the status career of dominant females' offspring.

Evolutionary Fundamentals of Human Stratification Systems

Many phenomena in social science must be viewed as ultimately Malthusian-Darwinian problems. The origin of dominance orders is bound to be located in the competition for scarce resources, reproductive as well as economic, and the differential ability of individuals to succeed in it (Lenski 1966: 31–32). The results of the competition are not random; they are recorded and ordered by natural selection. What is recorded, specifically, is the set of those traits that incline toward the struggle for valued resources and in each generation end by promoting the reproductive success of some competitors as against others. Viewing such traits in an intuitive key, social scientists refer to them as ambition, competitiveness, the need to rise, the need for power, political savvy, and so forth. Associated with them are such other tendencies as pride and arrogance. Together, these traits constitute the major elements of dominance orders. The basic feature of such arrangements is exploitation of the losers by the winners: what is sometimes referred to as parasitism (McNeill 1976; Machalek 1995, 1996). In sum, the struggle for existence and natural selection are the irreducible processes that join together to produce the adaptations that result in dominance orders and exploitation.

Exploitation varies both in degree and in kind. Given time, population growth, and the multiplication of resources, it can achieve fantastic forms and magnitude, and become associated with almost unimaginable techniques of superordination and subordination. At a parasitic extreme, once in power, dominant individuals and groups may appropriate all but the scraps of the resources of others. The need to acquire and consume, as T. Veblen (1899) showed so clearly, can become so "conspicuous" that even the accumulation of material resources can take on a subjective and insatiable character. The more we have, the more we want. Humans are to one another as ravenous apiarists are to honey bees; it is easier to appropriate the products of the labor of others than to produce them directly (Pareto 1916). Everywhere the tendency has been toward a division between those, always a minority, who have appropriated the richest supplies and those, always a majority, who must make do with the remainder, often the bare minimum needed for survival.

There is a widespread tendency among sociologists to assume that human beings are embarked on the road to an increasingly egalitarian distribution of resources. Evolutionary theory cautions against this notion although, when complemented by organizational theory and principles of population, it does help to predict an enlargement of the privileged group (see also Pareto 1906: chap. VII; Michels 1914). Technological innovation, for example, has engendered great wealth, and for a variety of related reasons the size of the middle classes has increased. But a certain percentage of people must make do with the insecurity of the daily bread, and most still must worry about having enough to live on in their old age, while a small number manage to amass almost unimaginable wealth. Modern society continues to feature high degrees of inequality, and the future promises nothing new in this respect.

Sexual Selection and Dominance Orders

Harking back to our discussion of evolutionary theory in chapters 4 and 5, we may stress once again that the competition for resources occurs on two distinctive but complementary levels. One refers to the struggle for the various resources that promote the organism's well-being and longevity; individuals compete for priority of access to food, preferred territories, influence, and such other resources that enhance their prospects for better health and greater individual satisfaction. The other level involves a competition for access to reproductive mates. From an evolutionary perspective, it is not sufficient to examine an organism's endowments strictly in terms of their contribution to health, longevity, and satisfaction. Of greater importance is how they inhibit or facilitate the survival of the organism's genetic heritage. The two levels of competition constitute the basic selection pressures that have governed the emergence and persistence of psychological adaptations underlying the rise and perpetuation of dominance orders. It bears reiterating the point, however, that of the two, one is the more fundamental, both factually and epistemologically. We must consider that organisms certainly compete for the wherewithals necessary for daily survival but, as E. Nagel pointed out in chapter 3, science develops on the basis of "remote" concepts. In short, the struggle for material resources may be viewed as a strategy of proximate devices ultimately utilized by organisms to secure mates and, thereby, to promote the "interest" of their genetic endowment. In short, sexual selection, the competition for mates, has played *the* crucial role in the evolution of dominance orders.

Sexual selection broadens and intensifies the struggle for existence. It also introduces among males the purest form of what may be termed coerced altruism into the game of life: the utilization of conspecifics, especially females, to exploit other males and thus select them out of the genetic population. Hence, the first structural sign of sexual selection is polygyny: the appropriation of multiple mates by some males. From an evolutionary perspective, polygyny, in turn, is the fundamental form of exploitation, for through it some males deprive others, sometimes the many, of the satisfaction of the primal need: a reproductive and often caring bond with a mate.

The other side of polygyny is the bias toward hypergyny, namely the tendency among females to favor mates enjoying high status and/or high resource-holding potential (Trivers and Willard 1973). As chapters 6 and 7 suggested, the evidence in favor of this observation is rich. Hypergyny is a direct consequence of anisogamy and intersexual selection, specifically of the "choosy" reproductive strategy that is inherent in the relativley limited female reproductive potential. One result of the joint action of polygyny and hypergyny is the submission of females to rich males, for to dominate desired resources is to dominate those who depend on them. And as we argued just above and in our brief discussion of patriarchy, another result, inextricable from the first, is that men dominate men in part by dominating inherently cooperative women. The radical feminist view of this subject is a bit too self-centered and not a little hypocritical and sanctimonious. It is not at all certain that women have been "forced" into a patriarchal arrangement.

We can say little with certainty about our distant past; but, as noted in chapter 6, estimates of polygyny for recent times indicate that it was practiced in about 83 percent of known human societies (e.g., Murdock 1967; Smith 1984), if not even higher (Low 1988b). Anisogamy, combined with our knowledge of size dimorphism between the two sexes (Klein 1989), suggests that ours has been a polygynous species all along its history (e.g., Diamond 1992; Wright 1994; Wrangham and Peterson 1996: 125). A direct relationship may be safely assumed between the degree of size dimorphism in species and the deviation of the breeding system from monogamy (Alexander et al. 1979: 402). That would indicate that we are still a polygynous species, though obviously to a reduced extent. While size dimorphism between the human sexes is still a fact, it appears that we have been evolving away from it (Cliquet 1984). The hypothesis transpires from consideration of the large size dimorphism existing in our nearest relatives, the chimpanzees. Not surprisingly, then, Betzig and Weber (1993) have found, on the basis of biographical data on members of the U.S. executive, legislative, and judicial branches, little or no support for the polygyny hypothesis over the last 200 years.

It would be rash to assume, however, that a fundamental effect of anisogamy and sexual selection has been eradicated altogether. A persisting degree of size dimorphism aside, it is necessary to distinguish between *de jure* polygyny and *de facto* polygyny. Previously encountered evidence on sex differences in marital infidelity, remarriage, and expectations in cohabiting unions, among other things, indicates that a degree of effective polygyny persists in modern society (see van den Berghe 1979; Pérusse 1993).

The anthropologist G.P. Murdock (1945) included status differentiation among his many cultural universals of human society, despite the occasional ethnographic reports of societies allegedly featuring equality. Evolutionary anthropologists have shown that there may have been much wishful thinking in the latter reports (e.g., Wright 1994: chap. 12). Dominance orders are a universal phenomenon. Among hunter-gatherer peoples, the best hunters may be no better off than the less skillful hunters in the share of meat they receive from a common pool. But while the better hunters may have an egalitarian stomach, they do not have an egalitarian reproductive urge. Hence, they philander more and produce more children than the less adept hunters. The means through which superior status is expressed vary across societies and over time. But the ancient facts of sexual selection appear to be far more constant.

Anthropologist N.A. Chagnon (1979: 377) has put the matter succinctly: "In a word, thinkers from industrialized communities are concerned with...the means of production—with material resources. Actors in tribal societies are concerned with sex, quality of mates, and the means of reproduction." Indeed, "equality of opportunity" in sociology typically refers to such factors as income, education, and mobility (e.g., Braddock and McPartland 1992). We would not wish to underestimate the needs of the stomach and other creature comforts. But Chagnon's focus is closer to the dynamics of evolution and to the fundamental motives that undergird human behavior. Sexual selection has been fierce. Chagnon (1979: 398, *passim*) finds that a small number of males, and through status inheritance the sons of these, sire a large portion of their society's children. Moreover, "differential reproductive success creates differential status, which, in turn, requires differential utilization of strategic resources" (Chagnon 1979: 378). Indeed, once a system of inequalities develops we may expect a mutual dependence between material resource acquisition, reproductive success, and social status. In complex societies, it is more likely that it is high status that begets high reproductive success. But even here, matters are not always so clear-cut. High status does not always correspond to the sociologist's measure of it. At the time of a quarrel, a brawler in a ghetto pool room, for example, may have low social status, but if he is successful in the fight, his status may rise, and so does his attractiveness to females. With few exceptions (e.g., Whyte 1943; Liebow 1967), studies of status have been insensitive to such contextual fundamentals.

The above comments raise serious questions about sociologists' view of social stratification. An evolutionary perspective demands that we not sacrifice millions of years and rich interspecific as well as intraspecific facts to a few hundred years of sociocultural development and the intellectual temporecentrism that has accompanied it. In most of the human past the concern that most directly related to dominance orders was not driven by the quest for economic resources. In relation to these, our ancestors enjoyed a high degree of egalitarianism. Indeed, they had few or no possessions to speak of by today's standards, and group members shared pretty much whatever they gathered and slaughtered. The discriminating resources were those that evolutionary theory underscores: *mates*. In nearly all of human history, this was the basic fact inextricably associated with competition, dominance, and dominance orders. It was precisely when the productive base first underwent critical expansion and stimulated economic exploitation that reproductive exploitation reached extraordinary degrees. For millennia unequal distributions of economic and political power became a major facilitator of the polygynous and hypergynous tendencies inherent in sexual selection.

A compelling text on reproductive exploitation and how this relates to hypergyny and socioeconomic status is Laura L. Betzig's *Despotism and Differential Reproduction: A Darwinian View of History* (1986; see also Betzig 1993a). Betzig, distinguished anthropologist and keen student of fitness theory, shows for many societies up to recent times that powerful men have appropriated extraordinarily large numbers of women. Moreover, they have conveyed power and hence enormous reproductive success to their sons. To a lesser extent, depending for example on rank, reproductive privilege has also favored those other men who have constituted the power base of the "despots." There have been times and places, for example among the Incas of Peru, when women were almost an exclusive right of the powerful and were apportioned in numbers corresponding to men's relative rank (Betzig 1986: 77). Some men, as in the case of imperial China until a little more than a century ago, were not only deprived of women; they were also lucky if they had enough money to have themselves castrated and thus have some hope of making a living as eunuchs in a harem.

The basic facts of exploitation—economic or reproductive or both—correspond to psychological adaptations that have long been forged by natural selection and its erstwhile agent, sexual selection. There is an ancient need to dominate. According to Alfred Adler (1932), "we shall always find in human beings…the struggle to rise from an inferior position to a superior position, from defeat to victory, from below to above. It begins in our earliest childhood; it continues to the end of our lives." Auguste Comte (1875–1877, 1896) termed it the "instinct to dominate."

The drive to enhance one's rank in the dominance order—the "climbing maneuver" (Lopreato 1984: 110–20) or the "sentiment of equality in inferiors" (Pareto 1916: sections 1220–1228)—is so powerful a force in the human brain that people have evolved to deceive themselves as well as others about its urgency. It is always more acceptable, and hence more effective, to seek a selfish aim by cloaking one's motives in the garb of the collective good. Deception of others is all the more effective when deceivers are taken in by their own deceit (e.g., Trivers 1971; Trilling 1972; Wright 1994: chap. 12). The failure to understand these mechanisms of the mind has led to numerous errors in sociology. Deceived by the revolutionaries' sophistries of collective interest, we still think of sociopolitical revolutions, for example, as phenomena of *massive collective action* executed for the good of the group. In fact, as the aftermath of one revolution after another has shown, what once appeared to be collective action was after all a *mere summation of individual actions* whose results would profit mostly, or exclusively, only the few (Lopreato 1984: 117). Little wonder, then, that some scholars have perceived the dynamics of social status in the very nature of human language. As is predictable from sexual selection, the concern for rank is far more obvious among males than among females—more marked in the exploitative, philandering sex than in the more monogamous one (e.g., Tannen 1990).

In conclusion of this section, natural selection, sexual selection, adaptations of dominance and submission or deference, polygyny, hypergyny, cheating, climbing, and dominance orders are ancient phenomena that are still with us today. There is no society that is not stratified to a recognizable degree. Moreover, while polygyny, the oldest and most direct effect of sexual selection, is *de jure* absent in the majority of today's national societies, *de facto* polygyny is amply attested to by serial monogamy (e.g., Lockard and Adams 1981; Smith 1984), among other mating patterns previously noted. We have seen, for instance, that divorce, the principal mechanism of serial monogamy, is less likely to be followed by female remarriage than by the remarriage of males, often to much younger, never-married women.

Technically speaking, polygyny, or polygamy in general, may be practiced even while "monogamously" married. A recent study in the U.S. (Laumann et al. 1994) found that, among married people, about 94 percent had been faithful in the past year. One year, however, is a fairly short time, and loses meaning when one considers the percentage of relatively newly married couples and the much larger percentage of old couples for whom fidelity may be as much a matter of age and opportunities as it is one of faithfulness strictly speaking. As we have already seen, the same study found that men reported far more sexual partners than females. This difference was greater among college graduates than high school graduates. Hence, the evidence of polygynous practice, whatever the cultural veneer beneath which it operates, continues to reveal a reproductive strategy rooted in anisogamy, both reinforcing and being reinforced by high status. Culture may intensify its expression or attenuate it, but it is unlikely that it can cancel it out altogether.

A large study of cohabitation and reproduction in modern Sweden underscores the point. Lindquist Forsberg and Tullberg (1995) have found that remating increased the number of children for men but not for women, thus supporting the hypothesis that serial monogamy represents the persistence of effective polygyny in societies where polygyny is *de jure* absent. Relatively resource-rich men, moreover, were more likely than poorer men to practice this *de facto* polygyny, thus exploiting poorer men. For instance, among individuals who reported never having had a cohabiting partner, 18.5 percent of women had one or two children whereas among males only 3 percent had any children at all. Again, the study found that among six socioeconomic categories of middle-aged males, significantly more unskilled laborers had neither a mate nor children than any other category (for example, 36.4 percent fatherless laborers as compared to only 9.7 percent for men in management). Even today, then, in one of the most egalitarian societies, rich material resources translate into mating success.

'Tis Nature

William Makepeace Thackeray writes in *The History of Henry Esmond:* "'Tis nature hath fashioned some for ambition and dominion, as it hath formed others for obedience and gentle submission." The lesson is a bit overextended, for it is often the case that the submissives of today are the dominants of tomorrow, and vice versa. The various adaptations that fuel dominance orders are not necessarily cast in stone; they may subsist in the same individual and used as opportunistic strategies according to circumstance. But it is the case that great writers often reveal an astonishing grasp of human nature.

The basic point of the present section may be stated very concisely. If behavior is to some degree the effect of ancient evolutionary forces, the fact should be observable in the machinery of the organism itself. Hence, if dominance orders are ultimately the byproduct of those forces, these may be expected to have fashioned life-cycle, organic mechanisms that express themselves in dominance-submission contexts. The foregoing two sections have emphasized male sexual selection and related facts, such as dominance and polygyny. Accordingly, in the few comments that follow, the focus will be on the male; and within this limitation we shall give a cursory glance primarily to what appears to be the hormone that is most salient in contexts of dominance orders, that is, testosterone (T), the major male sex hormone.

The case for a causal link between T and dominance is not entirely problem-free, but it is highly suggestive. In large part, the problem seems to be that T has consistent and fairly strong links to aggression (Meyer-Bahlburg 1981; Christiansen and Knussmann 1987) as well as dominance (e.g., Kemper 1990, 1994; Gray et al. 1991; Mazur 1994); and the relationship between the two is not unilinear. Aggression may depress as well as enhance the chances for dominance. Thus, Booth and Dabbs (1993) have recently reported a number of findings that, on the surface at least, indicate dominance-negative effects of high T. High-T men were less likely than men with more moderate T levels to marry and more likely to divorce. If married, they were more likely to have marital difficulties, to use violence, to avoid spousal interaction, and to have extramarital sex partners.

As those authors (1993: 464) point out, although aggression and dominance behaviors, and thus T, may be adaptive in terms of securing resources and status, if unchecked they may have opposite effects in situations that require high degrees of mutual dependence. Some support for the hypothesis of optimality implied here is provided by studies of inter-sex cognitive variations. Doreen Kimura (1992: 122; see also Becker et al. 1992), for example, reports a moderate optimum level of testosterone for maximal spatial ability among men. On the other hand, the sorts of findings reported by Booth and Dabbs (divorce, extramarital sex, etc.) may also be viewed as behaviors that are expected precisely of individuals actively *seeking* dominance and polygynous

opportunities. Unfortunately, we know more about the behavior of dominant individuals, who are relatively few, than about the behavior of the
much larger number of individuals who *would be* dominant. In this
sense, the study referred to here may have value beyond that underscored by its authors.

At any rate, it seems appropriate enough to distinguish between aggressive behavior (see Archer 1988) and dominant behavior, though A.
Mazur (1994: 38) has noted that, at least among primates, studies that
link testosterone to aggression "may also be interpreted as linking it to
dominance behavior." The involvement of physiological mechanisms
for the situational emergence, and most probably the evolution, of dominance orders is now fairly well established, and the role of testosterone
is becoming increasingly clear (e.g., Mazur 1985, 1994; Kemper 1990,
1994). For example, Mazur and Lamb (1980) have shown that tennis
players who won decisive matches experienced a rise in the T level,
while the reverse was true for losers. Moreover, there was no such rise
in players who had barely escaped defeat. These same scholars have
also found that, hours after graduation, medical students were already
recording their rise in status by experiencing a significant rise in the T
level (for analogous results, see also Elias 1981; Booth *et al.* 1989).
The upshot of findings in this area is that "there appears to be a reciprocal relationship between circulating testosterone and dominance behavior" (Mazur 1994). That makes good evolutionary sense. Hormones
elicit given behaviors, and these in turn react on hormones, modifying
their expression.

Mazur's (1994: 37) work appears to show that testosterone and other
neurohormonal mechanisms play an important role in status processes
only at the level of microsocial or face-to-face interaction. We cannot
strictly adhere to this restriction for several reasons. First, in keeping
with our adherence to methodological individualism, until such time as
we discover appropriate tools for the assessment of possible emergent
properties, we have no choice but to view macro structures as summa-
tions of fundamental, evolutionarily stable micro structures. Second,
individuals who dominate at macro levels are often the same persons
who previously dominated at the level of micro structures. The frater-
nity president later becomes a member of Congress. The president of
the student body becomes governor of his state. Analogous examples
are legion.

Mazur's point that other neurological mechanisms are involved in
eliciting status behavior appears to be well-founded. Recent research

in this complex area implicates the action of various neurotransmitters in the expression of "moralistic aggression," which refers to agonistic behavior directed toward those who fail to reciprocate (Trivers 1971). Such aggression "is a strongly predisposed behavior—we all get angry when others fail to own up to their reciprocal debts" (McGuire 1992: 32). More to the point, the likelihood that such behavior represents species-typical responses is especially relevant to discussions of dominance orders. These involve complex systems of asymmetric reciprocities. Dominant and subordinate statuses, along with a range of related behavioral strategies such as when and with whom to form an alliance, develop out of a complex set of cost-benefit calculations whereby organisms strive to make the most of their available talents and resources. To one degree or another, all relationships in dominance orders entail rendering assistance to others in return for some anticipated benefit, although how much one is willing to invest varies in accordance with one's rank.

Evidence is mounting that several neurotransmitters participate in this cost-benefit calculus. According to a brief but cogent review of relevant research (McGuire 1992), higher levels of seratonin, norepinephrine, and dopamine appear to be associated with lower levels of agonistic behavior, such as readier inclination to help others by lowering the perceived costs of such aid. By contrast, decreased activity levels of these neurotransmitters seem to contribute to heightened levels of aggression, to a lower likelihood of offering assistance to others, and to a higher probability that neutral behavior by others will be perceived as hostile or threatening. Such evidence needs to be interpreted cautiously. "It is…a big jump between events taking place at the cellular level and behavior carried out in the social arena. There are innumerable—probably thousands of—intervening physiological events" (McGuire 1992: 33). But there is now little doubt that various neurotransmitters condition the expression of aggression, and hence of dominance behavior.

Similar respect for uncharted complexity is due to the action of hormones; the link between T and status in a dominance order is not crystal-clear. But the evidence appears to favor the hypothesis that T is implicated in the adaptations that account for expressions of dominance and deference. These may vary from one social context to another—which is to say that the forces are variables—though more in some individuals than in others (Lopreato 1984: 161–76). Associated with these adaptations are what may be viewed as two major personality types. The ones are characterized by pride, expensive tastes, appropriative tendencies, even arrogance—or in Darwin's (1872) own language, "scorn, disdain, contempt, and disgust." The others are characterized by humility, self-abasement, modesty, submission. The traditional image of the poor peasant, hat in hand, begging favor of the haughty landlord, or merely bowing to the local gentry, describes in a nutshell the correlativeness of the two types.

We may add that the overbearing demeanor of the dominant human and the deferential posture of his subordinates have their counterparts among other animals (Darwin 1872). The dominant wolf, for example, holds his head, ears, and tail high. In his encounters with others, he carries a challenging demeanor (Wilson 1975: 280). Dominant male chimpanzees strut proudly and at times approach their troop like a roaring tank (de Waal 1982: chap. 2). Submissive ones crouch, bow, kiss hands, and beg for assurance. The utmost contrast between the two types is found in some species, for instance, chimpanzees, baboons, and macaques, where dominant males assert their superiority by a ritualized form of homosexual mounting, while the subordinates present their rumps as a sign of absolute submission, or a wish for reconciliation if offense has been taken by the superior animal (e.g., Dunbar 1988: 239; see also de Waal 1982; Smuts 1985; Goodall 1986a).

The Failure of Destratification Efforts

There are various kinds of evidence, both theoretical and factual, in favor of the hypothesis of stratification as an ancient and inevitable phenomenon. Facts indicate, for instance, that attempts at destratification made in some places and times have simply met with failure. This is precisely the result predicted by evolutionary theory. For a variety of reasons—including the fact, deeply embedded in the mind, that competition is stressful and dangerous—attempts at constructing societies free of grievous inequalities (e.g., the Owenites) have been numerous, especially in recent millennia. They have all failed. A more conspicuous setback is represented by so-called Marxist experiments in destratification (Lenski 1978; Jones 1978; Ulč 1978; Volgyes 1978). In the old USSR and its satellites, egalitarian doctrine had the effect of undermining the masses' incentive to compete for desired resources. This behavior combined with the eliticization of the doctrine to produce a monopoly of power by party oligarchs and thus to give rise to dominant classes that became even more abusive than those they had replaced.

This state of affairs developed faster than could have been predicted by political theory in 1917, and was described in dramatic strokes by Milovan Djilas (1957), the Yugoslav scholar who, as Marshall Tito's comrade in arms, and for a while political colleague, had an excellent chance to observe communist realities at close range. "Everything," according to Djilas, "happened differently in the USSR and other Communist countries from what the leaders...anticipated." The state, or governing class, grew stronger instead of withering away according to doctrine. Despite widespread collectivization and destruction of capitalist ownership, classes and class exploitation flourished. The old rulers were replaced by what Djilas termed a new class of owners and despots: the "political bureaucracy," also known as the *apparatchiki* and the *nomenklatura* (e.g., Parkin 1971: chap. 5; Volensky 1984). The dominance of this new class became heavier than its counterpart in capitalist society, for it grew steadily more impenatrable and accountable to no one but itself: "Open at the bottom, the new class becomes increasingly and relentlessly narrower at the top."

In time, a chasm developed between the humble masses and the new class. The latter came to own the country homes, special housing, access to richly stocked and inexpensive stores, freedom of movement, chauffeured limousines, and numberless other privileges for their children as well as themselves. The masses were deprived of all but the essentials, and often had to spend long hours in endless queues in order to obtain them. The secret police was ever on the alert to quash even minor expressions of discontent. If the disgruntled or merely those so suspected were artists, scientists, and other scholars, they faced a good chance of exile to Siberia or lengthy confinements in "psychiatric wards."

What is most remarkable about these facts is that sociologists, to the extent that they were interested in them at all, were far less perceptive than Milovan Djilas. Furthermore, it apparently never occurred to them that they were observing a profoundly vulnerable system of social relations. One sociologist, for example, asked "Is the classless society coming?" and answered that the "scope and force of the trend away from extreme differentiation are unmistakable. There are many clues," including "a pervasive, if still partial, change in the method of awarding medals and orders; a demand that the Soviet fashion journal concern itself less with evening gowns and furs and more with 'everyday' clothes" (Feldmesser 1966: 531). It was the time of Khrushchev, and Feldmesser was mistaking a little curve in the line for the line itself.

Alex Inkeles (1966) seems to have been a bit more perceptive, but the possibility of a classless society in the USSR was not entirely absent in his mind. "What then," he asked, "is the prognosis for the future development of the present structure of stratification?" The answer, we think, should have been something like this: "When, I don't know, but it can't be long before a system that is so contrived and thus assaulted from within will collapse entirely." Inkeles (1966: 526—emphasis added) viewed matters a bit differently:

> An unequivocal answer appears warranted. The present system of stratification seems to be not merely stable, but is of such an order that it would probably require a new social and political revolution to *restore* the kind of dynamism necessary to create even an approximation of a classless society defined in classical Marxist terms.

Such a verdict represents a huge equivocation. The "dynamism" was simply never there, or anywhere else, and could hardly be restored.

Elsewhere we find equally strong rejections of classless experiments, even though the futile means employed toward attainment were immensely more benign than those employed in so-called Communist societies. The Israeli kibbutzim provide a case in point. Starting around 1910, these communes set out to achieve a classless society and instituted a number of relevant normative principles, for example, collective ownership of property, central distribution of all goods according to need, communal eating, and, among others, a premium on manual labor as opposed to managerial positions. Matters then proceeded to develop in quite a different way. Already by the 1940s, a study by Eva Rosenfeld (1951; see also Cherns 1980) showed that a class structure was clearly in the making. Managerial positions received the highest honor, and reelection to them was a near-certainty. Two distinct social strata had developed. One, the managers, received special privileges, and their children received special educational opportunities. The other, the rank and file, suffered all manner of frustrations and humiliations. They also rankled under the suspicion that hard work was not rewarded fairly.

We have no special insight into what the distant future may hold. But if the history of our species and of its ancestry is prelude, inequality of access to desirables is an inevitable fact of nature, at least for the near future. Any attempt at egalitarianism must contend hopelessly with several evolutionary adaptations. People are not constituted to want equality for all. They are rather predisposed, to varying degrees, to seek advantages for themselves, often by replacing those who had successfully preceded them in the struggle. The oft-cited need for equality is in fact analogous to the force that, for example, impels a chimpanzee to attack and replace one above him in the dominance order. The major difference between humans and other animals is that our language makes us far more adept at hiding our real motives, often unknown even to ourselves, with sophistries of all sorts.

The basic force behind the evolution of dominance orders of all types has been Darwin's "struggle for survival," which, with some slight modification, we have represented with two types. One emphasizes the struggle for the resources needed to survive and prosper; the other underscores sexual selection as competition for mates. The two forces together resulted in the natural selection of specific adaptations for dominance orders: for example, the adaptations of dominance, deference, and social climbing. Concomitant with the emergence of these were the dominance orders and the polygyny and hypergyny practiced therein. These fundamental dynamics, along with some relatively recent factors implicated in the development of hypertrophic dominance orders, are represented in figure 8.1. This type of analysis is extraneous to existing stratification theory in sociology, including that found in the scholars discussed early in this chapter. Davis and Moore came closest to it with their accent on inevitability, but in the absence of an evolutionary perspective they failed to grasp the universal fundamentals.

In approaching the close of this chapter, we reiterate the point that we have deliberately stressed the prehistorical period of our hunting and gathering past. Until about 10,000 years ago, society was based on a subsistence economy that permitted little if any economic exploitation. As the ethnographic evidence suggests, however, there was probably plenty of reproductive exploitation that favored the great warriors, the great hunters, and other types of prestigious males (e.g., Hill and Hurtado 1996). Grievous economic exploitation was introduced only with the advent of the horticultural society some 10,000 years B.P. By then, enough technological innovations, including plant and animal husbandry, had accumulated to make possible permanent or semi-permanent settlements of relatively large populations, an economic surplus of sorts, and an increase in the division of labor (e.g., Lenski *et al.* 1991: chap. 6). The preexisting reproductive exploitation probably intensified as economic exploitation stimulated both polygyny and hypergyny (Betzig 1986).

What happened thereafter (the historical era)—beginning especially

FIGURE 8.1
The Evolution of Dominance Orders

	NATURAL SELECTION OF:		SALIENT CATALYSTS AND DEVELOPMENTS OF THE NEAR PAST	
PRIMEVAL CAUSES	PSYCHOLOGICAL ADAPTATIONS	ANCESTRAL SOCIAL FORMS	CATALYSTS	DEVELOPMENTS
Struggle for Existence (Competition for Material Resources)	Status Striving	Dominance Orders Featuring Reproductive Exploitation and Modest Levels of Economic Exploitation	Technological Acceleration	Rise of Relatively Rigid Social Classes
	Deference		Economic Surplus	Intensification of Economic and Political Exploitation, then Followed by Movement toward Greater Equality
			Population Explosion	
Sexual Selection (Competition for Reproductive Mates)	Polygynous Tendency	Polygyny	Large-Scale Warfare	Intensification of Reproductive Exploitation (de jure Polygyny), then Followed by De-Intensification of Reproductive Exploitation through de jure Monogamy
	Hypergynous Tendency	Hypergyny	Territorial Expansion and the Rise of Empires	Literacy

with the advent of the agrarian revolution some 5,000 years ago, and perhaps as early as the discovery of metals and the rise of the advanced horticultural society at least 7,000 years B.P.—is beyond the reach of anyone to describe and to explain in full. The fundamentals, however, remained. For millennia thereafter, both economic and reproductive parasitism by dominant individuals and classes reached extraordinary proportions. In recent centuries, however, several developments have acted to control to a considerable extent both types of exploitation. One is especially noteworthy. It refers to the discovery of the movable-type printing press. This technology fostered widespread literacy and the rise of a substantial intelligentsia, some of whom eventually came to act as the promoters and guardians of popular rights, though there have been many times when a populist ideology has in fact been utilized to promote narrow interests (Michels 1914). As a result, both economic and reproductive exploitation have decreased in intensity in very recent times. But the struggle for survival, of both types, has not thereby come to an end. Exploitation has become more subtle. The very rich today are billionaires, and many in the managerial class of modern industry and commerce have annual earnings in excess of some city budgets, whereas the average family must make do with far more modest incomes. It is perhaps civil rights that have improved most dramatically in recent centuries, ironically as capitalist society has become entrenched in many parts of the world.

A crucial by-product of this evolution has been the legal abolition of polygamy, a major feature of precapitalist, and preagrarian societies. But polygamy, especially its polygynous variety, has not disappeared. The old forces that impelled men toward philandering and women toward hypergynous preferences have contributed, in a manner predictable from evolutionary theory, to high rates of divorce and remarriage, especially among men. In the meantime, systems of stratification have become ever more complex, depending on a variety of factors, for example, population increase and heterogeneity, new knowledge, technological innovations, and the relationship between government, on the one hand, and religious, educational, and business institutions, on the other. It is certainly important to understand these developments and complexities, the focus of most stratification theorists. Shorn from their evolutionary background, however, they can only yield an ephemeral historiography.

Finally, any reasonable attempt at a general theory should contain the logic for the derivation of a body of falsifiable propositions. A select number of them are listed below. They are addressed to societal systems, but with slight or no modifications, most if not all apply to various other sorts of social organization as well. Some of the statements, we believe, will be unobjectionable from any sociological point of view. Others, we have no doubt, will strike quite a different chord. None, we trust, will tempt the reader to interpret them in an ideological key.

1. In any social system, desirable resources are always scarce, or so they are defined.
2. Competition for resources is a universal aspect of the human existence.
3. Some individuals succeed better than others in the competition for a variety of causes, including the fact that human beings are unequally endowed with the innate traits needed to compete with success.
4. In any dominance order there is a degree of status inheritance and favoritism.
5. In different degrees, people are power-seeking animals whose hunger for power increases in direct proportion with the power already commanded.
6. Success in the competition is at times a result of sheer merit, but more frequently it is a function of manipulating rules to one's own advantage.
7. Successful, that is, dominant, males are especially attractive to females, with the result that—in one way or another—they achieve greater than average reproductive success; and women continue to manifest their tendency toward hypergynous mating.
8. Men's tendency to exploit women in varying ways is only partially subject to cultural mitigation.
9. Destratification efforts do not succeed.
10. Class or collective movements are only apparently driven by collective interests.
11. Whatever the political form of a social system, power is concentrated in the hands of a few: the oligarchs.
12. Oligarchies are ever subject to challenges, often successful, from elements who covet power for selfish reasons but make appeals to collective interests.
13. Oligarchies seek to defend themselves with a variety of coercive and other techniques, including especially the cooptation of potential challengers.
14. The most successful challenges to established dominant groups derive from those who are in close proximity to the top.
15. Social systems, however rigidly stratified, feature a continuous flow of personnel from one stratum to another.
16. Dominance orders most of the time have the support of the populace because, among other reasons, they (a) bespeak opportunities for future

success; (b) maintain a tolerable degree of internal order; (c) provide some direction for future development; and (d) organize the defense against really or potentially hostile social systems.

9

The Clannish Brain

The common emphasis on socioeconomic phenomena in stratification theory has the virtue of sensitizing to the extraordinary economic transformations that have taken place since the horticultural revolution. But, as shown in the preceding chapter, such a focus restricts attention to fairly recent historical developments and detracts from a proper grasp of more ancient and fundamental facts. Moreover, contrary to common belief, social classes are generally less productive of conflict and thus of change—capital aspects of evolution—than status groups are. Max Weber, we may recall, showed some awareness of the fact when he argued that classes are normally not communities. By contrast, status groups do constitute communities, namely collectivities characterized by a consciousness of kind that yields concepts of "us" and "them," in-groups and out-groups. Weber's conceptualization of the status group thus bears a striking similarity to Sumner's (1906) work on primitive societies and the conflictual nature of intersocietal relations poignantly conveyed by his famous concept of ethnocentrism. The clan is the prototype of the status group. It is also the prototype of the ethnic group. That is why Weber (1921–1922: 389) understood the ethnic group to consist of members who "entertain a subjective belief in their common descent because of similarities of physical type or customs or both, or because of memories of colonization and migration."

Other sociologists have explicitly recognized ethnic groups as family-like teams in human evolution. V. Pareto (1902–1903), for example, argued in a critique of socialist systems that such cleavages as religious and ethnic differences are much older than classes and have played a far greater role in human evolution. Indeed, the psychological adaptation associated with ethnicity, ethnocentrism, and the conflict this entails may be viewed as primeval and ever-present aspects of inter-group relations, and hence as major mechanisms of human evolutionary history.

The subject is not pleasant. It concerns prejudice and hatred, among other less agreeable features of human nature. These powerful emotions can spring up in any social context, but in the last analysis they recall properties of clan living; hence, they are frequently stimulated by contact with "outsiders." Others are somehow different from us, and they may be viewed as threats to cherished ideals, long-established ways of life, and one's precious resources. They are not merely different; they are real or potential enemies.

Sacred texts, folklore, and ethnography as well as history offer abundant evidence that the peoples of the globe have participated only too keenly in the facts surrounding otherness. The name of many a preagricultural society translated into "human," while the appellation given to others indicated something of lesser quality (e.g., Sumner 1906: sections 16–18; Benedict 1934: 7; Barash 1979: 151). Our ancestors divided into nuclei of us and them—a fact that in time yielded the Greek concept of *ethnos*, referring to a specifiable stock or lineage of unique people. Ironically, sociologists in recent times have been a bit less perceptive, at times tending to view ethnos, or ethnicity, as a vanishing phenomenon, at others seeming surprised by its enduring or recurrent vitality. Like journalists who dramatize today one fad, tomorrow another, we have shown a marked tendency to favor the extremities of what may be termed the ethnic pendulum and hardly given attention to the affective force that propels the swing. Such a stance leaves us chasing history rather than anticipating it, as the following statement suggests. "At just the moment when most social scientists were anticipating the rapid extinction of the remaining significant differences among white ethnic groups [in the U.S.], these distinctions seemed suddenly to revive with startling intensity" (McLemore 1980: 325). The famous "melting pot" was off the burner. Cooking in its place was nothing other than "ethnic affirmation." In the land of "one Nation...indivisible," the ethnic fissures seemed to erupt into flash points of a civilizational tempest.

Our principal aim in this chapter is to argue the hypothesis that ethnicity, ethnocentrism, and ethnic conflict hark back to prehistoric, perhaps even prehuman times. They are phenomena of natural selection (e.g., Sumner 1906; Pareto 1916; van den Berghe 1981; Lopreato 1984; Irwin 1987; Hartung 1995). The inclination to cluster with those deemed similar to us and to stand in a relation of animus toward those who are different is a universal fact that expresses itself in different ways and to varying degrees. Given the clan origin of human society, it is almost certainly rooted in the fitness interests of individuals and thus in kin selection. The idea is not new in social science (e.g., Tylor 1871; Spencer 1892–1893), though it has certainly been forgotten if it was ever noticed. In discussing the various hypotheses of group formation in human history, V. Pareto (1916: section 1022) put it ingeniously as follows:

> But there is [another] hypothesis that explains the known facts much better. It considers the groups as natural formations growing up about a nucleus which is generally the family, with appendages of one sort or another, and the permanence of such groups in time engenders or strengthens certain sentiments that, in their turn, render the groups more compact, more stable, better able to endure.

Facts of ethnicity, as we shall see, reflect many ancient features of kinship and nepotistic favoritism. David Barash (1979: 141, 149) has implied the point with characteristic economy and elegance: "Kinship is a basic organizing principle in all human cultures" and thus "a powerful whisper within us."

Conceptual Note

The literature on ethnic phenomena is replete with terminological effusion intended to capture one sort of detail or other. In particular, several terms are sometimes treated as synonyms of ethnicity, although this "is the concept best able to tie" together the variety of related terms (Yinger 1994: 10). Race, tribe, nation deserve a brief visit at this point. Among those who argue on behalf of the distinctive nature of race, the purpose is typically to call attention to a history of oppression suffered by specific groups in multiracial societies (e.g., Wolf 1982; Omi and Winant 1986; Cornacchia and Nelson 1992). The historical experiences of American blacks and black South Africans, for instance, are portrayed as especially severe examples of group subjugation. Subsuming such cases under the general rubric of ethnic conflict allegedly masks or underestimates the magnitude of the human costs. The objection cannot be lightly gainsaid, but the issue is one of degree rather than kind. Our own position is that so-called racial features are particular ethnic markers that may enhance ethnocentrism and conflict. But even this qualification may not be absolutely necessary when we consider, for example, the intra-racial carnage that has been perpetrated in places like Rwanda. What is probably true is that races provide the outer limits of ethnic boundaries.

The meaning of tribe varies widely across cultural contexts (Yinger 1994: 22–24). The term may designate ethnic subpopulations of contemporary nations established at the collapse of colonial empires in the nineteenth and twentieth centuries. References to tribal hostilities are found in studies of various African nations (e.g., van den Berghe 1981; Horowitz 1985), among others, many of which attained political independence in the latter half of the twentieth century. New national borders were drawn by former colonial rulers who paid little if any heed to the traditional boundaries that marked long-standing lineage, linguistic, and political loyalties. Subsequent episodes of ethnic contention— for example, in Angola, the Sudan, Eritrea, Somalia, Burundi, Rwanda, Zaire—illustrate only too well the virulence of animosity when released from, if not intensified by, capricious suppression (Gurr and Harff 1994). Perhaps the most common usage of the tribe concept is found in the ethnographic literature. The subject here can get very complicated, but in general the term refers to an alliance of clans, namely the irreducible societal units whose origins may be traced to our hunting and gatherering ancestors. It is in this context that the concept of kinship is most unambiguously associated with the concept of ethnicity (e.g., Irwin 1987).

Nation is the most conceptually compound of the three terms under discussion. And with it go such emotive terms as nationalism, patriotism, and jingoism (e.g., Rose 1985). Some researchers use nation as a synonym for ethnic group, referring to a people united by bonds of common language, traditions, and conceptions of common descent (e.g., Smith 1986; Esman 1994). There is partial justification to this equation. With the explosion of the human population, starting some 10,000 years in the past, and the concomitant enlargement of the societal unit, reciprocal relations had to be extended over much broader networks of compeers. Growth was associated with economic expansion and the intensification of large-scale warfare (e.g., Alexander 1979, 1987; Melotti 1990: 242). Hence, the expanding sense of oneness was to a large extent motivated by real or perceived threats deriving from a common enemy. Making common cause became an organizational necessity. In this sense, R.A. Levine and D.T. Campbell (1972) are justified in viewing nation and nationalism as extensions of earlier forms of ethnicity and ethnocentrism and as expressions of the necessity for state leadership on the part of a large, elaborately organized, and heterogeneous social grouping.

To the extent, however, that the cohesion of provincials is occasioned by the threat from without, it may also be expected to dissolve when the threat subsides, thereby revealing the persistence of ancient nuclei and oppositions. Ethnic groups may exist within nations, and internal ethnocentrism may persist even in the presence of more extensive political loyalties. The point is clearly illustrated by the United States of America. Claims of equal opportunity and justice for all notwithstanding, it is a nation of deep and persisting ethnic cleavages (e.g., Shipler 1997). Among American sociologists, no one has captured this reality better than Milton Gordon (1964) in his classic study of assimilation in the U.S.

So much for problems of kindred concepts. What, specifically, does ethnicity refer to? There is no generally accepted view of it. But Pierre van den Berghe's *The Ethnic Phenomenon* (1981: chaps. 1–2), a major text on topics of this chapter, refers to two prevailing perspectives: the "primordialist" and the "instrumentalist." Proponents of the latter argue that ethnicity is but one kind of affiliation which varies according to situation, and is thus culturally manipulable (e.g., Barth 1969; Wallerstein 1974; Anderson 1983). This viewpoint is typical of those who are inclined to equate ethnicity with nationhood, with the result that for some writers ethnicity, though an old phenomenon, has of late been replaced by a demographic amalgamation produced almost entirely by cultural factors. According to E. Gellner (1994: 46), for instance, "pre-industrial complex societies were endowed with elaborate and fairly stable structures" supported by relations and terminologies of kinship. With the rise of modern technologies and corresponding changes in the nature of work, individuals were required to interact in and identify with broader social groupings wherein they were enlisted into a "literate, school-transmitted" culture. The internalization of such a culture constitutes "a person's identity, to a far greater extent" than was the case in the past. "In a sense, ethnicity has replaced kinship as the principal method of identity-conferment."

There is some equivocation in this statement, but the thrust is toward underscoring structural and cultural realities at the expense of kin relations. At any rate, this perspective is rejected by proponents of primordialism. These scholars hold that ethnicity is a more enduring and deeply historical phenomenon, rooted in appeals to common ancestry, language, and cultural traditions (e.g., Shils 1957). Here, too, the focus is often on the cultural bases of ethnicity or ethnic identity. But for some writers, ourselves included, the primordialist conception can be extended to argue that persistent ethnicity expresses a fundamental human need to identify with real or putative kin (e.g., van den Berghe 1981). Of course, the intensity of ethnic allegiance varies from situation to situation. Whether it expresses itself, and in what measure, depends in part on environmental factors with which it interacts. But however variable the phenomenon, it invariably involves "a significant element of [common] descent" (Horowitz 1985: 55; see also Smith 1986; Esman 1994; Williams 1994; Yinger 1994).

We hold with Pareto that ethnicity grows up "about a nucleus which is generally the family." This is the unavoidable evolutionary view (see van den Berghe 1981). But a strict concept of family or common descent, though always real to a degree, is relevant in inverse proportion to the size of the ethnic group. So, at one extreme, the ethnic group—perhaps best represented by the clan—refers mostly to a group of genetic kin. At the other extreme, typical of the megasociety, the ethnic group survives as a sort of breeding population wherein assortative mating, or homogamy, is widely practiced (Lopreato 1984: 331; see also Whitmeyer 1997). The biological substrate of ethnic bonds may be robust or tenuous, but it is ever present and lies deep in our species' ancestry.

Ethnographic observations on preagrarian societies accumulating in the nineteenth and early twentieth centuries led several scholars to posit a fundamental tendency to establish bonds of loyalty within the group and to adopt hostile attitudes toward outsiders. This theme was perhaps most fully explored at the turn of the century by W.G. Sumner (1906, 1911), the great American sociologist who coined the term ethnocentrism. Sumner argued that primitive societies are best understood as "small groups scattered over a territory," thereby focusing attention on the band or clan as the basic societal unit in our species' evolutionary past. The relative availability of resources and the degree to which external groups pose a threat may encourage two or more small bands to form "a group of groups" united by bonds of kinship, mutual assistance, commerce, marriage, and political alliance. "The insiders in a we-group are in a relation of peace, order, law, government, and industry, to each other. Their relation to all outsiders...is one of war and plunder, except so far as agreements have modified it" (Sumner 1906: section 13).

The "exigencies of war" with outsiders are of capital significance in facilitating a strong sense of in-group solidarity accompanied by attitudes of cultural superiority. Hence, the presence of actually or potentially hostile out-groups is a crucial selective pressure, encouraging psychological adaptations consistent with the needs for internal order and common defense: "Loyalty to the group, sacrifice for it, hatred and contempt for outsiders, brotherhood within, warlikeness without—all grow together, common products of the same situation" (Sumner 1906:

section 14). Accordingly ethnocentrism, "the technical name for this view of things in which one's own group is the center of everything, and all others are scaled and rated with reference to it" (Sumner 1906: section 15), is viewed as a natural response to environmental pressures that are themselves primary factors of societal evolutionary history. Groups composed of loyal individuals are better prepared to compete against those that are less well-integrated (e.g., Davie 1929; Lorenz 1966; Low 1993).

Such sentiments of group loyalty and mutual obligation are most accentuated in the family context. Ties to close genetic relatives are extraordinarily strong because they have been the most durable and efficient in serving selfish ends. To cooperate with and even sacrifice for those with whom we share a blood bond tend to serve inclusive fitness interests and thus obey the dictates of kin selection. Of course, when the family is no longer the organizational unit defining "we-ness," the sense of blood bond is vaguer and more diffuse. Still, it remains an existential necessity. It continues to fuel ethnocentrism and the behaviors that this motivates. Ethnic conflict is the crucial manifestation of ethnocentrism. Inasmuch as the latter was born in the ancestral clan, its action is most easily predictable where group divisions retain familistic traditions, as in so-called tribal societies. Where such traditions are diluted, as in rapidly changing industrial societies, ethnic conflict may normally take weaker and more deceptive forms, such as sly ethnic epithets or even such surrogates as the totemic simulations executed by sports rivalries between cities or between schools in the same city. But it may flare up even in such societies.

Ethnic Conflict in Sociology

The sociological literature on ethnic conflict is rich and nuanced. But it has been shackled by narrow vision and the failure to explore some promising leads, including Sumner's just noted work, V. Pareto's (1916: sections 1016–40) "sentiment" termed "persistence of relationships of family and kindred groups," M. Weber's treatment of status groups, M. Gordon's (1964; see also 1978) view of ethnicity as something more than a purely culturtal phenomenon, and more recently, P. van den Berghe's (1981) evolutionary analysis of the ethnic phenomenon. As this latter work plainly demonstrates, the impairment of vision is in the last analysis rooted in the sociologists' failure to enter the stream of the Darwinian revolution.

Melting Pot, Assimilation, and Sundry Theories and Facts

> America is God's Crucible, the great Melting Pot where all the races of Europe
> are melting and re-forming! Here you stand, good folks, think I, when I see them
> at Ellis Island, here you stand in your fifty groups, with your fifty languages and
> histories, and your fifty blood hatreds and rivalries. But you won't be long like
> that, brothers, for these are the fires of God you've come to—these are the fires of
> God. A fig for your feuds and vendettas! Germans and Frenchmen, Irishmen and
> Englishmen, Jews and Russians—into the Crucible with you all! God is making
> the American. (Zangwill 1909: 37)

This dithyramb was delivered by the protagonist of Israel Zangwill's popular play, *The Melting Pot*, first staged in New York City in 1908. The drama, reacting in part to an arrogant ideology of "Anglo conformity" (e.g., Gordon 1964: chap. 4), embodied great hopes for the future of the American nation. Due to massive waves of immigration during the latter half of the nineteenth century and the first two decades of the twentieth, American cities were developing into veritable mosaics of peoples speaking different languages, worshiping different gods, and subscribing to diverse beliefs and codes of conduct. How these ethnicities were to mesh into one people—an American Amalgam— was a question of profound historical, political, and sociological significance.

The melting pot metaphor soon came to be associated, without much justification, with one of the first efforts to construct a sociological theory of ethnicity: the so-called assimilation theory of the Chicago School. The inspiration was in part provided by the expectation that, while various problems would necessarily ensue from the introduction of the new immigrants into the old stock of peoples from Northwestern Europe, they would gradually admit of some solution. The recent arrivals came mostly from Southeastern Europe, and were in many respects decidedly different peoples. Predominantly Roman Catholic, Eastern Orthodox, or Jewish, they brought with them traditions that clashed with the established ways. Social and cultural heterogeneity was further compounded for the nation by increasing numbers of black Americans migrating from the rural south to northern cities. Broadened and deepened ethnic fault lines were thus established across the country, particularly in urban centers of new ethnic concentration.

According to sociologists at the University of Chicago—Park (1914), Thomas and Zaniecki (1918–1920), and Park and Burgess (1921)— ethnic prejudice and discrimination, gang delinquency, family disorganization, crime, and so forth were largely the results of uneven integration of immigrant ethnics into the mainstream of American culture. One of the key factors concerned the difficulty encountered by "backward" peoples, typically uprooted from peasant environments, in adapting to the ecological demands of the modern city.

The basics of the resulting model of race and ethnic relations are primarily attributable to R.E. Park and E.W. Burgess who outlined four major processes governing relations between groups, including ethnic groups: *competition, conflict, accommodation,* and *assimilation.* These authors argued that competition is "a universal phenomenon...defined in the evolutionary formula 'the struggle for existence'" (Park and Burgess 1921: 505). When competing organisms become aware of their respective intentions, competition turns into conflict, wherein "competitors identify one another as rivals or as enemies" (Park and Burgess 1921: 507).

Group conflict, however, is not necessarily permanent. Indeed, it may give way to accommodation wherein "the antagonism of the hostile elements is, for the time being, regulated, and conflict disappears as overt action, although [it] remains as a potential force." In short, accommodation is fragile and always incomplete. Animosities across ethnic lines may be suppressed for a time, as patterns of ethnic domination and subordination enter periods of relative stability. But with "a change in the situation, the adjustment that had hitherto successfully held in control the antagonistic forces fails" and conflict between groups resurfaces (Park and Burgess 1921: 665). Given the proper circumstances, however, such hostile tendencies may be reduced by assimilation, namely "a process of interpenetration and fusion in which persons and groups acquire the memories, sentiments, and attitudes of other persons and groups, and, by sharing their experiences and history, are incorporated with them in a common culture" (Park and Burgess 1921: 735). But again, there is no inevitable progression from accommodation to assimilation or the melting pot.

In fact, at least for Park, it was highly improbable that ethnic cleavages would blend and dissolve entirely. Permeating his work is the argument that ethnocentrism is deep-rooted "in the very nature of men and their relations to one another." Building on Sumner's insight, he (1928: 170) held that all of "our sentiments, love, loyalty, patriotism, homesickness, contempt, arrogance, hate, are based upon and supported by prejudices [presumably reflecting ethnocentrism, among other mental biases that] are part of the stuff from which our human life is made." If ethnocentrism is in the nature of the beast, so is the tendency, by definition, for the beast to stubbornly distinguish between in-groups and out-groups. Ethnic prejudices are subject to modification as a result of various factors, principally reductions in the "social distance" between members of different ethnic groups; but they are primordial in nature and thus unlikely to vanish altogether. In conclusion, like other early treatments of ethnic phenomena, this was a good beginning. There was assimilation—"interpenetration and fusion"—in Park's view, but assimilation was viewed as a process that, even if it should lead to "a common culture," would hardly result in a loss of fundamental identity: in an impairment of "homesickness" or of the *atavus* that in the "sentimental" mind persistently whispers, "Who are you, who are yours?"

Nearly half a century later, this combination of cultural accent and tribal atavism recurs with elegant cogency in one of the best statements on ethnic theory. Milton M. Gordon's (1964) *Assimilation in American Life* provided important clarifications on several varieties of ethnicity theory and in the process identified seven stages of assimilation. Compelling in Gordon's classification is the emphasis on primary group ties as essential to the attainment of high levels of assimilation. What had occurred in the U.S. up to the 1960s was a significant degree of acculturation. But along various dimensions of *structural affiliation*, substantial interpenetration across ethnic boundaries remained elusive. Accordingly, Gordon (1964: chs. 4–6) found little support for assimilation theories, such as Anglo-conformity and the melting pot, that had had strong appeal in some sociological circles.

Why this tenacity of ethnic parochialism? Gordon tended to view ethnicity as a primordial phenomenon. Moreover, while he never explicitly treated it as an evolutionary fact, he came close to such a perspective. "The "sense of ethnicity," he (1964: 24–25) argued,

> has proved to be hardy. As though with a wily cunning of its own, as though there were some essential element in man's nature that demanded it—something that compelled him to merge his lonely individual identity in some ancestral group of fellows smaller by far than the whole human race, smaller often than the nation— the sense of ethnic belonging has survived. It has survived in various forms and with various names, but it has not perished, and twentieth-century urban man is closer to his stone-age ancestors than he knows.

Like Park, Gordon avoided the trap of viewing ethnic rivalries in the modern world as mere vestiges of outmoded cultural traditions. Unfortunately, however, this latter view has afflicted many a contribution to the sociology of ethnicity, for example, theories of "the new ethnicity" in modern societies, especially American society (e.g., Glazer and Moynihan 1970; Novak 1972; Greeley 1974).

New ethnicity portraits vary in detail and emphasis, but all tend to focus on the fact that ethnic sentiments and ethnic conflicts have escalated in frequency and intensity in the latter half of the twentieth century. This resurgence has astonished many commentators, leading them to conclude that "something new has appeared"—something that allegedly distinguishes modern ethnic divisions from previous instances of "linguistic, national, religious, tribal, [and] racial" heterogeneity (Glazer and Moynihan 1975: 2). So, for some writers, ethnic animosities in modern societies are little more than expressions of underlying class antagonisms. Assessing the foundations of "peer group society" among residents of Boston's West End, H. Gans (1962: 230), for instance, claimed some forty years ago that they reflected primarily "economic and social positions that the Southern Italian and the West Ender have occupied in the larger Italian and American societies respectively." Specifically, Gans alleged that "the class hypothesis offers a better explanation than the ethnic one" for the basis of community solidarity.

For other authors, the new ethnicity represents a "new social form" of political interest group that has arisen in combination with the expansion of state power in industrial society (Glazer and Moynihan 1970: 16–17). "The welfare state and the socialist state appear to be especially responsive to ethnic claims" (Glazer and Moynihan 1975: 9). The "strategic efficacy of ethnicity" is located in its ability to serve as an efficient "organizing principle" for "making legitimate claims on the resources of the modern state" (Glazer and Moynihan 1975: 10–15). All of this may hold more than a kernel of truth. What is wrong with it is the extreme accent on the here-and-now and the associated obsession with the "something new," which diverts attention from the old that the new may be grafted on.

Another, and probably more common, variant of the new ethnicity thesis focuses on "ethnic collectivities...as bearers of differential cultural heritages" (Greeley 1974: 31). Such cultural bonds enable individuals living in large and complex societies to cope with an otherwise alienating and anomic environment. Ethnicity is thus portrayed as "one of the resources available to contemporary Americans [among others] for finding self-definition, social location, and preferential role" orientations; "ethnicity is one of the forms of *Gemeinschaft* that has survived in a rationalized, bureaucratized society" (Greeley 1974: 27). This conception stakes out a position that fairly conforms to evolutionary approaches to the topic. There is an inkling in it that the sources of ethnic attachment are traceable to times when humans lived in small, informal communities. But lacking is any explicit linkage between the idea and any evolutionary explanation. As a result, ethnicity in the megasociety appears as a significant but anachronistic feature of the modern world.

As in other areas of sociology, there has been no dearth of debates and nuances in the continuing attempt to understand phenomena of ethnicity. But in the end it is hard to detect any significant developments in the quality of theorizing. To a large extent, it is also difficult to clearly distinguish between one argument and another. What is easier to see is the sociologist's need to make capital of intuitively significant environmental circumstances, as can be noted in two other approaches to the analysis of ethnic conflict in industrial society, commonly referred to as the *segregation* and *competition* models.

According to the segregation view, which harks back about a quarter of a century, industrial development generates long-term improvements in average living standards so that even the most disadvantaged segments of multiethnic countries experience improved life chances as well as greater opportunities for political expression. Typically, however, economic development is not even, and some groupings may be relegated to relatively low-status occupations and depressed income levels "on the basis of observable cultural traits or markers" (Hechter 1975: 1154). Their collective lot may be better than what was enjoyed by their parents or grandparents. But, relative to other segments of the population, the less privileged may feel discriminated against and thus be concerned about falling still further behind.

To the extent that the disadvantaged do in fact share certain characteristics (e.g., linguistic, religious, physical), the relative deprivations associated with rising but frustrated aspirations may stimulate ethnic solidarity and political agitation. The outcome is said to be especially likely when the underprivileged are socially and/or territorially segregated by "internal colonialism" (Hechter 1975) or "split labor markets" (Bonacich 1972). Ethnic loyalties and related networks are thus portrayed as weapons wielded by the less fortunate in their quest to secure a greater share of societal resources. Nothing wrong with this view, as far as it goes.

Proponents of the alternative (competition) model rebut that ethnics are in fact likely to become disgruntled when their life chances improve relative to their previous superiors. Hence, the probability of ethnic clashes is predicted to increase as individuals of different ethnic backgrounds find themselves competing on a more nearly equal footing for economic and political resources (e.g., Nielsen 1985; Olzak and Nagel 1986; Olzak 1992). This view of ethnic conflict has been most commonly applied in industrial societies characterized by a history of immigration. The rationale is that initially immigrant minorities must contend with intense prejudice, ghettoization, and educational and occupational discrimination. Over time these barriers may weaken, and members of once oppressed ethnic minorities begin to compete on a more level playing field with ethnic dominants. "A core hypothesis from the competition perspective…is that *desegregation of labor markets intensifies ethnic competition, which in turn raises the rate of ethnic collective action*" (Olzak 1992: 3—emphasis in original). Further, such conflict is said to escalate especially when previously expanding economic opportunities begin to contract.

Again, there may be some validity to such perspectives on ethnic conflict. Moreover, they share a number of features. For example, both assume that there is something about ethnicity that joins individuals into cohesive groups to more efficiently pursue their interests. Both, however, beg the fundamental question: Why, seriously, does ethnicity remain a crucial feature of collective identity in the megasociety? If banding together in order to compete more effectively for valued resources was merely a matter of convenience or historical contingency, then other bases of common identity could just as easily define the boundaries between contending parties. Firms and corporations, trade unions, professional associations, political parties—these and other networks can, and in some instances do, serve as vehicles for promoting group interests. But few if any of these inspire the profound sense of in-group loyalty, the intense animosity toward outsiders, and the lasting potential for conflict associated with ethnicity.

There must be something unique about ethnic identity. This possibility apparently escapes attention because of a fundamental deficiency in both models. They are historiographic rather than scientific in nature. Like nearly all of sociology, they are constrained by an excessive focus on the historical and cultural details of relatively recent events. We wish that we could avoid repeating this basic complaint regarding sociological practice. But the fascination with events of the here-and-now bears all the hallmarks of a limited imagination and very possibly of a self-destructive tendency. Narrow vision obscures underlying uniformities that may exist between the recent events and comparable occurrences at other times (and places). The general is sacrificed in favor of the particular, and that is not the way of science. Sociology's explanatory potential stalls at the point of building descriptive and ephemeral models, while opportunities to construct a cumulative body of theory are repeatedly squandered.

The release of the imagination requires sensitivity to the fact that violent spasms of ethnic encounters have occurred throughout human history. Instances of forced emigration, population exchanges, deportation, and genocide are easily traceable to the very dawn of civilization, and no doubt have an even more ancient lineage. For example, during the reign of Tiglath-pileser III, ruler of Assyria in the late eighth century B.C., "about half the population of a conquered land would be carried off, and its place taken by settlers from another region" (Bell-Fialkoff 1993: 112). The policy continued under his successors and was eagerly imitated by leaders of ancient Babylon, Greece, and Rome.

European colonization of the Americas beginning in the late fifteenth century eventually led to one of history's most lurid instances of ethnic brutality. Exposure to previously unknown diseases, genocidal atrocities, and forcible expropriation of native lands took a heavy toll on Amerindian populations from which they have never recovered (e.g., McNeill 1976: chap. V; Diamond 1997). As this process was nearing its completion in the nineteenth century, ethnic tensions were heating up almost everywhere else in the world. In the Near East, for example, Turks sought to impose their dominion over Armenians, Greeks, and Kurds. Then the twentieth century merely followed suit, perhaps nowhere more violently than in the case of the Nazi persecution of Jews and other minorities, such as Gypsies and homosexuals. The facts of ethnic brutality are universal and recurrent.

Wherever we look, even today in the "global village," we find mixtures of peoples who have an awfully hard time living together. The statement applies to nearly all the nations of Asia and Africa. In South America, ethnic disputes have a somewhat lower profile (e.g., van den Berghe 1978), but a close examination reveals them there, too. One constant in that area of the world is "the problem of the Indios," which of late has been most apparent in Mexico and Peru. Facts across the globe reveal that we are a large species divided into innumerable little tribes and clans—an ethnic mosaic repeatedly cracking under violent attacks. This in effect was the message of a 1977 study of "ethnic conflict in the world today" published in the *Annals* of the American Academy of Political and Social Sciences (Heisler 1977).

Consider the degree of ethnic diversity and tension in some of the world's most populous nations. "India, Indonesia, and Brazil are...home to about 850, 670, and 210 languages, respectively" (Diamond 1997: 323). In the U.S., as any recent text on ethnic and racial relations illustrates, ethnic heterogeneity continues unabated and underlies various dimensions of political contention, perhaps most apparently in disputes about affirmative action. Nor is it very different in much of Europe. A recent study of ethnic minorities has singled out no fewer than 170 such entities on the European continent, Russia included, in a total population of about 822 million (Bregantini 1996: table 3). Everywhere they are uneasy neighbors. Even a country like Italy, among the most homogeneous anywhere, contains at least fourteen major minorities (Bregantini 1996: 10).

A survey of sixty-two recent instances of ethnic discord, a few dating to the early 1950s but most erupting during the past twenty years, estimates that by mid-1993 at least 3.5 million persons had lost their lives to ethnic hatred, while several million more had been forced to seek refuge away from their ancestral homes (Gurr and Harff 1994: appendix). In early 1993 there were about forty-eight ethnic wars in progress in the world. In the former Soviet Union alone there were 164 ethnic disputes concerning borders, and thirty of these had involved some form of armed conflict (Huntington 1996: 35). Ancient animosities based on sentiments of lineage, peoplehood—ethnicity—erupted almost immediately as soon as Soviet politics and military might relaxed the reins that ethnic cleavages had been straining in the first place.

The tragedy of the Balkans is only too well known for the ferocity of its acts and scenes. What may not be equally known is that the recent events that have so captured the human sense of horror have deeply entrenched roots (e.g., Bell-Fialkoff 1993). What is most remarkable, at least as far as sociology is concerned, is that sociologists were surprised by the dissolution of the old Yugoslavia and by the ubiquitous ethnic fires that were ignited in the emerging independent states. Perhaps more grievous still was the thunderbolt that struck "the science of social structure, function, and change" at the dismantling of the USSR and the emergence of such an extraordinary number of new nation-states, each of which must cope with its own internal ethnic fuses. If we insist on capturing the unique and disregarding the nature of the animal that is the human being, we shall be surprised again and again.

An Evolutionary Perspective

To put it mildly, then, the sociological "literature on ethnicity remains unsettled in its theoretical core" (Alba 1992: 583). Theory must come to grips with the roots, persistence, and universality of ethnicity if we are to gain an adequate grasp of the role it plays in human society. And to accomplish the deed, we must turn to aspects of evolutionary theory, particularly kin selection and kin altruism. To suggest that ethnicity, ethnocentrism, and ethnic conflict have their roots in kin selection is to assert that these phenomena have had adaptive significance, at least in the context within which human nature was forged and acted itself out until very recent times. The maximization principle predicts that organisms tend to preferentially direct resources toward their kin. Accordingly, we may predict that the capacity to somehow distinguish kin from unrelated others is a trait that will be selectively retained over the course of a species' evolution. After all, to preferentially bestow favors on kin depends on the ability to recognize them. Such kin-recognition mechanisms take many forms across insect, avian, and mammalian species, among others (e.g., Fletcher and Michener 1987). But they are present in all animal societies. This consideration leads back to Sumner's argument that humans are naturally inclined to distinguish between the in-group and the out-group and that this inclination dates back to our ancestors' lengthy existence in hunting and gathering bands. As another early scholar put it,

> Primitive man never looked out over the world and saw "mankind" as a group and felt his common cause with his species. From the beginning he was a provincial who raised the barriers high. Whether it was a question of choosing a wife or taking a head, the first and important distinction was between his own human group and those beyond the pale. His own group, and all its ways of behaving, was unique. (Benedict 1934: 7–8)

Indeed, parochialism harks back to the precultural era, as the ethnic-like rivalries of our primate cousins strongly suggest. In 1973, Jane Goodall (1986a: chap. 17) and her associates noticed that a distinct and smaller group of chimpanzees had splintered off from the Kasakela troop at the Gombe Stream Reserve. The offshoot was dubbed the Kahama community after the valley that constituted its home range. Beginning in 1974, a "series of violently aggressive episodes" were observed in which groups primarily composed of males from the larger Kasakela group systematically stalked and savagely attacked members of the Kahama community. The attacks, described in some detail by Goodall (1986a: 506–14), leave little doubt that the aggressors intended to cripple or even kill their victims. In fact, by 1977 the entire Kahama population had been wiped out.

According to Goodall (1986a: 525–28), the violence appeared to be rooted in the ability of chimpanzees to distinguish members of the in-group from those of the out-group and to behave in ways that reflected "ethnocentric" urges. Chimpanzees do not merely defend a territory. They "actually expend considerable energy in *creating* opportunities to encounter intruders at close range." Moreover, they "not only attack trespassers, but may…make aggressive *raids* into the very heart of the core area of neighboring groups" (Goodall 1986a: 528—emphasis in original). Accordingly,

> it is of considerable interest to find that chimpanzees show behaviors that may be precursors to pseudospeciation [i.e., ethnic differentiation] in humans. First, their sense of group identity is strong; they clearly differentiate between individuals who "belong" and those who do not. Infants and females who are part of the group are protected even if the infants were sired by males from other communities. Infants of females who do *not* belong may be killed…. The members of the Kahama community had, before the split, enjoyed close and friendly relations with their aggressors. By separating themselves, it is as though they forfeited their "right" to be treated as group members—instead, they were treated as strangers (Goodall 1986a: 532—emphasis in original).

There is good evidence that the tendency to dichotomize between friend and foe, ally and enemy, or simply the familiar and the unfamiliar is "elemental" (Wilson 1978a: 114). Animal studies show that predators, for instance, are frequently guided by the "oddity factor" or conspicuousness in the prey; danger lurks for the individual whose difference stands out from the crowd (Crook 1965). Xenophobic aggression is widespread among animals, so that, for example, the addition of unfamiliar conspecifics to a group typically has radically unsettling consequences (see van der Dennen 1987: 20–22 for a brief review). Likewise, human beings are more likely to aggress deviants than conformists (e.g., Freedman and Doob 1968). Why should that be so? It would not be sufficient to appeal to factors of the life cycle because we would run into the same old question as to how they came to be in the first place. We must take a deeper view of the question.

Back to the Clan

For millions of years hominid societies were organized primarily around ties of kinship. Judging by the size of contemporary hunter-gatherer societies, they consisted on the average of twenty-five to forty individuals, constituting extended kin groups (Ike 1987) and termed by some scholars "nucleus ethnic groups" (Shaw and Wong 1989). The evidence indicates that members lived in close proximity, cooperated intensely, and preferentially practiced cross-cousin marriage (e.g., Tindale 1974). Given these features, and the intersocietal conflicts that often attended them, kin selection pressures necessarily stimulated the evolution of adaptations that fostered bonds of nepotistic altruism within the clan and sentiments of fear, suspicion, and belligerence toward outsiders, especially those beyond the tribe if this organizational unit was in existence.

Nowadays, these psychological traits manifest themselves in numerous domains of the social life, and are conveniently observable in the behavioral development of the young. The infant, for instance, develops a close attachment to those who provide comfort and sustenance. That is one side of the coin. The other side exhibits fear of strangers (see van der Dennen 1987: 17–23 for a brief review). Xenophobia appears at around seven months of age; it peaks during the subsequent year, when recognition of, and attachment to, kin or other nurturers has been rather fully formed (e.g., Morgan and Ricciuti 1973; Freedman 1974). The fear of strangers soon diminishes as the child discovers the larger group, but its onset strongly indicates that we are born with an aversion toward people who will not readily remind us of those with whom we spent our earliest years.

Xenophobia has been repeatedly stimulated in human evolutionary time. As R. Alexander (1987: 78) has noted, "for humans, unlike any other species, other humans became the principal hostile force of nature—the principal cause of failure to survive or reproduce"; hence the old aphorism: *Homo homini lupus*—humans are wolves unto each other. But the weakening of early xenophobia in the child also implies that human beings are born with the ability to identify with a group that is larger than the immediate group of close kin. Reciprocal altruism is the basic manifestation of such an adaptation, and it has probably facilitated population increase as well as relationships extended beyond the family group. But note that its expression surfaces only after the appearance of the fear of strangers. The child is thus predisposed to widen its social horizons. But the more basic predisposition is more strictly familistic in nature, as indicated, further, by the fact that even young children show some degree of disdain for peers of different (racial) ethnic heritage (Aboud 1988). Moreover, within this context reciprocal altruism plays a double role. On the one hand, it tends to mitigate ethnic conflict by expanding conceptions of kindredness. On the other, this very amplification reinforces conceptions of us and them by setting up coalition boundaries.

These adaptations, epitomized by what is termed ethnocentrism, were forged in the clans of our primitive ancestors, and represent durable features of human nature. As Sumner noted, it was the exigencies of war with the out-group that probably constituted their crucial selection pressures. The "choice" was stark: either ethnocentrism and compactness or unilateral trust and elimination. Sumner's hypothesis is amply supported by the ethnographic record. Intertribal warfare has been common and typically conducted in the form of raids. "The adversary is stalked using hunting tactics and is surrounded. Surprise attacks on villages are often conducted in the early morning hours when the enemy is sleeping" (Eibl-Eibesbeldt 1989: 409). Such behavior has been widely noted in ethnographic accounts of hunter-gatherer, horticultural, and pastoral societies; and vivid descriptions have been reported, for example, for the Aranda of Australia, the Maori, the Yanomamö, the Melanasians of the San Cristobal Islands, the Eipo, the Murngin of Arnhem Land, and the Tsembaga of New Guinea, among many others (for brief summaries, see Eibl-Eibesfeldt 1989: 409–14).

Tribal warfare takes a tremendous toll. W.L. Warner's (1930) study of the Murngin showed that nearly 30 percent of the tribe's adult males had died in war. Among the Fore of New Guinea, 14 percent of the male population studied by J.H. Bennett and associates (1959) perished in wars. According to N.A. Chagnon (1988), who has studied the Yanomamö of South America for decades, 44 percent of males twenty-five years of age or older report having killed at least one person, and almost 70 percent of adults over the age of forty years report having lost a close relative in acts of war.

The proximate causes of intra- and intertribal wars are varied. Avenging the death of a compatriot, striving to gain greater access to game or other valued resources, plain hatred, and stealing the enemy's women have all been reported as reasons offered by tribal men as justifications for belligerence: "Whatever the individual reasons may be for aggressive motivation, the final result of aggressive group behavior is the dominance of one group over another, which in earlier times often led to the demise of the defeated group and even often today to driving them off the land" (Eibl-Eibesfeldt 1989: 416). Dominance and its attendant reproductive and material rewards may thus be viewed as among the chief motives for men cooperating in the risky behavior of waging war (e.g., Durham 1976). Chagnon's analysis of life histories, blood revenge, and warfare among the Yanomamö represents one of the best efforts to test this hypothesis. It shows that "kinship groups that retaliate swiftly and demonstrate their resolve to avenge deaths acquire reputations for ferocity that deter the violent designs of their neighbors." In addition, "men who demonstrate their willingness to act violently and to exact revenge for the deaths of kin...have higher marital and reproductive success" (Chagnon 1988: 986; see also tables 2, 3).

Episodes of intergroup warfare represent some of the most compelling evidence in favor of the hypothesis that ethnocentrism is a deep-seated feature of the human psyche. But it bears stressing that ethnic violence as such is only one and by no means necessary indicator of ethnocentrism. The absence of overt ethnic conflict cannot be taken as evidence that ethnocentrism is absent. The latter is more constant than the former, just as the propensity for X is always more common than X itself. The fact is well-illustrated by the !Kung San of Botswana, the famous "textbook example of the least violent end of the human cultural spectrum":

> While the !Kung, like most hunter-gatherers [today], do not have war or other organized group conflicts, their explicitly stated contempt for non-San people, for San people speaking languages other than !Kung, and even for !Kung in other village-camps who are not their relatives, makes it perfectly clear that if they had the technological opportunity and the ecological necessity to make war, they would probably be capable of the requisite emotions, despite their oft-stated opposition to and fear of war. (Konner 1982: 204)

Kin Selection and Altruism

Nepotistic favoritism is "wired in the brain"; it obeys the logic of the maximization principle. Kin selection theory and the facts surrounding it thus invite the hypothesis that ethnicity is an "extension of kinship, and, therefore, the feelings of ethnocentrism...associated with group membership are extensions of nepotism between kinsmen" (van den Berghe 1981: xi; see also Sumner 1906; Pareto 1916; Lopreato 1984: chap. 9). Human beings are ethnocentric ultimately because they are the descendants of organisms whose natural selection within a context of inter-group competition favored the installation of intense nepotistic favoritism. The human brain evolved in societies of twenty-five to forty individuals, whose broadest social horizon was the tribe, an aggregate of clans amounting to perhaps as many as 500 souls (Irwin 1987: 133–34). Even with the rise of great civilizations in the wake of the Neolithic revolution, much of human social life continued to revolve around the small village primarily composed of kith and kin. In terms of an evolutionary timetable, we are at present but a split second removed from this form of human organization. The brain has not changed in the meantime. Accordingly, the clan—the "'in-group' of intimates who think of each other as an extended family" (van den Berghe 1981: 25)—remains the prototype of the "natural" human group. But its tendency in history has necessarily been to open its boundaries to comprise a larger population. Where numbers matter, it is awfully counterproductive not to seek refuge in them. The expansion of social horizons did not, however, proceed indiscriminately. Expansion then moved preferentially in the direction of those who were somehow like us—those who in various phenotypic respects reminded us of "our own." This was an evolution toward today's amalgamation of ethnic groups.

The capacity to forge kinlike affiliations with an expanding range of people may be viewed as a generalization of nepotism under the direct pressure of the predisposition of "homologous affiliation" and the indirect action of "heterologous contraposition." The former concerns a "genetically based inclination to favor alliances...with others in direct proportion to one's degree of kinship and/or phenotypical similarity to these" (Lopreato 1984: 304). It is hardly surprising, therefore, that homogamy, or assortative mating, is highest for traits like race and religion, which most readily convey the message of kindredness (e.g., Rushton 1995: 70). The complement of the affiliation predisposition, heterologous contraposition, is a basic source of hostility toward outsiders. Defined as a "biologically based predisposition to have negative attitudes toward others on the basis of real or perceived differences that are typically, though not exclusively, of an ethnic nature" (Lopreato 1984: 332), contraposition works in conjunction with affiliation to produce and sharpen the boundaries between in-groups and out-groups:

> The more phenotypically (and, by implication, genotypically) similar two persons are to each other, the more they tend to attract each other and to practice mutual favoritism; conversely, the more phenotypically dissimilar they are, the more they tend to avoid each other and, as occasion arises, oppose each other's aims, moral standards, and the like. (Lopreato 1984: 332)

Ethnicity in the Megasociety

Until fairly recent times, the question of identity—who are my people?—was easily answered. We had long been, and were then still, members of a clan. Throughout most of our species' existence, one could readily say: "I am a Zuni, or an Arapesh, or a Kariera—these are my people—*the people*...." In short, the individual could locate "himself in a group which [was] a political unit...culturally uniform, and...the center of the universe, and within this group he [occupied] more specific relationships of kinship" (Gordon 1964: 19—emphasis in original).

Over the past 10,000 years, our species has steadily moved away from the clan as the principal form of societal organization. Today we live in societies with populations numbering in the hundreds of thousands, hundreds of millions, and at least in one case in excess of one billion. We are literally out of place, for we must move about these ever-more complex social worlds equipped with a brain designed to effectively operate an organism in the environment of the hunter-gatherer era. If our ancestors sharply differentiated the in-group from the out-group, we are inclined to do likewise, for the brain is still in the clan. But the answer to the question "Who am I?" is much more difficult to formulate.

The problem, if we may so call it, was created by the development of agriculture and the geographic expansion of political boundaries. Societies, if they survived, became increasingly heterogeneous, encompassing divisions between occupational specializations, social classes, rural workers and city dwellers, rulers and ruled, and so forth. For the first time in hominid history, we found ourselves living literally among strangers. The mind was obliged to expand by a long stretch its social horizons. And so our ancestors of the late Neolithic age began designating themselves as Assyrians, Egyptians, Hittites, and the like. Within each such broad circle of "us," far too many were really not us, if they were not altogether "them." The whisper within still demanded a more focused identity. The confusion, the sense of estrangement, must have been severe when we think of the extraordinary degree of shuffling and reshuffling caused by war, conquest, slavery, and migration—free or otherwise. Émile Durkheim placed in sociological center stage the anomie that accompanied the Industrial Revolution. The Agricultural Revolution was vastly more disruptive of peoples, their cultures, and their sense of moral well-being. It is such a pity that the sociological imagination is rarely challenged by past events.

Population and cultural disruption has continued for millennia. Consider even such relatively recent phenomena as the conquest of the New World, the intersocietal effects of the Protestant Reformation, the expansion and ultimate collapse of European empires, the development of a global slave trade, mass migrations, the emergence of the modern nation-state, the tremendous growth of cities and industries, and the numberless wars of devastation and dislocation. The accompanying shuffling has made it hard to answer the question, Who are my people? We have had to answer it in a variety of imperfect ways, but always somehow striving to identify one's clan. Adapted to the demands of our species' ancestral environment, we are nudged toward identification with what sociologists call primary groups. We try to isolate a narrow and manageable range of those who in some meaningful sense respond to the whisper within. If we cannot achieve the comfort of being with those who are strictly our own, we at least satisfy the need to be with those whose ways allow us to mimic to varying degrees feelings of kinship. It is ethnic ties that, more than anything else beyond the family group, help to satisfy this need.

Several factors enter into the dynamic of ethnic identification. Typically, members of an ethnic group identify with each other and enter into relatively strong relations of mutual dependence on the basis of (1) a common name; (2) a common set of historical experiences; and (3) a commitment to shared cultural traditions, e.g., distinctive cuisine, artistic and musical expressions, patterns of dress, and, perhaps most important of all, a common language (e.g., Smith 1986: chap. 2). The *sine qua non* of ethnic identity, however, is the appeal to common descent, often justified by long segments of communal life. In many contemporary societies the foundation of such appeal may be tenuous. But the need is there, and the mind will somehow justify the appeal.

Indeed, the human brain is well-equipped to solve this problem, especially in view of the fact that the sense of common identity is, like may other cognitive perceptions, mediated by symbols, such as names. Shared names represent one of the principal mechanisms of human kin recognition in humans. In his study of clan totemism, Durkheim understood the significance of this symbolic component of clan solidarity. Members of the clan, he (1912: 122—emphasis added) noted, "consider themselves united by a bond of kinship, but one which is of a very special nature. This relationship does not come from the fact that they have definite blood connections with one another; they are relatives from the mere fact that *they have the same name*." Durkheim's apparent dismissal of genetic relevance to kinship was an egregious error and, as we have remarked, may have contributed to the current crisis in sociological explanation. But he did grasp the actions of symbolic stimulators on the ancient mind. Common names inspire an attitude of mutual trust and obligation, thus encouraging a high degree of in-group solidarity (Isaacs 1975; Crippen and Machalek 1989; Shaw and Wong 1989).

While reliance on common group names introduces a certain degree of flexibility in establishing a sense of group identity, the sense of ethnic affiliation does not appear to be thoroughly elastic or entirely independent of a genetic basis. Ethnic groups have a history of homogamy and assortative mating. Accordingly, the average coefficient of genetic relatedness by descent between two members of the same ethnic group may be expected to be larger, by however minute a fraction, than that found on the average between two members of different ethnic groups.

Of course, the propensity to marry within the in-group varies across time and place. Studies of ethnic intermarriage in the U.S., for example, reveal that rates of homogamy vary directly with the degree of residential homogeneity, low levels of group acculturation, and the size of the ethnic group (namely the opportunity to choose one's own), among several other factors (e.g., Yinger 1994: 160). More to the point, the escalation of ethnic conflict typically intensifies homogamous patterns. According to D.L. Horowitz (1985: 61–62), for example, when "Kikuyu-Luo political relations grew more tense in Kenya, there was a virtual end to Kikuyu-Luo cohabitation and intermarriage"; furthermore, exogamy rates in "severely divided societies typically run below 10 percent of all marriages, and probably lower if only unions between the most-conflicted groups are counted."

One's choice of a marriage partner conveys a powerful message regarding the type of individual with whom one is most comfortable. But other choices reflect similar messages. Who are our friends? With whom are we most likely to join for an evening of camaraderie or an afternoon session of touch football? Whom do we prefer to have as neighbors, members of our own house of worship, and associates at our place of work? In these and other arenas of social life the preference to associate with similar others is widespread, and ethnicity remains one of the chief factors of similarity that channel our choices (e.g., van den Berghe 1981).

But the question remains: Among those living in large, heterogeneous societies how are such judgments formed? Lacking a detailed knowledge of the others' backgrounds, how do we determine if they share our group's history, traditions, and sense of oneness? The answer appears to be that we perceive these things in others, and we ourselves signal similar information to them, through what are called "ethnic markers." These reveal, sometimes clearly and at other times much more subtly, our respective ethnic identities and allegiances.

Pierre van den Berghe's (1981: 28–29) evolutionary analysis of ethnicity has provided a very helpful study of these markers. A first set of them refers to aspects of a "genetically transmitted phenotype." Certain physical characteristics very commonly signal common descent and one's ethnic identity. They include "skin pigmentation, hair texture, stature…[and] facial features," among others. These are the characteristics that are typically but not exclusively associated with "race." A second set of markers refers to features of the "man-made ethnic uniform." Sometimes referred to as "ethnic badges," these include various forms of body adornments such as clothing styles, headgear, body painting, tattooing, circumcision, tooth filing, and various forms of bodily mutilations (scarification, piercing, lip plugging, etc.). Finally, "behavioral" markers of ethnicity are revealed "by speech, demeanor, manners, [knowledge of] esoteric lore or some proof of competence in a behavioral repertoire characteristic of the group."

According to van den Berghe (1981: 29), each of these classes of markers "has a different set of properties and of structural consequences." Racial markers, for example, "can be expected to develop and thrive where genetically inherited phenotypes are the easiest, most visible and most reliable predictors of group membership" (van den Berghe 1981: 32). These markers may be "trivial in terms of fitness, abilities, aptitudes and temperament—indeed anything of social consequence" (van den Berghe 1981: 240). But in multiracial societies they are easy cues to perceive and are most resistant to modification. They may thus signal one's ethnicity fairly reliably.

Behavioral markers are also fairly stable and reliable, especially in contrast to ethnic badges, because they are less vulnerable to mimicry by others. Outsiders may readily adopt clothing styles, other bodily adornments, and even bodily piercings if their wish to invade a particular ethnic group is sufficiently strong, but it is quite another thing entirely to fake knowledge of language, accent, gestures, or social etiquette peculiar to a given ethnic group; the acquisition of these skills requires early exposure and several years of training. Given such experience, members of ethnic groups tend to develop tremendous pride in and affection for their people's cultural traditions—language, cuisine, music, art, and so forth. P. van den Berghe's (1989) own experiences as a cultural "stranger" leads him to poignantly observe that the "spontaneous joy of hearing one's mother tongue spoken when surrounded by strangers is probably a universal human experience. It is experienced even after a long exile. One may become quite proficient in a foreign language yet still fail to enjoy and experience it at the gut emotional level" (van den Berghe 1981: 34).

The emphasis on gut level reaction is particularly significant. We may recall that some proponents of the new ethnicity thesis emphasize the manner in which ethnic loyalties provide a sense of comfort, meaning, and belonging in social environments that are otherwise socially chaotic (e.g., Greeley 1974; see also Isaacs 1975). Indeed, ethnic markers trigger potent nepotistic adaptations that are the product of a brain adapted to the environment of the clan. Today we may live and work in societies featuring huge populations and tremendous status and role differentiation—conditions that engender weighty complexities in our daily lives. But amidst these intricacies, we behave as if we were programmed to live within narrower sociocultural environments. We simplify the complexities in various ways. Among the more widespread, however, are those rooted in ethnic allegiance. Given a nearly infinite array of choices regarding what to do and whom to do it with, we are inclined to gravitate more freely toward those who are like us and who as a result "take us back" to our ancestral home. By the same token, we are predisposed to respond with suspicion and prejudice toward those whose markers signal dissimilarity.

As human societies have grown in size and complexity, the significance of the ethnic markers has risen sharply. Lacking intimate knowledge of others, we are frequently impelled to rely on proxies that signify predictable characteristics in others. The reliance on ethnic markers is further stimulated by conditions that intensify ethnic rivalries. Consider an example from the American immigrant experience. Italians who immigrated around the turn of this century had left behind a society that had only recently achieved national unification, and was still burdened by signficant regional and community cleavages. Thus in the old country, loyalty to village, town, or region was frequently more intense than allegiance to the new nation. These narrow loyalties did not immediately vanish with the crossing of the Atlantic: "When the Italians came to the United States they imported a pitiful tendency to mistrust and avoid all those who did not share their particular dialect and customs" (Lopreato 1970: 104). Of course, the host society was not very sensitive to these regional divisions, and generally treated all Italian immigrants as if they were alike. This fact, in turn, encouraged immigrants from Calabria, Sicily, Campania, the Abruzzi, and other regions to deemphasize their differences and join in common cause so as to more effectively combat the hostilities directed toward them all. In short, despite the history of regional animus, the harsh experiences of discrimination and prejudice in the new world *"Italianized* them" (Lopreato 1970: 171). The regional markers—cuisine preferences, dialect, etc.—were not forgotten; but they were subordinated to general signs of a broader Italian ethnicity in view of a common and more distant stranger.

If increased emphasis on ethnic markers is in fact a corollary of heightened ethnic conflict, the fact does not bode well for the modern condition. Almost everywhere one looks, ethnic allegiances are rearing their ugly heads. We seem to be living in an era characterized by "a massive retribalization running sharply counter to all globalizing effects of modern technology and communications" (Isaacs 1975: 30). The globe may be shrinking; contact between diverse peoples and cultures may be increasing. But whether such changes facilitate greater cross-cultural understanding and tolerance is another question entirely. Indeed, it is just possible that these new features of the environment will have very different consequences. By stimulating kin-selected adaptations wired in the brain, they may very well cause humans to retreat more insistently into the comforting confines of their respective ethnic enclaves. In ways that really count, the globe is not likely to ever be a "global village."

A Note on World Order

Human history has a way of confronting sociologists and other types of social observers with some very great mysteries. For instance, we may recall that for about half a century two military giants and their respective satellites stared at each other with deep suspicion and threat of mutual annihilation. The rest of the world, "lying low" and kept aside by an apocalyptic threat that they had not instigated, held in awe the "titans shaking the world." Local suspicions and divisions everywhere seemed almost insignificant by comparison. And so the irony of that segment of history was that, while the potential for lethal danger had no precedent for its magnitude, it was a relatively peaceful period of human existence, though the fear of destruction had no precedent for its intensity, either.

Accordingly, when the Cold War came to an end some ten years ago, there was a global sigh of relief. Among scholars and politicians there was something else, too. There was a sense, widely lectured, that a "new world order" of peace and harmony was now upon us—according to some, under the aegis of Western liberal democracy, of course. Ideology had been dealt a fatal blow. Indeed, it was "the end of history" (Fukuyama 1989).

Alas, it was pure fantasy. As S.P. Huntington (1996) has cogently argued, with more than a dash of hindsight, the end of the Cold War marked the beginning of a great many hot wars. Much of the world became a battlefield where the armies fired with a distinctly ethnic enthusiasm. According to Huntington (1996: 20, *passim*), "culture and cultural entities, which at the broadest level are civilization identities, are shaping the patterns of cohesion, disintegration, and conflict in the post-Cold War world"; and human society is realigning around seven or eight civilizations. This is a largely intuitive estimate, but the general idea is well-grounded. It is sound precisely because Huntington recognizes that the building blocks of civilizations are ethnic groups. "People define themselves in terms of ancestry, religion, language, history, values, customs, institutions. They identify with cultural groups: tribes, ethnic groups, religious communities, nations, and, at the broadest level, civilizations" (Huntington 1996: 21)—but especially, nowadays, with ethnic groups. Thus: "In this new world, local politics is the politics of ethnicity; global politics is the politics of civilizations" (Huntington 1996: 28). In this "civilizational paradigm" something extraordinary happens to "the family." "A civilization is an extended family" at the center of which is a "core state," which, like a patriarch, provides the family members "with both support and discipline" (Huntington 1996: 156).

An evolutionary understanding of ethnicity provides solid support for some of Huntington's thesis (e.g., van den Berghe 1981; Lopreato 1984: especially chap. 9; Reynolds et al. 1987). Its basic error, truly imposing however, is that there was no need at all, beyond narrow historical convenience, to begin with the end of the Cold War. Human society has been moving toward civilizational alliances since the beginning of civilization, when population explosion; the rise of cities, nations, and empires; large-scale warfare; conquest; and migration destroyed the evolutionary equilibrium that for millions of years had existed in the clan-divided hominid species. Politics, therefore, is ethnic, whether it is local or civilizational. The civilization is merely the cultural umbrella of the ethnic group grown hypertrophic.

Propelled toward the megasociety and the civilization, the clannish brain has had to repeatedly redefine the ancestral and cultural boundaries of the clan. What has remained essentially constant is the need for identity by way of a distinction between us and them. The size of us necessarily varies roughly in direct proportion to the size of them. If to survive and obey the dictates of "the immortal replicator" means making common cause with a whole tribe, a nation, a Nation of nations, so be it. There is hardly a choice. Except, of course, for the option that those with whom we constitute the Nation, and the Civilization, whisper to us tunes that, more than those yelled by others, strike a chord that in the mind echoes back to the primeval home: the clan.

The ubiquity of ethnic conflict has, of course, captured the attention of sociologists and other social scientists. In fact, for some observers, it is the "defining mode of conflict" in the world today, involving savage disputes bred of ancient animosities and aspirations for political and cultural autonomy (e.g., Moynihan 1993). Others underscore such factors as "ethnically defined grievances, demographic threats, negative ethnic stereotypes, a history of ethnic domination, ethnic symbols, a reciprocal fear of group extinction, a *de facto* situation of anarchy, the military means to fight, and the political space for ethnic outbidding [i.e., mobilization]" (Kaufman 1996). There is a wealth of explanations in such analyses, including hints at evolutionary forces. It is hard, however, to clearly distinguish among them. They also tend to stress the "rational" elements of ethnic conflict. As a result, it is easy to fall to the temptation that "it may be easier to maintain inter-ethnic peace than many believe" (Kaufman 1996).

The nonrational aspects of ethnic conflict should come to mind even without benefit of evolutionary theory. Some facts are awfully suggestive. After the collapse of the Soviet Union, for example, some Latvian legislators sought to remove Russian corpses from their military cemeteries. What possible threat could those remains pose to the well-being of the Latvian people? Again, in 1988 a devastating earthquake hit Armenia, killing and injuring thousands of its citizens. They needed blood. But they refused to accept it from their Azerbaijani neighbors (Volkan 1997). Everywhere we observe "communities with adjoining territories, and related to each other in other ways as well, who are engaged in constant feuds and in ridiculing each other" (Freud 1930: 61).

Conclusion

Science is the art of "regressing" the why—inquiring into the more enduring causes of phenomena. The environmental conditions that trigger ethnic clashes vary considerably from time to time and place to place. They too are an important part of scientific explanation. But to transcend the level of mere historical description, they must be anchored to more constant tools of explanation. These refer to the evolutionary forces that confronted our distant forebears.

In conclusion, if we focus on the clans that our ancestors were organized into, we have good reason to assume that, for a variety of causes, some groups were more successful than others in the struggle for scarce resources. They, or better still the inherent traits that contributed to their success, inherited the world through the process of natural selection. Foremost among the causes of their success was in-group solidarity, which, while rooted in familistic psychological adaptations, was reinforced by the ever-present threat coming from without. This is another way of saying that in general the greater the ethnocentrism the greater the probability of survival, reproduction, and genetic representation in subsequent generations. That is, natural selection favored those who practiced intense kin altruism and its negative correlative, ethnocentrism, and may thus be said to have in part operated at the level of the kin group, as kin selection.

Equipped with these primeval adaptations, our clan progentiors entered the historical era and the megasociety with zealous conceptions of us and them. Paleogenetic evidence shows, however, that while societal organization has changed dramatically, our neurobiology is still back in the clan. In the continuing struggle for existence, we are still driven to make common cause with some and to suspect evil intentions in others.

But to make such common cause we must recognize commonality: we must be able to practice kin recognition. This capacity was mechanical, as Durkheim would say, in the ancestral group of kin. By contrast, today's society is a society of strangers. The whisper that echoes in our brain—Who am I?, Who are mine?—finds no easy answer. Yet it is insistent, and the urging accentuates awareness that the new society reflects the diversity of elements that have constituted it. One salient component of such diversity underscores the vitality of ethnic groups. Some strangers are less strange than others, after all. They are Jews rather than Christians, Christians rather than Muslims, Greeks instead of Italians, Tutsis instead of Hutus, Korean instead of Japanese. They are the kind of people that our ancestors might have married into. Their peculiarities of speech, religion, culinary preferences, and physical appearance, among other features, precipitate the ancient nepotism and ethnocentrism that are the hallmark of the clannish brain. These are the "ethnic markers," and through them we rejoin, in the midst of strangers, our ancestral group—or at least we are able to mimic feelings of belonging to it.

Which is to say that, at least for the foreseeable future, whatever the geopolitics of the times, the clannish brain will ever create the mischief that is its destiny by natural selection. Ethnic wars will be the constant of human history. Alliances and compactness will vary in time. History shows that ethnic groups have been the building blocks of nations and civilizations. The extraordinary paradox is that they also constitute the cracks along which nepotistic currents periodically rush to destroy societies and wreak havoc with civilizations. In large measure, the history of the human species has been, and will continue to be, a history of ethnic assemblies, ethnic collisions, and ethnic disorders. There is dailiness, immediacy of feeling and interest, in peoples' lives, and the echo of the clan's chant—the call of the wild—will continue to resound at the periphery of the immediate kin group. Too many human facts are here and now. Their lasting causes are there and then.

References

Aboud, F. 1988. *Children and Prejudice*. Oxford: Blackwell.

Adler, A. 1932. *What Life Should Mean to You*. London: Allen & Unwin.

Agger, B. 1994. Derrida for sociology? A comment on Fuchs and Ward. *American Sociological Review* 59: 501–5.

Ahlburg, D.A. and C.J. DeVita. 1992. New realities of the American family. *Population Bulletin* 47 (No. 2, August): 1–44.

Alba, R.D. 1992. Ethnicity. Pp. 575–84 in E.F. Borgatta, ed. *Encyclopedia of Sociology*. New York: Macmillan.

Alexander, J.C. 1994. How "national" is social theory? A note on some worrying trends in the recent theorizing of Richard Münch. *Theory* (Autumn): 2–8.

Alexander, R.D. 1971. The search for an evolutionary philosophy. *Proceedings of the Royal Society*, Victoria, Australia 84: 99–120.

———. 1979. *Darwinism and Human Affairs*. Seattle: University of Washington Press.

———. 1986. Ostracism and indirect reciprocity: The reproductive significance of humor. *Ethology and Sociobiology* 7: 253–70.

———. 1987. *The Biology of Moral Systems*. New York: Aldine de Gruyter.

———. 1988. Evolutionary approaches to human behavior: What does the future hold? Pp. 317–41 in L. Betzig, M. Borgerhoff Mulder, and P. Turke, eds. *Human Reproductive Behavior: A Darwinian Perspective*. Cambridge: Cambridge University Press.

———. 1990. Epigenetic rules and Darwinian algorithms: The adaptive study of learning and development. *Ethology and Sociobiology* 11:241–303.

Alexander, R.D., J.L. Hoogland, R.D. Howard, K. M. Noonan, and P.W. Sherman. 1979. Sexual dimorphism and breeding systems in pinnipeds, ungulates, primates, and humans. Pp. 402–35 in N.A. Chagnon and W. Irons, eds. *Evolutionary Biology and Human Behavior: An Anthropological Perspective*. North Scituate, MA.: Duxbury Press.

Allen, L.S. and R.A. Gorski. 1991. Sexual dimorphism of the anterior commisure and massa intermedia of the human brain. *Journal of Comparative Neurology* 312: 97–104.

Allen, L.S., M. Hines, J.H. Shryne, and R.A. Gorski. 1989. Two sexually dimorphic cell groups in the human brain. *Journal of Neuroscience* 9: 497–506.

Allen, L.S., M.F. Richey, Y.M. Chai, and R.A. Gorski. 1991. Sex differences in the corpus callosum of the living human being. *Journal of Neuroscience* 11: 933–42.

Allison, P.D. 1992. The cultural evolution of beneficent norms. *Social Forces* 71: 279–301.

Alpert, H. 1939. *Emile Durkheim and His Sociology*. New York: Columbia University Press.

Amato, P. 1989. Who cares for the children in public places? Naturalistic observation of male and female caretakers. *Journal of Marriage and the Family* 51: 981–90.

Anderson, B. 1983. *Imagined Communities: Reflections on the Origin and Spread of Nationalism*. New York: New Left Books.

Arafat, I. and B. Yorburg. 1973. On living together without marriage. *Journal of Sex Research* 9: 97–106.

Archer, J.E. 1988. *The Behavioural Biology of Aggression*. Cambridge: Cambridge University Press.

⸻, ed. 1994. *Male Violence*. New York: Routledge.

Arendt, H. 1959. *The Human Condition*. Garden City, NJ: Doubleday.

Arnhart, L. 1992. Feminism, primatology, and ethical naturalism. *Politics and the Life Sciences* 11: 157–70.

Aron, R. 1965. *Main Currents in Sociological Thought*, 2 vols. New York: Basic Books.

Axelrod, R. 1984. *The Evolution of Cooperation*. New York: Basic Books.

Bachrach, C.A. 1987. Cohabitation and reproductive behavior in the U.S. *Demography* 24: 623–37.

Backett, K. 1987. The negotiation of fatherhood. Pp. 74–90 in C. Lewis and M. O'Brien, eds. *Reassessing Fatherhood*. London: Sage.

Bailey, J.M., S. Gaulin, Y. Agyei, and B.A. Gladue. 1994. Effects of gender and sexual orientation on evolutionarily relevant aspects of human mating psychology. *Journal of Personality and Social Psychology* 66: 1081–93.

Baker, L.C. 1996. Differences in earnings between male and female physicians. *The New England Journal of Medicine* 334: 960–64.

Barash, D.P. 1979. *The Wisperings Within: Evolution and the Origin of Human Nature*. New York: Harper & Row.

⸻. 1982. *Sociobiology and Behavior*, rev. ed. New York: Elsevier.

Barry, B. and R. Hardin, eds. 1982. *Rational Man and Irrational Society*. Beverly Hills, CA: Sage.

Barth, F. 1969. Introduction. Pp. 1–38 in F. Barth, ed., *Ethnic Groups and Boundaries*. Boston: Little, Brown.

Bateman, A.J. 1948. Intrasexual selection in *Drosophila*. *Heredity* 2: 349–68.

Bauman, Z. 1988. Is there a postmodern sociology? *Theory, Culture, and Society* 5: 217–38.

Beck, E.M., P.M. Haran, and Tolbert, C.M. II. 1980. Industrial segregation and labor market discrimination. *Social Problems* 28: 113–30.

Becker, E. 1973. *The Denial of Death*. New York: Free Press.

Becker, G.S. 1976. *The Economic Approach to Human Behavior*. Chicago: University of Chicago Press.

⸻. 1981. *A Treatise on the Family*. Cambridge, MA: Harvard University Press.

Becker, J.B., S.M. Breedlove, and D. Crews, eds. 1992. *Behavioral Endocrinology*. Cambridge, MA: MIT Press.

Beigel, H.G. 1954. Body height in mate selection. *Journal of Social Psychology* 39: 257–68.

Bell, D. 1976. *The Cultural Contradictions of Capitalism*. New York: Basic Books.

Bell-Fialkoff, A. 1993. A brief history of ethnic cleansing. *Foreign Affairs* 72: 110–21.

Bellah, R.N, ed. 1973. *Emile Durkheim on Morality and Society*. Chicago: University of Chicago Press.

⸻. 1975. *The Broken Covenant: American Civil Religion in Time of Trial*. New York: Seabury Press.

Bellah, R.N., R. Madsen, W.M. Sullivan, and A. Swidler. 1991. *The Good Society*. New York: Knopf.

Bellah, R.N., R. Madsen, W.M. Sullivan, A. Swindler, and S.M. Tipton. 1985. *Habits of the Heart: Individualism and Commitment in American Life*. Berkeley: University of California Press.

Bem, S.L. 1993. *The Lenses of Gender.* New Haven, CT: Yale University Press.
Benbow, C.P. and J.C. Stanley. 1980. Sex differences in mathematical ability: Fact or artifact? *Science* 210: 1234–36.
———. 1983. Sex differences in mathematical reasoning ability: More facts. *Science* 222: 1029–31.
Benedict, R. 1934. *Patterns of Culture.* Boston: Houghton Mifflin.
———. 1946. *The Chrysanthemum and the Sword.* Boston: Houghton Mifflin.
Bennett, J.H., F.A. Rhodes, and H.N. Robson. 1959. A possible genetic base for Kuru. *American Journal of Human Genetics* 2: 169–87.
Bennett, N., A. Blanc, and D. Bloom. 1988. Commitment and the modern union: Assessing the link between premarital cohabitation and marital stability. *American Sociological Review* 53: 127–38.
Bereczkei, T. and A. Csanaky. 1996. Mate choice, marital success, and reproduction in a modern society. *Ethology and Sociobiology* 17: 17–35.
Berenbaum, S. and M. Hines. 1992. Early androgens are related to childhood sex-typed toy preferences. *Psychological Sciences* 3: 203–6.
Berger, P.L. 1963. *Invitation to Sociology: A Humanistic Perspective.* New York: Anchor Books.
Berk, S.F. 1985. *The Gender Factory.* New York: Plenum.
Bernard, J. 1987. Forword. In A. Simeone, *Academic Women.* South Hadley, MA: Bergin and Garvey.
Bernstein, I.S. and C.L. Ehardt. 1985. Intragroup agonistic behavior in rhesus monkeys. *International Journal of Primatology* 6: 209–26.
Betzig, L.L. 1986. *Despotism and Differential Reproduction: A Darwinian View of History.* New York: Aldine.
———. 1988. Mating and parenting in Darwinian perspective. Pp. 3–20 in L. Betzig, M. Borgehoff Mulder, and P. Turke, eds. *Human Reproductive Behaviour.* New York: Cambridge University Press.
———. 1989. Causes of conjugal dissolution: A cross-cultural study. *Current Anthropology* 30: 654–76.
———. 1993a. Sex, succession, and stratification in the first six civilizations. Pp. 37–74 in L. Ellis, ed. *Social Stratification and Socioeconomic Inequality. Volume 1: A Comparative Biosocial Analysis.* Westport, CT: Praeger.
———. 1993b. Review of *The Adapted Mind. Ethology and Sociobiology* 14: 397–402.
Betzig, L., and S. Weber. 1993. Polygyny in American politics. *Politics and the Life Sciences* 12: 45–52.
Bianchi, S.M. and D. Spain. 1996. Women, work, and family in America. *Population Bulletin* 51 (December): 1–48.
Bibb, R. and W.H. Form. 1977. The effects of industrial, occupational, and sex stratification on wages in blue-collar markets. *Social Forces* 55: 974–96.
Black, M., ed. 1961a. *The Social Theories of Talcott Parsons: A Critical Examination.* Englewood Cliffs, NJ: Prentice-Hall.
———. 1961b. Some questions about Parsons' theories. Pp. 268–88 in M. Black, ed. *The Social Theories of Talcott Parsons: A Critical Examination.* Englewood Cliffs, NJ: Prentice-Hall.
Blau, F.D. and M.A. Ferber. 1992. *The Economics of Women, Men, and Work*, 2nd ed. Englewood Cliffs, NJ: Prentice-Hall.
Blau, P.M. 1964. *Exchange and Power in Social Life.* New York: John Wiley and Sons.
Blau, P.M. and O.D. Duncan. 1967. *The American Occupational Structure.* New York: Wiley.

Bleiberg Seperson, S. 1995. What's wrong with sociology? Its public image. *Sociological Forum* 10: 309–12.

Bleier, R. 1984. *Science and Gender: A Critique of Biology and Its Theories on Women.* New York: Pergamon Press.

Blood, R.O. and D.M. Wolfe. 1960. *Husbands and Wives.* New York: Free Press.

Bloom, A. 1987. *The Closing of the American Mind.* New York: Simon and Schuster.

Blumer, H. 1969. *Symbolic Interactionism: Perspective and Method.* Englewood Cliffs, NJ: Prentice-Hall.

——. 1981. George H. Mead. Pp. 136–69 in B. Rhea, ed. *The Future of the Sociological Classics.* London: Allen & Unwin.

Boccia, M.L., M. Laudenslager, and M. Reite. 1988. Food distribution, dominance, and aggressive behaviors in bonnet macaques. *American Journal of Primatology* 16: 123–30.

Bonacich, E. 1972. A theory of ethnic antagonism: The split labor market. *American Sociological Review* 37: 547–59.

Booth, A. and J.M. Dabbs, Jr. 1993. Testosterone and men's marriages. *Social Forces* 72: 463–77.

Booth, A. and J. Edwards. 1980. Fathers: The invisible parent. *Sex Roles* 6: 445–56.

Booth, A., G. Shelley, A. Mazur, G. Tharp, and R. Kittock. 1989. Testosterone and winning and losing in human competition. *Hormones and Behavior* 23: 556–71.

Borgehoff Mulder, M. 1988. Reproductive success in three Kipsigis cohorts. Pp. 419–35 in T.H. Clutton-Brock, ed. *Reproductive Success: Studies of Selection and Adaptation in Contrasting Breeding Systems.* Chicago: University of Chicago Press.

Borgmann, A. 1992. *Crossing The Postmodern Divide.* Chicago: University of Chicago Press.

Bowlby, J. 1990. *Charles Darwin: A New Life.* New York: W.W. Norton.

Braddock, J.H., II and J.M. McPartland. 1992. Equality of opportunity. Pp. 554–63 in E.F. Borgatta, ed. *Encyclopedia of Sociology.* New York: Macmillan.

Braithwaite, R. B. 1964. *Scientific Explanation: A Study of the Function of Theory, Probability and Law in Science.* Cambridge: Cambridge University Press.

Brandon, G.S.F. 1962. *Man and His Destiny in the Great Religions.* Manchester: Manchester University Press.

Braudel, F. 1982 (orig. 1979). *The Wheels of Commerce.* New York: Harper & Row.

Bregantini, L. 1996. Ethnic minorities from the Atlantic to the Pacific. ISIG, Institute of International Sociology V (October): 8–12.

Bridges, W.P. 1980. Industry marginality and female employment: A new appraisal. *American Sociological Review* 45: 58–75.

Brinton, C. 1938. *The Anatomy of Revolution.* New York: Norton.

Brown, D.E. 1991. *Human Universals.* New York: McGraw-Hill.

Brown, D.M. 1955. *Nationalism in Japan.* Berkeley, CA: University of California Press.

Brown, J.K. 1970. A note on the division of labor by sex. *American Anthropologist* 72: 1073–78.

Buckle, L., G.G. Gallup, Jr., and Z.A. Rodd. 1996. Marriage as a reproductive contract: Patterns of marriage, divorce, and remarriage. *Ethology and Sociobiology* 17: 363–77.

Buffery, A.W.H. and J.A. Gray. 1975. Sex differences in the development of spatial and linguistic skills. Pp. 123–57 in C. Ousted and D.C. Taylor, eds. *Gender Differences.* London: Churchill Livingstone.

Bumpass, L.L. and J. Sweet. 1989. National estimates of cohabitation: Cohort levels and union stability. *Demography* 26: 615–25.

Bunge, M. 1987. Seven desiderata for rationality. Pp. 5–15 in J. Agassi and I.C. Jarvie, eds. *Rationality: The Critical View*. Dordrecht: Nijhoff.

Bury, J.B. 1955 (orig. 1932). *The Idea of Progress*. New York: Dover.

Buss, D.M. 1988. The evolution of intrasexual competition: Tactics of mate attraction. *Journal of Personality and Social Psychology* 54: 616–28.

———. 1989. Sex differences in human mate preferences: Evolutionary hypotheses tested in 37 cultures (with commentaries). *Behavioral and Brain Sciences* 12: 1–49.

———. 1994a. *The Evolution of Desire*. New York: Basic Books.

———. 1994b. The strategies of human mating. *American Scientist* 82: 238–50.

Buss, D.M. and M. Barnes. 1986. Preference in human mate selection. *Journal of Personality and Social Psychology* 50: 559–69.

Buss, D.M., R.J. Larsen, D. Westen, and J. Semmelroth. 1992. Sex differences in jealousy: Evolution, physiology, and psychology. *Psychological Science* 3: 251–55.

Buss, D.M. and D.P. Schmidt. 1993. Sexual strategies theory: An evolutionary perspective on human mating. *Psychological Review* 100: 204–32.

Caplan, A.L., ed. 1978. *The Sociobiology Debate*. New York: Harper & Row.

Carey, A.D. and J. Lopreato. 1994. Sociobiology and the wayward critic. *Sociological Perspectives* 37: 403–30.

———. 1995a. The biocultural evolution of the male-female mortality differential. *The Mankind Quarterly* XXXVI: 3–28.

———. 1995b. The evolutionary demography of the fertility-mortality quasi-equilibrium. *Population and Development Review* 21: 613–30.

Castro Martin, T. and L. Bumpass. 1989. Recent trends and differentials in marital disruption. *Demography* 25: 37–51.

Chafetz, J.S. 1984. *Sex and Advantage*. Totowa, NJ: Rowman & Allanheld.

———. 1990. *Gender Equity*. Newbury Park, CA: Sage.

Chagnon, N.A. 1979. Is reproductive success equal in egalitarian societies? Pp. 374–401 in N.A. Chagnon and W. Irons, eds. *Evolutionary Biology and Human Social Behavior: An Anthropological Perspective*. North Scituate, MA.: Duxbury Press.

———. 1980. Kin selection theory, kinship, marriage and fitness among the Yanomamo Indians. Pp. 545–71 in G. Barlow and J. Silverberg, eds. *Sociobiology: Beyond Nature/Nurture?* Boulder, CO: Westview Press.

———. 1983. *Yanomamo: The Fierce People*, 3rd ed. New York: Holt, Rinehard and Winston.

———. 1988. Life histories, blood revenge, and warfare in a tribal population. *Science* 239: 985–92.

Chagnon, N.A., M.V. Flinn, and T.F. Melancon. 1979. Sex ratio variation among the Yanomamo Indians. Pp. 290–320 in N.A. Chagnon and W. Irons, eds. *Evolutionary Biology and Human Social Behavior: An Anthropological Perspective*. North Scituate, MA: Duxbury Press.

Chance, M.R.A. and C.J. Jolly. 1970. *Social Groups of Monkeys, Apes, and Men*. New York: Dutton.

Cheney, D.L. and R.M. Seyfarth. 1990. *How Monkeys See the World*. Chicago: University of Chicago Press.

Cherlin, A.J. 1978. Remarriage as an incomplete institution. *American Journal of Sociology* 84: 634–50.

———. 1981. *Marriage, Divorce, Remarriage*. Cambridge, MA: Harvard University Press.

———. 1992. *Marriage, Divorce, Remarriage*, rev. ed. Cambridge, MA: Harvard University Press.

Cherns, A., ed. 1980. *Quality of Working Life and the Kibbutz Experience: Proceedings of an International Conference in Israel*, June 1978. Norwood, PA: Norwood Editions.

Chisholm, J.S. 1993. Death, hope, and sex: Life-history theory and the development of reproductive strategies. *Current Anthropology* 34: 1–12.

Christiansen, K. and R. Knussmann. 1987. Androgen levels and components of aggressive behavior in men. *Hormone and Behavior* 21: 170–80.

Clark, R.D. and E. Hatfield. 1989. Gender differences in receptivity to sexual offers. *Journal of Psychology and Human Sexuality* 2: 39–55.

Clignet, R. 1992. *Death, Deeds, and Descendants*. New York: Aldine de Gruyter.

Cliquet, R.L. 1984. The relevance of sociobiological theory for emancipatory feminism. *Journal of Human Evolution* 13: 117–27.

Cole, S. 1994a. Introduction: What's wrong with sociology. *Sociological Forum* 9: 129–31.

———. 1994b. Why sociology doesn't make progress like the natural sciences. *Sociological Forum* 9: 133–54.

Coleman, J.S. 1990. *Foundations of Social Theory*. Cambridge, MA: Belknap.

———. 1990–1991. The Sidney Hook memorial award address: On self-suppression of academic freedom. *Academic Questions* 4: 17–22.

———. 1992. Rational choice theory. Pp. 1619–24 in E.F. Borgatta, ed. *Encyclopedia of Sociology*. New York: Macmillan.

Collins, P.H. 1991. *Black Feminist Thought: Knowledge, Consciousness, and the Politics of Empowerment*. New York: Routledge.

Collins, R. 1975. *Conflict Sociology: Toward an Explanatory Sociology*. New York: Academic Press.

———. 1980. Weber's last theory of capitalism: A systematization. *American Sociological Review* 45: 925–42.

———. 1988. *Theoretical Sociology*. New York: Harcourt Brace Jovanovich.

———. 1989. Sociology: Proscience or antiscience? *American Sociological Review* 54: 124–39.

———. 1990. The organizational politics of the ASA. *American Sociologist* 21: 311.

———. 1998. The sociological eye and its blinders. *Contemporary Sociology* 27: 2–7.

Collins, R. and S. Coltrane. 1991. *Sociology of Marriage and the Family*, 3rd ed. Chicago: Nelson-Hall.

Coltrane, S. 1996. *Family Man*. New York: Oxford University Press.

Commander, L.K. 1909. The self-supporting woman and the family. *American Journal of Sociology* 14: 752–57.

Comte, A. 1830–1842. *Cours de Philosophie Positive*. Paris: Bachelier.

———. 1875–1877. *System of Positive Polity*. London: Longmans, Green.

———. 1896 (orig. 1854). *The Positive Philosophy of Auguste Comte*, 3 vols. (free translation and abridgement by H. Martineau). London: Bell.

Connell, R.W. 1987. *Gender and Power*. Stanford, CA: Stanford University Press.

Coombs, R.H. and W.P. Kenkel. 1966. Sex differences in mating aspirations and satisfaction with computer-selected partners. *Journal of Marriage and the Family* 28: 62–66.

Corballis, M.C. and I.L. Beale. 1983. *The Ambivalent Mind: The Neuropsychology of Left and Right*. Chicago: Nelson-Hall.

Cornacchia, E.J. and D.C. Nelson. 1992. Historical differences in the political experience of American blacks and white ethnics: An unresolved controversy. *Ethnic and Racial Studies* 15: 102–24.

Coser, L. A. 1971. *Masters of Sociological Thought*. New York: Harcourt, Brace, Jovanovich.

Cosmides, L. 1989. The logic of social exchange: Has natural selection shaped how humans reason? Studies with the Wason selection task. *Cognition* 31: 187–276.

Cosmides, L. and J. Tooby. 1989. Evolutionary psychology and the generation of culture, part II. Case study: A computational theory of social exchange. *Ethology and Sociobiology* 10:51–97.

Coughlin, E.K. 1992. Sociologists confront questions about field's vitality and direction. *Chronicle of Higher Education.* August 12, Section A: 5–7.

Crippen, T. 1987. The sources and evolution of social consciousness: Reconciling the contributions of Marx, Durkheim, and Mead. *Revue Européenne des Sciences Sociales* 25: 647–73.

———. 1988. Old and new Gods in the modern world: Toward a theory of religious transformation. *Social Forces* 67: 316–36.

———. 1992. An evolutionary critique of cultural analysis in sociology. *Human Nature* 4: 379–412.

———. 1994a. Toward a neo-Darwinian sociology: Its nomological principles and some illustrative applications. *Sociological Perspectives* 37: 309–35.

———. 1994b. Neo-Darwinian approaches in the social sciences: Unwarranted concerns and misconceptions. Sociological Perspectives 37: 391–401.

Crippen, T. and R. Machalek. 1989. The evolutionary foundations of the religious life. *Revue Internationale de Sociologie* 3 (nouvelle série): 61–84.

Cronin, H. 1991. *The Ant and the Peacock.* Cambridge: Cambridge University Press.

Cronk, L. 1991. Wealth, status and reproductive success among the Mukogodo of Kenya. *American Anthropologist* 93: 345–60.

Crook, J.H. 1965. The adaptive significance of avian social organizations. *Symposium of the Zoological Society of London* 14: 181–218.

Crook, J.H. and S.J. Crook. 1988. Tibetan polyandry: Problems of adaptation and fitness. Pp. 97–114 in L. Betzig, M. Borgehoff, and P. Turke, eds. *Human Reproductive Behaviour.* New York: Cambridge University Press.

Crow, J.F. and M. Kimura. 1970. *An Introduction to Population Genetics Theory.* New York: Harper & Row.

Cutts, S. 1994. The ambiguity of fatherhood. Honors thesis submitted to the Department of Sociology, University of Texas at Austin, Spring.

Dahrendorf, R. 1959. *Class and Class Conflict in Industrial Society.* Stanford, CA: Stanford University Press.

Daly, M. and M. Wilson. 1978. *Sex, Evolution, and Behavior.* North Scituate, MA: Duxbury.

———. 1983. *Sex, Evolution, and Behavior*, 2nd ed. Boston: Willard Grant Press.

———. 1988. *Homicide.* New York: Aldine de Gruyter.

Daly, M., M. Wilson, and S.J. Weghorst. 1982. Male sexual jealousy. *Ethology and Sociobiology* 3: 11–27.

Darwin, C. 1958 (orig. 1859). *The Origin of Species.* New York: New American Library, Mentor Books.

———. 1871. *The Origin of Species and The Descent of Man and Selection in Relation to Sex.* New York: Random House (undated collection).

———. 1965 (orig. 1872). *The Expression of Emotions in Man and Animals.* Chicago: University of Chicago Press.

———. 1902. *Journal of Researches.* New York: American Home Library.

Darwin, F. ed. 1885. *The Life and Letters of Charles Darwin.* London: John Murray.

Darwin, F. and A.C. Seward, eds. 1903. *More Letters of Charles Darwin.* New York: Appleton.

Datta, S. 1983. Relative power and maintenance of dominance. Pp. 103–12 in R.A. Hinde, ed. *Primate Social Relationships.* Cambridge: Cambridge University Press.

———. 1988. The acquisition of dominance among free-ranging rhesus monkey siblings. *Animal Behavior* 36: 754–72.
Davie, M.R. 1929. *The Evolution of War: A Study of Its Role in Early Societies.* New Haven, CT: Yale University Press.
Davies, J.C. 1962. Toward a theory of revolution. *American Sociological Review* 27: 5–19.
Davis, J.A. 1994. What's wrong with sociology? *Sociological Forum* 9: 179–97.
Davis, K. 1948. *Human Society.* New York: Macmillan.
———. 1953. "Reply." *American Sociological Review* 18: 394–97.
———. 1959. The myth of functional analysis as a special method in sociology and anthropology. *American Sociological Review* 24: 757–72.
Davis, K. and W.E. Moore. 1945. Some principles of stratification. *American Sociological Review* 10: 242–49.
Dawkins, R. 1979. Twelve misunderstandings of kin selection. *Zeitschrift für Tierpsychologie* 51: 184–200.
———. 1986. *The Blind Watchmaker.* New York: W.W. Norton.
———. 1989. *The Selfish Gene,* new ed. Oxford: Oxford University Press.
———. 1995. *River Out of Eden: A Darwinian View of Life.* New York: Basic Books.
de Beauvoir, S. 1952. *The Second Sex.* New York: Alfred A. Knopf.
Degler, C.N. 1991. *In Search of Human Nature.* New York: Oxford University Press.
de Lacoste-Utamsing, M.C. and R.L. Holloway. 1982. Sexual dimorphism in the human corpus callosum. *Science* 216: 1431–32.
de Lacoste-Utamsing, M.C. and D.L. Woodward. 1982. Sexual dimorphism in human fetal corpus callosum. Paper presented at the annual meetings of the Society for Neuroscience.
Dennett, D.C. 1995. *Darwin's Dangerous Idea.* New York: Simon & Schuster.
Denzin, N.K. 1991. *Images of Postmodern Society: Social Theory and Contemporary Cinema.* Newbury Park, CA: Sage.
———. 1997. Whose sociology is it? Comment on Huber. *American Journal of Sociology* 102: 1416–29.
Derrida, J. 1987. The ends of man. Pp. 125–58 in K. Baynes, J. Bohman, and T. McCarthy, eds. *After Philosophy: End or Transformation?* Cambridge, MA: MIT Press.
Devereux, E.C., Jr. 1961. Parsons' sociological theory. Pp. 1–63 in M. Black, ed. *The Social Theories of Talcott Parsons: A Critical Examination.* Englewood Cliffs, NJ: Prentice-Hall.
DeVore, B.I. 1965a. Male dominance and mating behavior in baboons. Pp. 266–89 in F.A. Beach, ed. *Sex and Behavior.* New York: Wiley.
———, ed. 1965b. *Primate Behavior.* New York: Holt, Rinehart & Winston.
de Vos, H. and E. Zeggelink. 1997. Reciprocal altruism in human social evolution: The viability of reciprocal altruism with a preference for "old-helping-partners." *Evolution and Behavior* 18: 261–78.
de Waal, F.B.M. 1982. *Chimpanzee Politics.* New York: Harper & Row.
———. 1986. The brutal elimination of a rival among captive male chimpanzees. *Ethology and Sociobiology* 7: 237–51.
———. 1989. *Peacemaking among Primates.* Cambridge, MA: Harvard University Press.
———. 1995. Bonobo sex and society. *Scientific American* 272: 82–88.
Diamond, J. 1992. *The Third Chimpanzee.* New York: HarperCollins.
———. 1997. *Guns, Germs, and Steel: The Fates of Human Societies.* New York: Norton.
Dickemann, M. 1979a. Female infanticide, reproductive strategies, and social strati-

fication: A preliminary model. Pp. 321–67 in N.A. Chagnon and W. Irons, eds. *Evolutionary Biology and Human Social Behavior: An Anthropological Perspective*. North Scituate, MA: Duxbury Press.

——. 1979b. The ecology of mating systems in hypergynous dowry societies. *Social Science Information* 18: 163–95.

Dion, K. 1981. Physical attractiveness, sex roles, and heterosexual attraction. Pp. 3–22 in M. Cook, ed. *The Bases of Human Sexual Attraction*. New York: Academic Press.

Dittman, R., M.H. Kappes, M.E. Kappes, and D. Borger. 1991. Congenital adrenal hyperplasia: I. Gender-related behavior and attitudes in female patients and sisters. *Psychoneuroendocrinology* 15: 401–20.

Djilas, M. 1957. *The New Class: An Analysis of the Communist System*. New York: Praeger.

Dobzhansky, T. 1973. Nothing in biology makes sense except in the light of evolution. *American Biology Teacher* 35: 125–29.

Dobzhansky, T., F.J. Ayala, G. Ledyard Stebbins, and J.W. Valentine. 1977. *Evolution*. San Francisco: W.H. Freeman.

Downey, J., A. Ehrhardt, R. Gruen, J. Bell, and A. Morishima. 1989. Psychopathology and social functioning in women with Turner syndrome. *Journal of Nervous and Mental Disease* 177: 191–201.

Duffy Hutcheson, P. 1996. *Leaving the Cave: Evolutionary Naturalism in Social-Scientific Thought*. Waterloo, Ontario: Wilfrid Laurier University Press.

Dunbar, R.I.M. 1988. *Primate Social Systems*. Ithaca, NY: Cornell University Press.

Dunbar, R.I.M. and E.P. Dunbar. 1977. Dominance and reproductive success among gelada baboons. *Nature* (London) 266: 351–52.

Duncan, B. and O.D. Duncan, with J.A. McRea, Jr. 1978. *Sex Typing and Social Roles: A Research Report*. New York: Academic Press.

Durham, W.H. 1976. Resource competition and human aggression, Part I: A review of primitive war. *Quarterly Review of Biology* 51: 385–415.

Durkheim, E. 1933 (orig. 1893). *The Division of Labor in Society*. New York: Macmillan.

——. 1958 (orig. 1895). *The Rules of Sociological Method*. Glencoe, IL: Free Press.

——. 1951 (orig. 1897). *Suicide*. New York: Free Press.

——. 1965 (orig. 1912). *The Elementary Forms of the Religious Life*. New York: Free Press.

——. 1956 (orig. 1924a). *Education and Sociology*. Glencoe, IL: Free Press.

——. 1953 (orig. 1924b). *Sociology and Philosophy*. Glencoe, IL: Free Press.

Eagly, A.H. 1995. The science and politics of comparing women and men. *American Psychologist* 50: 145–58.

Eals, M. and I. Silverman. 1994. The hunter-gatherer theory of spatial sex differences: Proximate factors mediating the female advantage in recall of object arrays. *Ethology and Sociobiology* 15: 95–105.

Easterlin, R.A. 1987. *Birth and Fortune*, 2nd ed. Chicago: University of Chicago Press.

Eaton, S.B., M. Shostak, and M. Konner. 1988. *The Paleolithic Prescription*. New York: Harper & Row.

Eaton, G.G. 1976. The social order of Japanese macaques. *Scientific American* 235: 97:106.

Eibl-Eibesbeldt. 1989. *Human Ethology*. New York: Aldine de Gruyter.

Elder, G.H. 1969. Appearance and education in marriage mobility. *American Sociological Review* 34: 519–33.

Eldredge, N. 1985. *Timeframes*. New York: Simon and Schuster.

Eldredge, N. and S.J. Gould. 1972. Punctuated equilibrium: An alternative to phyletic gradualism. Pp. 82–115 in T.J.M. Schoph, ed. *Models in Paleobiology*. San Francisco: Freeman, Copper.

Elias, M. 1981. Serum cortisol, testosterone, and testosterone binding globulin responses to competitive fighting in human males. *Aggressive Behavior* 7: 215–24.

Ellis, B.J. 1992. The evolution of sexual attraction: Evaluative mechanisms in women. Pp. 267–88 in J.H. Barkow, L. Cosmides, and J. Tooby, eds. *The Adapted Mind*. New York: Oxford University Press.

Ellis, B.J. and D. Symons. 1990. Sex differences in sexual fantasy: An evolutionary psychological approach. *Journal of Sex Research* 27: 527–55.

Ellis, L. 1995. Dominance and reproductive success among nonhuman animals: A cross-species comparison. *Ethology and Sociobiology* 16: 257–333.

———. 1996. A discipline in peril: Sociology's future hinges on curing its biophobia. *American Sociologist* 27: 21–41.

Engels, F. 1978 (orig. 1883). Speech at the graveside of Karl Marx. Pp. 681–82 in R.C. Tucker, ed. *The Marx-Engels Reader*, 2nd ed. New York: Norton.

———. 1888. Preface to the 1888 English edition of K. Marx and F. Engels. 1848. *Manifesto of the Communist Party*. Pp. 1–6 in L.S. Feuer, ed. *Marx and Engels: Basic Writings on Politics and Philosophy*. New York: Doubleday.

England, P.A. and I. Browne. 1992. Trends in women's status. *Sociological Perspectives* 35: 17–51.

England, P., M.S. Herbert, B.S. Kilbourne, L.L. Reid, and L.M. Megdal. 1994. The gendered valuation of occupational skills: Earnings in 1980 census occupations. *Social Forces* 73: 65–100.

Epstein, C.F. 1988. *Deceptive Distinctions*. New Haven, CT: Yale University Press.

Eriksen, J.A., W.L. Yancey, and E.P. Eriksen. 1979. The division of family roles. *Journal of Marriage and the Family* 41: 301–13.

Esman, M.J. 1994. *Ethnic Politics*. Ithaca, NY: Cornell University Press.

Euler, H.A. and B. Weitzel. 1996. Discriminative grandparental solicitude as reproductive strategy. *Human Nature* 7: 39–59.

Fabianic, D. 1991. Declining enrollments of sociology majors: Department responses. *American Sociologist* 22: 25–36.

Fausto-Sterling, A. 1992. *Myths of Gender*, rev. ed. New York: Basic Books.

Feingold, A. 1994. Gender differences in personality: A meta-analysis. *Psychological Bulletin* 116: 429–56.

Feldmesser, R.A. 1966. Toward the classless society? Pp. 527–33 in R. Bendix and S.M. Lipset, eds. *Class, Status, and Power*, 2nd ed. New York: Free Press.

Ferber, M.A. and H.M. Lowry. 1976. Women: The new reserve army of the unemployed. *Signs* 1: 213–32.

Findlay, C.S. and C.J. Lumsden. 1988. The creative mind. *Journal of Social and Biological Structures* 11: 3–55.

Finkelhor, D. 1980. Risk factors in the sexual victimization of children. *Child Abuse and Neglect* 4: 265–73.

Fisher, H.E. 1989. Evolution of human serial pairbonding. *American Journal of Physical Anthropology* 78: 331–54.

———. 1992. *Anatomy of Love*. New York: Norton.

Fitzgerald, T., A. Fothergill, K. Gilmore, K. Irwin, C.A. Kunkel, S. Leahy, J.M. Nielsen, E. Passerini, M.E. Virnoche, and G. Walden. 1995. What's wrong is right: A response to the state of the discipline. *Sociological Forum* 10: 493–98.

Fletcher, D.J.L. and C.D. Michener, eds. 1987. *Kin Recognition in Animals*. New York: Wiley.

Flinn, M.V. and R.D. Alexander. 1982. Culture theory: The developing synthesis from biology. *Human Ecology* 10: 383–400.

Ford, C.S. and F.A. Beach. 1951. *Patterns of Sexual Behavior*. New York: Harper and Row.

Fox, R. 1989. *The Search for Society*. New Brunswick, NJ: Rutgers University Press.

———. 1994. *The Challenge of Anthropology*. New Brunswick, NJ: Transaction Publishers.

Frank, R.H. 1988. *Passions Within Reason*. New York: W.W. Norton.

Freedman, D.G. 1974. *Human Infancy: An Evolutionary Perspective*. Hillsdale, NJ: Lawrence Erlbaum.

Freedman, J.L. and A. Doob. 1968. *Deviancy: The Psychology of Being Different*. New York: Academic Press.

Freese, L. 1994. The song of sociobiology. *Sociological Perspectives* 37: 337–73.

Freud, S. 1946 (orig. 1930). *Civilization and Its Discontents*. London: Hogarth.

Friedl, E. 1975. *Women and Men: An Anthropologist's View*. New York: Holt, Rinehart and Winston.

Fuchs, S. and S. Ward. 1994a. What is deconstruction, and where and when does it take place? Making facts in science, building cases in law. *American Sociological Review* 59: 481–500.

———. 1994b. The sociology and paradoxes of deconstruction: A reply to Agger. *American Sociological Review* 59: 506–10.

Fukuyama, F. 1989. The end of history. *The National Interest* 16: 3–18.

Furstenberg, F.F., Jr. 1987. The new extended family: Experiences in stepfamilies. Pp. 42–61 in K. Pasley and M. Ihinger-Tallman, eds. *Remarriage and Step-Parenting Today*. New York: Guilford Press.

———. 1988. Good dads—bad dads: Two faces of fatherhood. Pp. 193–218 in A. Cherlin, ed. *The Changing American Family*. Washington, DC: Urban Institute Press.

Furstenberg, F.F., Jr. and G.A. Condran. 1988. Family change and adolescent well-being: A reexamination of U.S. trends. Pp. 117–33 in A.J. Cherlin, ed. *The Changing American Family and Public Policy*. Washington, DC: Urban Institute.

Furstenberg, F.F., Jr. and G.B. Spanier. 1984. *Recycling the Family: Remarriage after Divorce*. Beverly Hills, CA: Sage.

Gamble, E.B. 1894. *The Evolution of Woman: An Inquiry into the Dogma of Her Inferiority to Man*. New York: G.P. Putnam's Sons.

Gans, H. 1962. *The Urban Villagers*. Glencoe, IL: Free Press.

Garai, J.E. and A. Scheinfeld. 1968. Sex differences in mental and behavioural traits. *Genetic Psychology Monographs* 77: 169–299.

Gaulin, S.J.C., D.H. McBurney, and S.L. Brakeman-Wartell. 1997. Matrilineal bias in the investment of aunts and uncles: A consequence and measure of paternity uncertainty. *Human Nature* 8: 139–51.

Gaulin, S.J.C., and A. Schlegel. 1980. Paternal confidence and paternal investment: A cross-cultural test of a sociobiological hypothesis. *Ethology and Sociobiology* 1: 301–9.

Gecas, V. 1976. The socialization and child care roles. Pp. 35–59 in F.I. Nye, *Role Structure and Analysis of the Family*. Beverly Hills, CA: Sage.

Gellner, E. 1994. *Encounters with Nationalism*. Cambridge, MA: Blackwell.

Genov, N. 1991. Toward a multidimensional concept of rationality: The sociological perspective. *Sociological Theory* 9: 206–11.

Gerstein, D. and D. Sciulli. 1987. Leading edges in social theory. *Perspectives* 10: 1–4.

Gibbs, J.P. 1994. *A Theory about Control*. San Francisco: Westview Press.

Giddens, A. 1973. *The Class Structure of the Advanced Societies.* New York: Harper & Row.

———. 1990. *The Consequences of Modernity.* Stanford, CA: Stanford University Press.

Giles-Sims, J. 1984. The stepparent role: Expectations, behavior and sanctions. *Journal of Family Issues* 5: 116–30.

Gillis, J.S. 1982. *Too Tall, Too Small.* Champaign, IL: Institute for Personality and Ability Testing.

Gillis, J.S. and W.E. Avis. 1980. The male-taller norm in mate selection. *Personality and Social Psychology Bulletin* 6: 396–401.

Gilman, C.P. 1911. *The Man-Made World; Or Our Androcentric Culture.* New York: Charlton.

Glazer, N. and D.P. Moynihan. 1970. *Beyond the Melting Pot*, 2nd ed. Cambridge, MA: MIT Press.

———, eds. 1975. *Ethnicity: Theory and Experience.* Cambridge, MA: Harvard University Press.

Glenn, N.D. 1997. A critique of twenty Family and Marriage and the Family textbooks. *Family Relations* 46: 197–208.

Glick, P.C. 1992. Marriage and divorce rates. Pp. 1188–99 in E.F. Borgatta, ed. *Encyclopedia of Sociology.* New York: Macmillan.

Goldberg, S. 1973. *The Inevitability of Patriarchy.* New York: Morrow.

Goldscheider, F.K. and L.J. Waite. 1991. *New Families, No Families? The Transformation of the American Home.* Berkeley, CA: University of California Press.

Goodall, J. 1971. *In the Shadow of Man.* Boston, MA: Houghton Mifflin.

———. 1986a. *Chimpanzees of Gombe.* Cambridge, MA: Harvard University Press.

———. 1986b. Social rejection, exclusion, and shunning among the Gombe chimpanzes. *Ethology and Sociobiology* 7: 227–36.

Goode, W.J. 1993. *World Changes in Divorce Patterns.* New Haven, CT: Yale University Press.

Gordon, M.M. 1964. *Assimilation in American Life.* New York: Oxford University Press.

Gorski, R.A., R.E. Harlan, C.D. Jacobson, J.E. Shryne, and A.M. Southam. 1980. Evidence for a morphological sex difference within the medial preoptic area of the rat brain. *Journal of Comparative Neurology* 193: 529–39.

Gould, S.J. 1978. Biological potential vs. biological determinism. Pp. 343–51 in A.L. Caplan, ed. *The Sociobiology Debate.* New York: Harper & Row.

Gould, S.J. and R.C. Lewontin. 1979. The spandrels of San Marco and the panglossian paradigm: A critique of the adaptationist programme. *Proceedings of the Royal Society* (London) 205: 581–98.

Gouldner, A.W. 1970. *The Coming Crisis in Western Sociology.* New York: Basic Books.

———. 1973. *For Sociology: Renewal and Critique in Sociology Today.* New York: Basic Books.

———. 1982. *The Future of Intellectuals and the Rise of the New Class.* New York: Oxford University Press.

Gove, W.R. 1995. Is sociology the integrative discipline in the study of human behavior? *Social Forces* 73: 1197–1206.

Gowaty, P.A. 1992. Evolutionary biology and feminism. *Human Nature* 3: 217–49.

Gray, A., D. Jackson, and J. McKinlay. 1991. The relation between dominance, anger, and hormones in normally aging men: Results from Massachusetts Male Aging Study. *Psychosomatic Medicine* 53: 375–85.

Graziano, W., T. Brothen, and E. Berscheid. 1978. Height and attraction: Do men and women see eye-to-eye? *Journal of Personality* 46: 128–45.

Greeley, A.M. 1974. *Ethnicity in the United States: A Preliminary Reconnaissance.* New York: Wiley.

Green, S.K., D.R. Buchanan, and S.K. Heuer. 1984. Winners, losers, and choosers: A field investigation of dating invitation. *Personality and Social Psychology Bulletin* 10: 502–11.

Gregersen, E. 1982. *Sexual Practices: The Story of Human Sexuality.* London: Mitchell Beazley.

Gregory, M.S., A. Silvers, and D. Sutch, eds. 1978. *Sociobiology and Human Nature.* San Francisco: Jossey-Bass.

Gross, H.E., J. Bernard, A.J. Dan, N. Glazer, J. Lorber, M. McClintock, N. Newton, and A. Rossi. 1979. Considering "a biosocial perspective on parenting." *Signs* 4: 695–717.

Grusky, D.B., ed. 1994. *Social Stratification.* Boulder, CO: Westview Press.

Gurr, T.R. and B. Harff. 1994. *Ethnic Conflict in World Politics.* Boulder, CO: Westview Press.

Gwartney-Gibbs, P.A. 1986. The institutionalization of premarital cohabitation: Estimates from marriage license applications, 1970 and 1980. *Journal of Marriage and the Family* 48: 423–34.

Habermas, J. 1987. *The Philosophical Discourse of Modernity: Twelve Lectures.* Cambridge, MA: MIT Press.

Haldane, J.B.S. 1932. *The Causes of Evolution.* New York: Harper.

Halfpenny, P. 1991. Rationality and the sociology of scientific knowledge. *Sociological Theory* 9: 212–15.

Halliday, T.C. and M. Janowitz, eds. 1992. *Sociology and Its Politics: The Forms and Fates of Disciplinary Organization.* Chicago: University of Chicago Press.

Hamilton, R.F. and L.L. Hargens. 1993. The politics of the professors: Self-identifications, 1969–1984. *Social Forces* 71: 603–27.

Hamilton, W.D. 1964. The genetical theory of social behaviour: I and II. *Journal of Theoretical Biology* 7: 1–52.

Handwerker, W.P. and P.V. Crosbie. 1982. Sex and dominance. *American Anthropologist* 84: 97–104.

Haraway, D. 1988. Situated knowledges: The science question in feminism and the privilege of partial perspective. *Feminist Studies* 14: 575–99.

Harcourt, A.H. and F.B.M. de Waal, eds. 1992. *Coalitions and Alliances in Humans and Other Animals.* Oxford: Oxford University Press.

Harris, L.J. 1978. Sex differences in spatial ability: Possible environmental, genetic, and neurological factors. Pp. 405–522 in M. Kinsbourne, ed., *Asymmetrical Function of the Brain.* Cambridge: Cambridge University Press.

Harris, M. 1968. *The Rise of Anthropological Theory.* New York: T.Y.Crowell.

Harrison, A.A. and L. Saeed. 1977. Let's make a deal: An analysis of revelations and stipulations in lonely hearts advertisements. *Journal of Personality and Social Psychology* 35: 257–64.

Hartmann, H.I. 1981. The family as the locus of gender, class, and political struggle: The example of housework. *Signs* 6: 366–94.

Hartung, J. 1982. Polygyny and the inheritance of wealth. *Current Anthropology* 23: 1–12.

———. 1995. Love thy neighbor: The evolution of in-group morality. *Skeptic* 2: 86–100.

Hawking, S.W. 1988. *A Brief History of Time.* New York: Bantam Books.

Hazelrigg, L.E. and J. Lopreato. 1972. Heterogamy, inter-class mobility, and sociopolitical attitudes in Italy. *American Sociological Review* 37: 264–77.

Heaton, T.B., S.L. Albrecht, and T.K. Martin. 1985. The timing of divorce. *Journal of Marriage and the Family* 47: 631–39.

Hechter, M. 1975. *Internal Colonialism: The Celtic Fringe in British National Development*. Berkeley, CA: University of California Press.
———. 1987. *Principles of Group Solidarity*. Berkeley, CA: University of California Press.
Hedges, L.V. and A. Nowell. 1995. Sex differences in mental test scores, variability, and numbers of high-scoring individuals. *Science* 269: 41–45.
Heilbrun, L. 1983. Feminist criticism in departments of literature. *Academe* (Sept.-Oct.): 11–14.
Heisler, M.O., ed. 1977. *Ethnic Conflict in the World Today. The Annals*. Philadelphia: The American Academy of Political and Social Sciences.
Hempel, C.G. 1968. The logic of functional analysis. Pp. 179–210 in M. Brodbeck, ed. *Readings in the Philosophy of the Social Sciences*. New York: Macmillan.
Henderson, L.J. 1935. *Pareto's General Sociology*. Cambridge, MA: Harvard University Press.
Hewitt, J.P. 1976. *Self and Society: A Symbolic Interactionist Social Psychology*. Boston: Allyn & Bacon.
Hewlett, B.S. 1988. Sexual selection and paternal investment among Aka pygmies. Pp. 263–75 in L. Betzig, M. Borgehoff Mulder, and P. Turke, eds. *Human Reproductive Behaviour*. New York: Cambridge University Press.
Hill, K. and A.M. Hurtado. 1996. *Ache Life History*. New York: Aldine de Gruyter.
Hill, M.R. 1996. Joan Huber, Irving Louis Horowitz, and the ideological future of objectivity in American sociology. *Sociological Imagination* 33: 228–39.
Hill, R.J. and P. Frank. 1986. *The Soviet Communist Party*. Winchester, MA: Allen and Unwin.
Hindes, B. 1988. *Choice, Rationality, and Social Theory*. London: Unwin Hyman.
———. 1991. Rationality and modern society. *Sociological Theory* 9: 216–27.
Hochschild, A. with A. Machung. 1989. *The Second Shift*. New York: Viking.
Hodge, R.W. 1981. The measurement of occupational status. *Social Science Research* 10: 396–415.
Holcomb, H.R., III. 1993. *Sociobiology, Sex, and Science*. Albany, NY: SUNY Press.
Homans, G.C. 1950. *The Human Group*. N.Y.: Harcourt Brace Jovanovich.
———. 1961. *Social Behavior: Its Elementary Forms*. New York: Harcourt, Brace & World.
———. 1964. Bringing men back in. *American Sociological Review* 29: 809–18.
———. 1967. *The Nature of Social Science*. New York: Harcourt, Brace & World.
———. 1974. *Social Behavior: Its Elementary Forms*, 2nd ed. New York: Harcourt Brace Jovanovich.
Homans, G.C. and C.P. Curtis, Jr. 1934. *An Introduction to Pareto: His Sociology*. New York: Knopf.
Hooks, B.L. and P.A. Green. 1993. Cultivating male allies: A focus on primates, including *Homo sapiens*. *Human Nature* 4: 81–107.
Horowitz, D.L. 1985. *Ethnic Groups in Conflict*. Berkeley, CA: University of California Press.
Horowitz, I.L. 1968. *Professing Sociology: Studies in the Life Cycle of Social Science*. Carbondale, IL: Southern Illinois University Press.
———. 1972 (orig. 1970). Social science mandarins. Pp. 414–30 in I.L. Horowitz, *Foundations of Political Sociology*. New York: Harper & Row.
———. 1977. *Ideology and Utopia in the United States, 1956–1976*. New York: Oxford University Press.
———. 1993. *The Decomposition of Sociology*. New York: Oxford University Press.
Howard, J.A., P. Blumstein, and P. Schwartz. 1987. Social or evolutionary theories? Some observation on preferences in human mate selection. *Journal of Personality and Social Psychology* 53: 194–200.

Hrdy, S.B. 1977. *The Langurs of Abu: Female and Male Strategies of Reproduction.* Cambridge, MA: Harvard University Press.

————. 1990. Sex bias in nature and in history: A late 1980s reexamination of the "biological origins" argument. *Yearbook of Physical Anthropology* 33: 25–37.

————. 1997. Raising Darwin's consciousness: Female sexuality and the prehominid origins of patriarchy. *Human Nature* 8: 1–49.

Huaco, G.A., 1963 A logical analysis of the Davis-Moore theory of stratification. *American Sociological Review* 28: 801–4.

Hubbard, R. 1990. *The Politics of Women's Biology.* New Brunswick, NJ: Rutgers University Press.

Huber, J. 1995. Institutional perspective on sociology. *American Journal of Sociology* 101: 194–216.

Huber, J. and G. Spitze. 1981. Wife's employment, household behaviors, and sex-role attitudes. *Social Forces* 60: 150–69.

————. 1983. *Sex Stratification.* New York: Academic Press.

Huntington, S.P. 1996. *The Clash of Civilizations and the Remaking of the World Order.* New York: Simon & Schuster.

Hurst, C.E. 1998. *Social Inequality: Forms, Causes, and Consequences.* New York: Allyn & Bacon.

Hutt, C. 1975. Neuroendocrinological, behavioural and intellectual differentiation in human development. Pp. 73–121 in C. Ousted and D.C. Taylor, eds. *Gender Differences.* London: Churchill Livingstone.

Huxley, J. 1942. *Evolution: The Modern Synthesis.* New York: Harper.

————. 1958. Introduction to the Mentor edition. Pp. ix–xv in C. Darwin, *The Origin of Species.* New York: Mentor Books.

Ike, B.W. 1987. Man's limited sympathy as a consequence of his evolution in small kin groups. Pp. 216–34 in V. Reynolds, V.S.E. Falger, and I. Vine, eds. *The Sociobiology of Ethnocentrism.* London: Croom Helm.

Imperato-McGinley, J., R. Peterson, T. Gautier, and E. Sturla. 1979. Androgens and the evolution of male gender identity among male pseudohermaphrodites with 5 alpha-reductase deficiency. *New England Journal of Medicine* 300: 1233–37.

Imperato-McGinley, J., M. Pichardo, T. Gautier, D. Voyer, and M.P. Bryden. 1991. Cognitive abilities in androgen-insensitive subjects: Comparison with control males and females from the same kindred. *Clinical Endocrinology* 34: 341–47.

Inkeles, A. 1966. Social stratification and mobility in the Soviet Union. Pp. 516–26 in R. Bendix and S.M. Lipset, eds. *Class, Status, and Power*, 2nd ed. New York: Free Press.

Irons, W. 1979. Cultural and biological success. Pp. 257–72 in N.A. Chagnon and W. Irons, eds. *Evolutionary Biology and Human Social Behavior: An Anthropological Perspective.* North Scituate, MA: Duxbury Press.

————. 1990. Let's make our perspective broader rather than narrower. *Ethology and Sociobiology* 11: 361–74.

Irwin, C.J. 1987. A study in the evolution of ethnocentrism. Pp. 131–56 in V. Reynolds, V.S.E. Falger, and I. Vine, eds. *The Sociobiology of Ethnocentrism.* London: Croom Helm.

Isaacs, H.R. 1975. Basic group identity: The idols of the tribe. Pp. 29–52 in N. Glazer and D.P. Moynihan, eds. *Ethnicity: Theory and Experience.* Cambridge, MA: Harvard University Press.

Jacobs, J.A. and R.J. Steinberg. 1990. Compensating differentials and the male-female wage gap: Evidence from the New York State Comparable Worth Study. *Social Forces* 69: 439–68.

James, T.W. and D. Kimura. 1997. Sex differences in remembering the locations of objects in an array: Location-shift versus location exchanges. *Evolution and Human Behavior* 18: 155–63.

Jeffrey, P. 1979. *Frogs in the Well: Indian Women in Purdah.* New York: Asia Book Corporation of America.

Joas, H. n.d. (circa 1992). The European state of the art. *Theory* (Newsletter of the Research Committee on Social Theory of the International Sociological Association) Unnumbered: 1–2.

Jolly, A. 1972. *The Evolution of Primate Behavior.* New York: Macmillan.

Jones, D. and K. Hill. 1993. Criteria of facial attractiveness in five populations. *Human Nature* 4: 271–96.

Jones, T.A. 1978. Modernization and education in the U.S.S.R. *Social Forces* 57: 523–46.

Josephson, S.C. 1993. Status, reproductive success, and marrying polygynously. *Ethology and Sociobiology* 14: 391–96.

Judd, C.M. and B. Park. 1993. Definition and assessment of accuracy in social stereotypes. *Psychological Review* 100: 109–28.

Kalleberg, A.L. and R.A. Rosenfeld. 1990. Gender inequality in the labor market: A cross-national perspective. Paper presented at the 12th World Congress of Sociology, Madrid.

Kamo, Y. 1992. Family roles. Pp. 671–73 in E.F. Borgatta, ed. *Encyclopedia of Sociology.* New York: Macmillan.

Kantrowitz, B. 1992. Sociology's lonely crowd. *Newsweek,* February 3: 55.

Karlin, S. 1969. *Equilibrium Behavior of Population Genetics Models with Non-Random Mating.* New York: Gordon and Breach.

Katz, M. and M. Konner. 1981. The role of the father: An anthropological perspective. Pp. 155–86 in M. Lamb, ed. *The Role of the Father in Child Development.* New York: Wiley.

Kaufman, S.J. 1996. Spiraling to ethnic war: Elites, masses, and Moscow in Moldova's civil war. *International Security* 21: 108–38.

Kawai, M. 1958. On the rank system in a natural troop of Japanese monkeys. I. Basic rank and dependent rank. *Primates* 1: 111–30.

Kawanaka, K. 1984. Association, ranging, and the social unit in chimpanzees of the Mahale Mountains, Tanzania. *International Journal of Primatology* 5: 411–34.

Kemper, T.D. 1990. *Social Structure and Testosterone.* New Brunswick, NJ: Rutgers University Press.

———. 1994. Social stratification, testosterone, and male sexuality. Pp. 47–61 in L. Ellis, ed. *Social Stratification and Economic Inequality,* vol. II. Westport, CT: Praeger.

Kennedy, P. 1987. *The Rise and Fall of Great Powers.* New York: Random House.

Kenrick, D.T. and R.C. Keefe. 1992. Age preferences in mates reflect sex differences in reproductive strategies. *Behavioral and Brain Sciences* 15: 75–133.

Kenrick, D.T., E.K. Sadalla, G. Groth, and M.R. Trost. 1990. Evolution, traits, and the stages of human courtship: Qualifying the parental investment model. *Journal of Personality* 58: 97–116.

Kertzer, D.I. 1988. *Ritual, Politics, and Power.* New Haven, CT: Yale University Press.

Khoo, S-E. 1987. Living together as married: A profile of de facto couples in Australia. *Journal of Marriage and the Family* 49: 185–91.

Kilbourne, B.S., P. England, and K. Beron. 1994. Effects of individual, occupational and industrial characteristics on earnings: Intersections of race and gender. *Social Forces* 72: 1149–76.

Kilbourne, B.S., P. England, G. Farkas, K. Beron, and D. Weir. 1994. Returns to skill, compensating differentials, and gender bias: Effects of occupational characteristics on the wages of white women. *American Journal of Sociology* 100: 689–719.

Killian, L.M. 1968. *The Impossible Revolution*. New York: Random House.

Kimura, D. 1992. Sex differences in the brain. *Scientific American* 268: 119–25.

Kimura, D. and R. Harshman. 1984. Sex differences in brain organization for verbal and non-verbal functions. Pp. 423–30 in G.J. DeVries, J.P.C. DeBruin, H.B.M. Uyling, and M.A. Corner, eds. *Progress in Brain Research*. New York: Elsevier.

Kinsey, A.C., W.B. Pomeroy, C.E. Martin, and P.H. Gebhard. 1953. *Sexual Behavior in the Human Female*. Philadelphia: W.B. Saunders Company.

Kitcher, P. 1985. *Vaulting Ambition: Sociobiology and the Quest for Human Nature*. Cambridge, MA: MIT Press.

Klassen, A.D., C.J. Williams, and E.E. Levitt. 1989. *Sex and Morality in the U.S*, ed. by H.J. O'Gorman. Middletown, CT: Wesleyan University Press.

Klein, R.G. 1989. *The Human Career: Human Biological and Cultural Origins*. Chicago: University of Chicago Press.

Knoke, D. and A.L. Kalleberg. 1994. Job training in U.S. organizations. *American Sociological Review* 59: 537–46.

Koford, C.B. 1963. Rank of mothers and sons in bands of rhesus monkeys. *Science* 141: 356–57.

Kompara, D.R. 1980. Difficulties in the socialization process of step-parenting. *Family Relations* 29: 69–73.

Konner, M. 1982. *The Tangled Wing: Biological Constraints on the Human Spirit*. New York: Holt, Rinehart and Winston.

Kuhn, T.S. 1957. *The Copernican Revolution*. Cambridge, MA: Harvard University Press.

——— 1962. *The Structure of Scientific Revolutions*. Chicago: University of Chicago Press.

Lack, D. 1947. *Darwin's Finches: An Essay on the General Biological Theory of Evolution*. Cambridge: Cambridge University Press.

———. 1968. *Ecological Adaptations for Breeding in Birds*. London: Methuen.

Lamb, M. 1987. The emerging American father. Pp. 3–25 in M. Lamb, ed. *The Father's Role: Cross-Cultural Perspectives*. Hillsdale, NJ: Lawrence Erlbaum.

Lancaster, J.B. 1986. Primate social behavior and ostracism. *Ethology and Sociobiology* 7: 215–25.

LaRossa, R. 1988. Fatherhood and social change. *Family Relations* 37: 451–57.

Lasch, C. 1989. *The Minimal Self: Psychic Survival in Troubled Times*. New York: W.W. Norton.

Lash, S. and J. Friedman, eds. 1992. *Modernity and Identity*. Cambridge: Blackwell.

Lash, S. and S. Whimster, eds. 1987. *Max Weber, Rationality, and Modernity*. London: Allen & Unwin.

Laumann, E., R. Michael, S. Michaels, and J. Gagnon. 1994. *The Social Organization of Sexuality*. Chicago: University of Chicago Press.

Lee, R.B. 1984. *The Dobe !Kung*. Chicago: Holt, Rinehart and Winston.

Leibowitz, L. 1978. *Females, Males, Families: A Biosocial Approach*. North Scituate, MA: Duxbury Press.

Lenski, G. 1966. *Power and Privilege: A Theory of Social Stratification*. New York: McGraw-Hill.

———. 1978. Marxist experiments in destratification: An appraisal. *Social Forces* 57: 364–83.

———. 1988. Rethinking macrosociological theory. *American Sociological Review* 53: 163–71.

Lenski, G., J. Lenski, and P. Nolan. 1991. *Human Societies*, 6th ed. New York: McGraw-Hill.

Lerner, G. 1986. *The Creation of Patriarchy*. Oxford: Oxford University Press.

————. 1988. Remarks quoted in the *Chronicle of Higher Education*, September 28: 7.

LeVay, S. 1993. *The Sexual Brain*. Cambridge, MA: MIT Press.

LeVine, R.A. and D.T. Campbell. 1972. *Ethnocentrism: Theories of Conflict, Ethnic Attitudes, and Group Behavior.* New York: Wiley.

Lévi-Strauss, C. 1944. The social and psychological aspects of chieftainship in a primitive tribe: The Nambikuara of Northwestern Matto Grosso. *Transactions of the New York Academy of Sciences* 7: 16–32.

Lewontin, R.C. 1974. *The Genetic Basis of Evolutionary Change*. New York: Columbia University Press.

————. 1979. Sociobiology as an adaptationist program. *Behavioral Science* 24: 5–14.

Lieberman, L. 1989. A discipline divided: Acceptance of human sociobiological concepts in anthropology. *Current Anthropology* 30: 676–82.

Lieberson, S. 1992. Einstein, Renoir, and Greeley: Some thoughts about evidence in sociology. *American Sociological Review* 57: 1–15.

Liebow, E. 1967. *Tally's Corner*. Boston: Little, Brown and Company.

Liesen, L.T. 1995. Feminism and the politics of reproductive strategies. *Politics and the Life Sciences* 14: 145–62.

Lindquist Forsberg, A.J. and B.S. Tullberg. 1995. The relationship between cummulative number of cohabiting partners and number of children for men and women in modern Sweden. *Ethology and Sociobiology* 16: 221–32.

Lipset, S.M. 1994. The state of American sociology. *Sociological Forum* 9: 199–220.

Littlefield, C.H. and J.P. Rushton. 1986. When a child dies: The sociobiology of bereavement. *Journal of Personality and Social Psychology* 51: 797–802.

Lockard, J.S. and R.M. Adams. 1981. Human serial polygyny: Demographic, reproductive, marital, and divorce data. *Ethology and Sociobiology* 2: 177–86.

London, K. 1991. Cohabitation, marriage, marital dissolution, and remarriage: United States, 1988. Advance data from Vital and Health Statistics of the National Center for Health Statistics, No. 194.

Lopreato, J., ed. 1965. *Vilfredo Pareto*. New York: T.Y. Crowell.

————. 1968. Authority relations and class conflict. *Social Forces* 47: 70–79.

————. 1970. *Italian Americans*. New York: Random House.

————. 1971. The concept of equilibrium: Sociological tantalizer. Pp. 309–43 in H. Turk and R.L. Simpson, eds. *Institutions and Social Exchange: The Sociologies of Talcott Parsons & George Homans*. Indianapolis: Bobbs-Merrill.

————. 1980. Introduction. Pp. xiii–xliv in V. Pareto, *Compendium of General Sociology* (orig. 1920, G. Farina, ed.). Minneapolis: University of Minnesota Press.

————. 1984. *Human Nature and Biocultural Evolution*. London: Allen & Unwin.

————. 1986. Notes on human nature and biocultural evolution. *Revue Européenne des Sciences Sociales* 73: 97–121.

————. 1988. Creativity and optimization. *Journal of Social and Biological Structures* 11: 109–13.

————. 1989a. The maximization principle: A cause in search of conditions. Pp. 119–30 in R.W. Bell and N.J. Bell, eds. *Sociobiology and the Social Sciences*. Lubbock, TX: Texas Tech University Press.

————. 1989b. Sociological theory: Is the crisis necessary? *Revue Internationale de Sociologie* 3 (nouvelle série): 161–86.

————. 1990. From social evolutionism to biocultural evolutionism. *Sociological Forum* 5: 187–212.

————. 1992. Sociobiology. Pp. 1995–2000 in E.F. Borgatta, ed. *Encyclopedia of Sociology*. New York: Macmillan.

Lopreato, J. and L. Alston. 1970. Ideal types and the idealization strategy. *American Sociological Review* 35: 88–96.

Lopreato, J. and P. Anthon Green. 1990. The evolutionary foundations of revolution. Pp. 107–22 in J. van der Dennen and V. Falger, eds. *Sociobiology and Conflict: Evolutionary Perspectives on Competition, Cooperation, Violence and Warfare.* London: Chapman & Hall.

Lopreato, J. and L.E. Hazelrigg. 1972. *Class, Conflict, and Mobility: Theories and Studies of Class Structure.* San Francisco: Chandler.

Lopreato, J. and L.S. Lewis. 1963. An analysis of variables in the functional theory of stratification. *Sociological Quarterly* 4: 301–10.

Lopreato, J. and M-y Yu. 1988. Human fertility and fitness optimization. *Ethology and Sociobiology* 9: 269–89.

Lorber, J. 1994. *The Paradoxes of Gender.* New Haven, CT: Yale University Press.

Lorenz, K. 1966. *On Aggression.* London: Methuen.

Louv, R. 1993. The crisis of the absent father. *Parents* 34: 54–58.

Low, B.S. 1988a. Pathogen stress and polygyny in humans. Pp. 115–27 in L. Betzig, M. Borgehoff Mulder, and P. Turke, eds. *Human Reproductive Behaviour.* New York: Cambridge University Press.

———. 1988b. Measures of polygyny in humans. *Current Anthropology* 29: 189–94.

———. 1992. Sex, coalitions, and politics in preindustrial societies. *Politics and the Life Sciences* 11: 63–80.

———. 1993. Ecological demography: A synthetic focus in evolutionary anthropology. *Evolutionary Anthropology* 1: 106–12.

———. 1995. Behavioral ecology, "sociobiology," and human behavior. Pp. 3–26 in M. Ember and C. Ember, eds. *Research Frontiers in Anthropology.* Hawthorne, NY: Prentice-Hall.

Low, B.S., A.L. Clarke, and K. Lockridge. 1992. Toward an ecological demography. *Population and Development Review* 18: 1–31.

Lueptow, L.B., L. Garovich, and M.B. Lueptow. 1995. The persistence of gender stereotypes in the face of changing sex roles: Evidence contrary to the sociocultural model. *Ethology and Sociobiology* 16: 509–30.

Lukes, S. 1973. *Émile Durkheim.* New York: Harper & Row.

Lumsden, C.J. and E.O. Wilson. 1981. *Genes, Mind, and Culture: The Coevolutionary Process.* Cambridge, MA.: Harvard University Press.

Maccoby, E.E. and C.N. Jacklin. 1974. *The Psychology of Sex Differences.* Palo Alto, CA: Stanford University Press.

MacDonald, W.L. and A. DeMaris. 1996. Parenting stepchildren and biological children: The effects of stepparent's gender and new biological children. *Journal of Family Issues* 17: 5–25.

Mach, E. 1974. *The Science of Mechanics.* LaSalle, IL: Open Court.

Machalek, R. 1986. The sociology of ultimate causation. *Revue Européenne des Sciences Sociales* 24: 79–95.

———. 1995. Basic dimensions and forms of social exploitation: A comparative analysis. Pp. 35–68 in L. Freese, ed. *Advances in Human Ecology.* Greenwich, CT: JAI Press.

———. 1996. The evolution of social exploitation. Pp. 1–32 in L. Freese, ed. *Advances in Human Ecology.* Greenwich, CT: JAI Press.

Machalek, R. and L.E. Cohen. 1991. The nature of crime: Is cheating necessary for cooperation? *Human Nature* 2: 215–33.

MacLean, P.D. 1973. *A Triune Concept of Brain and Behavior.* Toronto: University of Toronto Press.

Malinowski, B. 1926. *Crime and Customs in Savage Society*. New York: Dutton.
———. 1929. *The Sexual Life of Savages in North-Western Melanasia*. New York: Harcourt, Brace.
———. 1935. *The Foundations of Faith and Morals: An Anthropological Analysis of Primitive Beliefs and Conduct with Special Reference to the Fundamental Problems of Religion and Ethics*. Oxford: Oxford University Press.
Mannheim, K. 1940. *Man and Society in an Age of Reconstruction*. London: K. Paul, Trench, Trebner.
Margolin, L. and L. White. 1987. The continuing role of physical attractiveness in marriage. *Journal of Marriage and the Family* 49: 21–27.
Marshland, D. 1988. *Seeds of Bankruptcy: Sociological Bias against Business and Freedom*. London: Claridge Press.
Marx, J. 1995. Snaring the genes that divide the sexes for mammals. *Science* 269: 1824–25.
Marx, K. 1961 (orig. 1844). *Economic and Philosophical Manuscripts*. Pp. 90–196 in E. Fromm, ed. *Marx's Concept of Man*. New York: Ungar.
———. 1978 (orig. 1845). *Theses on Feuerbach*. Pp. 143–45 in R.C. Tucker, ed. *Marx-Engels Reader*, 2nd ed. New York: Norton.
———. 1934 (orig. 1850). *The Class Struggles in France, 1848–1850*. New York: International Publishers.
———. 1956 (orig. 1852). The Chartists. *New York Daily Tribune*, August 25. In T.B. Bottomore, ed. *Karl Marx: Selected Writings in Sociology and Philosophy*. New York: McGraw-Hill.
———. 1904 (orig. 1859). *A Contribution to the Critique of Political Economy*. Chicago: Charles Kerr.
———. 1967 (orig. 1867). *Capital*. New York: International Publishers.
Marx, K. and F. Engels. 1947 (orig 1845–1846). *The German Ideology*. New York: International Publishers.
———. 1959 (orig. 1848). *Manifesto of the Communist Party*. In L.S. Feuer, ed. *Marx and Engels: Basic Writings on Politics and Philosophy*. Garden City, NY: Anchor Books.
———. 1935. *The Correspondence of Marx and Engels*. New York: International Publishers.
Maryanski, A. and J.H. Turner. 1992. *The Social Cage: Human Nature and the Evolution of Society*. Stanford, CA: Stanford University Press.
Masters, R.D. 1989. *The Nature of Politics*. New Haven: Yale University Press.
Mauss, M. 1954 (orig. 1925). *The Gift*. London: Cohen & West.
Mayr, E. 1963. *Animal Species and Evolution*. Cambridge, MA: Harvard University Press.
———. 1972. Sexual selection and natural selection. Pp. 87–104 in B.G. Campbell, ed. *Sexual Selection and the Descent of Man*. Chicago: Aldine.
———. 1980. Prologue: Some thoughts on the history of the evolutionary synthesis. Pp. 1–48 in E. Mayr and W. Provine, eds. *The Evolutionary Synthesis: Perspectives on the Unification of Biology*. Cambridge, Mass.: Harvard University Press.
———. 1982. *The Growth of Biological Thought: Diversity, Evolution, and Inheritance*. Cambridge, MA: Harvard University Press.
Mazur, A. 1973. A cross-species comparison of status in small established groups. *American Sociological Review* 38: 513–30.
———. 1985. A biosocial model of status in face-to-face primate groups. *Social Forces* 64: 377–402.
———. 1994. A neurohormonal model of social stratification among humans: A microsocial perspective. Pp. 37–46 in L. Ellis, ed. *Social Stratification and Socioeconomic Inequality*. Westport, CT: Praeger.

Mazur, A. and T.A. Lamb. 1980. Testosterone, status and mood in human males. *Hormones and Behavior* 14: 236–46.

McBurney, D.H., S.J.C. Gaulin, T. Devineni, and C. Adams. 1997. Superior spatial memory of women: Stronger evidence for the gathering hypothesis. *Evolution and Human Behavior* 18: 165–74.

McGlone, J. 1980. Sex differences in human brain symmetry: A critical survey. *Behavioral and Brain Sciences* 3: 215–63.

McGuiness, D. 1976. Sex differences in organisation, perception, and cognition. Pp. 123–55 in B. Lloyd and J. Archer, eds. *Exploring Sex Differences*. New York: Academic Press.

———. 1985. *When Children Don't Learn*. New York: Basic Books.

McGuire, M.T. 1992. Moralistic aggression, processing mechanisms, and the brain: The biological foundations of the sense of justice. Pp. 31–46 in R.D. Masters and M. Gruter, eds. *The Sense of Justice: Biological Foundations of Law*. Newbury Park, CA: Sage.

McLemore, S.D. 1980. *Racial and Ethnic Relations in America*. Boston: Allyn & Bacon.

McNeill, W.H. 1976. *Plagues and Peoples*. New York: Anchor Books.

Mead, G.H. 1934. *Mind, Self, & Society*. Chicago: University of Chicago Press.

Mealey, L. 1985. The relationship between social status and biological success: A case study of the Mormon religious hierarchy. *Ethology and Sociobiology* 6: 249–57.

Melotti, U. 1990. War and peace in primitive human societies. Pp. 241–45 in J.van der Dennen and V. Falger, eds. *Sociobiology and Conflict*. London: Chapman & Hall.

Menand, L. 1996. How to make a Ph.D. matter. *The New York Times Magazine*, September 22: 78–81.

Merton, R.K. 1948. The position of sociological theory. *American Sociological Review* 13: 164–68.

———. 1949. *Social Theory and Social Structure*. Glencoe, IL: Free Press.

———. 1957. *Social Theory and Social Structure*, rev. ed. Glencoe, IL: Free Press.

———. 1968. *Social Theory and Social Structure*, enlarged ed. New York: Free Press.

Meštrović, S.G. 1996. The Balkanization of sociology. *Sociological Imagination* 33: 202–14.

Meyer, D.R. and J. Bartfeld. 1996. Compliance with child support orders in divorce cases. *Journal of Marriage and the Family* 58: 201–12.

Meyer-Bahlburg, H.F.L. 1981. Androgens and human aggression. Pp. 263–90 in P. Brain and D. Benton, eds. *The Biology of Aggression*. Alphen an den Rijn, The Netherlands: Sijhoff & Noordhoff.

Meyrriecks, A.J. 1972. *Man and Birds: Evolution and Behavior*. Indianapolis: Bobbs-Merrill.

Michels, R. 1959 (orig. 1914). *Political Parties*. Glencoe, IL: Free Press.

Millet, K. 1970. *Sexual Politics*. New York: Doubleday.

Mills, C.W. 1956. *The Power Elite*. New York: Oxford University Press.

———. 1959. *The Sociological Imagination*. New York: Oxford University Press.

Model, S. 1981. Housework by husbands: Determinants and implications. *Journal of Family Issues* 2: 225–37.

Moir, A. and D. Jessel. 1989. *Brain Sex*. New York: Doubleday.

Molotch, H. 1994. Going out. *Sociological Forum* 9: 221–39.

Money, J. and A.A. Ehrhardt. 1972. *Man & Woman Boy & Girl*. Baltimore: The Johns Hopkins University Press.

Morgan, G.A. and H.N. Ricciuti. 1973. Infant's response to strangers during the first year. In L.J. Stone, H.T. Smith, and L.B. Murphy, eds. *The Competent Infant: Research and Commentary*. New York: Basic Books.

Mosca, G. 1939. *The Ruling Class.* New York: McGraw-Hill.

Moynihan, D.P. 1993. *Pandaemonium: Ethnicity in International Politics.* New York: Oxford University Press.

Mueller, C.W., S. Kuruvilla, and R.D. Iverson. 1994. Swedish professionals and gender inequalities. *Social Forces* 73: 555–73.

Münch, R. 1994. The contribution of German social theory to European sociology. Pp. 45–66 in B. Nedelmann and P. Sztompka, eds. *Sociology in Europe: In Search of Identity.* New York: de Gruyter.

Murdock, G.P. 1937. Comparative data on the division of labor by sex. *Social Forces* 15: 551–53.

———. 1945. The common denominator of culture. Pp. 124–42 in R. Linton, ed. *The Science of Man in the World Crisis.* New York: Columbia University Press.

———. 1967. *Ethnographic Atlas.* Pittsburgh, PA: University of Pittsburgh Press.

Murstein, B.I. 1980. Mate selection in the 1970s. *Journal of Marriage and the Family* 42: 777–92.

Nagel, E. 1952. Problems of concept and theory formation in the social sciences. Pp. 43–64 in *Science, Language and Human Rights*, vol. 1. Philadelphia: American Philosophical Association.

———. 1961. *The Structure of Science.* New York: Harcourt, Brace, & World.

Namboodiri, K. 1988. Ecological demography: Its place in sociology. *American Sociological Review* 53: 619–33.

Nass, R. and S. Baker. 1991. Learning disabilities in children with congenital adrenal hyperpalsia. *Journal of Child Neurology* 6: 306–12.

Nedelmann, B. and P. Sztompka, eds. 1994. *Sociology in Europe: In Search of Identity.* New York: de Gruyter.

Nielsen, F. 1985. Toward a theory of ethnic solidarity in modern societies. *American Sociological Review* 50: 133–49.

———. 1994. Sociobiology and sociology. *Annual Review of Sociology* 20: 267–303.

Nisbet, R.A. 1969. *Social Change and History.* Oxford: Oxford University Press.

Novak, M. 1972. *The Rise of the Unmeltable Ethnics.* New York: Macmillan.

Oakley, A. 1997. A brief history of gender. Pp. 29–55 in A. Oakley and J. Mitchell, eds., *Who's Afraid of Feminism?* New York: The New Press.

O'Kelly, C.G. 1980. *Women and Men in Society.* New York: D. Van Nostrand.

Olshansky, S.J., B.A. Carnes, and C. Cassel. 1990. In search of Methuselah: Estimating upper limits to human longevity. *Science* 263: 634–40.

Olson, M. 1982. *The Rise and Decline of Nations.* New Haven, CT: Yale University Press.

Olzak, S. 1992. *The Dynamics of Ethnic Competition and Conflict.* Stanford, CA: Stanford University Press.

Olzak, S. and J. Nagel, eds. 1986. *Competitive Ethnic Relations.* New York: Academic Press.

Omi, M. and H. Winant. 1986. *Racial Formation in the United States.* New York: Routledge.

O'Neill, J. and S. Polachek. 1992. Why the gender gap in wages narrowed in the 1980s. *Journal of Labor Economics* 11: 205–28.

Pareto, V. 1965 (orig. 1902–1903). *Les Systèmes Socialistes.* Geneva: Librairie Droz.

———. 1963 (orig. 1916). *A Treatise on General Sociology* (also known as *The Mind and Society*), 4 vols. New York: Dover.

———. 1971 (orig. 1906). *Manual of Political Economy.* New York: Kelly.

Parish, A.R. 1996. Female relationships in bonobos (*Pan paniscus*): Evidence for bonding, cooperation, and female dominance in a male-philopatric species. *Human Nature* 7: 61–96.

Park, R.E. 1967 (orig. 1914). Racial assimilation in secondary groups. Pp. 114–32 in R.H. Turner, ed., *Robert E. Park on Social Control and Collective Behavior.* Chicago: University of Chicago Press.

———. 1967 (orig. 1928). The bases of race prejudice. Pp. 169–84 in R.H. Turner, ed., *Robert E. Park on Social Control and Collective Behavior.* Chicago: University of Chicago Press.

Park, R.E. and E.W. Burgess. 1921. *Introduction to the Science of Sociology.* Chicago: University of Chicago Press.

Parkin, F. 1971. *Class Inequality & Political Order.* New York: Praeger.

Parsons, T. 1937. *The Structure of Social Action.* New York: McGraw-Hill.

———. 1951. *The Social System.* New York: Free Press.

———. 1954. *Essays in Sociological Theory.* Glencoe, IL: Free Press.

———. 1964. Evolutionary universals in society. *American Sociological Review* 29: 339–57.

———. 1971. Commentary. Pp. 380–99 in H. Turk and R.L. Simpson, eds., *Institutions and Social Exchange: The Sociologies of Talcott Parsons & George C. Homans.* New York: Bobbs-Merrill.

Parsons, T. and E. Shils, eds. 1951. *Toward a General Theory of Action.* New York: Harper & Row.

Patai, D. 1998. Why not a feminist overhaul of higher education? *The Chronicle of Higher Education,* January 23: A56.

Paul, L., M.A. Foss, and M.A. Baenninger. 1996. Double standards for sexual jealousy: Manipulative morality or a reflection of evolved sex differences? *Human Nature* 7: 291–324.

Peel, J.D.Y. 1972. Introduction. Pp. vii–li in J.D.Y. Peel, ed., *Herbert Spencer on Social Evolution.* Chicago: University of Chicago Press.

Pérusse, D. 1993. Cultural and reproductive success in industrial societies: Testing the relationship at the proximate and ultimate levels. *Behavioral and Brain Sciences* 16: 267–83.

Peter's Atlas of the World. 1990. New York: Harper & Row.

Peterson, R.R. 1996. A re-evaluation of the economic consequences of divorce. *American Sociological Review* 61: 528–36.

Phelan, J. 1994. The paradox of the contented female worker: An assessment of alternative explanations. *Social Psychological Quarterly* 57: 95–107.

Piaget, J. 1970. *Genetic Epistemology.* New York: Columbia University Press.

———. 1976. *Behavior and Evolution.* New York: Pantheon.

Pinker, S. 1994. *The Language of Instinct.* New York: Morrow.

Popenoe, D. 1987. Beyond the nuclear family: A statistical portrait of the changing family in Sweden. *Journal of Marriage and the Family* 49: 173–83.

———. 1988. *Disturbing the Nest: Family Change and Decline in Modern Societies.* New York: Aldine de Gruyter.

Popper, K.R. 1961. *The Logic of Scientific Discovery.* New York: Basic Books.

Pruett, K. 1987. *The Nurturing Father.* New York: Warner.

———. 1993. The paternal presence. *Families in Society* 74: 46–50.

Pusey, A., J. Williams, and J. Goodall. 1997. The influence of dominance rank on the reproductive success of female chimpanzees. *Science* 277: 828–31.

Radcliffe-Brown, A.R. 1922. *The Andaman Islanders.* Cambridge: Cambridge University Press.

Raisman, G. and P.M. Field. 1973. Sexual dimorphism in the neuropil of the preoptic area of the rat and its dependence on neonatal androgen. *Brain Research* 54: 1–29.

Raleigh, M.J. and M.T. McGuire. 1989. Female influences on male dominance acquisition in captive vervet monkeys, *Cercopithecus aethiops sabaeus. Animal Behavior* 38: 59–67.

Reinisch, J.M. 1974. Fetal hormones, the brain, and human sex differences: A heuristic, integrative review of the recent literature. *Archives of Sexual Behaviour* 3: 51–90.

Remoff, H.T. 1984. *Sexual Choice.* New York: Dutton/Lewis.

Reskin, B.F. 1988. Bringing the men back in: Sex differentiation and the devaluation of women's work. *Gender and Society* 2: 58–81.

———. 1992. Work and occupations. Pp. 2253–60 in E.F. Borgatta, ed. *Encyclopedia of Sociology.* New York: Macmillan.

Reskin, B.F. and P.A. Roos. 1990. *Job Queues, Gender Queues: Explaining Women's Inroads into Male Occupations.* Philadelphia: Temple University Press.

Restak, R. 1979. *The Brain.* New York: Doubleday.

Reynolds, V., V.S.E. Falger, and I. Vine, eds. 1987. *The Sociobiology of Ethnocentrism.* London: Croom Helm.

Reynolds, V. and R. Tanner. 1983. *The Biology of Religion.* New York: Longman.

Riche, M.F. 1988. The postmarital society. *American Demographics* 10: 22–26.

Ridgeway, C.L. 1997. Interaction and the conservation of gender inequality: Considering employment. *American Sociological Review* 62: 218–35.

Ridley, M. 1993. *The Red Queen: Sex and the Evolution of Human Nature.* New York: Macmillan.

Rindfuss, R.R., S.P. Morgan, and G. Swicegood. 1988. *First Births in America: Changes in the Timing of Parenthood.* Berkeley, CA: University of California Press.

Rindfuss, R.R. and A. VandenHeuvel. 1990. Cohabitation: A precursor to marriage or an alternative to being single? *Population and Development Review* 16: 703–26.

Ritzer, G. 1997. *Postmodern Social Theory.* New York: McGraw-Hill.

Robinson, J.P. 1988. Who's doing the housework? *American Demographics* 10: 24–28.

Rodriquez-Ibanez, J.E. 1997. On sociological difficulties and national backgrounds. *Theory* (Newsletter of the Research Committee of the International Sociological Association), Spring: 6–7.

Rogers, M.F. 1998. *Contemporary Feminist Theory: A Text/Reader.* New York: McGraw-Hill.

Roos, P.A. 1985. *Gender and Work: A Comparative Analysis of Industrial Societies.* Albany, NY: SUNY Press.

Rose, R. 1985. National pride in cross-national perspective. *International Social Science Journal* 37: 85–96.

Rose, H. and S. Rose. 1969. *Science and Society.* Baltimore: Penguin Books.

Rosenblatt, P.C. 1974. Cross-cultural perspective on attraction. Pp. 79–95 in T.L. Huston, ed. *Foundations of Interpersonal Attraction.* New York: Academic Press.

Rosenfeld, E. 1951. Social stratification in a "classless" society. *American Sociological Review* 16: 766–74.

Rosenfeld, R.A. and A.L. Kalleberg. 1990. A cross-national comparison of the gender gap in income. *American Journal of Sociology* 96: 69–106.

Rosenfeld, R.A. and A.B. Sorensen. 1979. Sex differences in patterns of career mobility. *Demography* 16: 89–101.

Ross, C.E. 1987. The division of labor at home. *Social Forces* 65: 816–33.

Ross, C.E. and J. Mirowsky. 1996. Economic and interpersonal work rewards: Subjective utilities of men's and women's compensation. *Social Forces* 75: 223–46.

Rossi, A.S. 1977. A biosocial perspective on parenting. *Daedalus* 106: 1–31.

———. 1984. Gender and parenthood. *American Sociological Review* 49: 1–19.

Rotundo, A. 1985. American fatherhood: A historical perspective. *American Behavioral Scientist* 29: 7–25.

Rozin, P. 1976. The evolution of intelligence and access to the cognitive unconsciousness. Pp. 245–80 in J.M. Sprague and A.N. Epstein, eds. *Progress in Psychobiology and Physiological Psychology.* New York: Academic Press.

Rubin, G. 1975. The traffic in women: Notes on the "political economy" of sex. Pp. 157–210 in R. Reiter, ed. *Toward an Anthropology of Women.* New York: Monthy Review Press.

Rule, J.B. 1994. Dilemmas of theoretical promise. *Sociological Forum* 9: 241–57.

Ruse, M. 1979. *Sociobiology: Sense or Nonsense?* Boston: D. Reidel.

Rushton, J.P. 1995. *Race, Evolution, and Behavior.* New Brunswick, NJ: Transaction Publishers.

Russell, D. 1984. The prevalence and seriousness of incestuous abuse: Step-fathers versus biological fathers. *Child Abuse and Neglect* 7: 133–46.

Rytina, N.F. 1981. Occupational segregation and earnings differences by sex. *Monthly Labor Review* 104: 49–53.

Sadalla, E.K., D.T. Kendrick, and B. Vershure. 1987. Dominance and heterosexual attraction. *Journal of Personality and Social Psychology* 52: 730–38.

Saluter, A. 1991. Marital status and living arrangements: March 1990. *Current Population Reports*, Series P-20, No. 450.

Sanday, P.R. 1981. *Female Power and Male Dominance.* New York: Cambridge University Press.

Sanders, B., M.P. Soares, and J.M. d'Aquila. 1982. The sex difference on one test of spatial visualization: A nontrivial difference. *Child Development* 53: 1106–10.

Sanderson, S.K.. 1991. *Macrosociology: An Introduction to Human Societies.* New York: HarperCollins.

Sanderson, S.K. and L. Ellis. 1992. Theoretical and political perspectives of American sociologists. *American Sociologist* 23: 26–42.

Sawhill, I. 1976. Discrimination and poverty among women who head families. *Signs* 1: 201–11.

Schaller, G.B. 1972. *The Serengeti Lion: A Study of Predator-Prey Relations.* Chicago: University of Chicago Press.

Schoen, R. and R.M. Weinick. 1993. Partner choice in marriages and cohabitations. *Journal of Marriage and the Family* 55: 408–14.

Schulman, S.R. 1978. Kin selection, reciprocal altruism, and the principle of maximization. *Quarterly Review of Biology* 53: 283–86.

Scott, J. 1996. *Stratification and Power: Structures of Class, Status and Command.* Cambridge: Polity Press.

Seidman, S. 1991. The end of sociological theory: The postmodern hope. *Sociological Theory* 9: 131–46.

Sen, A. 1993. On the Darwinian view of progress. *Population and Development Review* 19: 123–37.

Shaw, R.P. and Y. Wong. 1989. *Genetic Seeds of Warfare: Evolution, Nationalism, and Patriotism.* Boston: Unwin Hyman.

Shelton, B.A. and D. John. 1993. Does marital status make a difference? Housework among married and cohabiting men and women. *Journal of Family Issues* 14: 401–20.

Shepher, J. 1983. *Incest: A Biosocial View.* New York: Academic Press.

Shettel-Neuber, J., J.B. Bryson, and C.E. Young. 1978. Physical attractiveness of the "other person" and jealousy. *Personality and Social Psychology Bulletin* 4: 612–15.

Shils, E. 1948. *The Present State of American Sociology.* Glencoe, IL: Free Press.

————. 1957. Primordial, personal, sacred, and civil ties. *British Journal of Sociology* 8: 130–45.

Shipler, D.K. 1997. *A Country of Strangers*. New York: Knopf.

Shostak, M. 1981. *Nisa: The Life and Words of a !Kung Woman*. New York: Random House.

Sica, A. 1993. Does PoMo matter? *Contemporary Sociology* 22: 16–19.

Simmel, G. 1950. *The Sociology of Georg Simmel*, ed. by K.H. Wolff. Glencoe, IL: Free Press.

Simons, H.W. and M. Billig, eds. 1994. *After Postmodernism: Reconstructing Ideology Critique*. Thousand Oaks, CA: Sage.

Simpson, G.G. 1949. *The Meaning of Evolution*. New Haven: Yale University Press.

Simpson, I.H. and R.L. Simpson. 1994. The transformation of the American Sociological Association. *Sociological Forum* 9: 259–78.

Singh, D. 1993a. Adaptive significance of female physical appearance: Role of waist-to-hip ratio (WHR). *Journal of Personality and Social Psychology* 65: 293–307.

————. 1993b. Is thin really beautiful and good? Relationship between waist-to-hip ratio (WHR) and female attractiveness. *Personality and Individual Differences* 16: 123–32.

————. 1993c. Body shape and women's attractiveness: The critical role of waist-to-hip ratio. *Human Nature* 4: 297–321.

Skinner, B.F. 1938. *The Behavior of Organisms*. New York: Appleton-Century-Crofts.

————. 1953. *Science and Human Behavior*. New York: Macmillan.

Small, M.F. 1992. The evolution of female sexuality and mate selection in humans. *Human Nature* 3: 133–56.

Smith, A.D. 1986. *The Ethnic Origins of Nations*. New York: Basil Blackwell.

Smith, D.E. 1987. *The Everyday World as Problematic: A Feminist Sociology*. Boston: Northeastern University Press.

————. 1990. *Texts, Facts, and Femininity: Exploring the Relations of Ruling*. New York: Routledge.

Smith, D.G. and S. Smith. 1988. Parental rank and reproductive success of natal rhesus males. *Animal Behavior* 36: 544–62.

Smith, R.L. 1984. Human sperm competition. Pp. 601–59 in R.L. Smith, ed. *Sperm Competition and the Evolution of Animal Mating Systems*. New York: Academic Press.

Smuts, B.B. 1985. *Sex & Friendship in Baboons*. New York: Aldine.

————. 1987. Gender, aggression, and influence. Pp. 400–12 in B.B. Smuts, D.L. Cheney, R.M. Seyfarth, R.W. Wrangham, and T.T. Struhsaker, eds. *Primate Societies*. Chicago: University of Chicago Press.

————. 1995. The evolutionary origins of patriarchy. *Human Nature* 6: 1–32.

Sober, E. 1984. *The Nature of Selection*. Cambridge, Mass.: MIT Press.

Sommers, C.H. 1994. *Who Stole Feminism? How Women Have Betrayed Women*. New York: Simon & Schuster.

Sorensen, A. and H. Trappe. 1995. The persistence of gender inequality in earnings in the German Democratic Republic. *American Sociological Review* 60: 398–406.

Sorokin, P.A. 1928. *Contemporary Sociological Theories*. New York: Harper & Brothers.

South, S.J. and K.M. Lloyd. 1995. Spousal alternatives and marital dissolution. *American Sociological Review* 60: 21–35.

South, S.J. and G. Spitze. 1994. Housework in marital and nonmarital households. *American Sociological Review* 59: 327–47.

Spain, D. and S.M. Bianchi. 1996. *Balancing Act: Motherhood, Marriage, and Employment*. New York: Russell Sage Foundation.

Spelman, E. 1989. *Inessential Women*. Boston: Beacon.
Spencer, H. 1864 (orig. 1851). *Social Statics*. New York: Appleton.
———. 1972 (orig. 1852). Population and progress. Pp. 33–37 in J.D.Y. Peel, ed. *Herbert Spencer on Social Evolution*. Chicago: University of Chicago Press.
———. 1915 (orig. 1857). *Essays: Scientific Political and Speculative*. New York: Appleton.
———. 1873. *The Study of Sociology*. London: Williams and Norgate.
———. 1906 (orig. 1876–1886). *The Principles of Sociology*, 3 vols. New York: Appleton.
———. 1892–93. *Principles of Ethics*. London: Williams & Norgate.
Stanley, S.M. 1981. *The New Evolutionary Time Table*. New York: Basic Books.
Stinchcombe, A.L. 1963. Some empirical consequences of the Davis-Moore theory of stratification. *American Sociological Review* 28: 805–08.
———. 1994. Disintegrated disciplines and the future of sociology. *Sociological Forum* 9: 279–91.
Sumner, W.G. 1906. *Folkways*. New York: Ginn.
———. 1911. *War and Other Essays*. New Haven, CT: Yale University Press.
Symons, D. 1979. *The Evolution of Human Sexuality*. New York: Oxford University Press.
———. 1989. A critique of Darwinian anthropology. *Ethology and Sociobiology* 10: 131–44.
———. 1990. Adaptiveness and adaptation. *Ethology and Sociobiology* 11: 427–44.
———. 1992. On the use and misuse of Darwinism in the study of human behavior. Pp. 137–59 in J.H. Barkow, L. Cosmides, and J. Tooby, eds. *The Adapted Mind*. New York: Oxford University Press.
Talbert, J. and C.E. Bose. 1977. Wage-attainment processes: The retail clerk case. *American Journal of Sociology* 83: 403–24.
Tam, T. 1997. Sex segregation and occupational gender inequality in the United States: Devaluation or specialized training? *American Journal of Sociology* 102: 1652–92.
Tannen, D. 1990. *You Just Don't Understand: Women and Men in Conversation*. New York: Morrow.
Tawney, R.H. 1926. *Religion and the Rise of Capitalism*. New York: Harcourt, Brace.
Taylor, C. 1989. *Sources of the Self*. Cambridge, MA: Harvard University Press.
———. 1991. *The Ethics of Authenticity*. Cambridge, MA: Harvard University Press.
Taylor, P. and N. Glenn. 1976. The utility of education and attractiveness for females' status attainment through marriage. *American Sociological Review* 41: 484–98.
Teachman, J.D. and K.A. Polonko. 1990. Cohabitation and marital stability in the United States. *Social Forces* 69: 207–20.
Therborn, G. n.d. (circa 1992). What about taking ourselves seriously? *Theory* (Newsletter of the Research Committee on Social Theory of the International Sociological Association) Unnumbered: 1–2.
Thiessen, D.D. 1996. *Bittersweet Destiny: The Stormy Evolution of Human Behavior*. New Brunswick, NJ: Transaction Publishers.
Thiessen, D.D. and B. Gregg. 1980. Human assortative mating and genetic equilibrium: An evolutionary perspective. *Ethology and Sociobiology* 1: 111–40.
Thiessen, D.D., R.K. Young, and R. Burroughs. 1993. Lonely hearts advertisements reflect sexually dimorphic mating strategies. *Ethology and Sociobiology* 14: 209–29.
Thomas, W.I. and F. Znaniecki. 1918–1920. *The Polish Peasant in Europe and America,* 5 vols. Boston: Richard G. Badger.
Thompson, P. 1989. *The Structure of Biological Theories*. Albany, NY: SUNY Press.

Thornhill, R. and S.W. Gangestad. 1993. Human facial beauty: Averageness, symmetry, and parasite resistance. *Human Nature* 4: 237–69.

Thornhill, R. and N.W. Thornhill. 1983. Human rape: An evolutionary analysis. *Ethology and Sociobiology* 4: 137– 73.

Thornton, A. and D. Freedman. 1983. *The Changing American Family*. Washington, DC: Population Reference Bureau.

Tiger, L. 1990. The cerebral bridge from family to foe. Pp. 99–106 in J. van der Dennen and V. Falger, eds. *Sociobiology and Conflict*. London: Chapman and Hall.

———. 1992. *The Pursuit of Pleasure*. Boston: Little, Brown and Company.

Tindale, N.B. 1974. *Aboriginal Tribes of Australia*. Berkeley, CA: University of California Press.

Tokuda, K. and G.D. Jensen. 1968. The leader's role in controlling aggressive behavior in a monkey group. *Primates* 9: 319–22.

Tönnesmann, W. 1987. Group indentification and political socialisation. Pp. 175–89 in V. Reynolds, V. Falger, and I.Vine, eds. *The Sociobiology of Ethnocentrism*. London: Croom Helm.

Tooby, J. and L. Cosmides. 1989. Evolutionary psychology and the generation of culture, Part I. Theoretical considerations. *Ethology and Sociobiology* 10: 29–49.

———. 1990. The past explains the present: Emotional adaptations and the structure of ancestral environments. *Ethology and Sociobiology* 11: 375–424.

———. 1992. The psychological foundations of culture. Pp. 19–136 in J.H. Barkow, L. Cosmides, and J. Tooby, eds. *The Adapted Mind*. New York: Oxford University Press.

Toran-Allerand, D. 1976. Sex steroids and the development of the newborn mouse hypothalamus and preoptic area in vitro: Implications for sexual differentiation. *Brain Research* 106: 407–12.

Townsend, J.M. 1989. Mate selection criteria: A pilot study. *Ethology and Sociobiology* 10: 241–53.

Townsend, J.M. and G.D. Levy. 1990a. Effects of potential partners' physical attractiveness and socioeconomic status on sexuality and partner selection. *Archives of Sexual Behavior* 19: 149–64.

———. 1990b. Effects of potential partners' costume and physical attractiveness on sexuality and partner selection. *Journal of Psychology* 124: 371–89.

Treiman, D.J. and K. Terrell. 1975. Women, work, and wages—trends in the female occupation structure. Pp. 157–99 in K.C. Land and S. Spilerman, eds. *Social Indicator Models*. New York: Sage.

Trefil, J. 1989. *Reading the Mind of God: In Search of the Principle of Universality*. New York: Charles Scribner's Sons.

Trilling, L. 1972. *Sincerity and Authenticity*. Cambridge, MA: Harvard University Press.

Trivers, R.L. 1971. The evolution of reciprocal altruism. *Quarterly Review of Biology* 46: 35–47.

———. 1972. Parental investment and sexual selection. Pp. 136–79 in B.H. Campbell, ed., *Sexual Selection and the Descent of Man, 1871–1971*. Chicago: Aldine.

———. 1985. *Social Evolution*. Menlo Park, CA: Benjamin/Cummings.

Trivers, R.L. and D.E. Willard. 1973. Natural selection of parental ability to vary the sex ratio of offspring. *Science* 1979: 90–92.

Tuchman, G. 1992. Feminist theory. Pp. 695–704 in E.F. Borgatta, ed. *Encyclopedia of Sociology*. New York: Macmillan.

Tumin, M.M. 1953. Some principles of stratification: A critical analysis. *American Sociological Review* 18: 387–94.

Turk, H. and R.L. Simpson, eds. 1971. *Institutions and Social Exchange: The Sociologies of Talcott Parsons & George C. Homans*. New York: Bobbs-Merrill.

Turke, P.W. 1989. Evolution and the demand for children. *Population and Development Review* 15: 61–90.

———. 1990a. Which humans behave adaptively, and why does it matter? *Ethology and Sociobiology* 11: 305–39.

———. 1990b. Just do it. *Ethology and Sociobiology* 11: 445–63.

Turner, C.F., H.G. Miller, and L.E. Moses, eds. 1989. *AIDS, Sexual Behavior and Intravenous Drug Use*. Washington, DC: National Academy Press.

Turner, J.H. 1984. *Social Stratification: A Theoretical Analysis*. New York: Columbia University Press.

———. 1985. *Herbert Spencer: A Renewed Appreciation*. Beverly Hills, CA: Sage.

———. 1989. The disintegration of American sociology. *Sociological Perspectives* 32: 419–33.

———. 1991. *The Structure of Sociological Theory*, 5th ed. Belmont, CA: Wadsworth.

———. 1996. American sociology: Can what was never coherently composed be decomposed? *Sociological Imagination* 33: 191–201.

Turner, J.H., L. Beeghley, and C.H. Powers. 1998. *The Emergence of Sociological Theory*. Belmont, CA: Wadsworth.

Turner, J.H. and A.R. Maryanski. 1979. *Functionalism*. Menlo Park, CA: Benjamin/Cummings.

Turner, S.P. and J.H. Turner. 1990. *The Impossible Science*. Newbury Park, CA: Sage.

Tylor, E.B. 1871. *Primitive Culture*. New York: Harper.

Udry, J.R.. 1994. The nature of gender. *Demography* 31: 561–73.

Udry, J.R. and B.K. Eckland. 1984. Benefits of being attractive: Differential payoffs for men and women. *Psychological Reports* 54: 47–56.

Ulč, O. 1978. Some aspects of Czechoslovak society since 1968. *Social Forces* 57: 419–35.

van den Berghe, P.L. 1974. Bringing beasts back in. *American Sociological Review* 39: 777–88.

———. 1978. *Race and Racism: A Comparative Perspective*, 2nd ed. New York: Wilcy.

———. 1979. *Human Family Systems: An Evolutionary View*. New York: Elsevier.

———. 1981. *The Ethnic Phenomenon*. New York: Elsevier.

———. 1989. *Stranger in Their Midst*. Niwot, CO: University Press of Colorado.

———. 1990. Why most sociologists don't (and won't) think evolutionarily. *Sociological Forum* 5: 173–85.

van den Berghe, P. and J. Whitmeyer. 1990. Social class and reproductive success. *International Journal of Contemporary Sociology* 27: 29–48.

van der Dennen, J.M.G. 1987. Ethnocentrism and in-group/our-group differentiation. A review and interpretation of the literature. Pp. 1–47 in V. Reynolds, V.S.E. Falger, and I. Vine, eds. *The Sociobiology of Ethnocentrism*. London: Croom Helm.

Vänhanen, T. 1992. *On the Evolutionary Roots of Politics*. New Delhi: Sterling Publishers.

Vaupel, J.W. 1988. Inherited frailty and longevity. *Demography* 25: 277–87.

Veblen, T. 1899. *The Theory of the Leisure Class*. New York: Macmillan.

Vining, D.R., Jr. 1986. Social versus reproductive success: The central theoretical problem of human sociobiology. *Behavioral and Brain Sciences* 9: 167–87.

Volensky, M. 1984. *Nomenklatura: The Soviet Ruling Class*. Garden City, NY: Doubleday.

Volgyes, I. 1978. Modernization, stratification and elite development in Hungary. *Social Forces* 57: 500–21.

Volkan, V. 1997. *Bloodlines: From Ethnic Pride to Ethnic Terrorism.* New York: Farrar Straus Giroux.

Waldrop, M.M. 1992. *Complexity: The Emerging Science at the Edge of Order and Chaos.* New York: Simon & Schuster.

Walker, K.E. and M.E. Woods. 1976. *Time Use: A Measure of Household Production of Family Goods and Services.* Washington, DC: American Home Economics Association.

Wallace, W.L. 1995. Why sociology doesn't make progress. *Sociological Forum* 10: 313–18.

Wallerstein, I. 1974. *The Modern World-System.* New York: Academic Press.

Walsh, A. 1995. *Biosociology.* Westport, CT: Praeger.

Walters, J.R. and R.M. Seyfarth. 1987. Conflict and cooperation. Pp. 306–17 in B.B. Smuts, D.L. Cheney, R.M. Seyfarth, R.W. Wrangham, and T.T. Struhsaker, eds. *Primate Societies.* Chicago: University of Chicago Press.

Ward, L.F. 1883. *Dynamic Sociology, or Applied Social Science, as Based upon Statical Sociology and the Less Complex Sciences,* 2 vols. New York: D. Appleton.

———. 1903. *Pure Sociology: A Treatise on the Origins and Spontaneous Development of Society.* New York: Macmillan.

Warner, W.L. 1930. Murngin warfare. *Oceania* 1: 457–94.

Weber, M. 1958 (orig. 1904–1905). *The Protestant Ethic and the Spirit of Capitalism.* New York: Charles Scribner's Sons.

———. 1946 (orig. 1919). Science as a vocation. Pp. 129–56 in H.H. Gerth and C.W. Mills, eds. *From Max Weber: Essays in Sociology.* New York: Oxford University Press.

———. 1968 (orig. 1921–1922). *Economy and Society,* 3 vols. New York: Bedminster Press.

———. 1961 (orig. 1923). *General Economic History.* New York: Collier Books.

———. 1949. *The Methodology of the Social Sciences.* Glencoe, IL: Free Press.

Weiner, J. 1994. *The Beak of the Finch.* New York: Alfred A. Knopf.

Weiss, K.W. 1990. The biodemography of variation in human frailty. *Demography* 27: 185–206.

Weitzman, L.J. 1981. *The Marriage Contract.* New York: Free Press.

———. 1985. *The Divorce Revolution.* New York: Free Press.

Wellington, A.J. 1994. Accounting for the male/female wage gap among whites: 1976 and 1985. *American Sociological Review* 59: 839–48.

West, C. and S. Fenstermaker. 1996. Doing difference. Pp. 357–84 in E.N-L. Chow, D. Wilkinson, and M.B. Zinn, eds. *Race, Class, & Gender: Common Bonds, Different Voices.* Thousands Oaks, CA: Sage.

West, C. and D.H. Zimmerman. 1987. Doing gender. *Gender and Society* 1: 125–51.

Western, M. 1994. Class structure and intergenerational class mobility: A comparative analysis of nation and gender. *Social Forces* 73: 101–34.

White, J.M. 1987. Premarital cohabitation and marital stability in Canada. *Journal of Marriage and the Family* 49: 641–47.

White, L.K. 1990. Determinants of divorce: A review of research in the eighties. *Journal of Marriage and the Family* 52: 904–12.

Whiting, B.B. and J.W.M. Whiting. 1975. *Children of Six Cultures.* Cambridge, MA: Harvard University Press.

Whitmeyer, J.M. 1997. Endogamy as a basis for ethnic behavior. *Sociological Theory* 15: 162–78.

Whitten, P.L. 1983. Diet and dominance among female vervet monkeys (*Cercopithecus aethiops*). *American Journal of Primatology* 5: 139–59.

Whyte, W.F. 1943. *Street Corner Society.* Chicago: University of Chicago Press.

Wiederman, M.W. 1993. Evolved gender differences in mate preferences: Evidence from personal advertisements. *Ethology and Sociobiology* 14: 331–52.

Wiederman, M.W. and E.R. Allgeier. 1993. Gender differences in sexual jealousy: Adaptionist or social learning explanations? *Ethology and Sociobiology* 14: 115–40.

Willhoite, F.H., Jr. 1975. Equal opportunity and primate particularism. *The Journal of Politics* 37: 270–76.

Williams, J.E. and D.L. Best. 1982. *Measuring Sex Stereotypes: A Thirty-Nation Study.* Beverly Hills, CA: Sage.

Williams, R.M., Jr. 1961. The sociological theory of Talcott Parsons. Pp. 64–99 in M. Black, ed., *The Social Theories of Talcott Parsons: A Critical Examination.* Englewood Cliffs, NJ: Prentice-Hall.

———. 1994. The sociology of ethnic conflicts: Comparative and international perspectives. *Annual Review of Sociology* 20: 49–79.

Wilson, D.S. 1994. Adaptive genetic variation and human evolutionary psychology. *Ethology and Sociobiology* 15: 219–35.

Wilson, E.O. 1971. *The Insect Societies.* Cambridge, MA: Harvard University Press.

———. 1975. *Sociobiology: The New Synthesis.* Cambridge, MA: Harvard University Press.

———. 1978a. *On Human Nature.* Cambridge, MA: Harvard University Press.

———. 1978b. What is sociobiology? Pp. 1–12 in M.S. Gregory, A. Silvers, and D. Sutch, eds. *Sociobiology and Human Nature.* San Francisco: Jossey-Bass.

———. 1984. *Biophilia.* Cambridge, MA: Harvard University Press.

———. 1986. Sociobiology and sociology converging: An evaluation of Lopreato's *Human Nature and Biocultural Evolution. Revue Européenne des Sciences Sociales* 24: 5–8.

Wilson, M. and M. Daly. 1987. Risk of maltreatment of children living with stepparents. Pp. 215–32 in R.J. Gelles and J.B. Lancaster, eds. *Child Abuse and Neglect: Biosocial Dimensions.* New York: Aldine de Gruyter.

Wilson, W.J. 1987. *The Truly Disadvantaged.* Chicago: University of Chicago Press.

Witelson, S.F. 1978. Sex differences in the neurology of cognition: Social educational and clinical implications. Pp. 287–303 in E. Sullerot, ed. *Le Fait Feminin.* Paris: Fayard.

Wolf, E.R. 1982. *Europe and the People Without History.* Berkeley, CA: University of California Press.

Wolf, W.C. and R.A. Rosenfeld. 1978. Sex structure of occupations and job mobility. *Social Forces* 56: 823–44.

Woods, J. and D. Walton. 1982. *Argument: The Logic of the Fallacies.* New York: McGraw-Hill.

Wrangham, R. 1997. Subtle, secret female chimpanzees. *Science* 277: 774–75.

Wrangham, R. and D. Peterson. 1996. *Demonic Males: Apes and the Origins of Human Violence.* New York: Houghton Mifflin.

Wright, R. 1994. *The Moral Animal: The New Science of Evolutionary Psychology.* New York: Pantheon Books.

Wright, S. 1969. *Evolution and the Genetics of Population,* 2 vols. Chicago: University of Chicago Press.

Wrong, D. 1994. *The Problem of Order.* New York: Free Press.

Yinger, J.M.. 1994. *Ethnicity: Source of Strength? Source of Conflict?* Albany, NY: SUNY Press.

Young, M.B. 1989. Chicken Little in China: Women after the cultural revolution. In S. Kruks, R. Rapp, and M.B. Young, eds. *Promissory Notes: Women in the Transition to Socialism.* New York: Monthly Review Press.

Zangwill, I. 1909. *The Melting Pot.* New York: Macmillan.
Zetterberg, H.L. 1963. *On Theory and Verification in Sociology.* Totowa, NJ:
    Bedminster Press.

Index of Names

Aboud, F. 264
Adams, R.M. 233
Adler, A. 233
Agger, B. 64
Ahlburg, D.A. 172, 175, 176, 182
Alba, R.D. 262
Alexander, J.C. 39
Alexander, R.D. 92, 107, 111, 125, 126, 127–29, 130, 224, 230, 250, 264
Allen, L.S. 147, 148
Allgeier, E.R. 155
Allison, P.D. 108, 110
Alpert, H. 51
Alston, L. 79, 118, 216
Amato, P. 188
Anderson, B. 251
Arafat, I. 185
Archer, J.E. 154, 236
Arendt, H. 61
Arnhart, L. 145
Aron, R. 38
Avis, W.E. 166
Axelrod, R. 18

Bachrach, C.A. 186
Backett, K. 189, 198–99
Bailey, J.M. 161, 165
Baker, L.C. 168, 203
Baker, S. 157
Barash, D.P. 110, 111, 118, 125, 136, 153, 248, 249
Barnes, M. 164
Barry, B. 55
Bartfeld, J. 190
Barth, F. 251
Bateman, A.J. 115
Bauman, Z. 61
Beach, F.A. 159
Beale, I.L. 152
Beck, E.M. 204
Becker, E. 54
Becker, G.S. 56, 194

Becker, J.B. 235
Beigel, H.G. 166
Bell, D. 60, 61
Bell-Fialkoff, A. 260, 261
Bellah, R.N. 15, 37, 52, 60, 61
Bem, S.L. 140
Benbow, C.P. 151
Benedict, R. 248, 262
Bennett, J.H. 265
Bennett, N. 186
Bereczkei, T. 181
Berenbaum, S. 157
Berger, P.L. 30, 54
Berk, S.F. 196
Bernard, J. 138
Beron, K. 204
Bernstein, I.S. 224
Best, D.L. 201
Betzig, L.L. 127, 162, 172, 174, 197, 230, 232, 241
Bianchi, S.M. 200
Bibb, R. 204
Billig, M. 60
Black, M. 19, 33–34, 35
Blau, F.D. 203
Blau, P.M. 27, 28, 57, 108, 194
Bleiberg Seperson, S. 49
Bleir, R. 142
Blood, R.O. 194
Bloom, A. 61
Blumer, H. 57–58
Boas, F. 13–14
Boccia, M.L. 221
Bonacich, E. 258
Booth, A. 188, 235, 236
Borgehoff Mulder, M. 162
Borgmann, A. 61
Bose, C.E. 204
Bowlby, J. 89, 93
Braddock, J.H., II 231
Braithwaite, R.B. 74
Brandon, G.S.F. 54

Braudel, F. 52, 53
Bregantini, L. 261
Bridges, W.P. 204
Brinton, C. 223
Brown, D.E. 130, 136, 201
Brown, J.K. 136
Browne, I. 204
Buckle, L. 177, 181, 182
Buffery, A.W.H. 152
Bumpass, L. 175, 183, 186
Bunge, M. 55
Burgess, E.W. 254–55
Bury, J.B. 5
Buss, D.M. 115, 119, 122, 129, 130, 136, 155, 159, 160, 161, 163, 164, 165, 166, 167, 168

Campbell, D.T. 250
Caplan, A.L. 111
Carey, A.D. 52, 72, 126, 171
Castro Martin, T. 175
Chafetz, J.S. 145, 195–96, 207
Chagnon, N.A. 153, 162, 219, 231, 265–66
Chance, M.R.A. 220
Cheney, D.L. 220, 225, 226
Cherlin, A.J. 172, 175, 176, 180, 183, 184, 190, 192
Cherns, A. 240
Chisholm, J.S. 72
Christiansen, K. 235
Clark, R.D. 161
Clignet, R. 119
Cliquet, R.L. 230
Cohen, L.E. 16, 18, 30, 52, 109
Cole, S. 37, 49, 70, 78
Coleman, J.S. 28, 43, 55, 71
Collins, R. 30, 45, 54, 58, 64, 74, 78–79, 136, 138, 159, 183, 207, 209
Coltrane, S. 159, 188, 194
Commander, L. 137
Comte, A. 5–6, 50–51, 65, 107, 233
Condran, G.A. 189
Connell, R.W. 136, 137, 144
Coombs, R.H. 168
Corballis, M.C. 152
Cornacchia, E.J. 249
Coser, L.A. 23
Cosmides, L. 13, 30, 50, 52, 74, 92, 109, 111, 113, 121, 126–28, 130
Coughlin, E.K. 45
Crippen, T. 52, 57, 72, 111, 126, 270

Cronin, H. 99
Cronk, L. 162
Crook, J.H. 162, 263
Crook, S.J. 162
Crosbie, P.V. 166
Crow, J.F. 159
Csanaky, A. 181
Curtis, C.P., Jr. 27
Cutts, S. 188

Dabbs, J.M., Jr. 235
Dahrendorf, R. 58, 208, 209
Daly, M. 92, 164, 174, 191, 192
Darwin, C. 4, 6, 8, 9, 10, 11, 12, 15, 16–17, 77, 79, 83–99, 104, 105, 106, 111, 112, 115, 117, 120, 125, 130, 137, 138, 181, 201, 218, 225, 238, 241
Darwin, F. 93
Datta, S. 220, 226
Davie, M. 253
Davies, J.C. 223
Davis, J.A. 13, 47, 49, 56, 59
Davis, K. 24, 26, 203, 209, 215–19, 224, 241
Dawkins, R. 63–64, 94–95, 106, 108, 119, 155, 169
de Beauvoir, S. 67, 192
Degler, C.N. 124, 137
de Lacoste-Utamsing, M.C. 147
DeMaris, A. 191
Dennett, D.C. 74, 124, 125
Denzin, N.K. 41, 61
Derrida, J. 38, 61
Devereux, E.C. 33
DeVita, C.J. 172, 175, 176, 182
DeVore, B.I. 220
de Vos, H. 110
de Waal, F. 141, 154, 211, 214, 220, 221, 222, 223, 224, 226, 238
Diamond, J. 108, 159, 230, 260, 261
Dickemann, M. 162, 170, 172
Dion, K. 168
Dittman, R. 157
Djilas, M. 212, 239
Dobzhansky, T. 83, 84, 85, 88, 89, 90, 92, 98, 101, 102–03, 117, 127, 130
Doob, A. 263
Downey, J. 156
Duffy Hutcheson, P. 50
Dunbar, E.P. 226
Dunbar, R.I.M. 220, 221, 225, 226, 238

Duncan, B. 195
Duncan, O.D. 195
Durham, W.H. 265
Durkheim, É. 13–18, 19, 24, 30, 31, 39,
    51–52, 62, 108, 191, 207, 218, 224,
    268, 269, 276

Eagly, A.H. 201
Eals, M. 152
Easterlin, R.A. 172
Eaton, G.G. 220, 223, 224, 225, 226
Eaton, S.B. 117
Eckland, B.K. 167
Edwards, J. 188
Ehardt, C.L. 224
Ehrhardt, A.A. 157
Eibl-Eibesfeldt, I. 135, 265
Elder, G.H. 167
Eldredge, N. 93–94
Elias, M. 236
Ellis, B.J. 159, 160
Ellis, L. 46, 49, 57–59, 220
Engels, F. 8, 9, 209, 211, 212, 223
England, P. 203, 204
Epstein, C.F. 112, 136, 141, 183
Eriksen, J.A. 195
Esman, M.J. 250, 252
Euler, H.A. 155

Fabianic, D. 66
Farkas, G. 204
Fausto-Sterling, A. 142, 147
Feingold, A. 201
Feldmesser, R.A. 239
Fenstermaker, S. 144
Ferber, M.A. 203, 204
Field, P.M. 148
Findlay, C.S. 178
Finkelhor, D. 191
Fisher, H.E. 175, 177
Fitzgerald, T. 138
Fletcher, D.J.L. 262
Flinn, M.V. 111
Ford, C.S. 159
Form, W.H. 204
Foucault, M. 38, 63
Fox, R. 13, 46
Frank, P. 212
Frank, R.H. 135
Freedman, D. 187
Freedman, D.G. 264
Freedman, J.L. 263

Freese, L. 126
Freud, S. 138, 275
Friedl, E. 193
Friedman, J. 61
Fuchs, S. 64
Fukuyama, F. 274
Furstenberg, F.F., Jr. 189, 191

Gamble, E.B. 137
Gangestad, S.W. 166
Gans, H. 257
Garai, J.E. 149, 150, 152
Gaulin, S.J.C. 155
Gecas, V. 195
Gellner, E. 251
Genov, N. 55
Gerstein, D. 35, 57
Gibbs, J.P. 59, 224
Giddens, A. 61, 209
Giles-Sims, J. 192
Gillis, J.S. 166
Gilman, C.P. 137
Glazer, N. 257
Glenn, N.D. 68, 144, 167
Glick, P.C. 175, 177, 181, 182
Goldberg, S. 171
Goldscheider, F.K. 195
Goodall, J. 154, 220, 221, 222, 223,
    224, 225, 226, 238, 262–63
Goode, W.J. 172, 175, 176, 181, 182,
    184, 190
Gordon, M.M. 251, 253, 254, 256–57,
    268
Gorski, R.A. 148
Gould, S.J. 93–94, 123–25
Gouldner, A.W. 58, 108, 191, 212
Gove, W.R. 65
Gowaty, P.A. 139
Gray, A. 235
Gray, J.A. 152
Graziano, W. 166
Greeley, A.M. 257, 272
Green, P.A. 9, 162, 226
Gregersen, E. 159
Gregg, B. 159
Gregory, M.S. 111
Gross, H.E. 146
Grusky, D.B. 207
Gurr, T.R. 250, 261
Gwartney-Gibbs, P.A. 184

Habermas, J. 38, 61

Haldane, J.B.S. 123
Halfpenny, P. 55
Halliday, T.C. 45
Hamilton, R.F. 70
Hamilton, W.D. 77, 104–06, 107–08, 117, 119, 129
Handwerker, W.P. 166
Haraway, D. 169
Harcourt, A.H. 220
Hardin, R. 55
Harff, B. 250, 261
Hargens, L.L. 70
Harris, L.J. 152
Harris, M. 6, 12
Harrison, A.A. 165
Harshman, R. 147
Hartman, H.I. 196
Hartung, J. 162, 248
Hatfield, E. 161
Hawking, S.W. 59
Hazelrigg, L.E. 217
Heaton, T.B. 175
Hechter, M. 28, 258
Hedges, L.V. 151
Heisler, M.O. 260
Hempel, C.G. 25–26
Henderson, L.J. 24, 28
Hewitt, J.P. 58
Hewlett, B.S. 161
Hill, K. 166, 241
Hill, M.R. 41, 55
Hill, R.J. 212
Hindes, B. 55
Hines, M. 157
Hochschild, A. 114, 195
Hodge, R.W. 208
Holcomb, H.R., III 122, 123, 124, 125, 126
Holloway, R.L. 147
Homans, G.C. 13, 27–30, 57, 74, 108, 194, 216
Hooks, B.L. 162, 226
Horowitz, D.L. 250, 252, 270
Horowitz, I.L. 4, 36, 49–50, 55, 56, 66, 69–70, 145, 207
Howard, J.A. 163
Hrdy, S.B. 139, 162, 171, 192, 197, 222
Huaco, G.A. 217
Hubbard, R. 112, 142–43
Huber, J. 4, 41, 49, 69, 195, 207
Huntington, S.P. 261, 274
Hurst, C.E. 209

Hurtado, A.M. 241
Hutt, C. 152
Huxley, J. 12, 91, 94, 101, 103

Ike, B.W. 263
Imperato-McGinley, J. 157–58
Inkeles, A. 240
Irons, W. 127, 130, 172
Isaacs, H.R. 270, 272, 273
Irwin, C.J. 248, 250, 266

Jacklin, C.N. 136, 152, 153
Jacobs, J.A. 201
James, T.W. 152
Janowitz, M. 45
Jeffrey, P. 162
Jensen, G.D. 223
Jessel, D. 156
Joas, H. 36
John, D. 196
Jolly, C.J. 220, 225
Jones, D. 166
Jones, T.A. 238
Josephson, S.C. 162
Judd, C.M. 201

Kalleberg, A.L. 36, 201
Kamo, Y. 194
Kantrowitz, B. 41
Karlin, S. 159
Katz, M. 198
Kaufman, S.J. 275
Kawai, M. 225
Kawanaka, K. 224
Keefe, R.C. 166
Kemper, T.D. 235, 236
Kendrick, D.T. 166
Kenkel, W.P. 168
Kennedy, P. 51
Kertzer, D.I. 221
Khoo, S-E. 183
Kilbourne, B.S. 204
Killian, L.M. 70
Kimura, D. 111, 122, 147, 149, 151, 152, 235
Kimura, M. 159
Kinsey, A.C. 174
Kitcher, P. 124–25
Klassen, A.D. 160
Klein, R.G. 230
Knoke, D. 36
Knussmann, R. 235

Koford, C.B. 225
Kompara, D.R. 192
Konner, M. 136, 148, 149, 153, 154, 156, 160, 198, 266
Kroeber, A.L. 56
Kuhn, T.S. 18, 84, 123

Lack, D. 87, 88
Lamarck, J.B. 11
Lamb, M. 189
Lamb, T.A. 236
Lancaster, J.B. 224
LaRossa, R. 188, 189, 190
Lasch, C. 61
Lash, S. 55, 61
Laumann, E. 160, 164, 173, 186, 234
Lee, R.B. 161
Leibowitz, L. 192
Lenski, G. 18, 47, 62, 66, 209, 212, 218, 221, 227, 238, 241
Lerner, G. 139
LeVay, S. 146, 148, 149, 156
Levine, R.A. 250
Levy, G.D. 167
Lévi-Strauss, C. 219
Lewis, L.S. 217, 218
Lewontin, R.C. 90, 124–25
Lieberman, L. 46
Lieberson, S. 76–77, 90
Liebow, E. 232
Liesen, L.T. 145
Lindquist Forsberg, A.J. 183, 234
Lipset, S.M. 49, 70
Littlefield, C.H. 155
Lloyd, K.M. 180–81
Lockard, J.S. 233
London, K. 185
Lopreato, J. 9, 13, 15, 24, 52, 54, 58, 72, 79, 80, 86, 111, 112, 114, 116, 118, 124, 126, 128, 130, 131, 159, 211, 214, 215–17, 218, 233, 237, 248, 252, 266, 267, 272–73, 274
Lorber, J. 140, 143, 144, 169–70, 187, 194, 197
Lorenz, K. 96, 131, 253
Louv, R. 189
Low, B.S. 72, 75, 162, 220, 230, 253
Lowry, H.M. 204
Lueptow, L.B. 201–02
Luhmann, N. 38
Lukes, S. 51
Lumsden, C.J. 30, 178

Maccoby, E.E. 136, 152, 153
MacDonald, W.L. 191
Mach, E. 124
Machalek, R. 16, 18, 30, 52, 75, 109, 228, 270
Machung, A. 114, 195
MacLean, P.D. 148
Malinowski, B. 24, 108, 110, 166
Malthus, T.R. 88
Margolin, L. 178–79, 180
Marshland, D. 45
Marx, J. 146
Marx, K. 6–9, 10, 19, 60, 62, 170, 209–12, 213, 214, 215, 218, 223
Maryanski, A.R. 26, 136, 187, 192
Masters, R.D. 135
Mauss, M. 108
Mayr, E. 90, 94, 98, 103–04, 123
Mazur, A. 223, 235, 236
McBurney, D.H. 152
McGlone, J. 147
McGuiness, D. 149, 152
McGuire, M.T. 222, 226, 237
McLemore, S.D. 248
McNeill, W.H. 228, 260
McPartland, J.M. 231
Mead, G.H. 13, 57–58
Mealey, L. 162
Melotti, U. 250
Menand, L. 40
Mendel, G. 91, 101–02, 105
Merton, R.K. 20, 23–26, 27, 28, 39, 44, 47
Meštrović, S.G. 37, 64
Meyer, D.R. 190
Meyer-Bahlburg, H.F.L. 235
Michels, R. 13, 220, 222, 228, 243
Michener, C.D. 262
Millet, K. 182
Mills, C.W. 34–35, 36, 57, 222
Mirowsky, J. 201
Model, S. 195
Moir, A. 156
Molotch, F.H. 62
Money, J. 157
Moore, W.E. 24, 203, 209, 215–19, 224, 241
Morgan, G.A. 264
Mosca, G. 13, 220, 222
Moynihan, D.P. 257, 275
Mueller, C.W. 201
Münch, R. 38–39

Murdock, G.P. 13, 136, 153, 161, 187, 192, 230, 231
Murstein, B.I. 168

Nagel, E. 25–26, 33, 35, 78, 118, 229
Nagel, J. 259
Namboodiri, K. 72
Nass, R. 157
Nedelmann, B. 38
Nelson, D.C. 249
Newton, I. 5, 29, 34, 35
Nielsen, F. 126, 259
Nisbet, R.A. 14
Novak, M. 257
Nowell, A. 151

Oakley, A. 140, 144
O'Kelly, C.G. 193
Olshansky, S.J. 72
Olson, M. 51
Olzak, S. 259
Omi, M. 249
O'Neill, J. 203

Pareto, V. 8, 13, 18, 19, 24, 27, 28, 31, 36, 53, 58, 83, 96, 131, 178, 214, 220, 222, 223, 228, 233, 247, 248, 249, 252, 253, 266
Parish, A.R. 141, 226
Park, B. 201
Park, R.E. 13, 254–56
Parkin, F. 239
Parsons, T. 6, 19–20, 27, 28, 30–34, 35, 39, 56–57, 58, 208
Patai, D. 140
Paul, L. 156
Peel, J.D.Y. 10
Pérusse, D. 173, 231
Peterson, D. 153, 154, 230
Peterson, R.R. 174
Phelan, J. 201
Piaget, J. 51
Pinker, S. 74
Polachek, S. 203
Polonko, K.A. 186
Popenoe, D. 183, 184
Popper, K.R. 124–25
Pruett, K. 189, 198
Pusey, A. 226

Radcliffe-Brown, A.R. 24
Raisman, G. 148

Raleigh, M.J. 222, 226
Reinisch, J.M. 151
Remoff, H.T. 164
Reskin, B.F. 200, 201, 207
Restak, R. 151
Reynolds, V. 135, 214, 274
Ricciuti, H.N. 264
Riche, M.F. 184
Ridgeway, C.L. 204
Ridley, M. 12, 136, 159
Rindfuss, R.R. 183, 184, 185, 186, 187
Ritzer, G. 64
Robinson, J.P. 193
Rodriquez-Ibanez, J.E. 39
Rogers, M. 145, 169
Roos, P.A. 200, 204
Rose, H. 74
Rose, R. 250
Rose, S. 74
Rosenblatt, P.C. 168
Rosenfeld, E. 240
Rosenfeld, R.A. 201, 204
Ross, C.E. 195, 201
Rossi, A.S. 145–46
Rotundo, A. 188
Rozin, P. 129
Rubin, G. 138
Rule, J.B. 47, 56
Ruse, M. 111, 122–23
Rushton, J.P. 155, 267
Russell, D. 191
Rytina, N.F. 204

Sadalla, E.K. 166
Saeed, L. 165
Saluter, A. 183
Sanday, P.R. 112
Sanders, B. 151
Sanderson, S.K. 46, 57–59, 66
Sawhill, I. 204
Schaller, G.B. 192
Scheinfeld, A. 149, 150, 152
Schlegel, A. 155
Schmidt, D.P. 160, 161, 165, 168
Schoen, R. 184
Schulman, S.R. 118
Sciulli, D. 35, 57
Scott, 208, 215
Seidman, S. 60, 61–63
Sen, A. 72
Seward, A.C. 93
Seyfarth, R.M. 220, 223, 225, 226

Shaw, R.P. 264, 270
Shelton, B.A. 196
Shepher, J. 119, 122
Shettel-Neuber, J. 155
Shils, E. 26–27, 30, 33, 251
Shipler, D.K. 251
Shostak, M. 161
Sica, A. 60, 61
Silverman, I. 152
Simmel, G. 13, 42, 58, 207
Simons, H.W. 60
Simpson, G.G. 91, 111, 130
Simpson, I.H. 45, 49, 70
Simpson, R.L. 27, 31, 45, 49, 70
Singh, D. 166
Skinner, B.F. 29
Small, M.F. 226
Smith, A.D. 250, 252, 269
Smith, D.E. 112, 138
Smith, D.G. 225
Smith, R.L. 230, 233
Smith, S. 225
Smuts, B.B. 139, 162, 171, 197–98, 220, 225, 226, 238
Sober, E. 96
Sommers, C.H. 138, 144
Sorensen, A.B. 201, 204
Sorokin, P. 13, 19
South, S.J. 180–81, 193, 196
Spain, D. 200
Spanier, G.B. 191
Spelman, E. 61
Spencer, H. 6, 10–13, 16, 19, 91, 212, 249
Spitze, G. 193, 195, 196, 207
Stanley, J.C. 151
Stanely, S.M. 9, 93, 95
Steinberg, R.J. 201
Stinchcombe, A. 59, 217
Sumner, W.G. 13, 41, 247, 248, 252–53, 262, 265, 266
Sweet, J. 183, 186
Symons, D. 92, 111, 121, 122, 126–27, 129–30, 159, 160
Sztompka, P. 38

Talbert, J. 204
Tam, T. 203
Tannen, D. 233
Tanner, R. 135
Tawney, R.H. 53
Taylor, C. 61

Taylor, P. 167
Teachman, J.D. 186
Terrell, K. 204
Therborn, G. 39
Thiessen, D.D. 124, 159, 167
Thomas, W.I. 254
Thompson, P. 90–91, 92, 122
Thornhill, N.W. 119
Thornhill, R. 119, 166
Thornton, A. 187
Tiger, L. 69, 185, 187
Tindale, N.B. 264
Tokuda, K. 223
Tönnesmann, W. 131
Tooby, J. 13, 30, 50, 52, 74, 92, 109, 111, 113, 121, 126–28
Toran-Allerand, D. 148
Townsend, J.M. 167, 168
Trappe, H. 201, 204
Trefil, J. 34, 64
Treiman, D.J. 204
Trilling, L. 233
Trivers, R.L. 15, 16, 18, 79, 92, 99, 108–09, 111, 114–16, 122, 170, 171, 191, 225, 230, 233, 237
Tuchman, G. 207
Tullberg, B.S. 183, 234
Tumin, M.M. 216
Turk, H. 27, 31
Turke, P.W. 72, 127, 130
Turner, C.F. 160
Turner, J.H. 4, 6, 11, 18, 26, 28, 30, 49, 56, 57, 62, 66, 67, 70, 136, 187, 192, 208, 209
Turner, S.P. 4, 49, 62
Tylor, E.B. 249

Udry, J.R. 72, 136, 167
Ulč, O. 238

van den Berghe, P. 4, 49, 52, 72, 80, 126, 131, 135, 136, 162, 164, 187, 207, 214, 231, 248, 250, 251, 252, 253, 260, 266, 267, 270, 271–72, 274
VandenHeuvel, A. 183, 184, 185, 186
van der Dennen, J.M.G. 263, 264
Vänhanen, T. 220
Vaupel, J.W. 72
Veblen, T. 228
Vining, D.R., Jr. 172
Volensky, M. 239

Volgyes, I. 238
Volkan, V. 275

Waite, L.J. 195
Waldrop, M.M. 30
Walker, K.E. 195
Wallace, A.R. 85, 93
Wallace, W.L. 49
Wallerstein, I. 25
Walsh, A. 136, 153, 156
Walters, J.R. 220, 223, 225
Walton, D. 76
Ward, L.F. 13, 137
Ward, S. 64
Warner, W.L. 265
Weber, M. 13, 19, 39, 52–55, 60, 62,
    209, 211, 213–15, 220, 247, 253
Weber, S. 230
Weiner, J. 87, 88
Weinick, R.M. 184
Weir, D. 204
Weiss, K.W. 72
Weitzel, B. 155
Weitzman, L.J. 174, 190
Wellington, A.J. 203
West, C. 144, 196
Western, M. 201
Whimster, S. 55
White, J.M. 183, 184
White, L. 178–79, 180
White, L.K. 176
Whitehead, A.N. 20
Whiting, B.B. 153
Whiting, J.W.M. 153
Whitmeyer, J.M. 72, 252
Whitten, P.L. 226

Whyte, W.F. 232
Wiederman, M.W. 155
Willard, D.E. 170, 230
Willhoite, F.H., Jr. 225
Williams, J.E. 201
Williams, R.M., Jr. 33, 252
Wilson, D.S. 127
Wilson, E.O. 30, 66, 74, 77, 96, 104,
    107, 111–12, 121–22, 124, 125, 126,
    130, 131, 141, 143, 220, 238, 263
Wilson, M. 92, 164, 191, 192
Wilson, W.J. 186
Winant, H. 249
Witelson, S. 147
Wolf, E.R. 249
Wolf, W.C. 204
Wolfe, D.M. 194
Wong, Y. 264, 270
Woods, J. 76
Woods, M.E. 195
Woodward, D.L. 147
Wrangham, R. 153, 154, 226, 230
Wright, R. 136, 159, 230, 231, 233
Wright, S. 159
Wrong, D. 55

Yinger, J.M. 249, 252, 270
Yorburg, B. 185
Young, M.B. 169
Yu, M-y. 72

Zangwill, I. 254
Zaniecki, F. 254
Zeggelink, E. 110
Zetterberg, H.L. 53, 76
Zimmerman, D.H. 196

Index of Subjects

Adaptation: in Spencer 10–11; in Durkheim 15; and equation with function in Merton 25–26; and Darwin's conception 85–90; as differential fitness in Darwin 95; ambiguous conception in Darwin 104; in some social insects 104–06; and maladaptive traits 104, 117–18, 119; and the fitness principle 117, *passim*; as relative and variable property of traits 117–18, 119, 121, 125, 130–31, 140; and reproductive success 120, *passim*; and human nature 120–22; defined 121, 125; and sex-differentiated traits of sensation, cognition, and emotion 149–56; see also Behavioral Predispositions.

Adultery: and sex-differentiated response 155, 174; and *de facto* polygyny 172–73; and frequency by sex 173; and divorce 174; see also Divorce, Marriage, Parental Investment.

Aggression: moralistic aggression 109, 237; in males 112, 153; and sex differences in neuroanatomy 148; and adaptive significance 154; and resource scarcity among primates 220–21; see also Dominance Orders, Male Dominance, Patriarchy, Primate Dominance Orders, Sex Differences, Sexual Selection.

Agricultural Revolution: 193, 197; and economic surplus and male dominance 197; and escalation of ruling-class exploitation 221, 243; and disruption of kin relations 250, 268–69.

Altruism: and Durkheim's theory of solidarity 18; and reproductive self-sacrifice 104–06; defined 107; conditions favoring its persistence 107; as selfish behavior 108–10; and self-

destruction 110; and the fitness principle 119–20; and sacrifice for family members 123–24; and coercion 229; and ethnic affiliation 262, 266–67; see also Kin Selection, Nepotism, Reciprocal Altruism.

Analogies: as a heuristic device 12; in Spencer 12; in Parsons 30.

Anisogamy: defined 113; law of 114; and relative parental investment 114; and initial parental investment 116; and predicted sex difference in nurturing offspring 116, 153, 187–88; and predicted sex difference in number of sex partners 160; and hypergyny 230; and male status-striving 234; chs. 5–7 *passim*; see also Hypergyny, Parental Investment, Parenting, Polygyny, Sexual Selection.

Anthropocentrism: 5; as a corollary of geocentrism 80.

Assimilation: in Gordon 251, 254; and interethnic relations 254–56.

Assortative Mating: and pair-bonds 159; and ethnicity 252, 267, 270; and ethnic conflict 270.

Behavioral Predispositions: neophobia 3, 83, 110; in Comte 5; in Spencer 10–11; and socialization 29–30, *passim*; and learning biases 29–30, 72–73; and resentment of capricious leadership 37; and creature comforts 37; denial of death 54; conformity 58, 73, 79; ethnocentrism 75, ch. 9 *passim*; symbolization 84; moralistic aggression 109, 237; sense of justice 109; cheater detection 109; gratitude 109; sympathy 109; friendship 109; guilt 109; and defense of reciprocal altruism 109; and male aggression 112, 115, 153–54; and male jealousy 115, 154–55; and female nurturing 116, 153, 156–57, 187–88, 190, 198; and nature of adaptive mechanisms 121; species-wide varieties of 122, 135; sex-specialized varieties of 122, 135, chs. 6–7 *passim*; evolutionary psychological approach to 126–30; as domain-specific psychological traits 126–30; urge to victimize 128; as adaptive specializations 129; and cultural universals as indicators of adaptive behavioral traits 130; dominance ch. 8 *passim*; deference 221–22, 234, 238; and cunning 222; and coercion 222–23; and ostracism 224; ambition 228; competitiveness 228; need to rise 228; need for power 228; pride 228, 238; and arrogance 228, 238; and need to acquire and consume 228, 238; instinct to dominate 233; climbing maneuver 233; sentiment of equality in inferiors 233; deception of self and others 233; xenophobia 263, 264; nepotism 264, 266–67; and blood revenge 265–66; homologous affiliation 267; heterologous contraposition 267; see also Adaptation, Human Nature.

Behaviorism: and Skinner's influence on Homans 29–30; and environmentalism 29–30; and evolutionary psychology 128; see also Exchange Theory.

Biological Determinism: and misconceptions of evolutionary theory 96, 123–24, 126; and radical feminist distortions of sociobiology 140, 143, *passim*; see also Interaction Principle.

Brain Anatomy: see Sex Differences.

Causal Analysis: priority of in Durkheim 14, 16; and grades of mechanisms 16; in Pareto 24; and confusion with functional analysis in Merton 25–26; in Weber 53–54; and proximate versus ultimate levels 75, 77, 176–78, *passim*; see also Functional Analysis; Laws, Scientific.

Cheating: in Durkheim 16, 18; in Homans 27; and reciprocal altruism 109–10; detection of 109; and adultery 172–73; and sex difference in cohabiting unions 186; in Marx 210–12; and privileges attending dominant rank 224–25; see also Adultery, Cohabitation, Dominance Orders, Exploitation, Marriage, Reciprocal Altruism, Reciprocity.

Child Care: see Parenting, Sex Differences.

Clan: and humans' evolutionary environment 73, 247; as prototype of ethnic group 247, 252, 263–66, 267; see also Status Groups.

Class Conflict: in Marx 8–9; and Marx's theory of 209–12; as key stress in social systems 212; in Weber 213–15; see also Coalitions, Collective Action, Exploitation, Resource Competition.

Class Consciousness: in Marx 7, 9, 209–12; in Weber 213–15.

Class Struggle: see Class Conflict.

Coalitions: and resource competition 8–9; and females' mitigation of male dominance in primates 141; and power in Weber 211, 214; in primate dominance orders 214, 220–22; see also Dominance Orders, Primate Dominance Orders.

Coefficient of Relatedness: and Mendel's laws of inheritance 102; in diploid and haplodiploid species 102, 105–06; and nepotism 104–06; see also Kin Selection, Nepotism.

Cohabitation: trends in 183; and alternative to marriage 184; and sociocultural trends 184–85; and sex difference in expectations from it 185; and costs and benefits 185–86; and sex difference in cheating 186; and dissolution of subsequent marriages 186; and female headed households 187.

Collective Action: and Marx's theory of class conflict 211, 212; as selfish action 233.

Competition: see Aggression, Class Conflict, Coalitions, Ethnic Conflict, Resource Competition, Sexual Selection.

Conflict: see Class Conflict, Ethnic Conflict, Resource Competition.

Conflict Theory: versus functionalism 58; in Marx 209–12; in Weber 213–15.

Conformity: in relation to consensus and conflict 58; as behavioral predisposition 73; adaptive significance of 79; see also Behavioral Predispositions, Cooperation, Reciprocity.

Cooperation: in Durkheim's theory of solidarity 15–16, 18; see also Kin Selection, Nepotism, Reciprocal Altruism, Reciprocity.

Cuckoldry: see Paternal Uncertainty.

Cultural Determinism: as hindrance to scientific development 14, 34, 38, 84, 110–11, *passim*; in Boas and Durkheim 13–14; and division of household labor 195–97; and the gendered workplace 203–05; see also Environmentalism; Laws, Scientific; Socialization; Social Structure.

Cultural Universals: as basis for inferring behavioral predispositions 130; and sex distinction 136; and male dominance 141; and sex-differentiated labor 141–42; and mate preferences 159; and women as primary providers of child care 187; and sex-differentiated household labor 192–93; and dominance orders 219; and status differentiation 231; and ethnocentrism 248; *passim*.

Deception: and false consciousness 7; and revolutionary leadership 233; and domination 238; and concealment of selfish motives 241; see also Behavioral Predispositions, Cheating, Self Deception.

Demography: and the future of sociology 72.

Destratification: and Marx's utopian vision 9; and failure to achieve gender equality 169–71; and failures of 238–44.

Differential Parental Investment: see Parental Investment.

Differential Socialization: see Sex Differences, Socialization.

Divorce: and adultery 174; and adaptive significance of 175, 177; and sociocultural explanations of 175–76; and proximate versus ultimate causes 176–78; and women's participation in labor force 176, 179–81; by age and sex of partners 176–77.

Dominance Orders: in Marx 7–9; based in sexual selection 115; as natural phenomena 207; in egalitarian societies 219, 231; defined 219–20; and allocation of reproductive resources 221; and social control 223–25; and behavioral predispositions 228, 231, 232–33, 238; and mate competition 229–34, 241; and status-striving 233; evolution of human species 241–45; see also Exploitation, Resource Competition, Primate Dominance Orders, Sexual Selection.

Double Standard: see Sexual Double Standard.

Elite Theory: and corresponding evidence in primates 220, 222; and universality of oligarchy 228–29; and dominance orders in recent centuries 243.

Emergent Properties: and Durkheim's metaphysics 13–15, 17–18, 52; in Parsons 30–32; and reification of society 30, 73–74, 209, 217–18; in the Davis-Moore theory of stratification 217–18; see also System Analysis.

Empiricism: in Comte 5–6; see also Laws, Scientific.

Enlightenment: and the rise of sociology 3; and its influence on sociology's Founders 5–13.

Environment of Evolutionary Adaptation (EEA): 127, 129, 130–31.

Environmentalism: and sociology's commitment to 4, *passim*; and cultural determinism in Durkheim 14; and socialization and social structure as causes of behavior 70, 72–74; in explanations of sex differences 136, chs. 5–8 *passim*; see also Cultural Determinism, Socialization, Social Structure.

Essentialism: and feminist rejection of biology 140; and alleged justification of male dominance 140, 144.

Ethnic Conflict: in Marx 8; in Pareto 8, 247; and kin selection 8; and failure to address contemporary global instances of 37; and ethnocentrism 75, 266, ch. 9 *passim*; and sociocultural explanations of 253–61; and its tenacity and universality 260–61; and its evolutionary foundations 262–67; among primates 262–63; and adaptive significance of 265–66, 266–67; and assortative mating 252, 267, 270; and population size and intersocietal contact 272–73; and the end of the Cold War 273–75.

Ethnic Identification: in Weber 247; in Pareto 247, 249; in Sumner 247, 262; and appeal to common descent 247, 269–70; in Gordon 256; in Benedict 262; and homologous affiliation 267; 269–73; and assortative mating 270; in van den Berghe 270–73; and role of ethnic markers 270–73; see also Clan, Status Groups.

Ethnicity: in Weber 214; and fitness interests and kin selection 248–49, 262, 264–67; and relation to race, tribe, and nation 249–51; and instrumentalist conceptions 251; and primordialist conceptions 251–52; in the megasociety 267–73; in civilizational conflict 271–75.

Ethnocentrism: and conflict 38; as a behavioral predisposition 75, 131; and intersocietal relations 247; in Sumner 252–53; as ancient adaptive trait 252–53, 255; and nepotistic favoritism 253; and heterologous contraposition 267; see also Behavioral Predispositions, Nepotism.

Evolution: Spencer's law of 10; and heredity, mutation, and natural selection 90–91, 101; and rhythmic nature of 95; see also Gradualism, Natural Selection, Punctuated Equilibrium, Sexual Selection, Speciation.

Evolutionary Psychology: and the fitness principle 126–31.

Exchange Theory: in Homans 27–30; versus functionalism 57; see also Behaviorism, Cooperation, Rational Choice Theory, Reciprocal Altruism, Reciprocity.

Exogamy: in hominids 197.

Explanation, Scientific: see Laws, Scientific.

Exploitation: in Marx 7, 210–12; and relations between men and women 171, chs. 7–8 *passim*; and access to resources in primate societies 220–21; and social parasitism 228–29; escalation of since Agricultural Revolution 241, 243; diminution of with the spread of literacy 243; see also Cheating, Dominance Orders, Reciprocal Altruism, Reciprocity, Resource Competition.

Family: see Cohabitation, Divorce, Kin Selection, Marriage, Nepotism, Remarriage.

Female Choice: see Sexual Selection.

Feminism: and postmodernism 60; and response to male aggression 112; and explanation of sex-differentiated behavior 113, chs. 6–7 *passim*; and biological approaches to sex differences 137–46; as a fragmented subject 137; and its revolutionary vision 138; and sociobiology 145–46; and rejection of science 169; as poor science chs. 5–7 *passim*; see also Cultural Determinism; Environmentalism; Socialization; Sociology, Crisis in.

Fertility: and evolutionary demography 72; and differential reproduction in Darwin 87, 90, 91, 93, 96; and sex differences in 115, 186–87, 234; age-dependency in women and probability of remarriage 182; see also Reproductive Success.

Fitness: see Adaptation.

Fitness Principle: defined 77, 118; and kin selection 107; as central principle of sociobiology 116–21, 128; upgraded statement of 118; theoretical basis of 119–20; and conscious motives 120; and male aggression 154; and sex difference in jealousy

154; and polyandry 162; and sex difference in remarriage 182–83; and sex difference in parenting 188; and ethnicity 248–49; and preferential treatment of kin 262; see also Altruism, Kin Selection, Nepotism, Parental Investment, Reciprocal Altruism, Sociobiology.

Functional Analysis: in Durkheim 14; in Merton 23–26; and failure of sociological theorizing 26; in Parsons 30–32; see also Causal Analysis; Laws, Scientific; Structural Functionalism.

Gametes: see Anisogamy.

Gender Stereotypes: and "social construction" of 143–46, 178–79; and polygyny, hypergyny 179; and division of household labor 195; as real gender differences 201–02; see also Sex Differences.

Generalizing Tendency: and scientific creativity 131; ethnicity as a generalization of nepotism 267.

Genetics: see Mendelian Genetics.

Geocentrism: 5; see also Anthropocentrism.

Gradualism: Darwin's alleged conception of 9, 93, 94–95; and punctuated equilibrium 93–95; see also Evolution, Speciation.

Harems: 197; see also Polygyny.

Heredity: see Evolution, Mendelian Genetics.

Historical Materialism: 7, 9.

Household Division of Labor: and universality of sex difference 192–93; and sociocultural explanations of sex differences 193–97; and differential resource contribution 193–95; and economic and biological factors 194–95; and differential cultural conditioning 195–97; and gender stereotypes 195; and differential socialization 195; 196; and anisogamy 196; and "doing gender" 196–97.

Human Nature: and adaptive traits 120–22; and evolutionary theory 121, 135, passim; and species-wide and sex-specialized adaptations 122; and domain-specific psychological adaptations 126–28; and patriarchy 136; and stratification theories 209; in Marx 211; see also Adaptation, Behavioral Predispositions.

Hypergyny: and sexual selection 115; and polygyny 161, 230; and mating success of high-status males 173; as effect of anisogamy and intersexual selection 230; see also Anisogamy, Mating Strategies, Parental Investment, Polygyny, Sexual Selection.

Ideology: in Comte 6–7; in Hegel 7; in Marx 7–8; as impediment to a scientific sociology 37, 41–42, 43–45, 49–50, 55–56, 58–64, 68–72, 112, 137–46, 169–71, 187–88, 194–97, 204–06, 207, 239–40, passim.

Inclusive Fitness: defined 106; and the fitness principle 118; see also Fitness Principle, Kin Selection, Sociobiology.

Inequality: see Class Conflict, Dominance Orders, Exploitation, Reproductive Success, Resource Competition.

Interaction Principle: misunderstandings of 59, 111; illustrated in the case of Darwin's finches 88; and proper view of natural selection 92, 96; and the invalidity of claims regarding biological determinism 96; definition 111; and cultural influence in sociobiology 111; and patriarchy 136, 143; and systemic nature of evolutionary reasoning 141, passim; and modification of male mating strategies 165; and ultimate, proximate explanation 176–78, 205–06, 227–45, 261–75, passim; see also Causal Analysis; Laws, Scientific.

Intersexual Selection: see Sexual Selection.

Intrasexual Selection: see Sexual Selection.

Jealousy: see Behavioral Predispositions, Paternal Uncertainty, Sex Differences.

Kin Recognition: and ethnic identity 262, 269–73, 276.

Kin Selection: and ethnicity 8, 107, 248–49, 261–67, ch. 9 *passim*; and mechanical solidarity 18; and Mendelian genetics 101–02; and theory of 104–06, 107; and inclusive fitness 106, 116–20, chs. 5–9 *passim*; and relatedness by descent versus conspecificity 108; and kin favoritism in inheritance 119; and solicitude of maternal versus paternal relatives 155; and polyandry 162; and blood revenge 265–66; see also Fitness Principle, Sociobiology.

Laws, Scientific: as essential explanation 4, 17, 59, 74–80; in Comte 5–6; in Marx 9, 218; in Spencer 10–11; as basis for cumulative, organized knowledge 13, 17–18, 124; and the failure of sociological theorizing 15, 18, 21, 22, 23, 26–27, 32, 34, 47, 50–56, 62, 83, 135, 145, 171, 176–78, 180–81, 184–85, 187, 188–90, 191–92, 193–97, 201, 202–05, 208–09, 215, 216–19, 224, 253–61; and functions of 17–18, 75–76, 121; in Homans 28–29, in Newton 34; and borrowing from related disciplines 74, 77, 79–80; and common misunderstandings of 78; and the fitness principle 116–20; and reductionism 120, 124; and theory of human nature 124–25; and feminist rejection of 145; and explanations of divorce 176–77; in Durkheim 218; and falsifiable predictions regarding dominance orders 244–45; see also Causal Analysis.

Leadership: and reproductive success 219, 231–34; and rewards in primate dominance orders 220–21, 226; and cheating 225, 228; see also Dominance Orders, Primate Dominance Orders, Reproductive Success.

Male Dominance: and sexual selection 115, 139–40; and fitness interests 139; near universality of in mammals 141; varying intensity of 141; and aggression 154; and number of sex partners 173; and the evolution of patriarchy 197–99; see also Coalitions, Cultural Universals, Dominance Orders, Patriarchy, Reproductive Success.

Malthusian Problem: and evolution in Comte 5; and evolution in Spencer 10; and Darwin's theory 88–89; and the fitness principle 118–19; see also Resource Competition.

Marriage: and anisogamy, parental investment, and sexual selection 171–74; as cultural universal 172; and *de facto* polygyny 172; and sex difference in adultery 172, 173; and monogamy 172; duration of 175; as reproductive alliance 178; and male stress on mate's physical appearance 178–79; see also Divorce, Remarriage.

Mate Preferences: among females 115, 159, 165–68, 175, 230, 232; among males 159, 165–68; and sex differences in desirable personality traits 163–65; and sex differences on fidelity 164–65; and sex differences in preferred age of prospective mate 165; and adaptive significance of sex differences 181.

Mating Strategies: and relative parental investment 114–15; and evolutionary psychology 128–29; and sex differences 159–68; and polygyny 159–62; and long-term versus short-term strategies 165; and male exploitation 171; and divorce 175–81; and sex differences in cohabitation 185–87; see also Anisogamy, Parental Investment, Sexual Selection, Sociobiology.

Maximization Principle: see Fitness Principle.

Mendelian Genetics: unknown to Darwin 91; principles of 101–02.

Methodological Reductionism: and scientific explanation 120, 124, 142, 275–76; see also Laws, Scientific.

Methodological Individualism: in Spencer 13; in Durkheim 15; in Merton 24; in Pareto 28, 31; in Homans 28–29; and behaviorist bias in Homans 29–30; Parsons' rejection of 31–32; and its absence in stratification theory 209; and deficiencies in Marx's theory of class conflict 211.

Modern Synthesis: as marriage of Darwinian and Mendelian science 12, 91, 102; and foundation of modern biology 102–03; defined 103; and clarification of Darwin's theory 103–04; see also Sociobiology.

Monogamy: as common form of marriage 161; as a socially imposed form 172; and size dimorphism 230; see also Marriage, Mating Strategies, Polygyny.

Mortality: and evolutionary demography 72; and women's longer life expectancy 137.

Mutation: see Evolution, Mendelian Genetics.

Natural Selection: and the rise of sociology 4; in Comte 5; in Marx 9; in Spencer 11; in Durkheim 14, 16–17, 18; and mutability of species 85, 86–87, 93; as uniform mechanism of evolution 85–86, 88–89; as Darwin's theory 85–96; and heritability of traits 87; and selective retention of trait variations 87, 89; as differential reproduction 87, 90, 91, 93, 96; and artificial selection 89; and basic elements of Darwin's theory 89–90; and the struggle for existence 89, 92; and other processes of evolution 90–93; as metaphor 92, 95–96; and gradualism 93–95; and the evolution of dominance orders 241–45; and ethnicity 248; see also Kin Selection, Sexual Selection.

Nepotism: and mechanical solidarity 18, 276; and the selfish basis of altruism 107–08; and ethnicity 253, 267; and ethnocentrism 264; as psychological adaptation 266; see also Fitness Principle, Kin Selection.

New Synthesis: see Sociobiology.

Parental Confidence: see Paternal Uncertainty.

Parental Investment: and relative contribution by men and women 113–14; theory of 114–16; initial and subsequent 116; and sexual selection 115–16; and the fitness principle 119–20; and sex difference in nurturing of offspring 153; and sex difference in number of sex partners 160; and sex difference in preferred personality traits of prospective mates 163–64; and sex differences in adultery 172, 173; and polygyny, hypergyny 179; and female specialization in care of offspring 187–88, 190; and sex-differentiated household labor 194; and dominance orders 229–34, 241; see also Anisogamy, Sexual Selection.

Parenting: and preferences for sex of offspring 170; and universal female specialization in 187; and anisogamy, differential parental investment 187–88, 190, 198; and paternal uncertainty 188; and the "new father" 188–89; and women's participation in labor force 188; and child support by absent fathers 189, 190; and female headed households 189, 190; and paternal involvement 189–90; and stepchildren 191–92; and mother's control over father's participation in 198–99; see also Anisogamy, Parental Investment, Paternal Uncertainty; Sexual Selection.

Paternal Uncertainty: and male jealousy 154–55, 174; and threat of cuckoldry 154, 174; and grandparents 155; and aunts and uncles 155; and men's desire for faithful mates 164–65; and men's abuse of wives 174; see also Kin Selection, Parental Investment, Sexual Selection.

Patriarchy: and explanation in sociology 136, 138; and human nature 136, 139; and female complicity in 139–40, 198; and sociobiological explanation of 139, 197–98; and polygyny 161; and nepotism, reciprocity 197; see also Environmentalism, Male Dominance.

Polyandry: and kin selection 162; see also Mating Strategies.

Polygyny: and sexual selection 115; cross-cultural distribution of 161–62, 230; and hypergyny 161–62, 230; and fitness benefits 162; de jure and de facto 172, 230–31, 234, 243;

in allegedly egalitarian societies 219, 231; and intense sexual selection 229–30; and size dimorphism 230; and despotic regimes 232; see also Anisogamy, Dominance Orders, Hypergyny, Mating Strategies, Parental Investment, Sexual Selection.

Population: in Comte's theory of evolution 5; in Spencer's evolutionism 10–11; in Durkheim's theory of evolution 15–16; and speciation 93, 95; and the adaptiveness of culture 131; and ethnicity 268; see also Demography, Fertility, Malthusian Problem, Mortality, Resource Competition.

Positivism: in Comte 5–6.

Postmodernism: and the denial of science 41; and sociology's crisis 59–64; as ideology 61, 62–63; and the misunderstanding of science 63–64, 65; and assessment of sex-differentiated household labor 196–97.

Power: and the postmodernist obsession 63, 65; see also Coalitions, Dominance Orders, Resource Competition.

Primate Dominance Orders: and oligarchy 220; and alliance formation 220, 222; and the dominants' privileges 220–21, 226; and means of maintaining dominant rank 221–22; and the role of adult females 222, 225–26; and social mobility 222–23; and functions of oligarchies 223–24; and status inheritance 225; common features of 227; see also Coalitions, Dominance Orders.

Principles, Scientific: see Laws, scientific

Psychological Adaptations: see Behavioral Predispositions.

Punctuated Equilibrium: and an analogous conception in Marx 9; and Darwin's alleged gradualism 93–95; criticisms of 94–95; see also Gradualism, Natural Selection.

Rational Choice Theory: and Homans' exchange theory 28; and failure of sociological theorizing 55–56.

Reciprocal Altruism: and organic solidarity 18; and conformity 79; theory of 109–10; conditions favoring its persistence 109; and threat of cheating 109–10; and relations between men and women 170; and divorce 176–78; and stepparenting 191; and alliances in status contests 222; and diminution of xenophobia 264–65; see also Altruism, Cheating, Nepotism, Sociobiology.

Reciprocity: and Durkheim's theory of solidarity 18; in Homans 27; and cheating 27, 109; and reciprocal altruism 108–09; evolutionary bases of 109; and stepfathers 191; and ethnic boundaries, ethnic conflict 264–65; see also Cheating, Cooperation, Reciprocal Altruism, Sociobiology.

Reductionism: see Methodological Reductionism.

Remarriage: sex difference in rates of 181; and men's social status 181; and male resources versus female reproductive value 182; and sex differences in age of new partner 12; and adaptive significance of sex-differentiated patterns 182–83; and sex-differentiated reproductive success 234.

Reproductive Success: and nepotism 77; in Darwin 87, 90, 91, 93, 96; and sex differences in 115; and fitness-enhancing behavior 119; and male dominance 139, 219, 231–32; and asymmetrical costs and benefits in pair-bonds 154, 185–87; and polygyny 162; and male status 173; and sex-differentiated effects of remarriage 234; see also Fertility, Inclusive Fitness.

Resource Competition: in Spencer 11, 212; in Marx 7, 210, 212; and the fitness principle 119; and male displays 167; in Weber 213; in Davis-Moore theory of stratification 218; and dominance orders 218, 227–34; and primate dominance orders 220–21; and acquiring mates 229; and ethnocentrism 252–53; and ethnic conflict 254–56; and warfare 265–66; see also see Dominance Orders, Malthusian Problem.

Revolution: Marx's theory of 8–9, 211.

Scientific Revolution: and the rise of sociology 3; and sociology's estrangement 23, *passim*; in social and biological disciplines 83; nature of 83–85; and the Modern Synthesis 103; and modern behavioral science 122–23.

Self-Deception: as impediment to theory construction in the social sciences 84, 111, 138; and adaptive mechanism in status contests 233; and domination 238; and concealment of selfish motives 241; see also Behavioral Predispositions, Deception.

Sex Differences: in aggression 112, 136, 153–54; and feminist approaches 113; in mating strategies 114–15, 159–68; in reproductive success 115; in mate attraction 136, chs. 5–8 *passim*; in pair-bond formation 136; in parenting 136, 187–92; in contribution to household labor 136, 192–99; in the workplace 136, 199–206; in brain anatomy 146–49; in sensation 149–51; in cognition 151–52; in emotions 152–54; in nurturing and possible adaptive significance 153, 198; in jealousy 154–55, 174; in number of sex partners 159–60; and their persistence 169–70; in fear of emotional desertion 174; in adultery 172, 173; in rates of remarriage 181; in expectations about cohabitation 185; in educational training 199–200; in occupational opportunities 200; in wages 200–01; in human capital investment 202–03; see also Anisogamy, Marriage, Parental Investment, Testosterone.

Sexual Development, Anomalies in: and social construction 144; Turner's Syndrome 156; androgen-insensitivity syndrome 156; congenital adrenal hyperplasia 157; 5-alpha reductase deficiency 157–58; as evidence against environmentalism 158–59.

Sexual Double Standard: and feminism on sociobiology 143, 182–83; and number of sex partners 161; and adaptive responses to adultery 174;

see also Patriarchy, Sexual Selection.

Sexual Selection: in Darwin 96–99; and peculiar phenotypic traits 97; and competition for reproductive mates 97, 98, 112–16, 159–68, 171–92, *passim*; and natural selection 98; intrasexual type 98, 115; intersexual type 99, 115; and sex-differentiated adaptive traits 99, 146–56, 159–68, 228, 234–38; and intensity of mate competition among males 115, 153–54, 159–62, 179–81, 220–22, 229–34, 241–45, 264–68; and parental investment 115–16; and the fitness principle 119–20; and sex-differentiated sensation 151; and sex-differentiated cognition 152; and paternal uncertainty 154; and polygyny, hypergyny 159–62, 229–30, chs. 5–8 *passim*; and mating strategies 159–68; and sex differences in the workplace 205–06; and husbands' loss of sexual interest in spouses 178–79; and dominance orders 229–34; and the evolution of dominance orders 241–45; see also Anisogamy, Natural Selection, Parental Investment, Paternal Uncertainty, Sex Differences.

Social Classes: and discrete dimension of resource allocation in stratification studies 208; see also Stratification, Social.

Social Constructionism: and feminist accounts of sex-differentiated behavior 143–45, 156; as basis of sex/gender distinction 143–44; as alleged basis of human emotions 156; and feminist views on mothering 187.

Social Evolution: in Comte 5–6; in Marx 7–9; in Spencer 10–11; in Durkheim 15–16; and modifications of male mating strategies 165; and sex-differentiated household labor 192–93; and dominance orders 241–45; and ethnicity 268–73.

Social Darwinism: 126; in Spencer 11; and environmentalist bias in sociology 14; as impediment to sociology's linkage with evolutionary science 17, 91.

Social Mobility: in Marx's theory of revolution 8–9, 211; in Weber 54, 214; and increasing opportunities for women 199–206; in the Davis-Moore theory 216–17; in primate societies 222–23, 225; and barriers to free circulation 228–29, 239–40, 243; see also Dominance Orders, Primate Dominance Orders.

Social Solidarity: Durkheim's theory of 15–17, 18; see also Kin Selection, Nepotism, Reciprocal Altruism.

Social Status: sociological measures of 231–32; see also Dominance Orders; Mate Preferences; Reproductive Success; Sex Differences; Stratification, Social.

Social Structure: static analysis in Comte 6; as intervening variables 52, passim; and the science of "social switches" 52, 180, chs. 2–3 passim; excessive emphasis on in studies of sex roles chs. 6–7 passim; excessive emphasis on in stratification theory 209–19; excessive emphasis on in studies of ethnic conflict 253–61; passim; see also Laws, Scientific.

Socialization: in sociology 21, 72–73, passim; in Homans 29; in Parsons 23; excessive emphasis on in studies of sex differences chs. 6–7 passim; see also Environmentalism; Interaction Principle; Laws, Scientific.

Sociobiology: and sociology at the frontier 84–85; and the study of social behavior 99, 122; and the discovery of kin selection 104; and reaction of social scientists 111; and invitation to the social sciences and humanities 111–12, passim; as remedy for temporecentrism 112; and anisogamy, parental investment, and sexual selection 112–16; and the fitness principle 118, 120; and critics 123–26; and explanation of patriarchy 139–40; and falsifiable predictions 142; see also Altruism, Kin Selection, Natural Selection, Reciprocal Altruism, Parental Investment, Sexual Selection.

Sociology, Crisis in: and betrayal of early promise 4, 17–20; and its cannibalization 4, 21, 42, 51, 56, 158–59; as widely recognized 4, ch. 2 passim; and quality of textbooks 19, 66–68, 126; defined 21–22; early signs of 23–24; and irrelevance in public policy debates 36–7, 40, 43–44; and ideological excesses 37, 49–50; and European sociologists 38–40; and complaints of non-academic sociologists 40; and weakened position in academe 41–43; and its denial 43–44, 46–47, 64–65, passim; and intellectual despotism 44–45, 70–71; and intrinsic incompetence 49; and irony of early ambitions 50–56; Comte's contribution to 50–51; Durkheim's contribution to 51–52; Weber's contribution to 52–55; and fragmentation 56–59; and postmodernism 59–64; and mediocrity 65–68; and political correctness 68–72, chs. 2–3 passim; and emphasis on socialization 72–74, passim; and emphasis on social structure 72–74, passim; see also Laws, Scientific.

Sociology, Early Promise: in Comte 5–6; in Marx 6–9; in Spencer 10–13; in Durkheim 14–17; and its betrayal 17–20.

Sociology, Rise of: in 18th and 19th centuries 3–4; and Darwinian theory 4; and Comte 5–6; and Marx 6–9; and Spencer 6, 10–13; and Durkheim 13–17; and the culture concept 110–11; see also Enlightenment, Natural Selection, Scientific Revolution.

Speciation: and rate 9; defined 87–88; and Darwin's finches 86–88; and transformation and diversification 90; and population isolation 93, 95; see also Evolution, Gradualism, Natural Selection, Punctuated Equilibrium.

Standard Social Science Model: 30, 50.

Status Groups: in Weber 214, 247; and the clan as prototype of 247, 252, 263–66, 267; see also Clan, Ethnicity.

Stepchildren: and risk of abuse by stepfathers 191–92.

Stratification, Social: and Marx's theory 209–12; and Weber's tri-dimensional theory 213–15; and functional theory of 215–19; ch. 8 *passim*; see also Coalitions, Class Conflict, Dominance Orders, Primate Dominance Orders, Resource Competition.

Structural Functionalism: waning influence of 6, 57; and Durkheim 14; and early critics 31, 32–34.

Struggle for Existence: in Marx 9; in Spencer 10–11; in Durkheim 16–17; in Weber 54–55; in Darwin 96–97, 117; in primate dominance orders 220, 228–34; and its persistence 276–77; see also Dominance Orders, Natural Selection, Resource Competition, Sexual Selection.

Survey Research: and excessive reliance in sociology 8, 44.

Symbolic Interactionism: versus functionalism 57–58.

System Analysis: in Spencer 12, 13; in Merton 25–26; in Parsons 30–32; in Weber 53–55; in evolutionary logic 54–55, *passim*; see also Emergent Properties.

Temporecentrism: as impediment to a scientific sociology 10; and feminists' view of patriarchy 139; in Marx 209–10, 212; in Weber 215; in the Davis-Moore theory of stratification 218; in general stratification theory 247; and treatments of ethnicity 248, 259–60; in the analysis of modern civilization 274.

Territory: and segregation between ethnic groups 252, 258; and defense by chimpanzees 262–63; and xenophobic aggression 265.

Testosterone: and sex difference in hypothalamus 148; and sex difference in aggression 153; and anomalous sexual developmental 156–58; and dominance behavior 235–38; and mating behavior 235.

Tribal Warfare: and ethnocentrism 252–53, 264; 264–66; and dominance 265.

Uniformitarianism: 86

Xenophobia: and aggression 263; and ethnic identification 263, 264.

Warfare: (see Tribal Warfare)

Workplace: and female social mobility 199–206; and the double standard 199–201; and causes of the double standard 201–06; and evolutionary foundations of sex differences in 205–06; see also Sex Differences.